QUESTIONING THE FOUNDATIONS OF PUBLIC LAW

In 2010, Martin Loughlin, Professor of Public Law at the LSE, published *Foundations of Public Law*, "an account of the foundation of the discipline of public law with a view to identifying its essential character". The book has become a landmark in the field, and it has been said, notably by one its major critics, that it now provides the 'starting point' for any deeper inquiry into the subject. The purpose of this volume is critically to engage with *Foundations*—conceptually, comparatively and historically—from the viewpoints of public law, private law, political, social and legal theory, as well as jurisdictional perspectives including the UK, the US, India, and Continental Europe. Scholars also consider the legacy and continuing relevance of *Foundations* in the light of developments in transnational law, global law and regional integration in the European Union.

Questioning the Foundations of Public Law

Michael A Wilkinson
and
Michael W Dowdle

•HART•
OXFORD • LONDON • NEW YORK • NEW DELHI • SYDNEY

HART PUBLISHING
Bloomsbury Publishing Plc
Kemp House, Chawley Park, Cumnor Hill, Oxford, OX2 9PH, UK
HART PUBLISHING, the Hart/Stag logo, BLOOMSBURY and the Diana logo are trademarks of Bloomsbury Publishing Plc
First published in Great Britain 2018

A catalogue record for this book is available from the British Library.
Library of Congress Cataloging-in-Publication data
Names: Wilkinson, Michael A., author. | Dowdle, Michael W., author.
Title: Questioning the foundations of public law / Michael A. Wilkinson and Michael W. Dowdle.
Description: Oxford [UK] ; Portland, Oregon : Hart Publishing, 2018. | Includes bibliographical references and index.
Identifiers: LCCN 2017056098 (print) | LCCN 2017056692 (ebook) | ISBN 9781509911684 (Epub) | ISBN 9781509911677 (hardback : alk. paper)
Subjects: LCSH: Public law. | Public law—Political aspects.
Classification: LCC K3150 (ebook) | LCC K3150 .W53 2018 (print) | DDC 342—dc23
LC record available at https://lccn.loc.gov/2017056098
ISBN: HB: 978-1-50991-167-7
ePDF: 978-1-50991-169-1
ePub: 978-1-50991-168-4
Typeset by Compuscript Ltd, Shannon
Printed and bound in Great Britain by CPI Group (UK) Ltd, Croydon CR0 4YY
MIX
Paper from responsible sources
FSC® C013604
To find out more about our authors and books visit www.hartpublishing.co.uk. Here you will find extracts, author information, details of forthcoming events and the option to sign up for our newsletters.

ACKNOWLEDGEMENTS

Thanks are due first and foremost to Martin Loughlin for helping to make this project happen. He handled the challenge of exploring his work with a broad array of commentators—both sympathetic and not so sympathetic—with tenacity and patience. It is testament to the interest that his *Foundations of Public Law* has aroused that we were able to garner contributors from such different disciplines and perspectives, all willing to give it a full and critical treatment. We would like to thank them for the huge amount of work they put into their chapters. And it is testament to the strength of *Foundations* that Martin was able to mount such a vigorous defence and one which sets the scene for further investigations.

This volume began with a conference at the National University of Singapore in March 2015, where we discussed the drafts that were to become the present chapters. The conference was made possible by Research Grant R-241-000-XXX-112 made under the Singapore Ministry of Education Academic Research Fund Tier 1. That grant supported the 'Review workshop for Martin Loughlin's Foundations of Public Law', which was held at NUS Law Faculty and we would like to thank the faculty for the support they provided.

We were fortunate to be able to publish a number of chapters in earlier versions in the journal *Jus Politicum: Revue de Droit Politique* and we would like to thank the journal and Denis Baranger in particular for facilitating that process.

We would also like to thank Samuel Tschorne, Signe Rehling Larsen and Anca Bunda for invaluable assistance with arduous editorial and bibliographical work.

Finally, thanks to Hart Publishing for their own patience and support in bringing this volume to fruition.

Mike Wilkinson and Mike Dowdle
London, October 2017

TABLE OF CONTENTS

Part V: The Comparative Critique

Part VI: The Response

CONTRIBUTORS

Denis Baranger, Professor of Public Law, University of Paris II Panthéon-Assas, France

Jacco Bomhoff, Associate Professor of Law, London School of Economics and Political Science, UK

Hauke Brunkhorst, Professor of Sociology and Head of the Institute of Sociology, University of Flensburg, Germany

Michael W Dowdle, Associate Professor of Law, National University of Singapore

Marco Goldoni, Senior Lecturer in Law, University of Glasgow, UK

Andrew Halpin, Professor of Law and Director of the Centre for Legal Theory, National University of Singapore

Bob Jessop, Distinguished Professor of Sociology, University of Lancaster, UK

Matthew John, Associate Professor and Executive Director, Centre of Public Law and Jurisprudence, Jindal Global Law School, India

Martin Loughlin, Professor of Public Law, London School of Economics and Political Science, UK

Panu Minkkinen, Professor of Jurisprudence, University of Helsinki, Finland

James Penner, Professor of Law, National University of Singapore

Mark Tushnet, William Nelson Cromwell Professor of Law, Harvard Law School, USA

Neil Walker, Regius Professor of Public Law and the Law of Nature and Nations, University of Edinburgh, UK

Michael A Wilkinson, Associate Professor of Law, London School of Economics and Political Science, UK

Anna Yeatman, Professor, Institute for Culture and Society, University of Western Sydney, Australia

Part I

Introducing the Foundations of Public Law

1

Questioning the Foundations of Public Law and Questioning *Foundations of Public law*

MICHAEL A WILKINSON AND MICHAEL W DOWDLE

I. Introduction

This book is about *Foundations of Public Law*, but also about the foundations of public law.[1] The chapters do more than just address Martin Loughlin's text; they examine broader issues surrounding the nature of the subject, its autonomy and its methodology, and the nature of the object with which it is so intimately associated; the modern state. Loughlin's *Foundations of Public Law*, however, represents a distinct if not unique attempt to outline the conceptual building blocks of both subject and object, and it is where we will begin.

Foundations of Public Law represents both a challenge and an opportunity for the discipline. It offers a thorough reworking of the study of public law, converting it into a wide-ranging, interdisciplinary investigation into the foundational elements and evolutionary character of the modern state. This is challenging in its rejection of the idea that public law can meaningfully be captured through juridical doctrine alone, or by a method of positivist jurisprudence more generally. Instead, it requires an approach that is capable of incorporating political philosophy, political sociology and state theory. Public law is recast through *Foundations* as integral *to* these disciplines. Conversely, by bringing public law into conceptual and discursive interplay *with* these other disciplines, it provides a vital opportunity to free public law from its own jurisprudential straitjacket.

Such a reworking demands critical interrogation. Can public law maintain its internal coherence if extended in this way? Does *Foundations* offer the normative resources to renew the discipline in the context of the many serious challenges it faces? Is *Foundations*' methodology a suitable one for understanding the concrete phenomena associated with public law? Can *Foundations* capture the idea of public law as it emerges and operates outside the European nation-state or after the exhaustion of the Westphalian paradigm? The purpose of this volume is to critically explore these questions, and to advance our understanding of

[1] Martin Loughlin, *Foundations of Public Law* (Oxford, Oxford University Press, 2010) (hereinafter '*Foundations*').

the challenges *Foundations* poses, as well as the opportunities it provides for the development of the discipline.

Foundations offers a reconstruction of public law at once traditional and radical. It presents public law not simply as a discrete set of juridical doctrines and practices but as an integral part of our capacity to make political sense of the world. Public law is not an autonomous legal discipline, nor a doctrinal offshoot of private law or common law; it is an essential feature of the modern political imaginary. Public law, in this account, is not derivative but foundational to the construction and maintenance of the modern idea of the state.

If it is commonplace that in modernity the idea of the state and its authoritative apparatus of rule anchors our political being, *Foundations* argues this to be a thoroughly *juridical* phenomenon, but one that cannot be grasped by focusing on the judicial branch of government or the positive law alone. It can only be grasped through an analysis of the key conceptual building blocks of political authority, along with a thicker historical contextualisation of their evolution over time.

The outcome of this contextualisation suggests that, although central to 'seeing and thinking like a state', to constructing a scheme of political intelligibility, this juridical phenomenon is vulnerable, even in danger of being eclipsed, subverted or transformed in contemporary conditions—partly due to material transformations in the nature and techniques of governing and partly due to the pressures on the nation-state as the primary locus of political power and authority.[2] But the prospective loss is also a result of the increasingly specialised and technical nature of the discipline of public law (and jurisprudence more generally), a retreat encapsulated in the turn to systematisations of positive public law, which has its analogues in general jurisprudence (in diverse schools of legal positivism and legal pluralism).

Foundations of Public Law attempts to redefine the discipline of public law away from a court-centric doctrinal jurisprudence concerned primarily with judicial review—whether in positivist or moralist guise—towards a 'political jurisprudence'. This proceeds by way of retrieval and refoundation of the discourse of public law and jurisprudence through a historical reconstruction of its origins and development.

In performing this radical reorientation of the enterprise of public law—radical only in the proper sense of uncovering and reclaiming its *roots*—*Foundations* draws on work in legal scholarship as well as writing in political theory, social theory, moral theory, state theory (*Staatslehre*), and political science. It does this in a historical rather than abstract orientation, integrating material from the UK, continental Europe, and the US, much of which has evolved independently, to offer an evolutionary narrative of public law, tracking the development of the modern state and the pressures it faces in the latter half of the twentieth century.

In the manner of this synchronic retrieval, *Foundations* develops a unique theoretical frame by incorporating writers in the cannon of political and legal philosophy—Hobbes and Rousseau, Kant and Hegel, Schmitt and Foucault, amongst many others—who have sought to uncover 'the laws of the political', or the basic rules and precepts of political association.

[2] See, eg C McAmhlaigh, N Walker and C Michelon (eds), *After Public Law* (Oxford, Oxford University Press, 2013).

Throughout *Foundations*, these giants of political philosophy are rendered central figures in the tradition of political jurisprudence and of a reconstructed public law.

For these reasons *Foundations* stands as deserving of special attention, not only from public law scholars, but also from political theorists, constitutional theorists, constitutional historians and all those interested in the fate of the modern constitutional state and the chances of its survival, renewal or transcendence. Even those who contest the particular claims made in *Foundations*, or doubt its overall endeavour, will not doubt that it contributes centrally to this project, if only, as one major critic notes, because it now provides the starting point for any deeper inquiry into the subject of public law.[3]

The purpose of this collection is to begin precisely such an inquiry. And it aims to do so in a thoroughly critical manner, taking neither the methodology nor the content of *Foundations* for granted. To pursue this aim, we have collected commentators from diverse traditions and disciplines to contest the claims—both general and particular—made in and by *Foundations*.

In the remainder of this introduction we first single out and examine in more detail two features in *Foundations* that stand out: the integration of law and politics into a coherent conceptual scheme, and the integration of the history of public law into the state's evolving political form. We then turn to consider, categorise and summarise the series of trenchant critiques made of *Foundations* in the chapters that follow. Serious doubts remain about the viability of the project of *Foundations* as a whole, as well as about its discrete claims; the doubts raised are conceptual and synthetic, methodological as well as particular. These doubts—and the critiques that generate them—will be categorised here under four headings: *methodological*, *normative*, *materialist*, and *comparative*, in an attempt to organise the critical reflections, and provide some coherence to the endeavour.

II. Law and Politics

Constitutional theory and public law scholarship commonly approach politics as outside the law, to be tamed or contained by law, or even as antithetical to the logic of the law. Political order is presumed to follow a distinct logic of power, or to inhabit the realm of fact as opposed to norm. Alternatively, it is ignored, occluded by a formalist or positivistic approach to the constitution of the polity. In normativist traditions, particularly in the liberal constitutional imagination, public law exists to protect the individual from interference by the political organs of the state; constitutional scholarship then consists in identifying, specifying or offering suggestions for the consolidation or improvement of these structures, explicating their interrelationship and their overall architecture.

Foundations suggests this ubiquitous vision to be distorting. Public law, understood in the broader sense of political jurisprudence, does not simply constrain the organs of the

[3] D Dyzenhaus, 'The End of the Road to Serfdom' (2013) 63 *University of Toronto Law Journal* 326. Other review articles include M Walters, 'Is Public Law Ordinary?' (2012) *Modern Law Review* 894–913; J Grant, *Times Literary Supplement*, 7 Oct 2010, 22–23; C Thornhill, 'Martin Loughlin, Foundations of Public Law' (2011) *Public Law* 673–79; B Mauthe and T Webb, 'Realism and Analysis Within Public Law' (2013) 34 *Liverpool Law Review* 27–46.

state; it creates, shapes and maintains them. It does so by establishing and sustaining the governing relationship, between rulers and ruled. And since this governing relationship is not exhausted by the positive law narrowly conceived, public law as political jurisprudence captures all aspects of its institutionalisation and regulation, and also, significantly, those occasions of abrogation or suspension of ordinary forms and norms.

Public law as seen through the lens of political jurisprudence thus consists in the fundamental laws and practices that structure the governing relationship as well as those prudential judgments required to maintain—or regain—stability in that relationship. The set of practices and the manner of their ordering is captured in the term *droit politique* or 'political right'. This might be usefully contrasted with what in the English-speaking world has emerged in the field referred to as 'general jurisprudence'. If the purpose of general jurisprudence is to provide an account of the systemic coherence of positive law as such, the purpose of *Foundations* is to provide an account of the socio-epistemic coherence of the laws of politics, of what gives claims to political authority traction—and of what undermines them—in the world of lived experience.

To capture the phenomenon of public law therefore demands an analysis that transcends the positive law. This is reconstructed through an account of the key building blocks of 'state', 'constitution' and 'government', as they emerge and evolve in concrete public law traditions (especially but not limited to the German tradition of *Staatslehre*) and in tandem with classical works of political theory, from Hobbes through to Foucault, which seek to explain or deconstruct the grounds of authority of the modern state.

It is from the practice and discourse of political right as a state- and polity-building exercise that the distinctive jurisprudence of public law is reconstructed. The task of this political jurisprudence is to make theoretical and practical sense out of the various relations and configurations of power and authority that emerge, enabling their recognition as a set of relatively coherent phenomena. But because of the inherently conflictual nature of the human condition—conflict over material as well as symbolic resources—the ways in which relative coherence and stability are achieved will perpetually evolve.

For the governing process to remain in productive tension, converting conflict into manageable contest, an overall unity of purpose and character needs to be established and maintained through representational devices. And the dominant mode this takes in the context of modern public law is the unity of the state and autonomy of the political on which its power and authority rests. The arrangements of public law thus contribute to the maintenance of the state as a political unity, one that discharges political responsibility to its subjects.

This political unity, according to Loughlin, can never be fully captured by rule-based categories, not least because conflict can never be fully or finally resolved. If 'the establishment of an autonomous domain of the political is therefore a historical achievement',[4] it is also a precarious one, particularly as through late modernity the legal-political coupling is put under increasing pressure from social, economic and geo-political developments.

The significance of this reconstruction—as well as the pressure it is put under—can be appreciated by considering that outside the Anglosphere, in both continental Europe and in Asia, the formational appeal of public law continues to exist precisely in its state-creating

[4] See also Loughlin, 'Political Jurisprudence' in chapter 2, ? of this collection.

and state-shaping functions. The same can be said of the public law of the European Union, where the polity-building function of the law, as well as its limits in performing this function, is well documented and continues to offer an experimental case in reconfiguring relations of political power and authority. *Foundations* thus facilitates the cross-fertilisation of public law scholarship, representing the most promising framework to date for integrating diverse experiences of public law into a common discourse rooted in the particular context of modern European state development.

III. The Evolution of the Modern State

To expand on this last claim, we can consider briefly a crude version of the exercise in historical reconstruction. There are two key foundational shifts that occur with the emergence of the modern state. The first is a change in the belief system on which political authority rests: political jurisprudence thus captures the process of secularisation of authority, corresponding to Weber's well known account of the process of modern 'disenchantment', involving a loss of faith in divine or substantive natural law. In a constitutional vernacular associated with the period of modern revolution, but which becomes widespread over time, 'We, the people' are the new foundation of political authority.

But *Foundations* rejects the equation of this process of secularisation with total positivisation of rules and norms, of the reduction of power to sheer coercive force, and the complete separation of fact and value. The normative power of the factual—including the symbolic imaginary—survives secularisation; disenchantment is far from total. This is nowhere more apparent than in the realm of public law, despite the pressures of modernisation. And the point of political jurisprudence is to capture in a scientific manner the ways in which the normative power of the factual is retained in the modern constitutional imagination (if also transformed in comparison to the medieval and the pre-modern understanding).

The second foundational shift that characterises the modern state is more material in nature: the evolution in the structures of power and authority necessary to produce and sustain a political community in the face of political and economic pressures. To respond comprehensively to military and other kinds of security threat and provide for the well-being of the people in conditions of economic scarcity requires the actual exercise of particular forms of governing power. This real power to dominate can be captured by the term, used initially by Spinoza, *potentia*, in contrast to a rightful claim to command and assert political rule understood as *potestas*.[5] The state cannot govern by *potestas* alone; the legitimacy of the governing relationship must be based on more than a claim to a formal right to rule, even as its authority becomes increasingly rationalised on the basis of legal rules and formal practices. The state must generate allegiance through its actual achievement of certain public goods—not least in order for its claim to rightful rule to be credible and match a corresponding set of beliefs in its legitimacy on the part of those who are ruled.

[5] B de Spinoza, *Tractatus Theologico-Politicus, Tractatus Politicus* (translated by RHM Elwes) (London, Routledge, c1951).

To put the point differently, authority requires both a claim to rightful rule and the compulsion or compliance that corresponds with actual obedience; authority is de jure and de facto. But for the purpose of understanding public law in terms of political jurisprudence, it makes little sense to make a formal separation of these elements. Authority is thus not a purely normative concept—reducible either to moral principle or positive law. Neither, however, is it a purely materialist concept that can be reduced to sheer coercion or violence or any other causal forces of nature. It must be based in political right and be able to produce political goods.

Potestas and *potentia* are interdependent and dialectical rather than alternatives; political authority 'is a product of their relationship'. And it is also an evolving beast. Political power and authority change over time with the evolution of the constitutional imagination and constitutional circumstances. *Foundations*' contribution here is to chart this in the language of public law as political right. Significantly, it insists that there will and can be no consensus on the nature of political right—on the correct manner of the production of political goods over time. As such, 'the law of the political cannot be an ethic of ultimate ends'. Political conduct 'involves a trade-off between rival and often incommensurable goods in circumstances where there is no authoritative principle or standard for resolving any dispute'.[6] Prudential judgment is therefore required; governing is an activity without end.

And yet throughout the twentieth century, this governing activity and the dialectical process on which it is based becomes increasingly fraught. More and more is required of the state in terms of both its normative and its factual legitimacy (*potestas* and *potentia*), just as its overall authority is increasingly called into question by processes of European integration and economic globalisation. So although the normative standards of rightful rule become increasingly demanding, as the governing arrangements of the state are increasingly called on to satisfy principles of democracy and the rule of law, so too do the expectations of its capacity to protect and enhance the welfare of its citizens in increasingly pressing conditions. This has led to the emergence of new forms of rule and regulation, as well as increasingly prescriptive formal and informal goal-setting. If the apparatus of rule of the modern state, both as a practical and as an ideological matter, is classically grounded in traditional legal categories—constitutional law, administrative law, competition law, and various aspects of private law—much of its standards are increasingly prescribed by soft or informal law. The disciplinary and regulatory character of its governing arrangements increasingly derives from routinisation, expectation and informal coercion rather than from threat of official state sanction.

As normative standards and practical expectations come into conflict with one another, particularly in times that are considered critical for the polity's identity or even survival, practices and methods of sustaining the governing relationship thus change and even transform the nature of the relationship and the practices and methods that undergird it. The challenge then is to grasp the juristic significance of these phenomena. This challenge is significantly aided with the conceptual edifice reconstructed in *Foundations*. But it also leaves open the question of whether the phenomenon of public law as it emerges into the twenty-first century has developed to the stage where it requires a new set of conceptual tools to be properly scrutinised and fully understood.

[6] See also Loughlin, 'Political Jurisprudence' in chapter 2, of this collection.

IV. Continuity and Critique

In synthesising diverse and sometimes competing intellectual traditions into a coherent whole which tracks the dynamics of state development, *Foundations* contributes to the very discourse of public law it identifies, precipitating further syntheses with new ideas and related phenomena. But the project, in its rather terse concluding sections, also calls into question the stability and durability of public law in contemporary social and political conditions, suggesting the enterprise of political jurisprudence is itself ripe for renewal. Critique is therefore necessary for continuity of the discipline, whether through integration, refinement or abandonment of the project of 'political jurisprudence'.

This collection begins with Loughlin's restatement of political jurisprudence, presenting in a condensed manner its key elements. It continues with the various critiques divided into four parts: methodological, normative, material and comparative. This division does not of course reflect any tight or neat separation, it merely serves a heuristic purpose—it exposes common themes, and often from positions that would otherwise seem heterogeneous, as well as opposing critiques from otherwise common positions. The collection then ends with a response to the chapters from Loughlin. But it is hoped that this is just the beginning of a new chapter in the development of the discipline of public law.

A. The Methodological Critique

The first set of critiques of *Foundations* is in some sense 'external' in that it questions its basic methodological approach and working assumptions. In different ways, each of the chapters under this heading cast doubt on the viability and desirability of a search for any singular, scientific account (however internally complex and differentiated) of an object that can be called 'public law' when the practices that come under that label constitute a contingent, complex and incommensurable set of experiences. *Foundations*, in this view, is ultimately an incoherent exercise in conceptualisation; moreover, to the extent it claims purity, it may be an ideological view of, even an apology for, the modern state's particular ruling forms and apparatus.

Andrew Halpin's critique is the most direct assault on the methodological underpinnings of *Foundations*. It questions both the possibility as well as the desirability of projecting a uniform concept of public law based on a master narrative of the modern state. Halpin thus challenges each of *Foundations*' key claims: the *autonomy* of public law, the possibility of a *science* of political right, political jurisprudence as the prudential *approximation* of this science, and public law as a *grammar* of political jurisprudence. For Halpin, the characteristics of public law are determined by particular social and political circumstances; there is no uniform conception of a state (or of its institutional branches) that undergirds public law. The attempt to impose one elides the variety of questions that public law needs to answer and of problems it is and might be called on to resolve. Since there is no single problematic that gives the modern state its raison d'être, public law loses any claim to autonomy. And if there were such a problematic, there is no reason to suppose it would be restricted to public as opposed to private law ordering. *Foundations*' arguments do not therefore establish the purity Loughlin claims for his account. On the contrary, since there are multiple concepts of public law, stained by their own ideological hues, it succeeds only in providing an account of one more, albeit dressed in a (spurious) garb of objectivity. This not only overlooks important local differences, skewing our understanding of public law as a particular phenomenon, but also is liable to elevate its own unwarranted trust in juristic forms to 'negotiate' social tensions at the expense of an authentic political hearing.

Panu Minkkinen argues that the problem with *Foundations*' own purportedly pure and scientific account of the negotiation of claims of political right through prudential judgment is that it is neither truly scientific nor explicitly political. The claim to offer a scientific account actually undercuts a key feature of the modern political and democratic imaginary, captured by Claude Lefort's characterisation of political democracy as holding open 'the empty space of power' (and which *Foundations* also advances in its account of public law emerging out of the secularisation of fundamental law). Maintaining the empty space of power demands active resistance to the totalising tendencies of modernity, including those offered by way of a purportedly scientific account of the prudential judgment of state discourse. There is no way of transcending politics in a manner consistent with this emptiness; the starting point to overcoming the antinomy would instead be to offer a 'metapolitics' of public law, Minkkinen drawing on French political theorists Jacques Rancière and Alan Badiou to suggest a possible way forward. The metapolitical alternative would regard science, including the 'science' of political negotiation that *Foundations* itself advances, 'as one divided and divisive element amongst others on the political stage.'

Jacco Bomhoff's methodological critique is less direct. But it also takes aim at the suggestion, explicit but underdeveloped in *Foundations*, that the modern state is autonomous or conceptually self-contained in the sense of marking a specific break and rupture with the theological frame of the medieval world that preceded it. Critiquing this basic methodological premise serves two purposes. First, it problematises the neat modernisation and securalisation thesis on which *Foundations* depends and second, it reveals aspects of the theological that remain embedded in the mode of political jurisprudence. Bomhoff explores a question that follows from this: does Loughlin's elision of the theological and the juridical in political jurisprudence undermine the broader endeavour to maintain irreconcilability and openness in the discourse of political right?

B. The Normative Critique

The next set of challenges casts doubt on whether *Foundations* does justice to the full panoply of normative concerns associated with the idea and practice of public law. In particular, it suggests that the occlusion of an ethical dimension leaves *Foundations* without the tools to address contemporary anti-statism, authoritarianism, and post-state problems that require global political coordination. In privileging a top-down discourse of *potentia* based on sovereignty, *Foundations* neglects the generation of power through pre-institutional acts of egalitarian solidarity or claims of subjective right. Its statist bias also undercuts the potential of public law as political right to respond to challenges of globalisation and of political community as it emerges in post-state forms more generally.

Hauke Brunkhorst's chapter challenges *Foundations*' basic prioritisation of a top-to-bottom dynamic of state formation and political development. In its place Brunkhorst resurrects the idea of *potentia* as social or communicative power, which emerges from the 'bottom-up', in the manner suggested by, for example, Hannah Arendt or Jürgen Habermas. *Foundations* thus overlooks the possibilities of a *rational* (more than prudential) grounding of public law in the communicative power of the people, a discursive process that *precedes* concrete order formation and reunites *voluntas* and *ratio*. This is advanced not only in order to hold open the possibility of emancipation, but to retrieve traditions of public law that *Foundations* alludes to in its early outline of political jurisprudence, but which 'go missing' as *potentia* becomes merely technical regulatory power in its later stages (a loss explained by *Foundations*' adoption of a meta-narrative of constituent power as state-sovereignty rather than as egalitarian solidarity).

From a very different perspective, James Penner also tackles the relationship between *potestas* and *potentia*, reframing it in the language of analytical philosophy. From there, Penner argues that, although it cannot be straightforwardly mapped onto the distinction between the moral and the ethical, or the right and the good, there is an analogy which suggest *potestas* is prior and non-negotiable and that *potentia* is derivative and negotiable. Kant's doctrine of right, as well as writers within the liberal tradition such as Nozick and Rawls, struggle with justifying the exercise of the state's *potentia*, because beyond establishing the rightful or civil condition *potentia* demands the making of complex ethical judgments about the well-being of citizens. Although Raz has a way of responding to this problem, it is not one that Penner finds convincing. Penner's critique, although a challenge to Loughlin's position that *potestas* and *potentia* are irreconcilable as a matter of human nature, thus also constitutes a profound challenge to the tradition of liberal political philosophy itself.

Anna Yeatman argues that to successfully revive the tradition of political right requires the retrieval not only of a practical and prudential discourse—as *Foundations* attempts—but also, as it rejects—precisely such an explicitly ethical discourse based on subjective right. The unification in the early modern imagination of state and subjective freedom (which through Spinoza and Hegel play a significant part in the construction of political jurisprudence) is lost along the way in *Foundations*, and once it recedes, the emergence of social law and a functionalist mindset comes to resemble 'the road to serfdom'.[7] Rather than suggesting the termination of the dialectic of *potentia* and *potestas* (and lamenting the 'destruction of the modern edifice of public law') we should instead view the rise of the social through the lens of an *evolution* of subjective right in an increasingly complex world, a further stage in the dialectic of *potentia* and *potestas*. Only then might contemporary neo-liberal anti-statism be properly contested, as it must be in order to conceive of the state as expressing a form of public freedom rather than merely patrimonial service. *Foundations*' equivocation and ultimate denial of any normative standpoint thus ultimately threatens to undermine its overall promise and leaves it impotent to respond to the challenge of neo-liberalism.

If Yeatman's injunction is to take anti-statism seriously in order to defend the state, Neil Walker's approach tackles a different problem, suggesting that post-statism must be taken more seriously in order to defend the need for political authority *beyond the state*. Walker thus takes the critique of Loughlin's refusal of a normative standpoint a step further, pursuing the increasing challenges that political community as such and in general faces

[7] See also Dyzenhaus (n 3).

in conditions of globalisation and Europeanisation. Walker suggests *Foundations* is too quick in rhetorically deflecting their significance. He queries first whether it has sufficient resources to explain what would count as a transformation or underlying shift in governing arrangements such that we would be in a position to consider constitutional forms beyond the state. The charge is that *Foundations* suffers from a settlement bias, a reinforcing pattern of 'deep imaginary and surface form, of the abstract and concrete'. As such Walker doubts, second, whether there is sufficient scope within its own hermeneutic to imagine alternative non-state forms of authority—not only those already in evidence, but those that are transparently required to deal with global problems such as climate change or threats to national and transnational security.

C. The Material Critique

There is a different set of challenges to *Foundations* that emerge from a quite distinct perspective which we group here under the rubric of 'materialism'. From this perspective, the problem with *Foundations* is that it presents conflicting claims over the common good in overly abstract terms, even naturalising in a Hobbesian fashion the human condition of antagonism and formalising the relationship between rulers and the ruled. In other words, rather than being insufficiently normative, *Foundations* is insufficiently concrete, in a sense that is familiar to critical theory and Marxist traditions. Rationalising the art of governing requires an account—missing from *Foundations*—of how concrete social conflict, real domination, and power dynamics are translated into and in turn shape the ordering and outcome of political negotiations and of the content of political right. *Foundations*, in other words, fails to account for the material, economic and geo-political phenomena that condition claims to political right, whether the interplay of concrete subjectivities from below, through, for example, class struggle or from above, through, for example, geo-political imperialism and interstate competition. From a materialist perspective, this omission betrays a residue of formalism and even ideology, privileging—or reifying—one particular but contingent form of rule, neglecting that the state (and the interstate system) is not only a political but also a political-economic, and geo-political order.

Bob Jessop presents a comprehensive overview of state theory from different disciplinary angles, including conceptual history, systems theory, historical materialism, ideology critique and institutionalism, which complement but also compete with *Foundations*' jurisprudential account. Jessop highlights that *Foundations* does not explain *why* its particular juristic categories come to settle and dominate in the way they do, why certain ideas and practices become embedded and hegemonic, and others fail or fade away. Nor does it consider whether the dominant position of ideas that do come to settle might be subject to an ideology critique. Does public law, for example, serve particular interests; does it entrench particular positions? What would an account of the foundations of public law look like if it considered the asymmetries of authority and domination inscribed in the particular constellations and relations between rulers and the ruled, as well as the state's strategic role in reproducing patterns of exploitation and oppression? Given the range of materials addressed by *Foundations*, it is surprising that this is not given more consideration, even if only to be dismissed.

Whilst complementing *Foundations*' adoption of a dialectic of authority and power, Marco Goldoni also suggests that its analytical framework is overly formal. Goldoni picks as an example its metaphor of public law as grammar, which elides the element of political agency at play in the generation of different grammars or even of an overarching 'Ur-grammar'. As a corrective, Goldoni proposes the integration into political jurisprudence of the political subjects whose actions are responsible for forging the content of the material constitution. Integrating these insights means more than merely emphasising the formal possibility of revolutionary interruption or 'disruption' of the status quo (a la Rancière); it requires analysing in greater detail the political-economic organisation of society, including those hegemonic forces that shape it. By establishing the 'conditions of visibility' of political subjects, the potential dividends of a focus on the material constitution can be fully cashed out, not by a crude reductionism of politics to causal economic forces but by an integration of economic and material features into the analysis of the evolving political constitution.

Michael A Wilkinson makes this material critique more explicit, asking what the autonomy of the political looks like from the perspective of the relationship between politics and economics. He suggests that the autonomy of the political should be understood as a continuous political struggle taken up in the conflict between democracy and capitalism. He takes a diachronic approach to explore the contextual evolution of the Western European state in the twentieth century, considering political-economic as well as geo-political material factors that condition the claims and exercise of political authority, specifically the severe stress in the interwar period as a result of internal (political economic) pressures of democratisation and class consciousness and external (geo-political) pressures of inter-state competition. The state that inhabited the constitutional landscape of the long nineteenth century is refounded on a new basis in Western Europe in the postwar period in the project of European integration, materially transforming the very foundation of *Foundations*: the modern state itself as well as the coupling of law and politics on which political jurisprudence depends.

D. The Comparative Critique

If the methodological critique suggested that *Foundations*' dependence upon a singular and uniform paradigm of the modern state fails to account for the actual diversity of political and public law forms as they have emerged across time and space, this suggestion only invites further specification of what these different forms are, where they might be found, and why they depart from the paradigm. It invites, in other words, a critique from the perspective of comparative public law. This section presents three very different case studies that each call into question any claim to universality, to public law reflecting a unitary ordering of political right based on the edifice of the modern European state: first, US public law with its written constitution rather than state foundation; second, French and UK administrative law based on court-centric practice that emerged sporadically and laterally, and finally Indian constitutional law with its mix of cultural particularity and postcolonial legacy. They suggest, in other words, that whilst *Foundations* may have offered an account of the 'foundations' of a very particular tradition of public law (although one that remains underspecified), it is far from having offered a persuasive account of the foundations of public law *per se*.

Mark Tushnet argues that the project pursued in *Foundations* arises out of distinctly parochial British concerns, specifically those emerging from the modernising pressures that the British style of governing has come under since the latter half of the twentieth century. In the US, by contrast, the answer to the question of public law's foundations is relatively trivial and uncontested: it is the written constitution, and popular allegiance to it, that constitutes the state and grounds the constitution of government. And because of its dominant position in the world economy, the US is not under the kind of pressure faced by the UK to negotiate relationships with supranational political entities like the EU that would force a questioning of its basic authority structure. As a result of its relative political isolationism, US constitutional culture has also remained relatively autarkic; it has not therefore faced the same need to reflect on its constitutional basis. *Foundations* thus scratches an itch that simply isn't (yet) felt in the US context.

Mathew John examines the foundations of public law in India, providing a non-European perspective on *Foundations*, but one that has been highly influenced by British colonial history. John argues that the kinds of constitutional pedagogy espoused in the British colonial-constitutional settlements imposed in India, and reflected in *Foundations*' own conceptual categories, has difficulty in capturing the social reality of Indian political culture as well as the distinct problem of minority rights that it has had to confront. In the presence of such entrenched inequality and difference, the autonomy of the political and the unity of the state on which it depends can only seem a distant dream. A different set of conceptual tools and analytical devices would therefore be required to capture its public law tradition.

Denis Baranger, on the other hand, picks two phenomena which arguably should be central to the vernacular of *Foundations*: British and French administrative law. Specifically he queries whether *Foundations* fully captures the emergence of the court-based jurisprudence which has generated administrative law in both jurisdictions. This, after all, is the law commonly referred to by 'public law' in a contemporary context, including administrative action, regulation, and judicial review. In Baranger's view, modern administrative law does not emerge out of a foundational process of 'political jurisprudence'; it is rather a 'lateral' development, emerging in a 'sporadic and peripheral' fashion. And yet it evolves into a feature that becomes central to the discipline of public law as a whole. In other words, the French and British fields of administrative law, despite their significant differences, have both developed outside any foundational narratives of 'the State' or of 'the Constitution', and they remain in that suspended state. This autonomy is best explained as a process of 'differentiation', the state distinguishing (or 'derogating') the exercise of its powers from private law ordering. But in that sense, public law is derivative rather than foundational. In conclusion, however, Baranger offers an olive branch, seeing in *Foundations*' project of elaborating a 'science of right ordering' a way of retrieving a 'foundational narrative' of the quest for (political) *justice*, which might be renewed in contemporary conditions in the face of increasing and evolving discretionary administrative powers.

2

Political Jurisprudence

MARTIN LOUGHLIN

I. Introduction

Political jurisprudence is a discipline that explains the way in which governmental authority is constituted. It flourished within European thought in the period between the sixteenth and nineteenth centuries and since the twentieth century has been in decline. That decline, attributable mainly to an extending rationalisation of life and thought, has led to governmental authority increasingly being expressed in technical terms. And because many of the implications of this development have been masked by the growth of an academic disciplinary specialisation that sacrifices breadth of understanding for depth of knowledge, sustaining the discipline has proved difficult. Since we may now have reached a critical period in which the influence of technique threatens entirely to subvert the intelligibility of the foundations of modern governmental authority, it seems an appropriate moment at which to reflect on the nature and significance of political jurisprudence.

II. Schools of Jurisprudence

Throughout the Middle Ages, jurists maintained a distinction between positive law, law made by the sovereign, and natural law (sometimes expressed as 'fundamental law'), law that made the sovereign. With the transition to modernity, the predominant meaning of law altered: as the authority of natural law waned, the term came to signify positive law, that is, rules of conduct expressing the will of the sovereign. The question of why one should obey the sovereign's laws—the issue on which natural law focused—did not disappear. What changed is that most jurists came to believe that the question lies beyond the bounds of legal cognition. The question remains, but it raises issues of a moral, political, or sociological character and is not one for legal science.

This position, commonly associated with the school of legal positivism, is directly challenged by political jurisprudence. It is true that in the modern era law is positivised and that public law emerges as a distinct body of positive law that establishes and maintains the activity of governing. But political jurists contend that the status and meaning of positive public law cannot be grasped without understanding the socio-political factors that condition governmental authority. Political jurisprudence, then, is a science that emerges as natural law is transformed, moral theology pushed to a private sphere, and the idea of fundamental law acquires a new meaning within the autonomous domain of the political. The nature of public law, it is contended, can be properly specified only from the perspective of political jurisprudence.

Political jurists are not alone in maintaining an anti-positivist stance and arguing that there is an intrinsic connection between legality and legitimacy. However, many who take a critical position with respect to legal positivism skew the nature of that connection by making two distorting shifts in orientation. Having become preoccupied with the expanding jurisdiction of courts, anti-positivist legal scholars often claim that law is, in its essence, a principle-embedded argumentative practice. They believe that the true character of law is revealed through an analysis of the rulings of the court acting as the 'forum of principle'. While this has become an important aspect of contemporary practice, this claim neglects a more basic modern function of law: that of establishing the institutions of government and equipping them with their powers of rule. Once this constitutive aspect of law is overlooked, a second distorting move soon follows: anti-positivists promote a moral rather than a political reading of that exercise. The basic task of public law, they maintain, is to explicate what are perceived to be the fundamental moral principles of a governmental regime, and these are invariably expressed in some catalogue of citizens' rights. The neglect of the more basic constructive dimension of law and the consequential foregrounding of one special institutional forum sets the frame for regarding law as a moral rather than a political discourse. This leads anti-positivists to conflate legality and legitimacy.

Political jurisprudence seeks to redress this imbalance. It is founded on the assumption that law is a dimension of the political. The political, it is maintained, is an autonomous universe of discourse, and it is able to build the power of that worldview only through the operation of its own fundamental laws. Legality and legitimacy are distinct but interrelated concepts. They must be drawn into an appropriate relation, but legitimacy—otherwise, authority—is a political concept, and one that should not be equated with legality.

Legal positivists treat the office of the sovereign as the ultimate authority, and this remains the case even in sophisticated accounts that rest the authority of law on some 'founding norm' or on a 'rule of recognition'. In those accounts, questions of legality and legitimacy are kept distinct. Anti-positivist normativists conflate the two. They do so by seeking to eliminate the sovereign altogether, replacing that figure with the self-sustaining authority of a corpus of values, norms and principles of an abstract, morally-laden legality. From the perspective of political jurisprudence, by contrast, the central object of inquiry is neither the sovereign as such, nor the unfolding integrity of a moral practice. Rather, it is the relationship that evolves between a 'people' and its office of government. It is this distinctively political relationship that holds the key to understanding the modern concept of fundamental law. The sovereign, it might be said, is above fundamental law only in the way that a building is above its foundations: tamper with the foundations and the building might collapse. Formally, the sovereign's authority to make (positive) law is unlimited. But the task of political jurisprudence is to specify those 'laws' that establish and condition a formally unlimited authority of positive law-making. This is the basic 'law' of 'the political'. This central investigation for political jurisprudence is the search for what I have variously called *jus politicum*, *droit politique* or, in English, 'the science of political right'.

III. The Nature of the Inquiry

I have advanced this inquiry in two ways—synchronic and diachronic—that are intended to be mutually reinforcing. In *The Idea of Public Law*, I sought to specify the conceptual building blocks of this subject.[1] These are: *the activity of governing*, the unique object of the subject (Ch 2); *politics*, the distinctive practice that evolves to manage the activity of governing (Ch 3); *representation*, the symbolic basis of public law (Ch 4); *sovereignty*, the modern representation of the autonomy of the political domain (Ch 5); *constituent power*, the juristic representation of *collective autonomy* in modern public law (Ch 6); and *rights*, the juristic representation of the principle of *individual autonomy* in modern public law (Ch 7). These elements were then drawn together to specify the distinctive method of public law as political reason, or *raison d'état* (Ch 8). And finally (Ch 9) I suggested that, since Kelsen presents a pure theory of positive law,[2] this account of the basic elements of *jus politicum*—which establishes a specific (ie autonomous) way of world-making—aspired to offer a pure theory of public law.

The second book, *Foundations of Public Law*, provided a thicker account of the texture of public law by presenting a historical reconstruction of its conceptual formation. It provides an account of the origins of the subject in medieval and early-modern jurisprudence (Pt I), examines the search for a modern science of political right (Pt II) and then explains how the fundamental laws of modern political reality that have evolved shape understanding of: (i) the nature of this mode of political association (the state: Pt III), (ii) the scope of its office of authority (the constitution: Pt IV), and (iii) its distinctive modes of action (government: Pt V).[3]

The basic argument made in *Foundations* is that the tensions inherent in this distinctive type of political association ensure that a science of political right can never be realised. This is for two main reasons. The first is attributable to the nature of political association, an issue which will be considered below in section V. The second, attributable to the nature of law, is addressed now. The basic point is that *jus politicum* must not be assumed to refer merely to a set of abstract normative principles, such as the principles of equal liberty. To count as law, these principles must be operationalised within actual regimes. Law is concrete and embedded. Realising both the normative power of facticity and the facticity of normative power is an altogether more challenging task. Rousseau had suggested that putting the law above man is a problem in politics similar to that of squaring the circle in geometry. If it can be solved, good government results. If not, then wherever people believe that the rule of law prevails, they deceive themselves: 'it will be men who will be ruling'.[4]

[1] Martin Loughlin, *The Idea of Public Law* (Oxford, Oxford University Press, 2003).

[2] Hans Kelsen, *Introduction to the Problems of Legal Theory* (BL Paulson and SL Paulson trans of first edn [1934] of *Reine Rechtslehre)* (Oxford, Clarendon Press, 1992).

[3] Martin Loughlin, *Foundations of Public Law* (Oxford, Oxford University Press, 2010).

[4] Jean-Jacques Rousseau, *Considerations on the Government of Poland and on its Projected Reformation* [1772] in his *The Social Contract and other later political writings* (edited by Victor Gourevitch) (Cambridge, Cambridge University Press, 1997) 177–260, 179.

But if this 'law of the political' cannot be discovered through normative abstraction, then neither is it a set of scientific laws of causation, not least because the world of the political presents itself as a domain of freedom. In *The Spirit of the Laws*, Montesquieu tried to explain political right in such causal terms but, as Rousseau noted, he had been 'content to discuss the positive right of established governments', which is a different matter.[5]

Some might therefore conclude that the idea of 'political right' refers only to a loose collection of prudential maxims, and this does not deserve the designation of 'law'. Before yielding to such pragmatism, it might be noted that Rousseau's innate pessimism derives in large part from his unworldly nature. In postulating an ideal—the general will—as the principle on which the state is founded, his thesis effectively guarantees that this principle of political freedom will become corrupted. Rather than assuming some immaculate conception, it is more realistic to inject a dose of historical materialism and explain political ordering as the product of the ongoing struggle to give precise institutional meaning to contentious principles of political right. The political domain is not a regime that has authoritatively legislated certain principles of right; it is a domain within which the tensions between contested expressions of *jus politicum* are continuously negotiated.

Jus politicum might therefore be defined as an expression of the immanent laws of the domain of the political. Causal laws, whether those of Montesquieu (factors of climate, commerce, spatial location, etc) or Marx (generated between the forces and relations of production), undoubtedly exert considerable influence in structuring the domain of the political. But *jus politicum* refers to that body of constitutive and regulative rules and practices that sustain the autonomous character of the domain of the political. These laws are distilled from political practice. The 'law of the political' is derived neither from the wisdom of the ancient Greeks nor from utopian thought experiments. Far from expressing an ideal arrangement of liberal-democratic norms, *jus politicum* can only be derived from lived experience.

From this perspective, the contrasting expressions of the 'law of the political' offered by such scholars as Bodin, Hobbes, Locke, Pufendorf, Montesquieu, Rousseau, Hegel and their followers all deserve acknowledgement. Claims to the authority of the sovereign will, the foundational importance of rights to life, liberty, and property, the influence of causal social laws, and the striving for equal liberty in solidarity are all capable of shaping the character of a political regime. But regimes invariably incorporate a variety of these formally incompatible precepts. The political domain expresses a distinctive mode of association but it remains open and indeterminate. Its discontinuities—between the appeal to the universal and the demands of the local, between the absolute and the conditional, between the formal and the material—can be neither eliminated nor reconciled: they can only be negotiated. *Jus politicum* does not just require an explication of certain principles of political right; of its nature, it expresses an endless tension between different conceptions and the manner of their institutionalisation at particular moments. Any reconciliation must be the result of practical reasoning and prudential judgment. This is an exercise in *juris-prudentiae*. And it is for this reason that the science of public law is best called 'political jurisprudence'.

[5] Jean-Jacques Rousseau, *Emile, or On Education* [1762] (translated by Allan Bloom) (New York, Basic Books, 1979) 458.

IV. The Political Domain

Modern western political thought has drawn much of its energy from a basic conundrum: that despite our common historical experience of regimes built on conflict, domination and the threat of disorder, we nevertheless feel the appeal of the idea of human association formed as an orderly, just and peaceful community. An influential strand of political thought devotes itself to the task of overcoming that gulf between reality and ideal. Drawing on earlier studies by the Stoics and medieval Christian scholars, this strand of thought is expressed most clearly in the work of certain Enlightenment writers who suggest that the laws of nature and the laws of reason can be reconciled. Reconciliation is achieved by realising a form of human association made accessible to us through the power of reason. Initially expressing an overarching, divinely-sanctioned unity, in its post-theological phase it presents itself as a set of principles of association that humans are impelled rationally to adopt.

The contemporary rights-orientated, anti-positivist stance I have outlined amounts to a reprise of this conviction. Political jurisprudence develops in opposition to this strand of thought. Sceptical about the possibility of reconciliation through transcendence, political jurisprudence recognises the unbridgeable nature of the gulf between reality and ideal. Political jurisprudence might acknowledge the influence of 'abstract universals' but it does not ignore 'necessary conditions'.[6] It appeals to reason but does not seek an escape from history. It presents itself as a practical discourse which, although orientated to norms, also has regard to pre-conditions, contexts and consequences.[7] Rather than advocating reconciliation through the promotion of some overarching moral sensibility, political jurisprudence seeks through phenomenological investigation to explain the immanent logic of political reason that sustains this distinctive way of ordering the world. What, then, are the underlying assumptions on which political jurisprudence rests?

We might start by recognising that the arrangement adopted when humans enter into some type of collective association is not determined by nature. Early-modern scholars occasionally used analogies drawn from nature, such as the beehive or the family, to demonstrate that human association takes a pre-determined hierarchical form.[8] Political jurists of the formative era, by contrast, recognised the need to found human association on some notion of equality. Too much should not be made of this criterion: the essential point they were making is that the right to rule exists neither as a divinely-ordained nor a natural right and that its justification required acceptance of formally-equal individuals. In order to express this point, they were obliged to draw a distinction between public and private.

[6] GWF Hegel, *Philosophy of Right* [1821] (translated by TM Knox) (Oxford, Clarendon Press, 1952) §§ 29–33. See Axel Honneth, *The Pathologies of Individual Freedom: Hegel's Social Theory* (Princeton, Princeton University Press, 2010) 15: 'here [in this section of *Philosophy of Right*] it becomes clear that the term *right* has the double meaning of a "necessary condition" and a "justifiable claim"'.

[7] See, especially, Ian Hunter, *Rival Enlightenments: Civil and Metaphysical Philosophy in Early Modern Germany* (Cambridge, Cambridge University Press, 2001).

[8] See, eg, John Locke, *Two Treatises of Government* [1680] (edited by Peter Laslett) (Cambridge, Cambridge University Press, 1988), the first treatise of which was a critical analysis of Robert Filmer's *Patriarcha*, which sought to show that paternal power and political power must be differentiated.

Bodin was the first of the early-modern scholars to retrieve the Aristotelian distinction between the household (*oikos*) and the polity (*polis*). He thereby opened up the possibility of differentiating between a natural hierarchy based on master and slave (or superior and inferior) operating in a private space, and a public domain involving an arrangement of government that, in the absence of divine or natural ordering, can properly be constituted only by an exercise of will.[9] When Hobbes presented Bodin's argument in a more systematic manner, he emphasised that this type of collective association is not drawn from nature: it is created by artifice, an exercise in imagination. The political domain is established through an exercise of imaginative representation and its mode of government is created through consent (though, in Hobbes' case, this was consent generated by fear).

This exercise of imagination draws on a specific philosophical anthropology. Hobbes's sketch of life without governing authority, a world of perpetual conflict, is exemplary of the anthropological scepticism maintained by political jurists. Even if we do not accept Hobbes' account, we might still recognise that his sources of human conflict—acquisitiveness, diffidence, and the striving for glory—are distinctive features of politically-orientated behaviour. Machiavelli had argued in similar fashion, claiming that humans are creatures of appetite and passion. Since rivalry, competition and conflict among humans is ingrained, resource scarcity is not some existential fact that drives us to compete; such scarcity is itself the consequence of human attributes. Similar assumptions underpin the work of political jurists.[10] Far from being inspired by an image of ideal order, they were driven by the threat of disorder. Political jurisprudence founds itself on the belief that conflict is an intrinsic feature of collective human association.

Political jurisprudence also rests its claims on the belief that humans are political animals. They are political animals by virtue of being sociable creatures who recognise the need to cooperate in order to flourish, but they are also driven to compete with one another as a means to their own satisfaction. They must therefore simultaneously cooperate and compete, and they compete not only over material goods but also for fame and glory. This need to compete over marks of esteem that require public acknowledgement suggests that politics—the struggle for power under conditions of mutual recognition—is intrinsic to the human condition.

Political jurists maintain that competition and conflict cannot be eliminated, and nor should we try to, since conflict and struggle are intrinsic to human freedom. Only through these struggles are the singular human qualities of autonomy, difference and distinction realised. Only then can individuals and groups assert themselves (ie, forge an *identity* in the world) and only through acknowledgement of that identity (ie, through *recognition*) do they acquire status within *a common world* (ie, affirm themselves as members of a common

[9] Jean Bodin, *The Six Bookes of a Commonweale* (translated by Richard Knolles, 1606, edited by Kenneth Douglas McRae) (Cambridge, Massachusetts, Harvard University Press, 1962) I. 2.

[10] James Madison, Alexander Hamilton and John Jay, *The Federalist Papers* I (edited by Kramnick) (London, Penguin, 1987) No 51: 'If men were angels, no government would be necessary' (Madison). His claim derives from J-J Rousseau, 'The Social Contract' in *The Social Contract and other Later Political Writings* (translated by V Gourevitch) (Cambridge, Cambridge University Press, 1997) Bk II, ch7 (68–69): 'To discover the best rules of society suited to each Nation would require a superior intelligence who saw all of man's passions and experienced none of them … It would require gods to give men laws.'

association). Political jurisprudence recognises that politics is an aspect of the human condition and is born of the need to manage rather than eliminate conflict.[11]

If the struggle for recognition is a central feature of political existence, it follows that the key to understanding the human condition is found not in nature but in historical experience. Humanity is not revealed by some fixed and abstract conception of human nature: human nature is the product of an evolving sense of mutual recognition. The political domain emerging from the dissolution of a medieval belief in the divinely-ordained, legally-prescribed intelligible cosmos is characterised by openness to historical contingency. It emerges because different ways of viewing the world are opened up: scientific, moral, economic, aesthetic, technical … and political. The political evolves as a specific type of interaction; political relations are not reducible either to moral or to socio-economic relations.

The autonomy of the political, then, expresses itself in a number of distinctions: as autonomy from a theological or religiously-derived worldview, exemplified by the replacement of the principle of 'one prince, one faith, one law' with that of a freedom of religious worship in a private sphere and the authority of a secular sovereign in the public; autonomy from the idea that force or conquest provide a sound basis for building a political society; autonomy from custom or tradition as the determinative source of legitimation; and autonomy from the idea that property equals sovereignty, that political power is reducible to economic power. The establishment of an autonomous domain of the political is a historical achievement.

If the autonomy of the political is a historical achievement, then so too are the concepts by which the political operates: these concepts amount only to a 'fragment of historical experience captured in words' and they 'bear the scars of political struggles'.[12] Although political concepts may express principles of universal aspiration, they can never shed their marks of historical particularity.

It follows that the law of the political cannot be an ethic of ultimate ends. Civil peace is achievable only when the moral convictions underpinning people's beliefs remain primarily in the private sphere. Consensus is generally reached only on outcomes rather than the reasons for them.[13] This is what Weber called an 'ethic of responsibility',[14] concerning

[11] Niccolò Machiavelli, *The Discourses* (translated by LJ Walker) (London, Penguin, 1970) Bk I.4 (p 113): 'those who condemn the quarrels between the nobles and the plebs, seem to be cavilling at the very things that were the primary cause of Rome's retaining her freedom … [I]n every republic there are two different dispositions, that of the populace and that of the upper class and all legislation favourable to liberty is brought about by the clash between them'. As scholars such as Arendt and Lefort have shown, the attempt in the modern world to bring about the elimination of social conflict leads only to totalitarianism. See, eg, Claude Lefort, *The Political Forms of Modern Society: Bureaucracy, Democracy, Totalitarianism* (Cambridge, Massachusetts, MIT Press, 1986) 79. Totalitarianism, he argues, 'is not a political regime: it is a form of society, that form in which all activities are immediately linked to one another, deliberately presented as modalities of a single world … that form in which, lastly, the dominant model exercises a total physical and spiritual constraint on the behaviour of private individuals'.

[12] Wilhelm Hennis, *Politics as a Practical Science* (translated by Keith Tribe) (Basingstoke, Palgrave Macmillan, 2009) 27.

[13] Note, eg, Merleau-Ponty's observation that the 'purity of principles not only tolerates but even requires violence': Maurice Merleau-Ponty, *Humanism and Terror* (translated by John O'Neill) (Boston, Beacon Press, 1969) xiii.

[14] Max Weber, 'Politics as a Vocation' in HH Gerth and C Wright Mills (eds), *From Max Weber: Essays in Sociology* (London, Routledge & Kegan Paul, 1948) 77–128, at 120–28.

how we are able to act responsibly and in accordance with the particular requirements of whichever life one finds oneself in.[15] Principles take us only so far; the political domain rests on cultural and contextual factors that permit the emergence of the idea that political conduct involves a trade-off between rival and often incommensurable goods in circumstances where there is no authoritative principle or standard for resolving any dispute.

V. The State

Political jurists recognised that in order to manage conflict and build authority some symbolic representation of the unity of the association is needed. This was Hobbes' objective in devising the figure of an omnipotent sovereign, and we see variants in Rousseau's concept of 'the general will' and also in the concepts of 'harmonic proportion' proposed by Bodin and Montesquieu.[16] Symbolic representation of unity diffuses those conflicts that threaten to undermine order and converts such conflicts into more manageable tensions. Generating a strong sense of political unity also performs the delicate task of maintaining order while permitting change. This is a necessary task but because the power of the traditional image of the prince as the majestic sovereign is eroded it proves difficult to sustain. The traditional image of the prince is supplanted by an abstract, rather ethereal notion of 'the people' as the source of ultimate authority. This is a much less powerful representational device, and it makes the maintenance of a sense of political unity a more uncertain and contingent undertaking.

Rather than simply resting on an ambiguous notion of 'the people' as the ultimate authority, political jurists devised an institutionalised expression of ultimate authority in the concept of the state. The autonomy of the political domain is made manifest in the juristic idea of the state. When a group are drawn together in common association, there comes a moment at which they are perceived as existing as a distinct people occupying a defined territory and subject to a governing authority. This arrangement is known as a state: the state is an expression of the scheme of association that characterises a people within a defined territory as being subject to an authoritative form of government. Individuals are conceived as subjects when passive, citizens when active, but never primarily as labourers, producers, consumers, or family members. Within this scheme, they realise freedom as a consequence of a struggle for recognition. Such political freedom is never absolute, but always contextual and conditional. And although freedom is realised through law, this expression refers to *jus politicum*, which operates as the code of the political domain.

The authority of this scheme is expressed in the concept of sovereignty, which recognises the absolute authority of the state to govern itself through positive law. Sovereignty expresses the autonomy of the political domain and the state's independent status in the political world. It establishes both the autonomy of states to regulate their own affairs through law and the principle on which modern international relations are conducted.

[15] See Wilhelm Hennis, 'Max Weber's "Central Question"' in his *Max Weber: Essays in Reconstruction* (translated by Keith Tribe) (London, Allen & Unwin, 1988) Ch 1.

[16] Bodin (n 9) Bk VI; CL Montesquieu, *The Spirit of the Laws* (translated and edited by A Cohler, B Miller and H Stone) (Cambridge, Cambridge University Press, 1989) Bk11, Ch 6.

This first develops as a *jus publicum europaeum* founded on a mutual acknowledgement of the inviolable domestic authority of sovereign states and mutual recognition of autonomous states in the international arena. This hegemony later assumes a global significance. Not subject to any common higher authority and conferring the right to make war (*jus ad bellum*), inter-state law evolves in the modern era to replace the medieval idea of 'just war' (*justa causa belli*). This distinctive political arrangement is recognised by the emergence of a body of public international law which regulates inter-state relations.

This juristic idea of the state should not be misunderstood: although comprising territory, people and ruling authority, it is not reducible to any one of these elements. Rather, the state is that which enables us to think systematically about governmental institutions and practices and the set of political relations with respect to people and territory that arise between them. The state is the regulatory idea that gives meaning to the workings of political life. And yet, when we inquire further into its character we encounter a fundamental ambiguity. The state can be properly grasped only as 'an unresolved tension between two irreconcilable dispositions'.[17] The state presents itself both as an arrangement of authoritative rules of conduct (*societas*) and as a corporate entity established in furtherance of designated purposes (*universitas*). These might be read as alternative images of the nature of the state since, although irreducible, they cannot be combined. But since they cannot stand as self-sufficient specifications, each must be embraced as the specification of the self-division of this key concept of the state. And this illustrates why it is in the nature of political jurisprudence that it operates to negotiate these intrinsic tensions in the political domain.

VI. Power and Authority

Jus politicum operates to maintain the authority of the state. That the state must possess authority is elementary: authority is the lifeblood of the state without which security, justice and liberty cannot be maintained. But in order to understand the concept of authority a distinction must be drawn between two concepts of power: *potestas*, the power generated by being-in-common and experienced as 'power to', and *potentia*, the ability to achieve intended effects, experienced as 'power over'. Authority is generated primarily by the former and deployed as the latter.

Potestas is a type of power intrinsic to political jurisprudence; it creates authority as a product of the people's capacity to act in common. Since it is the power created by drawing people together in a common undertaking, *potestas* is derived from the imaginative power of symbolic representation of a people existing in common association. *Potestas* is the power generated by the conviction that the association forms a unity, a collective singular: 'we the people'. This provides the foundation for collective security, not least because it is the source of the people's willingness, *in extremis*, to fight to preserve that mode of association.

The original source of *potestas* is some notion of a founding moment when a multitude conceives itself as forming a people. This notion is invariably shrouded in myth and legend,

[17] Michael Oakeshott, 'On the Character of a Modern European State' in his *On Human Conduct* (Oxford, Clarendon Press, 1975) 185–326 at 200–01.

and its power is generated through augmentation of these founding myths. That is, the power expressed in *potestas* rests on a foundation it does not itself establish. It draws on stories of peoplehood that generate a sense of common identity. This might be based on ethnicity, culture, language and shared history, but whatever its source it must be transformed into a common sense of *political* identity. This is what Rousseau meant by the need to promote a 'civil religion' able to instill the virtues of patriotism.[18] It also explains the importance of the modern notion of political nationalism.[19] *Potestas* maintains its vigour through reinforcement and augmentation of a foundational myth.

Potentia, by contrast, is the power deployed by government to control and regulate conflict, to maintain order, and to promote the public welfare. Governmental 'power over' its subjects is often regarded as domination, enforced obedience to rules. Weber was referring specifically to this when suggesting that from a sociological perspective one can define the state 'only in terms of the specific *means* peculiar to it, as to every political association, namely, the use of physical force'. In his elaboration, he defined the state as 'a human community that (successfully) claims the *monopoly of the legitimate use of physical force* within a given territory'.[20] But Weber here is describing the state only as an instrument of rule and consequently he analyses its power only as force. This distorts the juristic idea of the state and neglects the generational aspect of power created by action-in-common, power that renders the force of *potentia* 'legitimate'. *Potentia*, as 'power over' or domination, is a central element of political jurisprudence, but it is only the distributive aspect of a political power generated through *potestas*.

The essence of the political rests in the relationship between *potestas* and *potentia*. Carl Schmitt had defined the essential criterion of the political as the drawing of a friend–enemy distinction. This inclusionary–exclusionary criterion is critical to the formation of a sense of a people but this is only one of the elements of the building of an autonomous world of the political. State-building through *jus politicum* rests most importantly on the dynamic between *potestas* and *potentia*. This relationship is often expressed paradoxically: constraints on power generate power. This apparent paradox, first identified by Bodin,[21] is resolved once it is understood that constraints on governmental power (*potentia*) provide the decisive means of enhancing authority (*potestas*). *Potestas* is based on trust and allegiance, qualities strengthened by the imposition of controls and checks on officers of government. *Potentia* exercised in an unrestrained or arbitrary manner, by contrast, ends up corroding the basis of authority, leading to a loss of power (*potestas*).[22] For this reason, Montesquieu regarded despotism as the antithesis of political order and recognised the necessity of building political power through institutional development.[23]

[18] Rousseau (n 10) 142–151; Rousseau, 'Discourse on Political Economy' in Rousseau (n 10) 3–38 at 16–17.

[19] See Benedict Anderson, *Imagined Communities: Reflections on the Origin and Spread of Nationalism* (London, Verso, 2006).

[20] Weber (n 14) at 78.

[21] Bodin (n 9) 517.

[22] Friedrich Meinecke, *Machiavellism: The Doctrine of Raison d'État and its place in Modern History* (translated by D Scott) (New Haven, Yale University Press, 1957) 10: 'Power which gushes out blindly, will end by destroying itself; it must follow certain purposive rules and standards, in order to preserve itself and to grow.'

[23] See Montesquieu (n 16) esp Bks 8 and 11. Note also Machiavelli (n 11) Bk III.5 (p 396). 'From this princes should learn … that they begin to lose their state the moment they begin to break the laws and to disregard the ancient traditions and customs under which men have long lived'. Cf Michael Oakeshott, *The Politics of Faith and*

The 'law of the political' dictates that political power is enhanced by virtue of its institutionalisation.[24]

Political power is not a thing-in-itself; it is a product of the relationship between *potestas* and *potentia*. Contrary to Mao's claim, political power does not emanate from the barrel of a gun.[25] It is generated through the symbolic representation of political unity, which expresses itself in an institutional configuration of authority. As the state becomes more powerful, this institutional configuration becomes more complex and robust. Despotic power diminishes and infrastructural power increases.[26] Political power does not reside in any specific locus: it is generated through the relationship itself. This expresses the dynamic aspect of the political domain. Power (*potentia*) is a central feature of the state and is often deployed through the medium of positive law but it relies on a foundation of authority generated through the operation of 'political right'.

What about conquest? Although violent conquest (in contrast to domination) plays no direct role in political jurisprudence, the fact that the origins of order often spring from conquest makes force the dark shadow of political ordering. This is Hobbes' critical point about man's natural state being that of a perpetual 'war of all against all'. In this respect, he was following the ancients.[27] And although he uses this as the basis of an analytical exercise, it remains the 'original sin'.[28] Hobbes' point is reinforced by Rousseau's claim that the original acquisition is generally effected through force and only subsequently legitimated through institution. This renders the question of foundation particularly complicated: what some celebrate as liberation and the opening of a new era, others experience as defeat and subjugation.[29] Since political jurisprudence is rooted in the connection between

the Politics of Scepticism [c.1952] (edited by Timothy Fuller) (New Haven, Yale University Press, 1996) 35: 'the barbarism of order appears when order is pursued for its own sake and when the preservation of order involves the destruction of that without which order is only the orderliness of the ant-heap or the graveyard'.

[24] Freedom, like power, cannot be treated as some pre-existing condition: freedom is a status that is realised only within the state. Consequently, the sovereign's commands (ie positive law) cannot be conceived as imposing restrictions on some pre-existing freedom; such commands might equally be viewed as conditions for the realisation of freedom. The discourse of political right, operating to enhance the power of the public domain, strives to realise an equal liberty for all through an institutional arrangement that imposes a structure which constrains and disciplines individuals. The discourse of political right is simultaneously enabling and constraining. Rousseau concisely expressed this dilemma when claiming that the state 'cannot endure without freedom, nor freedom without virtue, nor virtue without citizens'. If we are able to create citizens, he added, we will realise liberty. But if we fail in this endeavour, we will create 'nothing but nasty slaves, beginning with the chiefs of the state'. Rousseau, 'Discourse on Political Economy' (n.18) at 20.

[25] Mao Tse Tung, 'Problems of War and Strategy', 6 November 1938 in *Selected Works, Vol II*, 224 (Marxists Internet Archive): 'Every Communist must grasp the truth: "Political power grows out of the barrel of a gun".'

[26] Michael Mann, 'The Autonomous Power of the State: Its Origins, Mechanisms and Results' (1984) 25 *Archives Européenes de Sociologie* 185–213 at 190.

[27] See, eg, Heraclitus (535–475BC): 'War is the father of all and king of all, and some he shows as gods, others as men; some he makes slaves, others free'. GS Kirk, JE Raven & M Schofield, *The Presocratic Philosophers: A Critical History with a Selection of Texts*, 2nd edn (Cambridge, Cambridge University Press, 1983) 193. See further, Thucydides, 'The History of the Grecian War' in W Molesworth (ed), *The English Works of Thomas Hobbes* (London, Bohn, 1843) Vol 8, 348: 'war is a most violent master'.

[28] For a Freudian reading, founded on the original patricidal pact that enables brothers to recognise themselves as equals, see: Panu Minkkinen, *Sovereignty, Knowledge, Law* (Abingdon, Routledge, 2009) 1–6.

[29] Weber (n 14) at 78: '"Every state is founded on force", said Trotsky at Brest-Litovsk. That is indeed right. If no social institutions existed which knew the use of violence, then the concept of "state" would be eliminated, and a condition would emerge that could be designated as "anarchy", in the specific sense of this word. Of course, force is certainly not the normal or the only means of the state—nobody says that—but force is a means specific to the state.'

the imaginary and the real, this problem cannot be ignored. Arendt was right to claim that violence has no role in political jurisprudence.[30] Political power is generated by institutionalisation and though it might be experienced as domination, domination must be differentiated from violence by virtue of its symbolic dimension and its promotion of collective ordering. Yet the application of force must always pose a threat to 'being-in-common', and therefore to power itself. This is why the science of political jurisprudence seeks to manage conflict, to overcome the original usurpation, to build authority, and to realise political right.

VII. Constitution

The domain of the political is not a discrete sphere of society in which institutionalised politics is undertaken: it refers to an entire world considered from the distinctive perspective of the political. Just as economists envision the sum of all human interaction as an economic calculus of profit and loss, or moral philosophers evaluate human interactions according to a moral calculus of good and evil, so too do political jurists conceive the entire world according to an increase or decrease in political power (generated by the relation between *potestas* and *potentia*). It is precisely because political power is potentially all-encompassing that a constitutional framework is required.

The concept of constitution has two distinct meanings. It refers first to the entire scheme of intelligibility of the political, that is, to the way in which the constitution of the state is formed. It refers second to the formal body of law, generally contained in a written document, which provides the template for the government of the state. The two concepts are related but distinct. Both are means by which political power is generated. But the first is articulated through *jus politicum*, while the second is expressed in positive law. It is this relation between these two concepts that gives the political domain its dynamic quality. The nature of this relation also indicates why there can be no fixed constitutional settlement. Constitutions serve both symbolic and instrumental purposes and they are constantly evolving in the light of political necessities.

VIII. The Logic of Political Jurisprudence

I have suggested that the various tensions intrinsic to the practice have to be negotiated. How is this done? The distinctive logic of the science of political jurisprudence is that of dialectic. Dialectic involves a duality, an opposition or conflict. It is a logic relating to the unity of opposites, and its primary objective is to elicit understanding rather than to

[30] Hannah Arendt, *On Revolution* (London, Penguin, 1973) 19: 'violence itself is incapable of speech … Because of this speechlessness, political theory has little to say about the phenomenon of violence and must leave its discussion to the technicians'.

demonstrate truth. Dialectic seeks to show how the interdependence of opposing forces is able to provide the basis for the relative stability and dynamism of structural configurations. Since it deals only with the meanings of the terms of discourse and does not seek to establish truths beyond this discourse, such truths as are established are relative to the practice.

The dialectical method of political jurisprudence specifies a relation of terms and although these are numerous, three primary forms might be highlighted. The first derives from the fact that the state draws on the sense of unity of common association but it acquires an institutional form only by dividing members from officers in a hierarchical arrangement of rulers and ruled. There is consequently a powerful tension between unity and hierarchy, between horizontal relations formed by the will to live in common and the vertical relations of domination and subordination. Aspects of this can also be seen in the tension between authority and liberty, but the most basic tension is between unity and hierarchy.

A second tension arises between the universal aspiration to equal liberty and the necessity of accepting historically-situated contingencies. This theme runs through Rousseau's writing. On the one hand, the ideal constitution of *The Social Contract* is a virtual exercise, yet it aspires to shape the formation of existing political regimes. On the other, actual constitutions might offer a glimpse of liberty through an expression of principles of right, but may serve only to mask the dominant power of ruling elites. However rational the idea of the state may be, it unfolds in history by means of decisions. Political jurisprudence exhibits the dialectic of reason and history, of universality and historicity.

The third tension is between the discursive claim to autonomy and the oppositions it must inevitably provoke. The political is asserted as an autonomous domain: it conceives the entire world in terms of its own distinct discourse. This involves a claim to the primacy of the political, which regulates all other domains of life (economic, religious, cultural, etc). Yet from the perspective of these other discourses, the political is reduced to a specific and limited domain, a sub-system of society that governs the relationship between rulers and ruled. Within political jurisprudence, the state is conceived as the entire scheme of intelligibility, but from outside the discourse it is merely the institutional apparatus of rule. The state is both the scheme that regulates other domains and that which is regulated by those other domains. As a discursive system, the political is a domain of dialectical elaboration but the dialectic is not complete unless subjected to the oppositions of its own discursive claims. Montesquieu's causal laws, for example, operate here to constrain the scope of the political. Political jurisprudence exhibits the dialectic of autonomy and heteronomy.

These dialectical tensions—unity and hierarchy, universality and historicity, and autonomy and heteronomy—are replicated in many of the propositions of political jurisprudence: between sovereignty and the figure of the sovereign, between the people-as-one and the people-as-the-governed, between the historic form of the nation-state and its universal aspirations, between 'power to' (*potestas*) and 'power over' (*potentia*), between *jus politicum* and positive law, between the constitution of the state and the constitution of the office of government, and so on. The philosopher who came closest to providing a systematic expression of dialectic as method was Hegel but he tied his method to an Absolute Idea in which all tensions are resolved. The notion that dialectic culminates in an ideal synthesis of these political tensions is implausible. On the contrary, the 'tragic' character of the political rests on the conviction that the dialectical method undertakes its work without any terminal point.

IX. Conclusion

Political jurisprudence is a modern discourse that has evolved since the late-sixteenth century. By the twentieth century, however, it was widely misunderstood. This was mainly attributable to the growth of academic specialisation. Various components of the practice were separated off into the new disciplines of political economy, political science, public administration, political philosophy and analytical jurisprudence. One consequence was that within public law many of the leading scholars maintained that the discipline could only acquire a professional and scientific status if confined to the study of positive law. That the golden era of writing systematic treatises of positive public law occurs during the latter half of the nineteenth century is not coincidental.[31]

The dominance of the school of legal positivism in modern public law has led to a considerable narrowing of the boundaries of juristic knowledge. This is graphically illustrated by the legal positivists' treatment of the idea of the state: the state is reconstructed as a legal person, an entity which possesses rights and duties. This personification of juridical order led to a considerable narrowing of the concept of the state, not least, by removing its intrinsically political aspects. This positivisation in the pursuit of scientific knowledge reaches its apotheosis in Hans Kelsen's theory of positive law, which 'purifies' sovereignty of all political aspects and treats state and legal order as synonymous.[32] It then becomes possible to treat public law as 'a pure and simple technology of rules'.[33]

This scholarly movement helped shape an intellectual environment in which 'the European liberal state of the nineteenth century could portray itself as a *stato neutral ed agnostico*' and could therefore 'see its existential legitimation precisely in its neutrality'.[34] It is therefore not surprising that the dramatic growth in the range of governmental activities in the early twentieth century generated a crisis in understanding. Often expressed as the corrosion of the 'rule of law' or the undermining of constitutional government, the growth in the scale of government in response to the challenges presented by industrialisation, urbanisation and the extension of the franchise generated a series of disputes over public

[31] In Germany: CF von Gerber, *Grundzüge eines Systems des deutschen Staatsrechts* (Leipzig, Tauchnitz,1865); Paul Laband, *Das Staatsrecht des deutschen Reiches* (Tübingen, Laupp, 3 vols 1876–82); Otto Mayer, *Deutsches Verwaltungsrecht* (Leipzig, Duncker & Humblot, 1895). In France: Maurice Hauriou, *Précis de droit administratif* (Paris, Sirey, 1892); Gaston Jèze, *Principes généraux du droit administratif* (Paris, Berger-Levrault, 1904); Raymond Carré de Malberg, *Contribution à la théorie générale de l'Etat* (Paris, Sirey, 1920). In Italy: VE Orlando, *Principii di diritto costituzionale* (Florence, Barbera, 1889); VE Orlando, *Principii di diritto amministrativo* (Florence, Barbera, 1891). In Britain, one looks no further than AV Dicey, *Introduction to the Study of the Law of the Constitution* (London, Macmillan, 1885).

[32] Hans Kelsen, *Das Problem der Souveränität und die Theorie des Völkerrechts* (Tübingen, Mohr, 1920); Kelsen (n 2).

[33] Olivier Beaud, 'L'État' in P Gonod, F Melleray and P Yolka (eds), *Traité de droit administratif* (Paris, Dalloz, 2011) vol 1, 207–67 at 213 [For the English version see: 'The State' *Sorbonne-Assas Law Review*: http://lawreview.u-paris2.fr/issue/2015/state (last accessed 17 October 2017)].

[34] Carl Schmitt, 'The Age of Neutralizations and Depoliticizations' [1929] in his *The Concept of the Political* (translated by G Schwab) (Chicago, University of Chicago Press, 1996) 80–96, at 88. Note that Schmitt also acknowledged the essential link between dialectic and the political. See, eg, ibid, 62: 'Hegel … remains everywhere political in the decisive sense. … Of a specifically political nature also is his dialectic of concrete thinking.'

law method.[35] But the impact of positivist scientific method on legal consciousness was such that it became very difficult to sustain the discipline of political jurisprudence after the early twentieth century. In place of a dialectical engagement, the relationship between the legal and the political was invariably conceived as an illegitimate attempt to cross the divide between norm and fact, between legal normativity and political science.

The impasse, then, was largely the product of the prevailing scientific method. Weber here is the pivotal figure. In adopting an instrumental conception of the state, reducing it to its specific means, and conceiving power in a purely material sense, Weber underplays the symbolic dimension of the juristic. He establishes a political sociology which, by conceiving law as an instrument of political domination (*Herrschaft*), effectively abandons the precepts of political jurisprudence. This insistence on a strict separation of facts and norms undermines the claim of 'the normative power of the factual'. Yet this formulation, transforming what exists and is tacitly accepted into a normative form, concisely expresses the way that political jurisprudence is able to do its work.[36] And it is able to maintain its symbolic power only so long as it is able to achieve this effect.

There are many threats today that erode the power of the discourse of political jurisprudence. One is a growing belief in technology as a neutral force and the consequential belief that law is now merely a technical instrument subject to a means-end rationale. This is corrosive because political jurisprudence is 'not just a *praxis prudentia*, and not just a craft'; it is also an achievement that remains 'deeply embedded in the adventure of Occidental rationalism'.[37] But that threat is now compounded by developments that threaten to displace the nation-state as the primary site of political power. This is not in itself the critical concern, especially as the juridical idea of the state is one of considerable flexibility and is not reducible to the material phenomenon of the nation-state. The main problem is that they threaten to undermine the power of the political imagination itself. These developments heighten the points of tension in the main dialectics of political jurisprudence: between unity and hierarchy (does the claim of political unity remain a decisive factor?); between universality and historicity (do universal claims remain historically grounded through the institution of the state?); between autonomy and heteronomy (is this autonomous worldview of the political still able to generate symbolic power?). These are real and powerful threats. The continuing value of political jurisprudence, it is suggested, is that it remains the most effective medium through which we might understand what presently is at stake.

[35] For the German literature on the *Methodenstreit*, see Arthur Jacobsen and Bernhard Schlink, *Weimar: A Jurisprudence of Crisis* (Berkeley, University of California Press, 2002). The related French debate is explained in Beaud (n 33). On the British disputes, see Martin Loughlin, *Public Law and Political Theory* (Oxford, Clarendon Press, 1992) esp Ch 7.

[36] Bourdieu expresses this point clearly in his lectures on the state when referring to the work of Spinoza: 'Spinoza speaks of what he calls the *obsequium*, a respect not for individuals, forms or people—but respect paid to the state or the social order. These "obsequious" acts display a pure respect for the symbolic order, which the social agents of a society, even the most critical, the most anarchistic, the most subversive, pay to the established order, all the more so as they do this without knowing it. As an example of this *obsequium*, I always propose the formulas of politeness or rules of conduct that are seemingly insignificant ... By respecting them, homage is paid not to the individual who is the apparent object of respect, but to the social order that makes this person respectable. This is the most fundamental tacit demand of the social order.' Pierre Bourdieu, *On the State: Lectures at the Collège de France, 1989–1992* (translated by D Fernbach) (Cambridge, Polity, 2014) 34–35.

[37] Carl Schmitt, *Ex Captivitate Salus: Erfahrungen der Zeit 1945/46* (Cologne, Greven, 1950) xx.

Part II

The Methodological Critique

3

Questioning a Uniform Concept of Public Law

ANDREW HALPIN

I. Introduction

In this chapter I focus on the claim, not associated with Martin Loughlin alone, that it is possible to identify a general and substantial understanding of Public Law which has a significant bearing on our efforts to comprehend individual instances of public law within particular political communities or jurisdictions. I concentrate on the arguments Loughlin puts forward in his book to advance a singular foundational understanding of public law,[1] but also refer to arguments raised fairly recently by Jack Goldsmith and Daryl Levinson in joining together constitutional law and international law as 'public law', which they regard as determining what a well-ordered, properly functioning state amounts to.[2]

The motivation for challenging a uniform concept of public law, attempted in different ways by Loughlin, and Goldsmith and Levinson, is based on three concerns. First, such a uniform concept detracts from the importance of local differences among individual cases of public law. Even where these differences are recognised, they are considered subservient to the master concept of public law. This produces a skewed analytical (descriptive) portrayal of public law, but also lends itself to assuming a general normative trajectory inherent in public law itself, serving to determine the well-ordered state. Second, the marginalisation of local differences distracts attention from the peculiar social and political conditions (conditions that in an important sense precede the legal) which determined the precise contours and characteristics of the public law of a particular political community or jurisdiction. Third, and despite Loughlin's rich array of disciplines and sources for his notion of public law, a uniform juristic concept of public law elevates the legal to a position that may become unstable, or possibly even dangerous: unstable, in that an unwarranted trust in the legal to 'negotiate' social tensions at the expense of a full political hearing for those tensions may destabilise the law by placing upon the law a burden it cannot effectively discharge, so leaving its responses lacking consistency and credibility; possibly dangerous,

[1] M Loughlin, *Foundations of Public Law* (Oxford, Oxford University Press, 2010) [hereafter *Foundations*].

[2] J Goldsmith and D Levinson, 'Law for States: International Law, Constitutional Law, Public Law' (2009) 122 *Harvard Law Review* 1791 [hereafter, 'Law for States'].

in that the machinery of the law may be employed to repress a fair political hearing of those tensions.

In pursuing these concerns here, I shall challenge four key positions adopted in *Foundations*:

1) the autonomy of public law;
2) the general relationship between a science of political right and public law;
3) the idea of political jurisprudence as a prudential approximation for a science of political right; and
4) the grammar of public law.

In the course of making these challenges, I shall attempt some wider reflections on the manner in which tensions within the political community or the law are negotiated and resolved; on the idea of a coherent conceptual scheme within a Wittgensteinian perspective on language; and on the puzzle of the strange confidence placed in the legal over the political. Or, to rephrase that last point as a question: why should public law succeed where ideology has failed?

II. A Preliminary Digression on Goldsmith and Levinson

Both *Foundations* and the article by Jack Goldsmith and Daryl Levinson referred to above look to public law to produce a well-ordered state. It is instructive to bring the efforts of Goldsmith and Levinson into the primary discussion of Loughlin for two reasons. Their work demonstrates that there is a more general tendency to assume a uniform concept of public law with normative connotations for our understanding of the state and, thereby, that this is not an idiosyncratic move by Loughlin. In addition, a closer examination of their work reveals a differentiated vocabulary of the state which undermines the claim to a uniform concept of public law.

Loughlin is concerned with public law as 'the right-ordering of the state'.[3] For Goldsmith and Levinson, there is a threshold role for public law in the form of key parts of constitutional law displaying the clarity required to 'recognise a functioning government or legal system',[4] and to establish 'the authority of domestic law in a well-ordered state'.[5] Alongside this work of what they take to be an incomplete system of public law,[6] Goldsmith and Levinson speculate on how a completed system of public law, taken to comprise both constitutional law and international law, might herald the emergence on the global stage of 'a new (super-)state'.[7] Relying on public law to determine a well-ordered state presumes not only a uniform concept of public law but also a uniform concept of the state.[8]

[3] *Foundations* (n 1) 9.
[4] 'Law for States' (n 2) 1819.
[5] 'Law for States' (n 2) 1799.
[6] 'Law for States' (n 2) 1821, 1863–64.
[7] 'Law for States' (n 2) 1864.
[8] The uniform concept of a state is helped along by referring to a sovereign state, in both works. For Goldsmith and Levinson, see below n 13. Loughlin invokes sovereignty explicitly when making the connection between a

Otherwise we should have different forms of public law for different forms of the state, well-ordered or otherwise. In much the same way as we could identify different forms of family law for different conceptions of the family, whether the conceptions be of a well-functioning family or otherwise.

The primary reliance on public law to promote the well-ordered state, rather than seeking the well-ordering of the state from other resources and then expecting that well-ordering to be reflected in the state's public law, places an unusual burden on this branch of law. Even if public law is regarded as qualitatively different from the rest of municipal law,[9] the suggestion that well-ordering is the province of the law suggests a pre-eminence for law in this area that would look strangely out of place elsewhere. Nobody would suggest that we should look to the law to *provide* us with the idea of a well-functioning family.

On the other hand, resorting to law appears to have its advantages, in cutting through the contestabilities of other resources. At one level, it is appropriate to recognise the distinctive role of law in cutting through these contestabilities by providing a determinate resolution of how the subject matter is to be dealt with, irrespective of the controversies that may subsist over that subject matter in moral, political, and other discourses. Law is distinctively 'heteronomous' in terminating these controversies, as Neil MacCormick put it.[10] However, that is not to say that law assumes an expertise to compete in these controversies and to vanquish all opposing views on their own terms. Law simply reflects a determinate resolution of the controversy as considered fitting by those who have the power and authority to settle the matter within a particular society. Family law organised around the central idea of *patria potestas* is not a legal invention, but a form of family law reflecting the allocation of power and authority in the ancient Roman patriarchal society.[11]

There is, accordingly, an improper opening for resorting to law as a settler of contestability through assuming that the legal resolution of controversy does actually definitively settle that controversy on its own terms: that family law provides the definitive form of a well-functioning family; that public law provides the definitive form of the well-ordered state. There may be less likelihood for impropriety in the case of family law, where law's past efforts are readily considered to have failed so dismally by modern lights. It appears that there is far greater likelihood for impropriety in the case of public law.

The prospects for such impropriety in public law are enhanced by a number of factors. Unlike family law, public law can be regarded as the development of a modern and enlightened age.[12] Unlike family law, public law can be regarded as a work in progress, not yet having attained the completed stage of other forms of municipal law, or 'domestic law' as Goldsmith and Levinson call them.[13] And unlike, say, family law—which clearly has dealt

uniform concept of public law and a uniform concept of a state: 'The concept of public law explicated in this book is today a universal phenomenon, if only because the entire world is now divided into an assortment of sovereign states, each of which has governing arrangements authorised by means of law' (*Foundations* (n 1) 2).

[9] Loughlin sees it as 'fundamental law' as opposed to 'ordinary positive law' *Foundations* (n 1) 1–2; Goldsmith and Levinson as 'public law' distinct from 'ordinary domestic law' ('Law for States' (n 2) 1795).

[10] N MacCormick, *Institutions of Law: An Essay in Legal Theory* (Oxford, Oxford University Press, 2007) 255–61 and his *Practical Reason in Law and Morality* (Oxford, Oxford University Press, 2008) 92, 198–99.

[11] For a modern example, take the treatment of married women's property within family law.

[12] 'a consequence of the processes of secularisation, rationalisation, and positivisation of fundamental law' (*Foundations* (n 1) 2).

[13] 'Law for States' (n 2) 1821, 1863–64.

with different forms of the family—public law can be regarded as dealing with a uniform concept of the (modern) state—or so it seems.

In their article, Goldsmith and Levinson do not consciously explore the notion of a state. They simply employ a constant term, amplified to be understood as a sovereign state.[14] Public law in their own twin recognition of it is a picture of international and constitutional law as 'dual systems of public law', as 'two sides of the same coin', relating to 'the "external" and "internal" manifestations of the sovereign state'.[15] Yet Goldsmith and Levinson's vocabulary is revealing in that it discloses a number of entities treated as synonyms for the state—that is to say, as the subject of public law.

Their differentiated vocabulary clearly raises the possibilities of recognising different aspects of a state, or different parts of a state. Their wider vocabulary extends to the following:

a. state;[16]
b. state actors;[17]
c. state institutions;[18]
d. political forces;[19]
e. political branches of government;[20]
f. government officials;[21] and
g. the people.[22]

Each of these is explicitly used to denote what is subject to public law.

Commonly, it is accepted that a modern state encompasses the different elements that Goldsmith and Levinson mention or allude to:

1) those who govern and those who are governed;
2) the different branches of government—the political (executive and legislature) and the legal (the judiciary);
3) different officers, institutions, and officials within the different branches of government;
4) the people as the governed or subjects, and the people as citizens or the electorate to whom government is accountable; and
5) majorities and minorities within the people of a state.

This differentiated vocabulary clearly raises possibilities of recognising different conceptions of a state. This is so for two reasons. First, the different elements just identified are

[14] Goldsmith and Levinson admit their initial focus is on the USA, but regard their observations as applying to 'other constitutional systems' ('Law for States' (n 2) 1800). The significance of sovereignty as a unifying factor is expressly noted: 'the idea of sovereignty was crucial to the creation of the centralised legal institutions of the state, for it was the concept that explained and legitimised the political authority of these institutions … Sharing common origins in the rise of the sovereign state, these dual systems of public law were invented to limit otherwise limitless state power, from the inside and from the outside' ('Law for States' (n 2) 1862–63).

[15] 'Law for States' (n 2) 1863, 1868.

[16] eg 'Law for States' (n 2) 1795. Here, as is frequently the case, the term appears in close proximity to alternative expressions.

[17] 'Law for States' (n 2) 1795.

[18] 'Law for States' (n 2) 1795.

[19] 'Law for States' (n 2) 1816.

[20] 'Law for States' (n 2) 1831.

[21] 'Law for States' (n 2) 1831.

[22] 'Law for States' (n 2) 1853.

configured in quite distinct forms across different (modern) states. There are significant differences regarding the branches of government and with regards to the officers, institutions, and officials that populate these branches of government. The status of citizenship, with its entitlements and responsibilities, is far from uniform. The emergence of recognisable majorities and minorities, and the severity of tensions between them, differs enormously according to specific historical and cultural conditions. Second, there are more than one set of possible relationships among these different elements (however configured), meaning that there is a variety of blueprints for a modern state. The variety of states, even in considering only those that are modern-day and are regarded as democratic, exhibits a corresponding diversity of bodies of constitutional law, or public law.[23]

The point being emphasised is that where we can recognise a body of public law as being a form of constitutional law, it cannot be a law that threatens the state—since its very role is to bring together the elements of a state in a way which allows them to exist together as *this state*. Where public law as constitutional law does operate, it therefore must serve to protect this state as against alternative forms of the state (which do not uphold this practice of democracy, which do not respect these minority rights, which are not federal, and so on). And if the sovereign is equated with the state, then constitutional law does not constrain the sovereign; it constrains that sovereign's usurper. Public law cannot occupy a duality: it cannot both protect the (actual) state and represent some cosmopolitan right-ordering of the state, in the way *Foundations* seeks to identify.

III. The Autonomy of Public Law

In contrast to Goldsmith and Levinson's differentiated vocabulary of the state which readily yields an array of concerns over the precise characteristics of the different aspects of the state and of their relationships (or ordering), Loughlin introduces the modern state as caught up in a single problem: 'reconcil[ing] claims of individual autonomy with the existence of a regime of public authority', that is to say, 'reconcil[ing] two equally powerful but contrary human dispositions: the desire to be autonomous and the desire to be a participant in a common venture'.[24]

Setting the stage for the emergence of modern public law as an abstract foundational question (rather than locating it in the conditions of the modern state) undoubtedly assists with procuring a uniform concept of public law. Yet the abstract formulation of the question is not sufficient to maintain uniformity in the responses, if those responses can range freely over the particular circumstances of each state, thus producing a variety of forms of

[23] The distinctive character of German public law, in its relation to EU law, is nicely illustrated in a decision of the German Federal Constitutional Court in 2009—*Bundesverfassungsgericht* (*BVerfG*), Case 2 BvE 2/08, Judgment of 30 June 2009 (English translation accessible at: www.bundesverfassungsgericht.de/entscheidungen/es20090630_2bve000208en.html (last accessed 17 October 2017)). The title of the commentary by Jo Murkens, 'Bundesverfassungsgericht (2 BvE 2/08): "We want our identity back"—the revival of national sovereignty in the German Federal Constitutional Court's decision on the Lisbon Treaty' [2010] *Public Law* 530, serves to emphasise the matter.

[24] *Foundations* (n 1) 11.

public law distinguished by the constitutional arrangements responding to each set of individual circumstances in working out how precisely the demands of individual autonomy and public authority are to be met.

Loughlin therefore has to insulate his concept of public law from the disturbance of individual circumstances by locating it in an autonomous sphere. As well as referring to an 'autonomous concept of public law',[25] Loughlin speaks of 'the political realm ... as an autonomous sphere'.[26] Public law (operating within that sphere) becomes 'a distinctive juristic discourse operating according to its own discrete logic'.[27] Public law also preserves the autonomy of the political sphere in which it operates: '[It] works to maintain the autonomous world of the public sphere, a sphere that achieves its distinctive position through arrangements that seek to reconcile claims of individual autonomy with the existence of a regime of public authority.'[28] It is this autonomy that allows for what Loughlin has labelled 'the "pure theory" of public law'.

In talking of autonomy, purity, and discrete logic, Loughlin provokes the questions as to how the separateness of public law emerged and what exactly it is being separated from. In the excerpt quoted above, it appears that by merely addressing the foundational question regarding individual autonomy and public authority, public law ensures the autonomy of the public sphere. But why should a response to this question enhance the autonomy of the sphere in which it is raised? Or require a discreet logic?

Further clues are provided by Loughlin's description of the emergence of the modern state and modern public law, as throwing off the shackles of religion,[29] natural law,[30] and the personal authority—together with the subjective wishes—of rulers.[31] This process consequently realigned the government of the state with the interests of the governed: 'an objective order—the state which the ruler was obliged to maintain'.[32] Even if these are accepted as the historical features which accompanied the creation of the modern state, the mere rejection of religion and/or natural law as providing the grounding for 'fundamental law', or the mere rejection of the individual right of rulers (to be replaced by a responsibility to the governed), does not necessitate that the public (fundamental) law of the new state should be autonomous. Being not dependent on religion or natural law; independent of the personal whims of the ruler—is accepted. Being not dependent on any values[33] or traditions

[25] *Foundations* (n 1) 2, 8.
[26] *Foundations* (n 1) 7, 8.
[27] Foundations (n 1) 2.
[28] *Foundations* (n 1) 10–11.
[29] *Foundations* (n 1) 7–8.
[30] *Foundations* (n 1) 158.
[31] *Foundations* (n 1) 8.
[32] *Foundations* (n 1) 8.
[33] For critical discussion of the feasibility of isolating public law from the morality of a society, as suggested in Loughlin's earlier *The Idea of Public Law* (Oxford, Oxford University Press, 2003), a precursor to *Foundations*, see Nicholas Barber's 'Professor Loughlin's *Idea of Public Law*' (2005) 25 *Oxford Journal of Legal Studies* 157. From Loughlin's perspective, Barber may be regarded as missing the point in stressing the contingent set of values that a particular system of public law is linked to and ignoring the transcendent quality of public law within that system, a quality that is agnostic to particular values. In this respect, Loughlin's 'pure theory of public law' appears to fully take a Kelsenian turn. This would amount to a double anomaly. To move from the discredited values of religion, etc, as the basis for fundamental law, to a value agnosticism is anomalous, when what might be expected would be a recognition of the actual values undergirding fundamental law (particularly where the authentic recognition of fundamental law is couched in value-laden terms, such as responsibility to the governed). Even more

embraced within a particular state; being independent of the particular circumstances within a particular society affecting the relationship between the government and the governed (including who precisely gets to count, and in what way, as the government and the governed),[34] simply does not follow as a matter of theory, and clearly has not followed as a matter of historical fact.[35]

Possibly, Loughlin is aware of the insufficiency of what we might term the historical premises, for he introduces an additional premise. This is the equality premise. Since the state and public law are not givens under religion, natural law, or the right of the ruler, Loughlin argues that they must be produced by the members of the state themselves: 'The public realm must function according to laws we have given ourselves'.[36] This step in itself would still be vulnerable to the elaboration of different possible renderings of ourselves in the different conditions of different states, along the lines indicated in the previous paragraph. Loughlin makes a further step. He adds to his description of the posited nature of public law[37] a normative conviction: 'that there is a mode of right-ordering of public life that free and equal individuals would rationally adopt'.[38]

The normative equality premise is specifically linked to the public sphere by Loughlin, through stressing its connection to liberty ('free and equal individuals'). Again, this involves two steps. One is analytical-descriptive: 'freedom is a status that is realised only within the state'.[39] The second is normative: 'The discourse of political right, operating to enhance the power of the public sphere, strives to realise an equal liberty for all'.[40]

There are two problems, however, in relying on this additional, equality premise to establish the autonomy of public law. The first is that there is no extant legal outworking of this premise such that it can be verified as a pure expression of the premise, untainted by 'impure' local conditions.[41] Whether this problem (which applies generally to Loughlin's enterprise for an autonomous public law based on political jurisprudence) can be surmounted will be considered at greater length below. The second problem is that if the equality premise is adopted, it does too much. If the members of a state are to be regarded as free and equal individuals whose status is taken to determine the scope and nature of public law, then that status would be equally effective in determining the scope and nature of private law, or 'ordinary positive law'.[42] How could free and equal individuals accept

anomalous would be, once having taken the Kelsenian turn, to continue maintaining the need for fundamental law. If the transcendent quality of law can be presupposed for positive law, without delving into the actual values of a particular system of law, then what need would there be for fundamental law as 'a prior source of authority' (*Foundations* (n 1) 2) to bring legality into play?

[34] On this point, consider the different positions of women, slaves, and the propertied/non-propertied classes within different modern states and at different times.

[35] Loughlin appears to want to avoid the historical messiness of actual states by discarding them as incapable of fully representing the theory of public law (*Foundations* (n 1) 158). However, the principal point being made here is that the theory itself does not follow from his (past historical) premises. A secondary point is to question why a theory with inadequate premises should be advanced when it is also at variance with the subsequent factual data.

[36] *Foundations* (n 1) 158.

[37] *Foundations* (n 1) 158.

[38] *Foundations* (n 1) 159.

[39] *Foundations* (n 1) 12.

[40] *Foundations* (n 1) 12.

[41] *Foundations* (n 1) 11, 158–59, 164.

[42] *Foundations* (n 1) 2.

anything less? Legal rights in general, not just constitutional rights, would be determined in accordance with this premise.[43] But this would mean that the 'distinctive position' of the public sphere, together with its autonomy, would be lost.

IV. Relating a Science of Political Right to Public Law

The failure to instantiate the equality premise is simply the other side of the coin to the ineffectual efforts to work out the science of political right. In ideal conditions, where success had replaced failure, public law would have simply reflected the understanding provided by a science of political right.[44] In the less than ideal conditions we find ourselves in, the relationship between the two becomes more subtle. Public law now takes on remedial work to cover the deficiencies of the search for a science of political right.[45]

Loughlin spends chapters 4 and 5 charting the lack of success in establishing a science of political right. He considers this intellectual failure to be caused by the essential irreconcilability of individual autonomy and participation in a joint venture[46]—an inability to answer authoritatively what was introduced at the beginning of section III as the foundational question. The foundational question poses both a practical imperative and a theoretical conundrum.

In order to set up the modern state, some accommodation has to be made for both the individual interests of its members and the limitation of those interests in establishing governance of the state. Since this accommodation cannot be imposed by some external authority (such as divine law, natural law, the right of the ruler), it is sought by means of intellectual reflection on these two features of the state. The intellectual reflection, being deprived of an authoritative framework which forces a practical compatibility on the two (these are the appropriate interests members of a society can expect to enjoy, this is the proper exercise of governmental power within a society—as ordained by divine law, etc), treats the two as separate requirements for a society.

Once separated from a common framework, the features inevitably become opposing objectives. Considered on their own terms, they become irreconcilable. Individual autonomy is opposed to public authority; or, with participation in a common venture.[47] Loughlin summons public law to effect a prudential fix of the irreconcilable, whilst still

[43] Just such an argument for legal rights is made by Pavlos Eleftheriadis, *Legal Rights* (Oxford, Oxford University Press, 2008). For further discussion, see my review in (2011) 121 *Ethics* 652. Significantly, Barber (n 33, at 164) comments on the chapter on rights in Loughlin's *The Idea of Public Law*: 'The easy way in which the moral slides into the political in this part of the book makes it hard to isolate either concept' above n 32.

[44] A glimmer of this prospect is permitted when the relationship between public law and political right is introduced by Loughlin (*Foundations* (n 1) 2).

[45] *Foundations* (n 1) 158.

[46] *Foundations* (n 1) 11.

[47] *Foundations* (n 1) 11. In the course of his book, Loughlin employs different forms of the elements in tension (the irreconcilables) within the foundational question: individual autonomy and public authority (*Foundations* (n 1) 11); autonomy and participation in a common venture, or, freedom and belonging (*Foundations* (n 1) 11); *societas* and *universitas* (*Foundations* (n 1)160); liberty and power, or, enablement and constraint (*Foundations* (n 1) 178).

aiming to retain the elevated status of the inquiry into their reconcilability (hence the autonomy of public law). We shall examine more closely the details of his fix in this and the following section, but an anticipatory critique can be offered already. Why attempt to fix the irreconcilable, when the more obvious response to the absence of an authoritative framework that has been lost due to the rejected conventions of a former age, is to look for a fresh framework? That line of inquiry might well take a turn into multiple frameworks, each based on the particular conditions of a society which combine to produce distinctive understandings of, and then effect a practical compatibility between, the interests of members and the exercise of government. The uniformity of public law is, again, at stake.

In this section, we shall consider the basic mechanism of Loughlin's fix, whereby he treats public law through the idea of political jurisprudence as a prudential approximation for a science of political right. In the next section, we shall explore the image of the grammar of public law, which is developed by Loughlin as a way of maintaining some fidelity to the theory of political right whilst acknowledging the practical realities of public law—a prudential approximation which he casts as a process of negotiation between the irreconcilable:

> And since this disjuncture between freedom and belonging can be neither eliminated nor reconciled, it can only be negotiated. In one sense, this negotiation does not itself amount to the explication of right: it involves an exercise of prudential judgment. Consequently, rather than treating public law as the unfolding of a science of political right, it is best expressed as an exercise in political jurisprudence. But another way of putting this is to say that the discourse of political right involves the elaboration of a prudential language through which that negotiation is effected.[48]

This negotiation involves some downgrading of the ideal science of political right, captured by the expression 'political jurisprudence', but importantly the fidelity to political right is preserved by viewing political right ('the discourse of political right'—a marker for the forthcoming image of grammar) as being involved in the production of political jurisprudence ('a prudential language'—another marker) and hence implicated in the process of negotiation.

This latter point is of crucial importance to Loughlin's endeavour. If, faced with the irreconcilable claims of individual autonomy and public authority, a process of negotiation were implemented as a means of exiting the impasse, that negotiation would quite reasonably be expected to tone down the claims of each side in order to bring about a reconciliation. 'You cannot go for autonomy, but I can allow you protection of a number of individual interests you hold dear'. 'You cannot keep hold of unlimited authority, but I can permit you to keep hold of considerable powers to enable effective government'. That, of course, would destroy the premises of a science of political right, and move us through negotiation to a quite different foundation (or set of foundations) for public law. Loughlin's foundational question gets replaced by a more prosaic question. What sort of settlement of powers between the government and the governed will work here?

Actually, the prosaic question is more elaborate, as has already been suggested in section II. The settlement of powers will not be negotiated simply between two parties, but between different factions and elements of both the government and the governed. The fact that both sides can be split up into (internally) opposing groups has repercussions not

[48] *Foundations* (n 1) 11.

simply for the process of negotiation that has been downgraded to deal with the prosaic question. What works here will involve a complex series of negotiations. This complexity also has implications for Loughlin's attempt to keep the process of negotiation still focused on the fundamental question, concerned with the issue of political right in the abstract.

The way Loughlin portrays the process of negotiation is not as an attempt to get the parties to back down from their irreconcilable demands (as suggested in the prosaic negotiation above), but as an attempt to allow the irreconcilable to be held in a state of tension. When dealing with the irreconcilable in terms of individual autonomy and public authority, or freedom and belonging, Loughlin stresses that the negotiation amounts to 'developing the most effective apparatus we can that acknowledges the power of these competing claims'.[49] Somehow both claims are to be maintained. Subsequently, when he reflects the same irreconcilables in Oakeshott's distinction between *societas* and *universitas*[50] Loughlin explicitly invokes Oakeshott's imagery of tension: 'The state can be grasped as "an unresolved tension between the two irreconcilable dispositions"'.[51] And public law remains held *within* this tension by means of 'a political imagination which is itself constituted in a tension between them'.[52]

When picking up in this later passage on the role of negotiation undertaken by political jurisprudence, Loughlin points to the variety of theories and practices of public law that have occurred. These different instances are still regarded as 'distinctive expressions of the polarities of a bifurcated discourse'.[53] That is to say, in their different ways, they employ the political imagination to occupy a point in tension between the two irreconcilables. However, what is negotiated, according to Loughlin, is not a compromise between the irreconcilables. The exercise of political jurisprudence has as its task 'to negotiate between the various conflicting accounts of political right that form part of its evolving discourse'.[54]

The signalling of discourse prepares us for the discussion of grammar in the next section, but before commencing that topic there is more to be said about Loughlin's portrayal of a tension between irreconcilables, and the technique of negotiation he attributes to political jurisprudence. Two irreconcilable states may be portrayed in a state of tension (say, a tension between the demands of home and the demands of the office) in a meaningful way at the point of posing a dilemma. The dilemma is found in a question confronting a person (how much time to spend at home and at the office). When the question is answered the irreconcilable states cannot be reconciled but the dilemma can be resolved (my home life is more important to me so I shall spend less time at the office). The resolution, while not reconciling the irreconcilable, breaks the tension.

[49] *Foundations* (n 1) 11.

[50] *Foundations* (n 1) 160–64.

[51] *Foundations* (n 1) 160.

[52] *Foundations* (n 1) 163 citing M Oakeshott, 'On the Character of a Modern European State' in his *On Human Conduct* (Oxford, Clarendon Press, 1975) 200–01, 320. Loughlin's use of Oakeshott's tension can be contrasted with the account provided by N Bhuta, 'The Mystery of the State: State Concept, State Theory and State Making in Schmitt and Oakeshott' in D Dyzenhaus and T Poole (eds), *Law, Liberty and State: Oakeshott, Hayek and Schmitt on the Rule of Law* (Cambridge, Cambridge University Press, 2015) 10, 30–34. Bhuta takes Oakeshott's tension to be resolved at different times in different ways, more favourable to *universitas* or *societas*, and concludes (at 37) on 'the impossibility of separating the dynamics of order creation from contingent historical determinations and uncontrollable exogenous and endogenous forces'. See n 58 below.

[53] *Foundations* (n 1) 164.

[54] *Foundations* (n 1) 164.

That illustration of tension might be considered too simple, as involving a single stark choice between the irreconcilables, to convey the complexities involved in the formation of a state. A different setting for the recognition of tension, which may be more pertinent to our present interests, occurs when an attempt is made to provide an accurate description of complex materials which appear to exhibit contrary tendencies. How do we describe the common law? Hanoch Dagan suggests that the empirical reality of the common law can be captured by three tensions: between power and reason, between science and craft, and between tradition and progress. He describes these tensions as 'constitutive and irresolvable'.[55] At a general level, such tensions convey a meaningful picture. However, when dealing with a particular instance of the common law, maintaining these tensions would be absurd. If the tensions were preserved, no law would ever emerge. On the occasion of a specific judgment, the tension between a traditional and a progressive response must be resolved in favour of one or the other.[56] As with the more simple case, the competing characteristics remain irreconcilable but the tension is broken.

In the light of these two examples of states of tension being meaningful at one stage but redundant or absurd at another stage, the question to ask is whether Loughlin can meaningfully maintain the tension confronted by a science of political right at the stage of political jurisprudence. There are three reasons for doubting that this can be done. First, if the science of political right has been accurately represented at the start of section III as dealing with an abstract foundational question, then the tensions found in the question (regarded as posing a dilemma) would not normally be expected to survive the production of an answer.[57] Second, the abstract condition of the question could be linked to a general picture of the domain of a science of political right, but a detailed exposition of the science would have to deal with particular arrangements that could not emerge with the tension intact.[58] Third, the exercise of political jurisprudence amounts to making a prudential judgment,[59] and it is difficult to see how a prudential judgment, bearing a juristic character, could be made without resolving the tension here, any more easily than a common-law judgment could be made without resolving the tensions identified by Dagan as intrinsic to the common law.

These reflections on the manner in which things are held, or portrayed, in a state of tension as between irreconcilables, only for the tension to be broken in a practical resolution by

[55] H Dagan, *Reconstructing American Legal Realism & Rethinking Private Law Theory* (Oxford, Oxford University Press, 2013) 14–15.

[56] For further discussion, see my review of Dagan's book in (2014) 11 *No Foundations: An Interdisciplinary Journal of Law and Justice* 138.

[57] This representation of the science of political right inverts a suggestion made by Loughlin when commenting on the futility of the search for a science of political right: 'this is because political right offers a conceptual *solution* to a set of recurrent issues in political experience, and a conceptual answer to a practical question offers no solution at all' (*Foundations* (n 1) 159, emphasis added). Here, I suggest that the search for a science of political right is formulated as an abstract theoretical *question*, which must then be related to a set of practical outworkings or solutions that are offered by political jurisprudence to the abstract question initially posed.

[58] There are grounds for taking Oakeshott, above n 52 to be endorsing this picture of the tension between *societas* and *universitas*. It is the 'political imagination' that is 'constituted in a tension between them' (at 320), and this may be regarded as encompassing the general or abstract inquiry as to the nature of a modern European state (Oakeshott (n 52)). However, when it comes to specific instantiations of 'the still puzzling associations called modern European states', we find that the notions or 'analogies' of *societas* and *universitas* are to be found among them 'in ever changing proportions' (at 326), no longer in a state of tension.

[59] *Foundations* (n 1) 164.

exiting the tension at some point more favourable to the one side than the other,[60] might be considered opportunistic. However, at the very least, they require in response a clarification of how the secondary stage of political jurisprudence can maintain the tension found at the initial stage of pursuing a science of political right, in a way that differs from the illustrations provided here. If, as we noted earlier in this section, the process of deriving political jurisprudence amounts to a 'negotiation' of the 'disjuncture between freedom [*societas*] and belonging [*universitas*]'[61] then such clarification would need to describe how this negotiation can reach an outcome which preserves the tension rather than breaks it (in the way described above). Loughlin does not provide such clarification. Instead, he depicts a process of negotiation between 'various conflicting accounts of political right'.[62] This misses the point, for there is nothing to suggest that each of these accounts has not exited the tension in the kind of practical resolution described above. Hence a (negotiated) choice between them would simply pick out one way of breaking the tension rather than another. What Loughlin requires is a negotiation that engages directly with the irreconcilables themselves, and as an outcome sustains the tension between them.

Alongside the challenge raised by these arguments requiring a fuller account of the nature of the tension between *societas* and *universitas* and of the way in which it is resolved (or negotiated), there is a quite different argument against Loughlin's preservation of tension. This relies on a point that Loughlin himself regards as central to his view of public law: 'freedom is a status that is realised only within the state';[63] 'power and liberty become correlative terms'.[64] This characteristic of public law is enough in itself to break down the irreconcilables of individual autonomy and public authority, of liberty and power. Taken together with the elaboration introduced above in considering the prosaic question, that a settlement of powers will not be negotiated simply between two parties but between different factions and elements of both the government and the governed, Loughlin's recognition of the correlativity of power and liberty has startling implications.

Whilst it might be possible to keep a tension between individual liberty and governmental power at the general level of describing the complexities of a modern state, and indeed still pose the fundamental question for the science of political right in terms of this tension, when it comes to the particular grant of an individual liberty any such tension is resolved in the practical correlativity of power and liberty. However, consider just how it will be resolved. A rich merchant and a slave have different levels of liberty while the liberty of each is dependent on the exercise of governmental power; the merchant and the slave enjoy different degrees of autonomy but neither's autonomy can exist outside of participation in a state.[65] So, it now appears that the real work on resolving the abstract tension lies not in taking up an imaginary position within the tension, but in contesting precisely where the

[60] With 'proportions' skewed one way or the other, to use Oakeshott's terminology above n 58.
[61] *Foundations* (n 1) 11.
[62] *Foundations* (n 1) 164.
[63] *Foundations* (n 1) 12.
[64] *Foundations* (n 1) 178.
[65] The classes of merchants and slaves are not unknown within the modern era in which the science of political right has emerged as a serious inquiry, and are accordingly fit subjects to introduce into a study of the practical ramifications of how the fundamental abstract question/tension is addressed/resolved. For a more contemporary illustration of the differentiated yields from practical resolutions of the tension, consider the contrasting positions of propertied and non-propertied, Northerners and Southerners, Catalans and Spanish.

tension is to be broken: whose benefit (and whose detriment) will be advanced in practice by selecting particular combinations (resolutions) of power and liberty in some cases and different combinations (resolutions) in other cases.

Loughlin has two rejoinders that might be made to counter the weakened condition in which political jurisprudence has been presented. One is to strengthen political jurisprudence by appeal to the equality premise. This is actually mentioned by Loughlin at the precise point at which he links liberty to the power of the state: 'equal liberty for all'.[66] But this is an additional premise, which skews the simple 'disjuncture between freedom and belonging' that political jurisprudence is supposed to negotiate.[67] In addition, it is attended by its own problems, noted at the end of section III above. The other rejoinder is to refer to the grammar of public law as being capable in some way of mounting a rescue of political jurisprudence.

V. The Grammar of Public Law

The grammar of public law introduced in the final section of Chapter 6 dealing with political jurisprudence, and more specifically public law as political jurisprudence, is accordingly the grammar of political jurisprudence.[68] The image of grammar is a powerful one as it conveys the simultaneous possibilities of flexibility and control. Grammar does not definitively determine speech, but it can nevertheless inform us whether speech is correct; it provides 'instruction in the appropriate ways to use a language'.[69] So too, then, the grammar of political jurisprudence does not determine precisely how the fundamental question is answered, how the tension between liberty and power is to be resolved. That was an outcome expected from the now abandoned quest for an objective science of political right. Nevertheless, the grammar of political jurisprudence can be referred to in order to establish whether a particular instantiation of political jurisprudence (a specific exercise of prudential judgment) does involve 'the correct use of [these] terms'.[70]

Loughlin's turn to grammar is a serious candidate for rescuing political jurisprudence from the weakened condition it acquired in section IV. It enables a recognition of the diverse experiences of the practice of public law, or political jurisprudence, while retaining an informative role for theory in addressing those practices and even assessing their correctness. In particular, the image of grammar is seen by Loughlin as allowing for the tension or 'struggle between opposing dispositions' within the foundational question of a science of political right to be responded to in different ways without overturning the tension.[71] Or, we might add, without permitting the response to degenerate into the kind of prosaic resolutions contemplated in section IV above.

[66] *Foundations* (n 1) 11.
[67] *Foundations* (n 1) 12.
[68] It is referred to in the additional abstract for Ch 6 provided in the e-book as 'the grammar of the practice [of political jurisprudence]'.
[69] *Foundations* (n 1) 178.
[70] *Foundations* (n 1) 178.
[71] *Foundations* (n 1) 179.

The richness of grammar is not compatible with providing political jurisprudence with a 'conceptual scheme in a simple logical form'.[72] Instead, Loughlin looks to Wittgenstein. He refers specifically to only understanding the language of political jurisprudence by referring to 'a form of life'; and thus to the need to consider the 'background conditions' of an exercise of political jurisprudence; and to the 'context-dependent and purpose-relative' nature of that exercise, as a use of language.[73] Given the variables involved in the different contexts in which political jurisprudence is practised, it is not surprising that Loughlin recognises that 'alternative grammars are conceivable' yielding 'discrepant meanings'.[74]

Nevertheless, Loughlin holds on to the value of his theoretical inquiry. He sees it as providing the skill to extend the practice of political jurisprudence 'to cover unusual cases or situations that appear exceptional', which is required in 'the world of public law today'.[75] As for his methodology, having abandoned simple logical forms, Loughlin reverts to a 'more or less logical ordering' he has associated with the grammatical form of language, manifested in 'displaying a coherent conceptual scheme':[76]

> In these circumstances, the inquiry into the foundations of public law is best furthered by examining the ways in which such terms have come to be deployed in the discourse of public law and showing how they can best be ordered into some relatively coherent conceptual scheme.[77]

The relatively coherent conceptual scheme must be understood in the light of his preceding comments as taking on a Wittgensteinian perspective, but this creates a basic problem for the direction in which Loughlin seeks to take his theoretical enterprise.

It is clear that Wittgenstein allowed for a language practice to be used for training,[78] so the idea of a corrective grammar is not at all alien to his thought. And for that training to be effective a 'relatively coherent conceptual scheme' to cover the correct use of the language can reasonably be assumed. However, there are two important qualifications to be made. First, Wittgenstein explicitly rejects the necessity of having a complete conceptual scheme.[79] So devising a theoretical conceptual scheme along Wittgensteinian lines will not provide the benefit Loughlin claims for his theory of political jurisprudence, of dealing with novel cases. A corrective grammar can be related to existing practice of the language, but new uses are up for grabs. The existing practice of the language is linked by Wittgenstein to 'a form of life',[80] as Loughlin acknowledges.[81] Accordingly, the grammar (or relatively coherent conceptual scheme) for the language practice of one form of life will differ from the grammar (or relatively coherent conceptual scheme) for the language practice of another conflicting form of life. This poses a deeper problem for Loughlin.

[72] *Foundations* (n 1) 179.
[73] *Foundations* (n 1) 178–79.
[74] *Foundations* (n 1) 179.
[75] *Foundations* (n 1) 179.
[76] *Foundations* (n 1) 178.
[77] *Foundations* (n 1) 179–80.
[78] L Wittgenstein, *Philosophical Investigations* (Oxford, Wiley-Blackwell, 2009) §§189–90, 692.
[79] 'If someone were to draw a sharp boundary I could not acknowledge it as the one that I too always wanted to draw, or had drawn in my mind. For I did not want to draw one at all' ibid §76.
[80] ibid §§ 19, 23, 226, 241.
[81] *Foundations* (n 1) 178, fn 95.

Loughlin wants to derive a theoretical grammar of political jurisprudence from examining the 'competing grammars' found 'in the discourse of public law'.[82] But there is no basis in Wittgenstein's approach to support this. For Wittgenstein there is one practice with its own form of life and its distinctive grammar; there is another practice with its own form of life and its distinctive, competing grammar. That is it. The coherent conceptual schemes which we have identified with a Wittgensteinian grammar can only be located in a practice. A coherent conceptual scheme cannot be derived by imposing theoretical coherence on the conflicting languages of different practices. That is not to say that an alternative practice (even a hypothetical one) could not be constructed as a composite of two previous practices. The point is that the new practice (and its grammar) would compete on the same level as the preceding practices; that it would not acquire a superior status of theory. Such a move would have been anathema to Wittgenstein.[83]

Loughlin's grammatical turn is not then capable of yielding at the theoretical level a uniform grammar for public law, as the basis for a uniform concept of public law. Different grammars for different practices will produce different concepts of public law. And the practical settings for political jurisprudence will not preserve it from the impure, degenerative factors that Loughlin's failed ascent to theory would have protected it from.

In the absence of a uniform grammar, could there be some looser constraint on the different forms of public law that emerge, on the different exercises of prudential judgment that political jurisprudence makes? The other linguistic image employed by Loughlin is discourse, which is also suggestive of the simultaneous possibilities of flexibility and control we attached to grammar. The possibility of a unifying control is particularly strong where the focus is on a controlling discourse that emanates from a single recognised source. And this is precisely how the lingering influence of political right (despite its failed scientific status), as noted in section IV above, is expressed: as 'the discourse of political right' within which prudential judgment is exercised;[84] and as an 'evolving discourse' of 'various conflicting accounts of political right'.[85] Yet this alternative image can no more guarantee a uniform discourse than the rejected image of grammar could secure a uniform grammar. If it transpires that the source (the basic tension within political right) is capable of generating conflicting responses (dependent on where and how that tension is broken), we are left with a similar variety of discourses.[86]

[82] *Foundations* (n 1) 179.

[83] Elsewhere, in dealing with competing theories, Loughlin affirms a rejection of an external, authoritative role for theory: 'These are competing theories, and since there seems no prospect of discovering the Archimedean point from which objective authority can be determined, the search for a science of political right becomes a journey without end', *Foundations* (n 1) 159. Since by taking a Wittgensteinian approach the theories have been grounded in the practices, the sentiment should have a similar impact on competing practices.

[84] *Foundations* (n 1) 11.

[85] *Foundations* (n 1) 164.

[86] Loughlin appears to recognise this problem but switches between images, allowing for alternative or competing grammars, while keeping a singular discourse of public law, and then relying on a theory of public law to produce an ordering of the terms of that discourse into a 'relatively coherent conceptual scheme' (*Foundations* (n 1) 179–80)—without indicating why the competing grammars should not be linked to competing discourses, and even to competing relatively coherent conceptual schemes.

VI. Why the Juristic Turn?

Loughlin's ambitious investigation into the foundations of public law is motivated by the failed quest for an objective science of political right, which (as we noted at the beginning of section IV) is fully charted by him. By making the turn to a juristic form of prudential judgment in political jurisprudence, Loughlin attempts remedial work to fix the deficiencies of a science of political right (see section IV above) without being captivated by the false enticements of ideology. His concern accordingly becomes to promote a pure theory of public law 'shorn of ideological considerations'[87] so as to establish the autonomy of the political realm grounded on the autonomy of public law (see section III above). And this requires a uniform concept of public law. A central claim of this essay is that such purity has not been established by Loughlin's arguments, and in responding to these arguments much has been discovered to support the alternative proposal made here that there exist multiple concepts of public law, coloured by the local circumstances of their individual emergence, including prevailing ideologies.

It seems strange that there should be an attempt to transcend these local circumstances, or the peculiar social and political conditions (including prevailing normative considerations) that precede the emergence of a particular state with a particular legal constitution, by resorting to the law that these circumstances and conditions have formed. It would appear far more natural to seek the objective science of the state in an understanding of the pre-legal political factors, in an objective political science. This attempt has been made, and not only in seeking the science of political right. Ironically, there are grounds for thinking that expressing the conceptual branch of a pure political science was the original aspiration for ideology at its inception in the writings of Antoine Destutt de Tracy after the French Revolution.[88] Subsequently, it became obvious that such an aspiration was doomed and ideology as a term was broadened out to convey the various partisan conceptual schemes of different political perspectives or traditions.

Loughlin's position is clear in its explicit disavowal of ideology in a partisan sense, and of any pretension found in 'overarching claims of the right and the true'.[89] Where his position remains ambivalent is in the role he accords to public law, in producing a remedial or prudential response to the failings of political science. If the science of political right has failed, then the remedial work that follows this discovery can take two quite distinct forms. On the one hand, the remedy can be to return us as close as is now possible to the original aims that we now concede are not realisable in an absolute sense: we are satisfied with an approximation where perfection is not attainable. On the other hand, the remedy may be to find something else to meet the objective that the original effort has failed to deliver: we give up on the ideal altogether and turn to something that actually works.

[87] *Foundations* (n 1) 10.

[88] See M Freeden, *Ideology: A Very Short Introduction* (Oxford, Oxford University Press, 2003) 4–5; M Festenstein and M Kenny (eds), *Political Ideologies: A Reader and Guide* (Oxford, Oxford University Press, 2005) 7; E Kennedy, '"Ideology" from Destutt De Tracy to Marx' (1979) 40 *Journal of the History of Ideas* 353. For wider discussion of the relationship between ideology and law, see A Halpin, 'Ideology and Law' (2006) 11 *Journal of Political Ideologies* 153.

[89] *Foundations* (n 1) 465.

Similarly, when the remedial work is characterised as prudential, the particular prudence involved is open to conveying moral strains of what is appropriate in exercising governance over others,[90] or to conveying realistic strains of what can be made to work.[91] Following this ambivalence through to Loughlin's proclaimed foundational status of public law, the foundation may then be either a justificatory one or a pragmatic one. That is to say, the theory of public law has a more modest objective of identifying an effective apparatus of government under the law, or a grander objective of developing the most effective apparatus we can. Loughlin chooses to add that normative embellishment.[92]

The recognition of a normative, justificatory aspect for public law has also been detected in Loughlin's equality premise, discussed in section III above, despite (as was noted there) the impurity of its local implementations. But the debasement of a pure, or autonomous, discipline of public law in its local instantiations turns away from the justificatory side of its ambivalent character, leaving it to be dominated by its pragmatic side. The danger then is that the justificatory side is wholly unfounded, and spurious claims to purity or objectivity in the case of public law will do as much damage as have false pretensions to an objective science of political right, or a scientific status for ideology.

Loughlin's ambivalence over the role of public law, wavering between a simply pragmatic and a full-blooded normative account, serves to conceal this danger. But the real test of the credentials of Loughlin's account of public law lies not in unravelling this ambivalence. It lies in challenging the basis for a uniform concept of public law that is capable of bearing the foundational political status he is minded to give it. Through making this challenge, the conclusion reached in this chapter is that we have discovered nothing to suggest that public law can succeed where ideology has failed.

[90] See Loughlin, quoting Oakeshott, 'moral and prudential guardianship' (*Foundations* (n 1) 161).

[91] See Loughlin, 'a prudential language through which that negotiation is effected' (*Foundations* (n 1) 11).

[92] *Foundations* (n 1) 11, the same normative addition is made when Loughlin describes public law in terms of a 'prudential discourse of political right' being 'an essential precondition of our ability *successfully* to make those negotiations' (*Foundations* (n 1) 13, emphasis added). It is clear at that point that the success is measured in normative, not merely pragmatic terms.

4

The Tragic Politics of Public Law

PANU MINKKINEN

I. Introduction

The starting-point that I have chosen is the claim that Loughlin's body of work—from *The Idea of Public Law* through to *Foundations* and beyond—is not merely nominally foundationalist, but is also foundationalist in its aspirations.[1] Loughlin states in the introduction to *Foundations* that it is an 'exercise in retrieval' in the sense that it aims to 'rediscover the earlier discourse on political right and assess its relevance in the contemporary world'.[2] This is only a half-truth because *Foundations* not only 'rediscovers' and 'assesses' something, but it also—and perhaps even for the most part—'refounds' whatever it has found. It 'reconstitutes' its object of study, perhaps even 'constitutionalises' it.[3] From the very start, *Foundations* is a book about instauration, about lost origins and the possibility of their reestablishment if only in slightly modified ways.

Throughout the course of its chapters—which make up a genuine *tour de force* in the history of ideas—*Foundations*, then, aspires to reestablish an earlier understanding of public law, one that crosses historical eras as easily as it does jurisdictional borders. The essential characteristic of this particular understanding of public law is, as Loughlin frequently emphasises, that it is a 'science of political right'. Loughlin's foundationalism thus seeks to overcome or at least to deflate the binary opposition between science and politics. On the one hand, *Foundations* like *The Idea*—or, rather, the theory in which both books take part—subscribes to a certain 'Kantianesque' epistemology that Loughlin shorthands as 'pure theory'. 'Kantianesque' because it isn't always clear which *Critique* is the engine. Although Hans Kelsen himself does not figure prominently in *Foundations*, and although the few

[1] M Loughlin, *The Idea of Public Law* (Oxford, Oxford University Press, 2003) [hereafter *The Idea*]; M Loughlin, *Foundations of Public Law* (Oxford, Oxford University Press, 2010) [hereafter *Foundations*]. In addition, see M Loughlin, 'The Nature of Public Law' in C MacAmhlaigh, C Michelon and N Walker (eds), *After Public Law* (Oxford, Oxford University Press, 2013) 11–24; M Loughlin, 'The Concept of Constituent Power' (2013) 13 *European Journal of Political Theory* 218; M Loughlin, 'Modernism in British Public Law, 1919–79' (2014) *Public Law* 56; M Loughlin, 'The Constitutional Imagination' (2015) 78 *The Modern Law Review* 1.

[2] *Foundations*, ibid, 10.

[3] M Loughlin, 'What is Constitutionalisation?' in P Dobner and M Loughlin (eds), *The Twilight of Constitutionalism?* (Oxford, Oxford University Press, 2010) 47–69.

references to 'purity' are restricted to the Introduction,[4] one should ask why Loughlin has decided to hold on to such a loaded term. The answer may be fairly simple. *Foundations* is part of a *scientific* theory, an epithet that Loughlin cultivates with a certain sense of defiance despite all its misleading connotations in the English language.[5]

On the other hand, the discipline of public law that *Foundations* represents—or, rather, that it seeks to reestablish—is a scientific theory of the *political* dimension of a legal phenomenon. This is how *Foundations* runs into the antinomy that it needs, if not to resolve, then at least to appease. Loughlin cannot simply ignore the fact that, *sensu stricto*, there can be no epistemologically purified theory of the political, that is, a pure theory that could somehow distance itself appropriately from the political right that it intends to study, at least not if we are to understand politics in the way Loughlin wants to. And, indeed, Loughlin concedes at the outset that a science of political right is 'strictly speaking … unachievable'[6] and that its irreconcilable antinomy can only be 'negotiated'[7] through prudential judgement. Hence the approach is characterised as 'political jurisprudence', that is, a prudential stance in relation to law and politics.[8]

By 'prudentially negotiating' this irreconcilable antinomy, Loughlin arrives at a very particular understanding of politics as 'government'. In *Swords and Scales* Loughlin had already specified politics as the way in which humans resolve disputes 'by self-reflection and deliberation on the appropriate pattern of collective life'.[9] This specification is a choice or normative preference that frames the whole theory. *Foundations* itself does not discuss 'the political' in much detail. In the Introduction,[10] and in various sections of the book, Loughlin does, however, specify that the new element in *Foundations* is its two-fold understanding of political power as both that which is contained and that which, in its very containment, enables. To view public law through the normativist lens of legal positivism will capture well the institutional competences into which power has been contained, something that Loughlin elsewhere calls 'negative constitutionalism'.[11] But contained and simultaneously institutionalised, power also takes on a 'positive constitutionalist' dimension. In *Foundations*, Loughlin's definition of this enabling dimension of political power is the following:

> Political power is a special type of power created by the drawing together of people in a common undertaking. This type of power is founded on the 'consent' of the people, is rooted in trust, and is generated through the imposition of controls and checks on those who hold positions of authority. In this sense, political power is created through the ways in which governing power is institutionalised.[12]

[4] Save one that Loughlin somewhat misleadingly annexes to his discussion of Kant's *practical* reason, see *Foundations* (n 1) 130–31.

[5] On the German tradition of 'legal science' and its significance, M Loughlin, 'In defence of *Staatslehre*' (2009) 48 *Der Staat* 1.

[6] *Foundations* (n 1) 11.

[7] *Foundations* (n 1) 11.

[8] See Loughlin, 'Political Jurisprudence', chapter 2 of this volume. See also *The Idea* (n 1) 163.

[9] M Loughlin, *Sword and Scales. An Examination of the Relationship between Law and Politics* (Oxford, Hart Publishing, 2000) 7.

[10] *Foundations* (n 1) 11–12.

[11] Loughlin, 'The Constitutional Imagination' (n 1) 17.

[12] *Foundations* (n 1) 11–12.

For Loughlin, what makes power 'political' is, then, a 'common undertaking' that has the ability to collect individuals together into something resembling a 'people'. It is this 'consensual' understanding of politics that I would like to contest. Loughlin has already responded to a similar critique elsewhere,[13] but my focus here is slightly different. In particular, I will explicate my reservations about Loughlin's understanding of politics by contrasting it with two 'agonistic' alternatives: with Claude Lefort's notion of 'the political'[14] and Jacques Rancière's understanding of politics as 'dissensus'.[15]

Both Lefort and Rancière play, in fact, a certain—albeit very minor—role in the overall development of Loughlin's theory. Unlike Loughlin, however, they approach the political phenomenon with a certain 'embeddedness' that I will call 'metapolitical'.[16] Pierre Bourdieu once commented on the 'improbability' of sociology as a science by pointing out how sociologists are always 'at stake' in their own objects of research.[17] This, I would add, is true of all the human sciences. In other words, *the knowledge that 'science' produces about politics participates in the lifeworld phenomenon of politics that it studies*, even when politics is understood in agonistic or polemical terms. This is what I mean by 'metapolitical' as a political account of the political. Schmitt, to take the example closest to Loughlin, cannot present his friend–enemy distinction[18] as an epistemologically 'purified' *a priori* conceptual binary that precedes the act of it being made. Making the distinction is in itself a political act, a 'polemical intervention' that discerns (*krinein*, *ent-scheiden*) the opposites and, in Schmitt's case, by so doing, also nominates and publicises its own 'enemy', that is, a divisionless and hence seemingly depoliticised liberal legal science.

This is where, I contend, Loughlin falls short. By trying to formulate political right as a 'science of the political', the theory ends up in the 'negotiated' territory that is 'government' which strictly speaking is neither 'scientific' nor 'political'. The alternative would be to work out something resembling a 'metapolitics of public law', as intimated by Rancière. I conclude by reviewing Loughlin's position through the lens of Max Weber's 'vocation lectures'.[19] As with Weber, Loughlin's attempt to 'negotiate' the opposition of science and politics through 'government' gives the theory a 'tragic' character. I will finally elaborate on this tragic element with the help of Massimo Cacciari.[20]

[13] See Emilios Christodoulidis' critical remarks on *The Idea* (n 1) in his 'Public Law as Political Jurisprudence: Loughlin's "Idea of Public Law"', in E Christodoulidis and S Tierney (eds), *Public Law and Politics. The Scope and Limits of Constitutionalism* (Aldershot, Ashgate, 2008) 35–45 and Loughlin's reply in his 'Reflections on *The Idea of Public Law*' contained in the same volume at 47–66.

[14] C Lefort, *The Political Forms of Modern Society. Bureaucracy, Democracy, Totalitarianism* (Cambridge, Polity, 1986); C Lefort, *Democracy and Political Theory* (Cambridge, Polity, 1988).

[15] J Rancière, *Disagreement. Politics and Philosophy* (Minneapolis, University of Minnesota Press, 1998) [hereafter *Disagreement*]; J Rancière, *Dissensus. On Politics and Aesthetics* (London, Continuum, 2009).

[16] See A Badiou, *Metapolitics* (London, Verso, 2011); *Disagreement*, ibid, 81–90.

[17] P Bourdieu, *Sociology in Question* (London, Sage, 1993) 9.

[18] C Schmitt, *The Concept of the Political* (Chicago, University of Chicago Press, 2007).

[19] The classic 'anti-Parsonsian' translations by H Gerth and C Wright Mills have been published as M Weber, 'Politics as a Vocation' in *From Max Weber: Essays in Sociology* (Abingdon, Routledge, 2009) 77–128 and M Weber, 'Science as a Vocation' contained in the same volume at 129–56.

[20] M Cacciari, 'Weber and the Politician as Tragic Hero' in his *The Unpolitical: On the Radical Critique of Political Reason* (New York, Fordham University Press, 2009) 206–38.

II. 'The Whirlwind of Rights'

Claude Lefort's name often comes up in discussions about politics, from Ernesto Laclau and Chantal Mouffe's critical theory of the hegemony of radical democracy[21] to the post-Heideggerian analyses of Philippe Lacoue-Labarthe and Jean-Luc Nancy.[22] The main reason is the distinction that he popularised between *le politique* or politics as a form of regime—usually translated as 'the political'—and *la politique* or politics understood as social agency, conflict-ridden by opposing and often irreconcilable interests—usually translated as 'politics'.[23] While 'politics' in the latter sense can be understood as the antagonist competition for power in its usual guises, Lefort's 'the political' is, in turn, the way in which a given society represents its own unity to itself as a collectivity. Commenting on Raymond Aron, whose radical liberalism is a major source of inspiration here,[24] Lefort notes how the term 'the political' is used in at least two ways:

> In a first meaning, this term designates a particular domain of the social ensemble; it delimits the source of authority, the conditions and means of its exercise, and the range of its competences. In a second meaning, the *political* refers to the social ensemble itself, for the entire collectivity is affected by conceptions of the nature of power and the mode of the exercise of government [...] decisions made at the top have repercussions in all domains of social life but also [...] the representation of authority in the particular sector of politics circulates in some manner throughout the social ensemble. It is in this second sense that it becomes relevant to affirm a 'primacy of the political,' no matter the society under consideration.[25]

Drawing on both the phenomenology of Maurice Merleau-Ponty[26] and the psychoanalytic theory of Piera Aulagnier,[27] Lefort maintains that 'the political' not only shapes (*mise-en-forme*) collective life into more or less permanent social relations, but that it also stages (*mise-en-scène*) individual interpretations of those relations. Only collective relations

[21] E Laclau and C Mouffe, *Hegemony and Socialist Strategy. Towards a Radical Democratic Politics* (London, Verso, 2001).

[22] P Lacoue-Labarthe and JL Nancy, *Retreating the Political* (London, Routledge, 1997).

[23] See also M Plot (ed), *Claude Lefort: Thinker of the Political* (Basingstoke, Palgrave Macmillan, 2013). More generally, O Marchart, *Post-Foundational Political Thought. Political Difference in Nancy, Lefort, Badiou and Laclau* (Edinburgh, Edinburgh University Press, 2007); W Breckman, *Adventures of the Symbolic. Post-Marxism and Radical Democracy* (New York, Columbia University Press, 2013) 139–82 in particular, and M Breaugh and others (eds), *Thinking Radical Democracy. The Return to Politics in Post-War France* (Toronto, University of Toronto Press, 2015).

[24] See R Aron, *Democracy and Totalitarianism* (London, Weidenfeld and Nicolson, 1968).

[25] C Lefort, 'The Political and the Social' in his *Complications. Communism and the Dilemmas of Democracy* (New York, Columbia University Press, 2007) 113–14.

[26] Especially the posthumous M Merleau-Ponty, *The Visible and the Invisible. Followed by Working Notes* (Evanston, Northwestern University Press, 1968) edited by Lefort himself. Lefort's affiliation with his phenomenologist mentor is analysed in detail in B Flynn, *The Philosophy of Claude Lefort. Interpreting the Political* (Evanston, Northwestern University Press, 2005). On Merleau-Ponty's late philosophy and law, WS Hamrick, *An Existential Phenomenology of Law: Maurice Merleau-Ponty* (Dordrecht, Springer, 1987).

[27] eg P Aulagnier, *The Violence of Interpretation. From Pictogram to Statement* (Hove, Brunner-Routledge, 2001). For her psychoanalytic take on totalitarianism, P Aulagnier, *L'apprenti-historien et le maître-sorcier. Du discours identifiant au discours délirant* (Paris, PUF, 1993) 237–54. Aulagnier, originally trained by Lacan, was at one point married to Cornelius Castoriadis, Lefort's collaborator from the *Socialisme ou Barbarie* period, 1947–1958. See C Memos, *Castoriadis and Critical Theory. Crisis, Critique and Radical Alternatives* (Basingstoke, Palgrave Macmillan, 2014) 26–45.

and individual interpretations can together provide form and meaning (*mise-en-sens*).[28] The dimensions of 'politics' and 'the political' are interwoven into one another in the sense that the antagonistic or conflictual element of political action is always reflected in society's representation of itself, and vice versa. Neither dimension can exist independently of the other.

The two modern political 'regimes' that Lefort has elaborated in detail, namely totalitarianism and democracy, share a kinship, but operate in diametrically opposite ways. In both, 'the political' functions as a symbolic constitution in so far as it locates society's unity in a particular point of power. As regimes, both totalitarianism and democracy attempt to resolve the same problem, namely to come to terms with the empty space that has been left behind once the claim to the transcendental nature of the King's divine power has lost its capacity to represent the corporeal unity of the body politic. Following the symbolic decapitation of the monarch and the dissolution of the kingdom that he represented, power appears as an empty space. Democracy, Lefort maintains, leaves that space empty. In the absence of kings, those who exercise power can only be mortals who occupy its positions temporarily or who can invest themselves in it only by force or by cunning. Unity is unable to efface social division. This division is, Lefort claims, the true nature of democracy as a political regime:

> Democracy inaugurates the experience of an ungraspable, uncontrollable society in which the people will be said to be sovereign, of course, but whose identity will constantly be open to question, whose identity will remain latent.[29]

In other words, the antagonistic and conflictual nature of 'politics', keeping the symbolic space of power empty, is what characterises 'the political' of the democratic regime. Totalitarianism, on the other hand, is an attempt to fill that space, to unify society by placing society itself in the empty space left behind after the regicide and dissolution of the body politic. With violence and repression, totalitarianism attempts to 'weld power and society back together again, to efface all signs of social division, to banish the indetermination that haunts the democratic experience'[30] or, in other words, to abolish the 'politics' that would maintain the emptiness of that space. This also has a constitutional dimension. Lefort's democratic state goes beyond the limits traditionally assigned to the *état de droit*. It tests out rights which have not yet been incorporated in it, it is the theatre of a contestation, whose object cannot be reduced to the preservation of a tacitly established pact but which takes form in centres that power cannot entirely master.[31]

Democracy is, then, the form of society in which the relationship of law to power is always external. In this 'savage democracy' law is, as Miguel Abensour explains, no longer thought of as an instrument of social conservation, but as a revolutionary source of authority for a society that constitutes itself as the indeterminate entity it is and will always be. In this sense, law is always in excess of what has been established, and once constituted,

[28] C Lefort, 'The Permanence of the Theologico-Political?' in his *Democracy and Political Theory* (Cambridge, Polity, 1988) 217–21.

[29] C Lefort, 'The Image of the Body and Totalitarianism' in his *The Political Forms of Modern Society* (n 14) 303–04.

[30] ibid, 305.

[31] Lefort, 'Politics and Human Rights' (n 14) 258.

the constituent force will always reemerge in order to both reaffirm existing rights and to create new ones:

> A political stage opens according to which there is a struggle between the domestication of rights and its permanent destabilisation-recreation via the integration of new rights, new demands that are henceforth considered as legitimate. According to Lefort, it is the existence of this incessantly reborn protest, this whirlwind of rights, that brings democracy beyond the traditional limits of the 'State of right' [*État de droit, Rechtsstaat*].[32]

A *droit politique* indeed in the sense that, for Lefort, human rights—and even rights more generally—demand specifically a *politics* of human rights, equivalent to a democratic politics. Lefort cannot accept the critique of the early Marx[33] that sees rights merely as a consequence of the decomposition of society into isolated monadic citizens. Even social separation is a modality of man's relation to others. The 'state of right', as Lefort understands it, introduces a 'disincorporation' of both power and right rather than their complete separation. And so the 'state of right' will always include within itself an 'opposition in terms of right':

> The rights of man reduce right to a basis which, despite its name, is without shape, is given as interior to itself and, for this reason, eludes all power which would claim to take hold of it whether religious or mythical, monarchical or popular. Consequently, these rights go beyond any particular formulation which has been given of them; and this means that their formulation contains the demand for their reformulation, or that acquired rights are not necessarily called upon to support new rights.[34]

Of the 'agonists' discussed here, Lefort is, perhaps, initially the furthest from Loughlin. This might be due to Lefort's phenomenological framework which is dissonant to Loughlin's more formal approach. In *Foundations*, Loughlin does mention Lefort in passing while discussing the political theology of medieval and modern constitutionalism: 'When Lefort refers to the modern democratic foundation as an "empty place", it is precisely because there is no longer an external authority that underwrites political existence.'[35] To my mind, Loughlin here misses Lefort's point about the relationship between the empty space and *democracy*. For Lefort, democracy is not merely the absence of an external authority once God has been pronounced dead. Such an absence would simply represent the post-theological vacuum from which both totalitarianism and democracy follow as archetypal variations of modern political regimes. If totalitarianism is the frenzied attempt to fill that empty space with unifying structures that would abolish the social divisions of politics, then democracy and 'right', by contrast, are measured by their ability to keep that space empty. In Lefort's scheme, democracy and 'right' are, in other words, marked by the *resistance* or *opposition* against the totalitarian tendencies of modern capitalism to fill the space, and the name of that resistance is 'politics'.

[32] M Abensour, 'Appendix: "Savage Democracy" and the "Principle of Anarchy"' in his *Democracy against the State. Marx and the Machiavellian Moment* (Cambridge, Polity, 2011) 108 [translation modified].

[33] See K Marx, 'On the Jewish Question' in *Marx. Early Political Writings* (Cambridge, Cambridge University Press, 1994) 28–56.

[34] Lefort (n 31) 258. Also C Lefort, 'Human Rights and the Welfare State' in his *Democracy and Political Theory* (n 28) 21–44; C Lefort, 'International Law, Human Rights, and Politics' in (2013) 22 *Qui Parle* 117–37 and Flynn (n 26) 164–84.

[35] *Foundations* (n 1) 48.

In a more recent article Loughlin already comes closer to the point. He notes:

> Constituent power exists only insofar as it resists institutionalised representation. Claude Lefort notes that modern democracy leads to the creation of the 'empty place' of the political. The problem is not that it is empty, but that the space is crowded with the many who claim the authentic voice of constituent power. This is his point: legitimacy must be claimed in the name of the people, and the question of who represents the people remains the indeterminate question of modern politics. The function of constituent power is to keep that question open, not least because 'the people-as-one' is the hallmark of totalitarianism.[36]

With this notion of constituent power, Loughlin clearly aligns himself with Lefort's idea of the political of democracy as an empty space and of a democratic 'constituent' subject whose identity is constantly kept in question. But unlike Lefort, Loughlin's 'relational method', as he calls it in this instance, is more concerned with resolving a normativist–decisionist dispute than with democracy as an object of study. By 'constitutionalising' the political domain, by bringing the order of government to the 'crowded space', Loughlin's theory runs the risk of promoting what Lefort would regard as the totalitarian tendencies of modern capitalism rather than putting them into question. Constitutionalisation fills and coagulates the space of politics. My point here is not that this would be a position that Loughlin explicitly adopts but, rather, a consequence of the epistemological premises of the theory. The political remains subservient to the scientific rationality of the theory, whereas the metapolitical alternative would have regarded science, including Loughlin's own theory, as one divided and 'divisive' element among others on the political stage.

III. The Polemical Intervention

Jacques Rancière addresses the relationship between politics and the disciplines that study it in more open terms.[37] He begins his book *Disagreement* with the hypothesis that 'what is called "political philosophy" might well be the set of reflective operations whereby philosophy tries to rid itself of politics, to suppress a scandal in thinking proper to the exercise of politics'.[38] This scandal does not concern merely philosophy in the narrow sense but all 'disciplines' dealing with political phenomena. In order to test this hypothesis, Rancière must then differentiate something that can be specified as 'politics' distinguishing it from all that is normally called by that name but for which Rancière famously reserves the term 'police'.

The distinction itself is well covered ground, but let us simply remind ourselves that for Rancière 'police' includes such phenomena as legislative acts, court decisions, initiatives by ministries and other governmental bodies, as well as public administration, or, to put it in a

[36] Loughlin, 'The Concept of Constituent Power' (n 1) 233–34. The article includes further less explicit references to Lefort's notion of the 'people-as-one'.

[37] See P Bowman and R Stamp (eds), *Reading Rancière* (London, Continuum, 2011); J-P Deranty (ed), *Jacques Rancière. Key Concepts* (Durham, Acumen, 2010); T May, *The Political Thought of Jacques Rancière. Creating Equality* (Edinburgh, Edinburgh University Press, 2008).

[38] *Disagreement* (n 15) xii. On Rancière's politics, see also J Rancière, *Hatred of Democracy* (London, Verso, 2006) and J Rancière, *On the Shores of Politics* (London, Verso, 2007).

single 'metaphorical condensation', government. As with Michel Foucault's (clearly related) notion of governmentality,[39] Rancière's government by 'police' does not necessarily imply a pejorative quality—'police' can deliver worthy objectives such as education, public health and social security—but it refers to a certain rationality of government:

> The police is thus first an order of bodies that defines the allocation of ways of doing, ways of being, and ways of saying, and sees that those bodies are assigned by name to a particular place and task; it is an order of the visible and the sayable that sees that a particular activity is visible and another is not, that this speech is understood as discourse and another as noise.[40]

So how, then, is government by 'police' different from the 'real thing'? In his 'sixth thesis', Rancière describes two ways of 'counting' or of 'accounting for' the parts that make up a community. The first, that is, 'police', considers only 'real' groups as they are defined by differences in their 'functions, places and interests' accounting for the entire social body and excluding the possibility of any remnant or supplement. One can hardly avoid hearing a certain echo of Lefort's notion of totalitarianism here.[41] The second way of counting, that is, 'politics', is a way of disrupting the seemingly totalising nature of 'police'. 'Politics' counts 'a part of those without part'.[42] It is worth noting how Rancière's reference to 'counting' and 'accounting for' resonates with the rationality of scientific enquiry. Government by 'police' accounts for the social body as the sum total of its constituent parts and their respective qualifications.[43]

In other words, government by 'police' represents a way of counting that excludes the possibility of any remainder. All and everything must be accounted for. As a symbolic constitution of the social order, the principle of 'police' is equivalent to 'the absence of void and of supplement'.[44] 'Politics', on the other hand, in Rancière's terms, is the disruption of the social order that government by 'police' represents. Because an order built on the principle of 'police' is hierarchical by nature, it is based on relations of inequality that both constitute and legitimate the social order as a form of domination. The principle of 'politics', by contrast, is equality, and it furnishes the logic for disruptive interruptions into the workings of government by 'police':

> The essence of politics consists in disturbing this arrangement by supplementing it with a part of those without part, identified with the whole of the community. Political dispute is that which brings politics into being by separating it from the police, which causes it to disappear continually either by purely and simply denying it or by claiming political logic as its own. Politics, before all else, is an intervention in the visible and the sayable.[45]

[39] Elaborated in particular in M Foucault, *Security, Territory, Population: Lectures at the Collège de France, 1977–1978* (Basingstoke, Palgrave Macmillan, 2007) and M Foucault, *The Birth of Biopolitics: Lectures at the Collège de France, 1978–1979* (Basingstoke, Palgrave Macmillan, 2008). On Rancière's assessment of the affinities, see his *Disagreement* (n 15) 28–29.

[40] *Disagreement* (n 15) 29.

[41] On the similarities and differences, see O Marchart, 'The Second Return of the Political: Democracy and the Syllogism of Equality' in Bowman and Stamp (n 37) 129–33.

[42] J Rancière, 'Ten Theses on Politics' in his *Dissensus* (n 15) 36.

[43] Rancière, 'The Subject of the Rights of Man' in his *Dissensus* (n 15) 70.

[44] Rancière (n 42) 36.

[45] Rancière (n 42) 36–37.

This is all well covered ground. But the contrast illuminates something essential about Loughlin's theory. In his response to Emilios Christodoulidis's criticism of *The Idea*, Loughlin himself takes up Rancière because he feels that there is a certain kinship with the arguments put forward by Christodoulidis.[46] In a (very insufficient) nutshell, Christodoulidis claims that in reading Schmitt, Loughlin mistakenly draws from the friend–enemy distinction and the autonomy of a 'first order' of the political a 'second order', as the governing that regulates the social conflicts inherent in political life.[47] Christodoulidis's metapolitical point, as I see it, is that in order to remain political in Schmitt's polemical meaning of the word, Loughlin's 'second order', that is, the management of social conflicts through government, must rest on the same distinction as the 'first order'. In other words, the governmental pacification of social conflicts must itself be seen as part of a 'social conflict'.

Loughlin's riposte is that whatever the merits of Christodoulidis's claims, the criticism misses its mark and serves more as a justification for the critic's own 'revolutionary politics'. Now drawing on Rancière, Loughlin readily admits that *The Idea* had no intention of engaging in the radical politics of justice, freedom or equality but that 'it tries to explain the ways in which, through instituted order, these terms are played out'.[48] And so Loughlin can conclude that 'for those who adhere to the possibility of a revolutionary politics being realised, the word 'politics' in the book can be replaced by the term 'the police' without any loss of cogency in its argument'.[49]

The tone of Loughlin's counterargument seems unnecessarily defeatist because it does not take the challenge on but, rather, withdraws into its own comfort-zone. And here again, I think that he does not fully appreciate the meaning of the question regarding the theory's metapolitical qualifications. This issue becomes clearer if we contrast Rancière's point to a less-known article that he has written on his 'method'. There Rancière, writing about himself in the third person, defines 'method' in a Heideggerian sense as a path. Not as a path that one follows but, rather, as the path that one has to carve out in order to show 'how idealities are materially produced'.[50] Rancière characterises this approach as one that does not produce 'theories of' but, rather, 'interventions on': 'They are polemical interventions. This does not only mean that they take a political stance. This means that they imply a polemical view of what ideas are and do.'[51] And further on, he presents democracy as such a polemical idea:

> 'Democracy' is not the concept of a form of power that has been betrayed or misinterpreted. It was, from the very beginning, the object of a struggle. Democracy was invented as a polemical name, designating the unthinkable power of the multitude of those who have no qualification for governing [...] To speak of democracy, this means to speak of the struggle about the word, to draw the map of a battlefield.[52]

[46] Although the observation may be plausible, Christodoulidis does not, in fact, deal with Rancière in this instance. See however E Christodoulidis, 'Against Substitution: The Constitutional Thinking of Dissensus' in M Loughlin and N Walker (eds), *The Paradox of Constitutionalism. Constituent Power and Constitutional Form* (Oxford, Oxford University Press, 2007) 189–209.

[47] Christodoulidis (n 13) 41–42. This distinction is made in *The Idea* (n 1) 37–42.

[48] Loughlin, 'Reflections' (n 13) 62.

[49] Loughlin, 'Reflections' (n 13) 62.

[50] J Rancière, 'A Few Remarks on the Method of Jacques Rancière' (2009) 15 *Parallax* 114.

[51] ibid, 116.

[52] ibid.

Rancière does not, then, dismiss this idea of a 'method', as reducing his work to 'revolutionary politics', which was the gist of Loughlin's riposte to Christodoulidis. If a political phenomenon like democracy is polemical by nature, then any 'scientifically' motivated approach worth its name will by necessity 'intervene' in the struggles that make up the phenomenon itself. There is no 'external' scientific position available in relation to a political phenomenon. Preferring to stay in the background, the author of *Foundations* tries to avoid making this intervention explicit.

But we can, once again, detect flirtations with the metapolitical position in Loughlin's more recent work. He will, for example, be well aware of Schmitt's argument that even an epistemologically veiled claim about the disinterested position of the scientist—ie, any claim to a 'pure theory'—is in itself a polemical challenge because it asserts a superiority in relation to the allegedly partisan position that is being challenged.[53] This will, then, apply logically even to Schmitt's own definition of politics regardless of whether he openly professes it or not. And although Loughlin is still unwilling to fully embrace the consequences of this position for his own work, the arguments for developing a 'metapolitics of public law' are clearly there.

IV. Tragic Metapolitics

My point, to conclude, has been that *Foundations* starts off with an impossible task, namely to present a scientific theory of a political phenomenon. Instead of looking deeper into this strained relationship, Loughlin attempts to reconcile the antinomy with a form of practical reasoning that he calls 'government'. As such, it satisfies neither the criteria of rigorous science in the Kantian sense that Loughlin frequently alludes to, nor the criteria of politics, if he chooses to align himself with his Schmittian sources of inspiration. I've further tried to argue that in his more recent work Loughlin is beginning to approach the antinomy in new ways, which would suggest a rethinking of the place of politics.

Loughlin's dilemma is, of course, very similar to Max Weber's. But while Weber attempted to clarify the nature of the abyss that separated the scientist from all political commitments, Loughlin is, perhaps, too quick to bridge that gap. And in that sense *Foundations* falls short of its aims. I have suggested that in Loughlin's work after *Foundations* there are already signs of a 'metapolitics of public law' that would allow him, if not to resolve, then at least to investigate the antimony in more detail, before he allows it to sublate dialectically. As it now stands, however, there is something 'tragic' about Loughlin's impasse. In an introduction to the Italian edition of Weber's vocation lectures,[54] Massimo Cacciari notes how, for Weber, the vocations of the scientist and of the politician are in open conflict with one another. The conflict is an 'insurmountable contradiction'[55] that excludes the possibility of

[53] Schmitt (n 18) 65–66, *cf* Loughlin (2017) 'Politonomy' in J Meierhenrich and O Simons (eds) *The Oxford Handbook of Carl Schmitt* (New York, Oxford University Press, 2007) 570–91.

[54] M Cacciari, 'Weber and the Politician as Tragic Hero', originally M Cacciari, 'Introduzione' in M Weber, *La scienza come professione. La politica come professione* (Milano, Oscar Mondadori, 2006) v–lx.

[55] ibid, 207. The analogy to Loughlin's starting point is worth noting here.

any overriding principle that would unify the two. Loughlin tries to bridge this divide with reference to 'prudence' and 'practical reason'. The Weberian scientist's will to knowledge, Cacciari continues, is grounded in decision, but her vocation is also tragic in the sense that while that decision cannot be inferred from values, it is intrinsically rooted in them. In answering her call, the scientist takes on a duty to pursue 'pure' value-free knowledge and the normative nature of this duty aligns her with the politician. Science provides judgements based on the observation of regularities but it cannot choose between values or prioritise them. Unable to decide between values, the vocation of the scientist can never elevate scientific rationality beyond values:

> Even the scientist decides, but he decides to understand the struggle of values without taking part in it for anyone, in the exercise and within the limits of his own research. However, in already undertaking a research he has *decided*, and therefore his relation to other vocations is a priori, original. A relation without confusion, absolute distinction without separation.[56]

The Weberian politician, on the other hand, specifically deals with values, promoting the ones that she has chosen. But in their opposing positions on values, the scientist and the politician are not enemies in the polemical sense, one that would include the destruction of the adversary as an end. The one is required to 'tolerate' the other. For Cacciari, this polarity or irresolvable antinomy between science and politics is what defines the tragic nature of Weber's modernity. And I have suggested that Loughlin's *Foundations*—the theory rather than the book—is tormented by a similar antinomy and that the attempts at resolving it are insufficient. In Cacciari's account, Weber's two protagonists, the scientist and the politician, occupy two different citadels that are incompatible with one another. The conflicting relationship between the two is a *stasis*, historically connected in their origins, and yet continuously perplexed by one another, a 'brotherly enmity between the city of science and the city of politics'.[57] It is tragic enmity because no battle can assume annihilation as its end. No science can overcome the antinomy: 'The antinomy has no other choice than that of being understood.'[58] In Loughlin's case, I have contended, a 'metapolitics of public law' may provide a starting point for such an understanding.

[56] ibid, 211.
[57] ibid, 213.
[58] ibid, 212.

5

Immanence and Irreconcilability: On the Character of Public Law as Political Jurisprudence

JACCO BOMHOFF

I. Introduction

Public law, Martin Loughlin has long argued, is fundamental law. It is the law that institutes the sovereign. And in its modern liberal form, it is the law that sustains 'the autonomous world of the public sphere'.[1] In *Foundations of Public Law*, Loughlin presents an intricate genealogical and conceptual account in which this modern public law emerges to answer questions of political theology by way of a 'political jurisprudence'. My argument in this article is that this account does not take its own crucial strands of 'religion' and 'law' sufficiently seriously, in revealingly similar ways. The resulting, radically immanent, conception of public law, I claim, is not only unrealistic, but also hinders rather than supports Loughlin's own ambition for political jurisprudence as guarantor of the 'irreconcilable' within society.

Three claims as to the character of modern public law, developed throughout *Foundations*, are central to this argument. First, Loughlin's public law is resolutely secular. The book depicts the birth of an autonomous domain of the political as the outcome of a grand process of secularisation. In this, Loughlin broadly follows the radical account of a transition from 'heteronomy' to 'autonomy' in Marcel Gauchet's *The Disenchantment of the World*.[2] In this story, the law sustaining political autonomy can evidently no longer be the religious fundamental law familiar to medieval jurists.[3] Religion in modernity, as the book puts it, merely 'lives on as culture, and no longer as a basic structuring force of collective organisation'.[4] It is important to note even at this early stage that Loughlin adds a revealing *coda* to his secularisation story in his closing pages. There, he identifies a more

[1] M Loughlin, *Foundations of Public Law* (Oxford, Oxford University Press, 2010) [hereafter *Foundations*] 10, 232.

[2] M Gauchet, *The Disenchantment of the World* (translated by O Burge) (Princeton, Princeton University Press, 1997).

[3] *Cf Foundations* (n 1) 158 (seeing this as 'axiomatic').

[4] *Foundations* (n 1) 8.

recent threat to modern public law in terms of a 'return of the religious'. This return, which is not dated with any precision, takes the form of the rise of 'the social', and is manifested in 'overarching claims of the right and the true', voiced, apparently, with growing fervour.[5]

Second, public law is law. It is a form of 'juristic' discourse. This term is not defined in the book, but appears to refer to a familiar catalogue of what we might call legalistic characteristics and values. However, it is also clear that if public law is to remain fundamental in any meaningful sense, it cannot merely encompass the bare '*lex*' of posited law. And so instead, Loughlin argues, modern public law takes a distinctive politico-juridical form: that of 'a prudential discourse of political right'. This is public law as political jurisprudence: as '*droit politique*' (in Rousseau's terms), or as 'the *jus* of *lex*' (in Oakeshott's).

Third, and most importantly, public law is 'unresolvable confrontation'—in its form, function, and aspiration.[6] The book's central concern is to recover and maintain public law as a form of discourse through which a range of enduring central dilemmas over 'matters of common existence' can be expressed and negotiated, but through which also, crucially, their reconciliation or elimination can be forever deferred.[7] Loughlin sees these dilemmas as all related to a supposedly universal 'disjuncture between freedom and belonging'.[8] But more important—and more easily defended—than the precise substance of any specific binary opposition identified, I would argue, is the overall character of his undertaking, as committed to recognising and safeguarding public law's irreducibly paradoxical logic and its essential openness and open-endedness.[9] Public law thus *contains* conflict, in the double sense of the verb 'to contain'.[10] Borrowing an expression from Hent de Vries, it is what allows us to 'dwell in contradiction', together.[11]

In what follows, I ask three broad questions with regard to these dimensions to the character of public law. First, if political jurisprudence is indeed, as Loughlin puts it, a 'kind of secularised natural law', then how exactly is it secular?[12] Second, if public law is to be a

[5] *Foundations* (n 1) 465.

[6] *Foundations* (n 1) 465.

[7] eg *Foundations* (n 1) 156 (quite literally 'forever': see the reference to 'perpetual conflict'). Safeguarding this essential openness to contradiction is Loughlin's only explicitly identified normative commitment (see *Foundations* (n 1) 13). Having framed his argument as—predominantly—an exercise in retrieval and reconstruction, Loughlin tells us almost nothing about the connections between his notion of 'unresolvable confrontation' and broadly similar ideas in normative political philosophy, such as, most importantly, Rawls' overlapping consensus (for a brief allusion, see *Foundations* (n 1) 365). These possible linkages will also remain outside the scope of this response. I should note, though, that some of the work drawn on below in support of a critique of Loughlin—in particular that of the anthropologist Talal Asad and the political theorist William E Connolly—is also, explicitly or implicitly, critical of Rawls. See further WE Connolly, *Why I Am Not A Secularist* (Minneapolis Minnesota, University of Minnesota Press, 1999).

[8] *Foundations* (n 1) 11, 13.

[9] *Cf* J-P Dupuy, *The Mark of the Sacred* (Stanford, Stanford University Press, 2003) 17. Positing the 'universality' of any particular binary simply imposes at a meta-level a form of precisely the absolutism that Loughlin seeks to avoid.

[10] This emphasis on the double meaning of the verb is taken from Jean-Pierre Dupuy and Louis Dumont. See Dupuy, ibid, 5.

[11] H De Vries, 'On General and Divine Economy: Talal Asad's Genealogy of the Secular and Emmanuel Levinas's Critique of Capitalism, Colonialism, and Money' in D Scott and C Hirshkind (eds), *Powers of the Secular: Talal Asad and His Interlocutors* (Stanford, Stanford University Press, 2005) 131. See also M Gauchet, 'Tocqueville' in M Lilla (ed), *New French Thought: Political Philosophy* (Princeton, Princeton University Press, 1994) [hereafter, 'Tocqueville'] 103 ('the existence of the irreconcilable within society').

[12] *Foundations* (n 1) 231.

'juristic discourse' sustained by 'lawyers and legal modes of thinking', but if it is, at the same time, threatened by positive law and excesses of 'legalism', then in what ways exactly is political jurisprudence still law?[13] And third, most importantly: if political jurisprudence does indeed both require and facilitate a lasting commitment to openness, to contradiction, and to 'unresolvability', are the chances of sustaining public law's paradoxical logic in fact best supported by insisting on its secular and juristic qualities in the way Loughlin frames them?

The argument offered in response starts from the claim that in his focus on retrieving and defending the autonomous and foundational character of public law in the modern age—*after* religion and *against* mere positive law, as it were—Loughlin does not take either religion or law sufficiently seriously. This is to say that he does not treat them as discourses and fields with their own histories and practices, internal dynamics and forms of efficacy. Ironically, it is precisely because Loughlin develops such a richly nuanced understanding of the politico-jurisprudential as a discursive modality—the register of a 'prudential discourse of political right'—that the book's essentialising take on what are, at least to some extent, two parallel registers—of the religious and of the juridical—is so striking.[14] The main reason for this flattening gaze may be that although both religion and law are assigned important, even crucial, roles in the narrative of *Foundations of Public Law*, these roles remain highly specific and circumscribed. This is where the relation to the third dimension of political jurisprudence noted above—its positive embrace of 'unresolvability'—becomes important. In more general terms, the principal danger to the vitality of paradoxes and of reflexive or dialectical relationships is some externally imposed finality, or closure. The main such threats of closure Loughlin identifies stem from what we might call two types of fundamentalism. There is, first, the more 'formal' fundamentalism of an exclusively positivistic and legalistic understanding of public law.[15] And second, there is the more 'substantive' fundamentalism of absolutist religious ideas and values, and more recently, the perfectionism of what Loughlin calls 'the social'. Loughlin's public law, as the 'the ineffable idea of the *jus* of *lex*', then, must continuously resist attempts at re-grounding through either a 'purely formalistic notion' of law or through the 'importation of substantive values derived from natural law'.[16]

Intriguingly, it may well be that these two fundamentalist challenges, of legalism and value-absolutism, are related, and also that they are both of particular salience in the present moment.[17] In a 2009 article, the anthropologist John Comaroff observed a 'simultaneous fetishism of the law and the assertive rise of religiosity in the age of neoliberalism'.[18] Part of what Comaroff means is that recent decades of intense juridification—of constitution-writing, of international human rights litigation, of investment arbitration,

[13] *Foundations* (n 1) 308.

[14] 'Modality' is used here in the basic sense of a mode of engagement with the world. *Cf* AB Seligman, RP Weller, MJ Puett and B Simon, *Ritual and its Consequences: An Essay on the Limits of Sincerity* (Oxford, Oxford University Press, 2008) x.

[15] *Foundations* (n 1) 297.

[16] *Foundations* (n 1) 232.

[17] These parallels and possible relationships between positivism and value-absolutism are not addressed explicitly in the book. Nevertheless, in my view it is one of the achievements of Loughlin's work to furnish examples of these parallel movements and to stimulate reflection on their relationship. See also below n 20.

[18] J Comaroff, 'Reflections on the Rise of Legal Theology: Law and Religion in the Twenty-First Century' (2009) 53(1) *Social Analysis* 193, 194ff.

and so on—have also been a period of an increased significance of religious formations in the public sphere, notably in places like the United States, West- and North-Africa and the Middle East.[19] Comaroff also suggests, however, that these are not merely parallel movements, but that we are in fact witnessing different forms of the 'mutual infusion of law and religion'. '*Pace* Carl Schmitt', he argues in response, 'it is not just about *political* theology that we ought to be vexing ourselves. It is also about *legal* theology'.[20] One question motivating my commentary on Loughlin's work is whether taking 'legal theology' seriously, as the encounters and analogies, clashes and parallels, between the religious and the juridical, is something that *Foundations of Public Law* does. My sense is that it does not. Rather, in his effort to answer a problem cast as *political theology* by way of *political jurisprudence*, it is not just religion, or law, but *legal-*, or *juridical theology* that becomes the missing leg in Loughlin's genealogical and conceptual triangles.

These parallel critiques of Loughlin's constricted views of religion and law, and of his neglect of their intertwined existence in juridical theology, occupy sections II, III and IV of this chapter. Section V then goes on to argue that his insistence on the secular and juridical character of political jurisprudence are, in fact, merely two aspects of a more general assertion of public law's autonomy, or more precisely: its immanence. Immanence is used here in the sense of Weber's '*Eigengesetzlichkeit*'—as the 'internal and lawful autonomy', of different spheres of life.[21] Religion, when understood as absolute, comprehensive exteriority—'heteronomy', in Gauchet's terminology—threatens this autonomy. The juridical, taken as an instrument available for appropriation, supports it, while any danger posed by its own formal absolutism has to be a threat that can be contained. Against this background, this section discusses two related areas of difficulty.

The first concerns the idea of immanence itself.[22] This theme arises because, in spite of the—perhaps partly polemical—emphasis on purely immanent logics in *Foundations of Public Law*, the character of *droit politique* as actually developed in the book does in fact rely on various forms of exterior authority, heteronomy, or indeed: transcendence. Key examples are the givenness of language, shared conceptions of past and future, and especially, as described earlier, the character of the juridical form. These elements are in need of recognition and exploration. Not least because they offer suggestive parallels to some of the work Loughlin examines in his reconstruction of political jurisprudence, notably the writings of Jean-Jacques Rousseau.

[19] ibid.

[20] ibid. Another way of capturing these parallel turns towards religion (and the assertion of religious identities in particular) and towards law, is by seeing both as part of an 'overwhelming concern with sincerity' that marks our age; with 'sincerity' understood as 'an overwhelming concern with 'authenticity,' with individual choice,' and by the projection of a 'totalistic, unambiguous vision of reality "as it really is"'. See Seligman et al (n 14) (n 14) 8–9, 42, 118, 122–24; and further section V, below. A third, similar, diagnosis is offered by Alain Supiot, who decries the simultaneous phenomena of a 'flood of individual rights' (somewhat confusingly called 'legal nihilism'), and 'religious fanaticism' as two sides of the same 'temptation of fundamentalism'. See A Supiot, *Homo Juridicus* (London, Verso, 2007) xxi, xxv. These three perspectives—of legal theology, sincerity, and fundamentalism—differ in important ways, but they also share similar themes.

[21] CW Mills and HH Gerth (eds), *From Max Weber: Essays in Sociology* (New York, Oxford University Press, 1958) 328.

[22] *Foundations* (n 1) uses both 'transcendence' and 'exteriority', apparently as synonyms. 'Heteronomy' is used by Gauchet, but does not figure in *Foundations*, despite the centrality of 'autonomy' to the book's argument.

The second area of difficulty concerns the relationship between immanence and irreconcilability as twin aspects of the character of political jurisprudence. On this point, I argue that Loughlin's rigid insistence on the immanent character of public law, in the end, undermines rather than strengthens the possibility of sustaining the kind of contained conflict he strives for. This argument draws together the understanding of religion presented, with an extension of Loughlin's own emphasis on paradox and ineffability, and it contains two claims. The first is that *ritual* may have an important role to play in safeguarding openness and contradiction. This may be counter-intuitive. Ritual, after all, is often associated rather with formalism, dogma, and cohesion. But recent anthropological work emphasises how ritualised action can also help defer closure and counteract the fundamentalism that comes with the 'drive to wholeness'.[23] Through ritualised action, these anthropologists suggest, 'absolutes' imposed from outside, can be replaced with 'shared subjunctives' construed partly from within. More specifically, and this is my second claim, it is through such forms of acting that individuals and collectives may be able to construct and maintain vital pockets of 'in-betweenness'.[24] This is space—mostly metaphorical and discursive, sometimes actual—that belongs neither entirely to the social, nor fully to any individual. Such sites can never be comprehensively occupied or represented by any person, any group, or by society itself. This means that, from the perspective of both individuals and the collective, they offer an *empty* space that appears as simultaneously immanent and transcendent. They are islands, in other words, of transcendence-within-immanence.

This emphasis on the significance of these themes, of 'unoccupiability', 'inbetweenness', and ritual, finally, suggests two important possibilities that *Foundations of Public Law* does not admit. First, that the religious may not be a mere absolutist threat to public law, but could also, through its links to ritualisation, be supportive of public law's requisite open-endedness.[25] And second, conversely, that the perils of legalism, so deeply embedded within the discursive modality of the juridical, may be far more difficult to contain than Loughlin seems to allow.

II. Taking Religion Seriously: Political Jurisprudence as *Secular*

In *Foundations of Public Law*, religion is both utterly central and curiously absent. The same is true for law, as I will argue in section IV. These parallel absences have important implications for what Loughlin is able to say about the character of public law as a secular prudential discourse of political right.

Religion's centrality, first, is perhaps most immediately noticeable in the way the work of the French philosopher Marcel Gauchet quite literally bookends Loughlin's argument.[26]

[23] *Cf* Connolly (n 7) 141, 143; Seligman et al (n 14). See further section V.

[24] See further section V.

[25] As should become clear below, this is a very different argument from the well-known claims developed by Tocqueville, Ernst-Wolfgang Böckenförde, Robert Bellah, and others, on religion as a guarantor of social cohesion.

[26] eg *Foundations* (n 1) 6–7, 48, 63, 84, 103, 465.

It is Gauchet's grand narrative of the 'disenchantment of the world' that Loughlin turns to for an account of the dynamics of differentiation and separation said to underpin the emergence of an autonomous domain of the political.[27] Gauchet also furnishes the timing of the relevant decisive historical change in outlook, with his claim that after 1700 the 'age of religion as a structuring force' of collective organisation 'is over'.[28] More generally, Loughlin's thesis of a recent 'return of the religious, albeit in a different form' has a clear analogue in a depiction Gauchet offers, in his work on Tocqueville, of a twentieth-century 'return of the religious principle', as 'the full and entire reconciliation of society to a predetermined truth' under totalitarianism.[29] Most importantly, Gauchet's identification of a fundamental incompatibility between 'religion' and 'democracy' provides the template for the character of political jurisprudence itself. Religion, for Gauchet, means appeals to 'the external' and 'the absolute' as sources of authority—precisely the transcendence and the fundamentalism that Loughlin rejects. Democracy, in stark contrast, enables and organises 'the existence of the irreconcilable within society'.[30] Loughlin's public law, as noted before, then becomes the prudential public discourse that assures this essential unresolvability.

My claim in this section is that by following Gauchet so closely, Loughlin commits himself to a historical and philosophical perspective that does not take religion seriously, in three related senses of that phrase.[31]

First, since Gauchet's original publication—and more particularly, during the decade or so leading up to Loughlin's book—there has been a sustained attack on the 'easy assumption' that public life today is 'basically secular'.[32] This has been an extended scholarly moment of 'searching critique' for 'long-accepted discourses of modernity and enchantment', as well as for the teleological paradigms on which these tend to rest.[33] Traditional periodisations—the idea of an 'enchanted' middle ages and the notion of a 'decisive cultural rupture' at the end of the seventeenth century—as well as the conceptual vocabulary of 'secularisation', 'secularism', and 'the secular' have all come to be seen as much less stable than assumed previously.[34] Loughlin, however, continues to rely on a version of the classical narrative that is now among the most radical in the field, subscribing fully to the teleology of 'a progressive and thorough modern secularisation' of law.[35] In *Foundations of Public Law*, history

[27] *Foundations* (n 1) 6–7, 63.

[28] *Foundations* (n 1) 48.

[29] *Foundations* (n 1) 465; 'Tocqueville' (n 11) 106.

[30] 'Tocqueville' (n 11) 103, 108 ('The radical originality of democratic society [...] is always to question itself'); *Foundations* (n 1) 465.

[31] See further S Shortall, 'Lost in Translation: Religion and the Writing of History' (2016) 13(1) *Modern Intellectual History* 273 [hereafter 'Lost in Translation'].

[32] C Calhoun, M Juergensmeyer, J Vanantwerpen, 'Introduction' in C Calhoun, M Juergensmeyer and J Vanantwerpen (eds), *Rethinking Secularism* (Oxford, Oxford University Press, 2011) 3; WF Sullivan, RA Yelle, M Taussig-Rubbo, 'Introduction' in WF Sullivan, RA Yelle and M Taussig-Rubbo (eds), *After Secular Law* (Stanford, Stanford University Press, 2011) 1; M Riesebrodt, 'Fundamentalism and the Resurgence of Religion' (2000) 47 *Numen* 266–87.

[33] M Saler, 'Modernity and Enchantment: A Historiographic Review' (2006) 111 *The American Historical Review* 692, 700; A Walsham, 'The Reformation and "The Disenchantment of the World" Reassessed' (2008) 51 *The Historical Journal* 497, 504, 528.

[34] ibid. See also Sullivan et al (n 32) 2; Calhoun et al (n 32) 3 ('Until quite recently, it was commonly assumed that public life was basically secular'); Walsham, ibid, 499 ('In recent years [...] the notion that the Reformation was a powerful catalyst of the "disenchantment of the world" has been seriously questioned and qualified').

[35] *Foundations* (n 1) 84, 63. Gauchet's theory has been described as '*the only* modern theory of secularisation' to posit the 'disappearance' of religion. See Philip Gorski, 'Historicising the Secularisation Debate: Church, State,

moves forward '*because of* God's withdrawal' from 'a secularising world'. And secularisation is a broadly coherent project, propelled by jurists actively '*undertaking*' a 'transition to modernity'.[36]

Second, religion figures in *Foundations of Public Law* in some sense as a 'transhistorical constant'—as 'an independent variable that affects other aspects of human life while itself eluding historical change'.[37] This constancy is not immediately obvious. After all, religion *disappears* in an important sense in Louglin's account, only to resurface again 'in a different guise', later in modernity. But this narrative still incorporates an understanding in which, first, religion's role appears to be largely unchanging during the long period of its initial reign, and in which, second, there exists in fact some identifiable, deeper, underlying religious element that is capable of resurrection in some recognisable sense, even after a long period of absence. For the first part of this story, the long period of pre- and early-modernity, the book tells us virtually nothing about religion's character, content, form, or modes of efficacy, apart from the abovementioned references to 'the absolute other' as a form of authority. Religion, for Loughlin and Gauchet, as for Kant and Schmitt, is theology; and theology is dogma.[38] But this abstract and timeless conception cannot do justice to religion as a historical phenomenon. It can explain neither its earlier capabilities as a 'structuring force', nor why and how this efficacy would have been lost. It does not account for any variation in religious doctrines and practices or in their significance to individual and collective life.[39] For the later part of the story, there is a second consideration, which is that if religion is to remain potent as a threat today, as Loughlin claims that it does, then it has to be 'more than just the obsolete vestige of a distant past'.[40] There apparently is, in other words, something underneath religion's changing appearance—'the religious'—that is granted 'a transhistorical status that is denied to other historical formations—in particular

and Society in Late Medieval and Early Modern Europe, ca. 1300 to 1700' (2000) 65(1) *American Sociological Review* 138, 141. This is even taking into account his concession of the survival of religion in 'the personal sphere', or as Loughlin puts it with a different emphasis, 'as culture'. Fallers Sullivan et al (n 32) 9. Note: In this respect, it is striking how much more Loughlin tells us about the historical settings in which his protagonists were writing, than about the immediate context for his own theory. What Loughlin offers us is a theory of public law heavily invested in the idea of a secular, autonomous public sphere, at precisely the time when the notion of the 'demarcation' of religion from such a sphere, both as a historical occurrence and a present day phenomenon, is increasingly uncertain.

[36] *Cf Foundations* (n 1) 84 (emphases added).

[37] 'Lost in Translation' (n 31) 275. This theme is central to the work of Talal Asad. See, eg his *Genealogies of Religion* (Baltimore, Johns Hopkins University Press, 1993).

[38] *Cf* G Hammill, 'Blumenberg and Schmitt on the Rhetoric of Political Theology' in G Hammill and JR Lupton (eds), *Political Theology and Early Modernity* (London and Chicago, University of Chicago Press, 2012) 87. See also 'Tocqueville' (n 11) 98–99 ('intellectual constraint' coming from 'a body of dogmatic beliefs sheltered from the disputes of experience').

[39] Note: Where Gauchet writes of the central importance of the development of 'the State', he means to refer not just to the development of nation states in Western Europe that Loughlin has in mind, but also to the very first instances of public administration, found around 3000 BC. See, eg M Gauchet, *Le Désenchantement du Monde* (Paris, Édition Gallimard, 1985) 20 ('*l'emergence de l'Etat [...] comme l'evenement majeur de l'histoire humaine*', refers to '*quelque part autour de 3000 avant J.-C. en Mesopotamie et en Egypte*', 22. See also 21: '*cinquante siècles de politique contre la religion*'.). For criticism, see also M Riesebrodt: 'by placing the seeds of secularisation into the rise of the early empires, secularisation becomes the logical outcome of the reconfiguration of religion as soon as the paradise of "primeval" society is lost' (M Riesebrodt, 'Book Review' (1999) *American Journal of Sociology* 1526).

[40] *Cf* 'Lost in Translation' (n 31) 279 (discussing opposite, but structurally identical, claims as to religion's continued relevance).

social and political ones'.[41] In a sense, this is a case of taking religion *too* seriously, by according it, as James Chappel has put it, 'a special reprieve from history'.[42] This 'transhistorical constant' view of religion is commonly associated with the work of Alexis de Tocqueville. It is a view that is often criticised for its—explicit or implicit—attribution, to religion, of a positive, socially integrative force.[43] Tocqueville himself famously wondered 'whether man can ever support at the same time complete religious independence and entire political freedom', and was drawn to the conclusion that 'if a man is without faith, he must serve someone and if he is free, he must believe'.[44] Loughlin and Gauchet, of course, draw the diametrically opposite conclusion: that true political freedom comes only with religion's demise, and the transition from transcendence to immanence—from heteronomy to Kantian autonomy, from an '*ordre subi*', in Gauchet's terms, to an '*ordre voulu*'.[45]

The structural parallel between these two positions prompts a third, related, critique: that *Foundations of Public Law* ignores the internal dynamics and ambiguities *within* the field of religion, as well as the difficulties of imposing any clear boundary between religious and non-religious phenomena. In the world of *Foundations of Public Law*, it is always possible to identify an idea, a practice, or a form—most broadly: a discourse—as 'religious' or not. The same goes for the identification of discourses as 'juristic', on which more below. But precisely what it is that makes a discourse 'religious'—or 'juristic'—is nowhere explained. And any attempt at such an explanation is bound to run into serious difficulty. To begin with, recent historiographical scholarship has emphasised striking instances of the 'heteronomous intellectual practices of the early modern period'. This work effectively undermines the notion of any clear historical and conceptual break—a 'great separation'—between ostensibly secular discourses of politics and law on the one hand and religion on the other, during that time.[46] Of special relevance for Loughlin's genealogy in this regard are the writings of Thomas Hobbes. For Hobbes, in a nuanced reappraisal by the historian Jonathan Sheehan, '"theology" and "law" were equally potent schemes for thinking [the] containment' of the commonwealth, and its preservation in the face of disorder and disintegration.[47] Even more fundamentally, what emerges from this reassessment, as Sheehan explains, is that 'theology, like politics, is not an essence, but a set of claims that appear in time'.[48] This idea, that religious utterances and symbols 'cannot be understood independently of their historical relations with nonreligious symbols or of their articulations in and of social life', is central to the work of the anthropologist Talal Asad.[49]

41 ibid. For this perspective see, eg *Foundations* (n 1) 19 (raising the question of 'to what extent do religious and symbolic impulses [...] continue to permeate our subject?'; describing 'theological questions' in abstract terms as 'driven by an appeal to the power of the One, and the need to mediate both between the visible and the invisible, and between the temporal and the eternal'; and remarking that 'the extent to which these impulses live on in the guise of new beliefs and representation remains in question today').

42 Cited in 'Lost in Translation' (n 31) 275.

43 'Lost in Translation' (n 31) 275 (discussing the work of Brad Gregory).

44 'Tocqueville' (n 11) 2.I.5, 512.

45 Gauchet (n 39) 15.

46 For the term 'the great separation', see Mark Lilla, *The Stillborn God: Religion, Politics and the Modern West* (New York, Knopf, 2007).

47 J Sheehan, 'Assenting to the Law: Sacrifice and Punishment at the Dawn of Secularism' in Sullivan et al (n 32). See also Walsham (n 33) 511 ('English monarchs continued to be seen as conduits of thaumaturgic power').

48 Sheehan, ibid, 77.

49 T Asad, 'The Construction of Religion as an Anthropological Category' in *Genealogies of Religion: Discipline and Reasons of Power in Christianity and Islam* (Baltimore, Johns Hopkins University Press, 1993) 53–54.

In his well-known critique of Clifford Geertz's symbolic approach to religion, Asad has called for attention to the 'authorising processes' of power and discipline, by which religious meaning is constructed in the world.[50] '[T]he theoretical search for an essence of religion', Asad writes, 'invites us to separate it conceptually from the domain of power'.[51] And it is through power, in a wide range of forms—including worldly and ecclesiastical laws, sanctions, and the disciplinary activities of social institutions and of individual bodies—that in Asad's view, "religion" is created'.[52] Even if one does not accept this critique in its most stringent version, it is easy to see how attention to the diverse range of processes by which religious meanings are created, is bound to throw up all kinds of difficult boundary questions. Questions, that simple binary oppositions—between religion as a powerful structuring force of collective organisation and religion as mere culture, or between religion as domesticated culture and religion as recurrent threat—cannot adequately address.

III. Autonomy and Ambivalence

Two main reasons animate this extended discussion of the position of religion in *Foundations of Public Law*, and of the book's position in the wider contemporary landscape of secularisation scholarship. I should emphasise that these go beyond highlighting the disjunction in Loughlin's work between, on the one hand, an acknowledgment of the fuzziness of any boundaries between the medieval and the modern, or the sacral and the secular, and, on the other, the centrality of precisely such a break, in conceptual terms, for his overall project.[53] They concern rather, first: the possibilities for a historicised and comparative understanding of the idea of 'autonomy' in general, in order to better grasp the notion of autonomy of the political more specifically; and, second: the appreciation of the irreducibly ambivalent character of religious phenomena, in contrast to the one-dimensional emphasis on the-absolute-as-constraint, emphasised by Gauchet and Loughlin.

First, as mentioned earlier, Loughlin is deeply invested in the idea of autonomy for the public sphere. That autonomy is closely interwoven with—supported by and generative of—a highly distinctive and similarly autonomous notion of specifically *political* power. Now, one thing Asad's work does is to show how historiographical and conceptual questions concerning the elaboration of this political autonomy find important parallels in the construction of an analogous autonomy for religion. Religion itself, in other words, comes to be included in the list of domains for which the construction of their—relative—autonomy needs to be interrogated. That perspective is radically different from the classical differentiation account, followed by Loughlin, in which religion figures merely as a background out of which modern specialised domains, like literature or art or science, and of course politics, emerge.[54] The relevant shared question is succinctly raised by the editors of a collection on *Political Theology and Early Modernity*,[55] which appeared around the same

[50] ibid.
[51] ibid 29.
[52] ibid 37.
[53] See, eg *Foundations* (n 1) 17.
[54] See, eg *Foundations* (n 1) 7.
[55] See above n 38.

time as Loughlin's book. 'How does politics remain distinct from the content and practices of ethics, economics, and culture, while nonetheless bearing on them', these editors ask, '*and how does politics share this difference with religion*'?[56] By casting religion merely as shackles to be thrown off, Gauchet, and following him, Loughlin, foreclose an important avenue for exploring precisely this type of question. For the editors of the political theology collection, 'grasping what is distinctive' about religion and, in their example, art, as 'forms of human expression' requires 'some kind of formal and phenomenological accounting'.[57] This kind of formal analysis of course lies at the heart of *Foundations of Public Law*, and Loughlin's own earlier *The Idea of Public Law*. Curiously, however, this approach only extends to the domain and the discourse of political jurisprudence; not to religion, nor, as I will claim below, to law. But attending more carefully to the way religious phenomena come to be authorised as religious, as well as to the roles of power and discipline in the construction of the category of 'religion' and the differentiation of the domain of 'the religious', is bound to be significant for a project so invested in a parallel autonomy for the political.[58] Without such a comparative and relational approach, it will be difficult to move beyond mere *assertions* of differences between a 'secularisation of power' and a 'transfusion of sacrality into politics', for example, or between divine grace as 'bolstering' as opposed to 'creating' a sovereign's status.[59] And our understanding of the idea of 'autonomy' is likely to remain ahistorical and importantly incomplete.[60]

Second, there is the problematic association of religion with the idea of the absolute. It is important to re-emphasise that the secularisation narrative described earlier has a central role to play in Loughlin's story. Secularisation and secularism render necessary, enable, and ultimately determine the character of, an anti-foundationalist conception of the foundations of public law. Secularisation provides the narrative in which the reign of absolute values, externally imposed, is replaced by a public discourse in which everything is always and continually up for prudential revision in a debate among equal participants. On this view, then, religion can only ever be understood as *the absolute* and the external—the 'absolute other' in Gauchet's phrase.[61] And religious power only ever works to *constrain*, as opposed to the rules of public law, which always simultaneously, and paradoxically, both enable and restrict.[62]

This story, however, ignores a diametrically opposite view of religious discourses and their social efficacy. Like Loughlin's and Gauchet's account, this alternative view has its roots in both history and philosophy. But instead of a one-sided emphasis on religion as constraint, this view stresses rather 'the irreducibly ambiguous ways in which religious

[56] Hammill and Lupton (n 38) 4 (emphasis added).

[57] Hammill and Lupton (n 38) 6. For a similar perspective, see 'Lost in Translation' (n 31) 284 (calling for 'an appreciation of the way in which religious discourses interact with, but are not exhausted by, the political, social, and cultural contexts of their production').

[58] Also because it will show how 'political' forces have long been bounded up with the demarcation of 'religious' spheres. See, eg Walsham (n 33) 522 (noting, for example, how 'political, rather than intellectual, forces' were significant in provoking a 'loss of credibility' for demonology and witchcraft during the early-modern period).

[59] For a more detailed discussion of examples of such 'migrations of the holy', see Walsham (n 33) 111ff.

[60] See *Foundations* (n 1) 39 for these references.

[61] 'Tocqueville' (n 11) 108.

[62] See, eg *Foundations* (n 1) 178. See, eg 'Tocqueville' (n 11) 110 (religion as 'ultimate limits').

discourses operate historically, at once constraining and enabling their subjects'.[63] Adopting a historical understanding of theology 'not as a passive entity or thing, but dynamic process', this view emphasises that 'ambivalence and contradiction', doctrinal tension and disagreement, 'should not be regarded as anomalies but normalities'.[64] On this reading, any association between religion and absolutism becomes contingent rather than necessary, certainly as a matter of history. Going further, the philosopher of religion Hent de Vries has argued that what he calls 'dwelling in contradiction'—and what Loughlin might call living with, or in, paradox—'is the "modality" of the spiritual life, the religion of adults'. Now, whether, with de Vries, one sees this kind of radical openness as *the* core characteristic of religion—'always and everywhere'—or whether one adopts a more moderate view, allowing at least as much room for contradiction as it does for dogma, and for empowerment as it does for constraint; in both cases, any equation of religion with the absolute dissolves. In fact, on the more moderate view, religion, as both enabling *and* limiting, as pushing towards universality *and* as a 'destructuring movement away from unity', comes to resemble very closely the character of political jurisprudence as described by Loughlin. The religious, like the political—even as *an inflection of* the political, perhaps[65]—rather becomes available as one more resource, conceptually and historically, for developing precisely the kind of prudential discourse for life lived in common, in contradiction, that Loughlin cares about.

IV. Taking Legalism Seriously: Political Jurisprudence as *Law*

The notion that political jurisprudence, as a 'prudential discourse of political right', must be a *juristic* discourse, is as central to Loughlin's account as the idea that this public law must be a secular phenomenon. But what is it, precisely, that makes a discourse 'juristic'? What, in other words, makes public law, *law*? That, in *Foundations of Public Law*, is far less clear. This is not for want of invocation of the appropriate terms. The autonomy of the public sphere, Loughlin says, is 'sustained by its own politico-*legal* norms and practices'.[66] These norms and practices—*droit politique*—form a 'singular type of juristic discourse'.[67] Its vision of the 'right-ordering of public life' is a juristic concept'.[68] It obeys a 'juristic logic' and offers a 'juristic frame' for political judgement.[69] It cannot, of course, be the aim of this section to restate or clarify what Loughlin means by 'public law' in the broader sense of '*Recht*' or '*droit*', as elucidated by Hegel and Rousseau, and so many other writers in the long Western tradition that 'flourished from the late-sixteenth to the early-nineteenth centuries'.[70]

[63] 'Lost in Translation' (n 31) 281. See also 275 (noting 'the political ambivalence of religious phenomena: the way they function as sites of empowerment as well as constraint, and inclusion as well as exclusion').
[64] Walsham (n 33) 527.
[65] De Vries (n 11) 131.
[66] *Foundations* (n 1) 86–87 (emphasis added).
[67] *Foundations* (n 1) 231.
[68] *Foundations* (n 1) 159 (in an account of 'authority').
[69] *Foundations* (n 1) 237, 400.
[70] *Foundations* (n 1) 9, 111ff (on Rousseau).

That, after all, is what *Foundations of Public Law*, as a whole, is about. What I am rather concerned with here is the insistence that this tradition is concerned with 'a category of *juristic* thought',[71] especially as Loughlin is equally insistent that the vitality and significance of this category of thought depends entirely on it *also* being something else, something more, than just positive law.[72]

These terms—'juristic', and 'legal', in particular—are nowhere defined. As was the case with 'religion' in the previous section, and again in marked contrast to the great care taken to elaborate the character of *droit politique* itself, the identification of phenomena as 'juristic', and of actors as 'jurists', is simply taken as given. The book does, however, offer a number of indirect, partial answers. Juristic, to begin with, references a '*rationalist commitment*'.[73] Law brings with it ideas of *order* and *regularity*, often by analogy with laws of nature, and a sense of '*scientific discipline*'.[74] It is associated with the Hobbesian idea of '*command*'.[75] Juristic accounts are concerned with the constitution of *authority*.[76] They are *normative*, in that they are not merely backward-looking historical investigations, but are concerned also, at least in part, with ideals. But juristic also carries the meaning of *practical*, in the sense that law is *dynamic*, but also in the sense that juristic accounts are concerned, at least in part, with social *reality*, rather than merely operating on the level of political philosophy or morality.[77] Juristic, finally, also appears as a simple shorthand for *secular*.

We get a particularly clear idea of the kinds of commitments involved in the adoption of a juristic frame, in Loughlin's discussion of Tocqueville's views on the role of lawyers in American democracy. For Tocqueville, lawyers, by their training, acquire 'certain habits of order, a taste for formalities, and a kind of instinctive regard for the regular connection of ideas, which naturally render them very hostile to the revolutionary spirit and the unreflecting passions of the multitude'.[78] 'Without this admixture of lawyer-like sobriety with the democratic principle', Tocqueville continues, 'I question whether democratic institutions could long be maintained'.[79] These passages, both quoted in *Foundations of Public Law*, raise two rather different questions. The first, to be discussed only briefly here, concerns the tension between, on the one hand, the book's embrace of these limits on democracy set by 'lawyers and legal modes of thinking', and, on the other, its forceful rejection of apparently very similar limits on the 'political world' set by the 'spirit of religion' that Tocqueville also sees as indispensable.[80] Here, it seems Loughlin could offer at least two defences. He might argue, first, that this inconsistency is only apparent, since the boundaries set by 'lawyers and legal modes of thinking' operate on the level of 'culture', and his account fully accepts that religion 'lives on as culture' in modernity, even when it has lost its efficacy as a 'structuring force' in society. In part for the reasons discussed in the previous section, however, I do not think this binary distinction between 'mere culture' and something supposedly altogether

[71] *Foundations* (n 1) 9 (emphasis added).
[72] Among many instances, see, eg *Foundations* (n 1) 237 (discussing Heller).
[73] *Foundations* (n 1) 98, 307 (emphasis added).
[74] *Foundations* (n 1) 110, 73 (emphasis added).
[75] *Foundations* (n 1) 88 (emphasis added).
[76] *Foundations* (n 1) 159.
[77] *Foundations* (n 1) 112 (Rousseau, contrast with pure political philosophy).
[78] Cited in *Foundations* (n 1) at 307.
[79] *Foundations* (n 1) at 307.
[80] *Foundations* (n 1) 308–10; Tocqueville, *Democracy in America* (translated by GE Bevan) (London, Penguin Books, 2003) 55–56.

more foundational can be maintained. Alternatively, Loughlin might say that the two kinds of boundaries are fundamentally different in that the juristic is entirely immanent, whereas the religious relies on some form of transcendence. This argument, and the understandings of immanence and transcendence it depends on, will be taken up in the next section.

What I want to focus on here is a second question raised by Loughlin's embrace of Tocqueville's view of law and lawyers. This is the question of the prospects for a political jurisprudence that is able, in the longer run, to capture the benefits of the juristic form, without falling prey to the legalism that constitutes the flip side of that very form. Loughlin's invocation of law, it should be emphasised, is entirely instrumental. The 'form of law' is what invests the political discourse of right ordering 'with rational form, *i.e.* with universality and determinacy', so as to become the opposite of mere individual 'subjective conviction'.[81] But while political jurisprudence relies on this juristic form, it is, simultaneously threatened by 'legalism' and 'the triumph of ordinary law'.[82] I am much less certain than Loughlin appears to be, however, that these dangers can be kept at bay. Does not invoking law—the juridical form, the authority of lawyers—mean that we get *all* of law? This, I would argue, is what taking law seriously, as a form and as a discursive field with its own internal dynamics, suggests. Loughlin's discussion of the state shows this very clearly. The concept of the state, Loughlin argues, 'is the entity that gives us access to the nature of modern political reality and provides the key to understanding the nature of public law. It forms a scheme of intelligibility [...]'.[83] But of course, as Loughlin also recognises, this scheme itself, this 'comprehensive way of seeing, understanding, and acting in the world', is itself an intellectual construct, of a very particular kind.[84] And as Pierre Bourdieu writes, it must be

> impossible to give a genealogy of Western society without bringing in the determining role of jurists brought up on Roman law, capable of producing this *fictio juris* [...]. The state is a legal fiction, produced by lawyers who produce themselves as lawyers by producing the state.[85]

The way these lawyers have created this fiction—and, with it, themselves as a professional class, as recognised also by Tocqueville—is through what Bourdieu calls 'the imposition of form'.[86] That form, for all Loughlin's protestations that 'law' here should refer to 'public law' in his broader sense, is the Western legalist form, of ruleness and autonomousness. And that form also, whether for political, social, or metaphysical reasons, has a force of its own. A force that, as the anthropologist Harry Walker argues in recent work, often 'exceeds people's capacities to manage or control it'. 'Like magical power, it surpasses the intentionality of even the most potent practitioners'.[87] Loughlin's instrumental invocations of the juridical form do not take these fetishistic qualities into account.[88] If law is invoked

[81] *Foundations* (n 1) 148, quoting Hegel.
[82] *Foundations* (n 1) 297.
[83] *Foundations* (n 1) 208.
[84] *Foundations* (n 1) 208.
[85] P Bourdieu, *On the State: Lectures at the Collège de France, 1989–1992* (edited by P Champagne, R Lenoir, F Poupeau and M-C Rivière and translated by D Ferbach) (Cambridge, Polity, 2014) 55.
[86] ibid, 57ff.
[87] H Walker, *Justice and the Dark Arts: Law and Shamanism in Amazonia* (2015) 117(1) *American Anthropologist* 47, 55. The argument here is not that no individual jurist can master all of law, but rather that invoking legal forms may bring consequences that surpass the intentionality of legal practitioners, both individually and collectively.
[88] *Cf* ibid; Comaroff (n 18); C Tomlins and J Comaroff, '"Law As ...": Theory and Practice in Legal History' (2011) 1 *University of California Irvine Law Review* 1039.

to rationalise and stabilise a political discourse meant to remain prudential, its form *will also* push towards closure. If law is relied on to maintain a political discourse meant to remain open and diverse, the juridical form *will also* impose centralisation.[89] Even if the conceptual vocabulary of law is invoked because, after the supposed demise of religion, we have no other words left to express the kind of amalgam intended, of rationality, universalism, normativity, authority, etc, we have to realise that this juristic vocabulary is not innocent.[90]

In closing this section, it is necessary to acknowledge one last issue, which bears on the consistency between the perspective adopted here, on law, and the one developed in the previous section, on religion. This is the question of whether 'juristic' and its cognate concepts and terms will have meant roughly the same thing to all the actors on the long historical arc traced in Loughlin's book. Is arguing that the juristic form will bring with it certain inherent tendencies that may overwhelm both individual and collective actors, not akin to adopting the 'historical constant' view criticised earlier for religion? This is a difficult question, and one that cannot be fully answered here. It does seem at least plausible, however, that law and religion are different on this point, at least in the Western legal tradition.[91] This is because the long arc of that tradition is itself built around, and constantly propagates, the idea of law as a historically constant form. The notions of law as a 'self-sustaining system of rules defined by reason'; of the legal order as 'separate and specialised technique of governing social relations'; and of legal science as 'an analytical approach to power and its rational normalisation'; all have their foundation in Roman law.[92] These were all notions that Loughlin's protagonists were familiar with; they often in fact invoked Roman law legal terms for these very qualities. And so the danger that references to historical actors as a 'jurist', or to historical sources as law (*lex*) will be a-historical, therefore, seems considerably smaller than the corresponding danger for references to, say, the authority of an early-modern monarch as being 'secular' in nature.[93]

V. Taking Exteriority Seriously: Public Law as *Immanent*?

Loughlin, then, presents political jurisprudence as a resolutely immanent phenomenon—a discourse free from any form of exteriority. Medieval government may have 'received its authority from transcendent source'. But the authority of modern government is firmly

[89] Walker (n 87) 55.

[90] It is noteworthy, finally, that the basic question of why Loughlin's protagonists of political jurisprudence *turned to law at all* is never raised or answered in *Foundations*. Compare in this regard Ian Williams's recent observations in his review of Daniel Lee's *Popular Sovereignty in Early Modern Constitutional Thought*: '[A]n important question was begged and never addressed: why use legal material, language and ideas at all? Not all early-modern theorists did. Did legal material determine the issues raised and conclusions reached, or was it used instrumentally, justifying conclusions reached (or sought) for other reasons?' See 80(2) *Modern Law Review* 382.

[91] But see for an important caveat Tomlins and Comaroff (n 88) 1069.

[92] See A Schiavone, *The Invention of Law in the West* (Cambridge MA, Harvard University Press, 2012) 11–13.

[93] ibid, 201.

'located in immanent necessities'.[94] The break between these two perspectives, for Loughlin, following Gauchet, is what constitutes 'the deepest ever fracture in history'.[95] Throughout this article, I have sought to argue that such a categorical distinction, between immanence and transcendence, cannot be maintained. Section II questioned the idea that the religious is entirely outside or above the control of individuals and collectives, notwithstanding Gauchet's and Loughlin's strident portrayal of 'the essence of religious thought' as 'the external' and 'the unchangeable'.[96] As historiographical and anthropological work shows, religion is simply too enmeshed with different forms of power and discipline to be understood as entirely transcendent in such a sense. Section IV, in turn, sought to cast doubt on the idea that law, even when 'acknowledged to be a human construct', is entirely within human control.[97] Law's hypostatised character and its fetish-like qualities render such pure immanence implausible.

Both religion and law, rather, appear as phenomena that are 'neither completely autonomous, nor completely constructed'.[98] Taken together, these discussions of religion and law in fact suggest that, at least for such domains of *individual*-making, *collective*-making, and *meaning*-making, it may be impossible to draw any general distinction between immanence and transcendence in the first place.[99] Once identified, this basic ambivalence turns out to pervade other elements of Loughlin's account of public law as well. The role played by language in *Foundations* is a good example. Recall that, for Loughlin, the discourse of political right is 'a language' needed for communication over matters of common existence. Loughlin links this formulation to Charles Taylor's similar notion of the need for a language to sustain a 'common space of evaluation' among individuals.[100] Taylor importantly argues that such a language cannot belong to any one individual speaker—it must, as he writes, be '*our* language'. And as such, he concludes, it 'has to be constituted by conversation *between us*'.[101] This is surely a major insight, as Loughlin also acknowledges. But it does not fully capture the extent to which such a language, its terms and its structures, will *also* already have to exist prior to any particular conversation.[102] Rather than being a purely immanent phenomenon, then, language combines all these elements in itself—of agency, both individual and collective, but also of heteronomy, or transcendence, as something both 'within us' and 'outside us'.[103]

The same basic ambivalence that is central to the character of religion, of law, and of language generally, I want to suggest, also marks the character of the special language of

[94] *Foundations* (n 1) 7.

[95] *Foundations* (n 1) 7 citing Gauchet (n 2) 28/55.

[96] *Cf Foundations* (n 1) 6–7.

[97] *Foundations* (n 1) 7.

[98] B Latour, *On the Modern Cult of the Factish Gods* (Durham NC, Duke University Press, 2011) 8.

[99] *Cf* ibid, 28.

[100] *Foundations* (n 1) 155.

[101] C Taylor, 'Hegel's Ambiguous Legacy for Modern Liberalism' (1988) 10 *Cardozo Law Review* 865, cited in *Foundations* (n 1) 155.

[102] For a broad statement to this effect, see Supiot (n 20) 7 ('We are all subject to the heteronomy of language. It constitutes the condition of any discussion and thus cannot itself be debated'). See also *Foundations* (n 1) 31 (on the role of Latin).

[103] See R Rappaport, *Ritual, Religion and the Making of Humanity* (Cambridge, Cambridge University Press, 1997) 49 (citing Stanley Tambiah). See also Bourdieu (n 85) 45 on language as a 'repository of social philosophy'.

political right. While the rules of the grammar for this language are indeed, as Loughlin writes, 'rules that *we* have devised', that cannot be *all* they are.[104] The discourse of public law as political jurisprudence is something we have built, but that also goes beyond us.[105] That political jurisprudence may indeed be best understood in such a paradoxical, dual sense is suggested by the work of the originator of the term *droit politique*: Jean-Jacques Rousseau. When Rousseau writes '*il faudrait des Dieux pour donner des loix aux hommes*',[106] he is not signalling some manifest impossibility, as perhaps suggested more strongly by his other famous aphorism, that placing 'law over man' would be akin to attempts to 'square a circle'.[107] Instead, Rousseau goes into great detail to set out the requisite qualities of his Legislator as a figure straddling the immanence–transcendence boundary.[108] In one especially revealing formulation, Rousseau writes that for a people to come to be truly ruled by law it would be necessary that '*l'effet pût devenir la cause*': 'that men should be *before* the law, what they are to become *by* the law'.[109] This is precisely the kind of paradoxical and reflexive dynamic that Loughlin emphasises throughout *Foundations*, as part of the distinctiveness of political jurisprudence. But the fact that the reversal of cause and effect that Rousseau invokes is a signature characteristic of the logic of fetishisation, suggests that more is involved here than the fully immanent idea of 'reflexivity' that Loughlin invokes.[110] Instead, I would argue, following Jean-Pierre Dupuy, that what Rousseau's work demonstrates is the uncanny ability of human societies to 'produce their own exteriority'.[111] These are forms of *projected* exteriority, however, that are essentially ambivalent: they involve forms of 'self-exteriorisation', or, in Dupuy's terms, 'self-transcendence'.[112]

One way of framing this argument is as a simple extension of Loughlin's own approach. If paradox lies at the very foundations of the public sphere, why would this same feature not also constitute that sphere as simultaneously immanent and transcendent, with boundaries at once firm and permeable, determinative of its identity *and* endlessly to be negotiated? We can also put this the other way around: It could well be that this reflexive and ambivalent conception of the relations between the register of political jurisprudence and alternative modalities, offers the best chance of securing the kind of commitment to openness and paradox that Loughlin seeks to maintain within public law. And so, the questions we should be asking would be these. First, if some form of exteriority is unavoidable, is there any way

[104] *Cf Foundations* (n 1) 178.

[105] *Cf* Latour (n 98) 16.

[106] JJ Rousseau, *Du Contrat Social* (1762), II, 7 (*Oeuvres Complètes, La Pléiade* III, 381) [hereafter *Contrat Social* and *OCP*].

[107] *Foundations* (n 1) 132.

[108] *Contrat Social* (n 106) II, 7; *OCP* III, 383 ('*Ainsi l'on trouve à la fois dans l'ouvrage de la Législation deux choses qui semblent incompatibles: une entreprise au-dessus de la force humaine, & pour l'exécuter, une autorité qui n'est rien*'.). See for a subtle characterisation of the '*volonté générale*' as '*à la fois immanent et transcendent*', L Scubla, 'Est-il Possible de Mettre la Loi au dessus de l'Homme? Sur la philosophie politique de Jean-Jacques Rousseau' in J-P Dupuy (ed), *Introduction aux Sciences Sociales* (Paris, Ellipses, 1998) 131. For Scubla, the general will is based on a 'common interest', formed through the simultaneous exclusion of all individual interests—a common interest, therefore, at once within and outside all citizens, rather than some generalised aggregation of all their individual preferences (ibid).

[109] *Contrat Social*, II, 7; *OCP* III, 383. See also Scubla, ibid, 134. Own translation, emphasis added.

[110] *Cf* Bourdieu (n 85) 32; *Foundations* (n 1) 12, and many other instances.

[111] Dupuy (n 9) 2.

[112] ibid, 9, 15.

to think through its character as something that is fundamentally different from the ideas of 'the absolute' and 'the unchangeable' decried by Loughlin? And second, if there is a way to conceive of exteriority in such a way, what does this mean for the character of public law and our approach to its understanding? The answers I would like to suggest to these questions—in the form of 'ritual' and the 'in-between'—are developed, tentatively, in the remainder of this section.

VI. Ritual and 'In-between' Spaces

The project, then, is to take Loughlin's search for a discourse of public law that can ward off any form of *absolutisation* in the public sphere largely *on its own terms*, with the friendly amendment that the role of contradiction and ambivalence should be extended to the boundaries of that sphere itself. What would be the characteristics of such a discourse?

It seems that certain conceptions of ritual and ritualisation are particularly well suited to the kind of engagement with irreconcilability that Loughlin envisages. This argument begins with a view of ritual as one particular 'modality' of engagement with the world, rather than any 'discrete realm' of action.[113] That, I would suggest, may also be the most productive way of thinking about public law (as well as about law more generally, and religion, but this is beyond the scope of this article). At least on some views, one important characteristic of the modality of ritual—and of the practice of ritualisation—is that, using an unavoidably ugly term, it '*precises* ambiguities, it neither overcomes them nor relaxes them'.[114] As the authors of '*Ritual and its Consequences*', a collective essay written around the time of Loughlin's book, argue, 'the ritual mode has a built-in ability to abide with the inevitable ambiguities of life, even within an equally inevitable impulse toward an ever delayed—yet also never abandoned, desire for wholeness and totality'.[115] What makes this suggestion especially interesting is the fact that these authors appear to share a diagnosis of a cultural, political, and social climate of around the turn of the twenty-first century that seems close to the one animating Loughlin's exercise to retrieve a lost discourse for the prudential negotiation of the tensions of common existence. 'The reaction to the cultural and economic forces of globalisation, the re-emergence of religious commitments and ethnic identities throughout the world', these authors argue, 'all suggest the failure of our existing cultural resources to deal with ambiguity, ambivalences, and the gentle play of boundaries that require both their existence and their transcendence'.[116] Ritual preserves and emphasises ambiguities and tensions, such as those between tradition and innovation,

[113] Seligman et al (n 14) x.

[114] Seligman et al (n 14) 7, citing Jonathan Z Smith.

[115] Seligman et al (n 14) 112; See also at xi ('a unique way of accommodating the broken and often ambivalent nature of our world'). Other writers in anthropology who have also highlighted connections between ritualisation and ambivalence and contradiction include Victor Turner and Vincent Crapanzano. For a general discussion, see C Bell, *Ritual: Perspectives and Dimensions* (Oxford, Oxford University Press, 2009) 39–40, 57. For a normative defence of a political philosophy with very similar features, see Connolly (n 7).

[116] Seligman et al (n 14) 10.

between agency and submission, between different roles of individuals, and between the individual and the collective. The ritual mode is able to achieve such states of 'dwelling in contradiction' through the creation of 'shared subjunctives'. These are '*as if* worlds' of 'social convention and authority beyond the inner will of any individual'.[117] For the authors of '*Ritual and its Consequences*', 'what constitutes society—what makes the social a sui generis entity, irreducible to any other—is [...] a shared "could be"', the 'mutual illusion of the sort that all rituals create'.[118] It is important to note that this 'subjunctively shared arena' is a '*space in between*. It is not a place where individual entities dissolve into a collective oneness', of the kind Durkheim designated through his notion of 'effervescence'.[119]

This last point is important in relation to the other question raised earlier, of how to understand exteriority in a way that sustains rather than abrogates productive tension and contradiction. Recall that Loughlin defines 'the social', as a principal danger to the vitality of political jurisprudence, as absolute and comprehensive claims of the right and the true. Such overriding claims of course do feature prominently in contemporary public discourse, and they may well be on the rise, as Loughlin suspects. Here, however, is a portrayal of 'the social' in terms of a shared 'could be': as the diametrical opposite of any 'totalistic, unambiguous vision of reality "as it *really* is"'.[120] This, in other words, is 'the social' as tentative, fragmented, and always provisional, rather than in any sense 'absolute', or 'unchanging'. An alternative form of exteriority now also comes into view. What political jurisprudence—through ritual—may be able to do, I would suggest, is to actively construct, by way of a shared imagination, a kind of transcendence-within-immanence: a space that 'belongs neither to the self nor the other'; neither to the individual, nor to the collective.[121] These 'in-between' spaces are public law's exteriority within itself. And their constitutive feature is precisely that they are *not* marked by any definite substantive content, person, or group, but by a form of absence. What political jurisprudence sustains and protects, then, are pockets of *emptiness*: 'in-between' spaces that cannot be occupied by any individual speaker, or by any set of substantive values, and that cannot be entirely subjected to rules, or legislated away.[122]

Further development of the character of these 'in-between' spaces, and their logics of *un*-occupiability and *un*-representability, has to remain beyond the scope of this article.[123] For now, a helpful analogy can be found in the way ritual liturgies are similarly able to instil shared experiences of 'time out of time'. These are intervals during which one form of time—'sacred' time, or 'festival' time, for example—is marked off from, moves differently from, but also remains dependent on, 'ordinary time'.[124] During such periods of transcendence-within-immanence, contradictions can be played out rather than definitely resolved. This is also how I would characterise the space for confrontation opened up, ideally, in political jurisprudence. It is also worth noting that these themes find resonance

[117] Seligman et al (n 14) 7, 11, 20.
[118] Seligman et al (n 14) 23.
[119] Seligman et al (n 14) 26 (emphasis added).
[120] Seligman et al (n 14) 8.
[121] *Cf* Seligman et al (n 14) 50.
[122] *Cf* Seligman et al (n 14) 180 (referring to 'pockets of order').
[123] For a rich, normative, account of a political philosophy with such features, see again Connolly (n 7).
[124] *Cf* Rappaport (n 103) 216.

in broader anthropological, historical and philosophical writing.[125] Take for instance this interpretation of the famous 'empty throne' of the Ashanti in the work of the anthropologist AM Hocart:

> [F]or a limited time the chief of state will occupy an inviolable place. Like the king of the Ashanti, who sits under [his throne] because no one can sit on it, he will be, so to speak, placed under the protection of the general will, without at all being able to identify himself with it. [He is] neither supreme leader, nor representative of the sovereign, but *guardian of an empty place from* which no one can talk *because no one can occupy it*.[126]

Loughlin himself, in his essay on *The Constitutional Imagination*, cites Claude Lefort's depiction of the 'locus of power' in modern government as 'an empty place'.[127] This is a form of emptiness that remains after, in Loughlin's words, 'the transcendent figure of the sovereign is effaced'.[128] If I understand him correctly, Loughlin would see his project as the elaboration of a form of public law that is able to 'fill' this modern 'vacuum'; though, crucially, without any resort to exteriority or absolutes. As he describes the challenge: 'It may indeed be empty, but the place remains'.[129] But would it not be more in keeping with Loughlin's own arguments to argue that it is rather *maintaining* these spaces as empty ground, protecting them against occupation and forever deferring their dissolution, that constitutes the task for which public law as political jurisprudence may be uniquely suited?

VII. Conclusion

There are no foundations, Loughlin tells us in *Foundations of Public Law*. It is *droit politique* all the way down. There is fundamental law, but there cannot be any fundamentalism. Public law's purpose is precisely to prevent, by postponing indefinitely, any kind of grounding in absolutes. It can only do this if it can safeguard *its own fundamental-ness*. Doing that, Loughlin argues, requires an immanent discourse of irreconcilability.[130]

On the first point, I have argued that given Loughlin's general outlook of favouring openness and paradox, the categorical affirmation that public law *has to be* entirely immanent is incongruous. If the 'radical originality of democratic society' really is 'always to question itself',[131] should this questioning not also be extended to the way the boundaries of the

[125] Notably in Hermann Heller's idea of an ethical foundation to law which 'has content, though one which is not prescribed by any particular philosophy or ideology' (as discussed in D Dyzenhaus, *Hermann Heller and the Legitimacy of Legality* (1996) *Oxford Journal of Legal Studies* 651. See also De Vries (n 11) 132 (presenting the 'central referent' in religion as 'unconquered, unoccupied').

[126] Lucien Scubla, cited in Dupuy (n 9) 149.

[127] M Loughlin, *The Constitutional Imagination* (2015) 78(1) *Modern Law Review* 11; also in Dupuy (n 9) 148.

[128] Loughlin, ibid.

[129] ibid.

[130] In this article, I have taken Loughlin's objective of assuring irreconcilability through public law on its own terms. I have not discussed possible objections to that overall project, such as that the discourse of public law construes an abstract concept of a public sphere rather than any actual, genuinely open, sphere itself; or the idea that speaking of public law reveals more about the speakers than about what is spoken of (*cf* Asad (n 49); Bell (n 115) 4; *cf* also Bourdieu (n 85) 28, on the 'divinisation effect' of neutrality, 28).

[131] *Cf* 'Tocqueville' (n 11) 108.

discourse of political right are conceived?[132] And so, instead of the pursuit of an impossible radical immanence, we may do better trying to understand political jurisprudence as generative of, and supported by, a highly particular kind of exteriority: an un-occupiable, in-between space for public discourse that is simultaneously, and from different perspectives, transcendent and immanent.

On the second issue, I have claimed that the concern to safeguard irreducibility and to prevent the elimination or reconciliation of the vital contradictions of living together, may draw support from the practices of ritual. Ritualised modes of acting may be uniquely well-suited to a world where identities and boundaries are in need of both constant affirmation and transgression, so as to both allow for their existence and to guard against their absolutisation. Ritualisation is also an appropriate frame for understanding the kind of reflexivity that Loughlin places at the heart of political jurisprudence. It offers an understanding of dynamics through which men and women can be made before law what they ought to become through law. Ritual, after all, is often a key site for the construction of both normality and of normativity, *and* for dialectical movement between the two.[133]

This turn towards ritual has important implications for the study and the practice of public law as political jurisprudence. For one, it sits somewhat uneasily with Loughlin's own turn towards symbolism in his more recent work on *The Constitutional Imagination*.[134] The strands of anthropological work he draws on there, notably the symbolic anthropology of Clifford Geertz, have been criticised for assuming and emphasising forms of coherence and harmony of ideas that are difficult to reconcile with Loughlin's own arguments in support of contradiction.[135] Apart from Geertz's insights, then, further work on the discourse and the practice of political jurisprudence might draw on other anthropological work, such as that by Edmund Leach on the 'grammar' of ritual, or by Talal Asad—cited earlier—on practice and discipline.[136]

Most importantly, the ritualisation perspective serves as a useful reminder that negotiating the tensions of common life requires effort. 'Ritual is endless work', it has been said, 'but it is among the most important things we humans do'.[137] Much the same could be said of our efforts to maintain a genuinely open register of public reason, in the form of a prudential discourse of political right. That discourse, though, as I have argued, may have to be somewhat more *like religion*, and somewhat less *like law*, than Loughlin envisages.

[132] *Cf* Connolly (n 7) 5–8, 19–46.

[133] The game analogy in David Dyzenhaus's discussion of Heller is illustrative for its closeness to ritual dynamics. See Dyzenhaus (n 125) 654.

[134] Loughlin (n 127). Note that *Foundations*, despite its explicit mentions of the importance of 'practice', in fact offers very little discussion of any such practices, apart from some mention of early coronation rituals.

[135] *Cf* Bell (n 115) 28–30; Asad (n 49).

[136] *Cf* Bell (n 115) 68, 79.

[137] Seligman et al (n 14) 182.

Part III

The Normative Critique

6

Concrete Order Formation or Rational Will Formation? Constituent Power as the *Ratio* of *Voluntas*

HAUKE BRUNKHORST

I. The Dialectic of *Potestas* and *Potentia*

One of Martin Loughlin's basic assumptions is that modern law in general, and public law in particular is *immanent* in the sense that it can no longer be justified transcendentally (eg by reference to God, natural law, or transcendental subject). Therefore, all references to the ancient understanding—the 'dignified aspect',[1] and the 'dignified façade'[2]—of public law are a 'masking of reality'[3] or, as one might say with the German sociologist Rudolf Stichweh, they are just a transitionary semantics (*Übergangssemantik*).[4] In their way, Loughlin and Stichweh corroborate an old Marxist argument: after the basic structure has accomplished the 'transference of the other into immanence',[5] 'the entire immense superstructure is more or less rapidly transformed'.[6] After the crumbling of the transcendental façade, however, there is still some need for justification or grounding of the positive law of the legally institutionalised political 'community' (*Gemeinschaft*).[7] The constitution is not just a contract.[8] Public law has a foundational and legitimising character that is not identical with its own legality. This foundation takes us back to the idea of constituent power.

Once institutionalised as political organisation (ie a state), the foundational character of political right protects the community (*universitas*) from the pressure of society (*societas*), especially from the blackmailing power of the economy, at least as far as the

[1] M Loughlin, *Foundations of Public law* (Oxford, Oxford University Press, 2010) [hereafter *Foundations*] 100.
[2] ibid 157.
[3] ibid 158.
[4] R Stichweh, 'Professionen in einer funktional differenzierten Gesellschaft' in A Combe and W Helsper (eds), *Pädagogische Professionalität* (Frankfurt, Suhrkamp, 1996) 49–69.
[5] *Foundations* (n 1) 49.
[6] K Marx, *A Contribution to the Critique of Political Economy* (Chicago, Charles H Kerr & Company, 1904), 12. 'Immense' in German is '*ungeheure*' and hesitates in the Marx text a bit between 'immense' and 'uncanny'.
[7] *Foundations* (n 1) 199f. Loughlin refers with 'community' to Tönnies' famous distinction between '*Gemeinschaft*' (community) and '*Gesellschaft*' (society).
[8] *Foundations* (n 1) 275ff.

political organisation can enforce its own autonomy (be it as politonomy, public autonomy or functional autonomy).[9] The constitutional constraints against social systems enable the *potestas* of the state to augment its own technical and disciplinary *potentia* that (in a first meaning of *potentia*) is mere technical power, and itself societal and not political.[10] The power of technical *potentia* has a strong tendency to destroy its master, the *potestas* of the state, that which is truly and originally political. One of the branches of the state that paradigmatically represents the 'managerial mindset' of *potentia* is the legal profession.[11] The system of courts is not, thus, what Alexander Bickel famously labelled the 'least dangerous branch'.[12] On the contrary, for Loughlin, the original sin of the modern constitutional state is *Marbury v Madison*, leading to the progressive positivisation of political right and the decay of the political and politonomy.[13] The *Rechtsstaat* comes to colonise the *Staatsrecht*, and its ideological assumption of neutrality opens the door for all kinds of particular social interests to dominate.[14] The technical and disciplinary power of *potentia* (now organised by private-public partnerships) ultimately subsumes the authority of *potestas*.[15] With this negative dialectic, developed in the last chapter, the book ends.[16]

One could already ask here why Loughlin refers only to the reflexive and systemic versions of technical power as domination (that he finds in the works of Léon Duguit, Michael Mann, Michel Foucault and Philipp Gorski), instead of returning to the alternative version of *potentia* that he had distinguished in Chapter 6 on 'Political Jurisprudence'.[17] This alternative version of *potentia* characterised by Loughlin as 'power to' (with Arendt and Habermas), as distinct from 'power over' (Mann, Foucault) and which is 'rooted in the intersubjective generation of solidarity' is gradually lost in later chapters.[18] But constituent power, in particular, is a 'power to'. Moreover, the guarantee of egalitarian solidarity (as 'power to') is an essential characteristic of and, indeed, Loughlin's *main justification* for

[9] See B Jessop's and M Wilkinson's contributions to this volume, in chapters 10 and 12 respectively.

[10] With the distinction between 'society' and the political that is the 'state', Loughlin goes back to Hegel and German statutory positivism (*Staatswillenspositivismus*—see below), and their basic distinction between '*Staat*' and '*Gesellschaft*', hesitating a bit between Hegel and Tönnies. However, the hesitation makes sense because Hegel's state is a form of '*Gemeinschaft*' but (in contrast to Tönnies') a modern one (that would have brought back the best of the classical meaning of *polis* and *res publica* to modernity). In Tönnies' more robust Hobbesianism, the modern state clearly is at the peak of *societal* advances, but this is exactly what Hegel calls a *Not- und Verstandesstaat* ('external state' or 'a state subservient to necessity').

[11] See M Koskenniemi, 'Constitutionalism as Mindset: Reflections on Kantian Themes about International Law and Globalization' (2006) *Theoretical Inquiries in Law* 8/1, 9–36.

[12] A Bickel, *The Least Dangerous Branch. The Supreme Court at the Bar of Politics* (New Haven, Yale University Press, 1986); see *Foundations* (n 1) 362f.

[13] *Marbury v Madison* 5 US (1 Cr) 137 (1803); *Foundations* (n 1) 289ff.

[14] *Foundations* (n 1) 312ff.

[15] *Foundations* (n 1) 407ff. On the colonisation of the state and the political lifeworld by the global economy, and in particular through private-public partnerships, see T Judt, *Ill Fares the Land* (New York, Penguin, 2010) and C Crouch, *The Strange Non-Death of Neoliberalism* (Oxford, Polity, 2011).

[16] Loughlin's diagnosis resembles not only that of Judt and Crouch who see the cause of colonisation of the political sphere by the economy in the politically enforced globalisation of financial capitalism, reinforced by the neoliberal episteme, and in the welfare state the main weapon of defence of a democratic political sphere. It also strongly overlaps with that of Arendt, Forsthoff and Schmitt, who consider colonisation as the result of the socialisation of the state by social welfare, pluralist representation of interests and social democracy. Loughlin seems to hesitate between the progressive and the neoconservative diagnosis without being able to resolve the ambivalence.

[17] *Foundations* (n 1) 164–71.

[18] *Foundations* (n 1) 169f.

the state. He assumes, as Hannah Arendt did in the immediate aftermath of World War II, that the 'sovereignty of the nation-state which once was supposed to express the sovereignty of the people' is 'the greatest bulwark against the unlimited domination of bourgeois society, and ... the introduction of imperialistic politics in the structure of Western states'.[19]

II. *Nomos* and the Genealogy of Political Power

My criticism is more fundamental: Loughlin's own conception of 'power to' as intersubjective generation of solidarity must in any case include much more than political power alone. The point is that 'power to' also stems from the social, belonging to the sphere of society, and emerging from it. 'Power to' dates back to a time and place long before the origin of the ancient state. Following Schmitt's genealogy, one might trace it back to the (agrarian) use of *nomos* and *nemein* as land grabbing and concrete ordering of the soil in ancient Greece and with Schmitt one might then take *nomos* to be the determining origin of all formations of state and state sovereignty, ancient and modern. In this context, Schmitt's argument is of particular relevance because Loughlin, despite his distance to Schmitt's elitist thinking, remains indebted to Schmitt's genealogy (and similar genealogies). Schmitt's argument can be briefly reconstructed. For Schmitt, the origin of the ancient and modern state dates back to the Greek terms *nomos* and *nemein* that refer to land grabbing (*Landnahme*) for reasons of agrarian settlement.[20] Once land grabbing becomes a normatively (tacitly) accepted division of the soil, the ('illegal') appropriation and occupation of land (*Landnahme*) shades into ('legal') land ownership (*Landbesitz*): the three original meanings of the Greek *nemein*, 'appropriation', 'division' and 'pasture' coincide. One can call this coincidence in the terminology of Schmitt (and Hauriou) the 'concrete ordering' of the space of the earth that is the origin of 'the political' and the state.

As becomes evident from a functional sociological perspective, however, this so-called 'origin' is at most a 'pre-adaptive advance' (to use Luhmann's terminology) that can only become relevant for the much later functional differentiation of the political system when it occurs in a plurality of different cases and at many different places across the globe. Moreover, pre-adaptive advances might vanish without any effect, evolution could completely change their original meaning in light of functional differentiation. Pre-adaptive advances ('origins'), on this sociologically informed account, have at most a minor significance for later developments, and they lack any significant power to determine history.

Schmitt's genealogy then is nothing other than an instance of conceptual idealism (*Begriffsidealismus*). Schmitt's (and Hauriou's) 'concrete ordering' is concrete and (literally) 'down to earth' in exactly the way Rousseau's famous 'first man' concretely orders the space of the soil. The 'first who, having enclosed a piece of ground, bethought himself of saying *This is mine* ['appropriation' of 'pasture'/ agricultural land], and found people ... to believe

[19] Arendt's 1948 diagnosis was already the same as Loughlin's, ie that the sovereignty of the nation state 'now (is) threatened from all sides' H Arendt, *Die verborgene Tradition* (Frankfurt, Fischer, 1976) 29.

[20] C Schmitt, *Der Nomos der Erde* (Berlin, Duncker & Humblot, 1988) 36–51.

him ['division']', constituted the first concrete order, and with it the paradigm (or model) for the formation of law and state.[21] Enclosing a piece of ground and finding people to accept it as mine are the concrete operations which constitute a first kind of customary law. From here, only a few logical steps of generalisation, abstraction and differentiation are required to arrive at the meaning of *nomos* as 'abstract law', a concept that covers the whole variety of legal forms: customary, natural, common, positive law, and so on. Eventually, people living in cities in the Peloponnese began to draw a distinction between the (proto-private) 'eco-nomy' that is the 'law of the *oikos*' (household), and the public *polito-nomy* that is the 'law of the *polis*' (the political organisation of the city). It is to that extent that *nomos* as land grabbing and concrete ordering is the origin of the political sphere and the state.[22]

But which state? Sociologically speaking, the evolutionary origin of the ancient (Eurasian and Middle-/South-American) formation of states (city-states, empires, etc) is the Agrarian Revolution about 10,000 years ago. If state formation actually began with a kind of land grabbing and concrete ordering of the earth, land ownership and tenure, it rapidly proceeded (simultaneously in several areas of the globe) to social class differentiation, together with the formation of centralised bureaucracies and political domination. No *nomos* (in the original Greek sense) without class-rule.[23] So far, Schmitt's genealogy is more or less compatible with the sociology of social and political evolution. However, what emerged in the aftermath of the agrarian revolution was a very specific kind of state that Schmitt takes for the origin not only of the imperial Greek city-state and the ancient states and empires in general (which were all based on social stratification, political domination, and a huge variety of slave labour), but of any political and state formation and, it is argued, this original usurpation and concrete ordering determines the state throughout its social evolution. Once the first act of land grabbing and the speech-act 'this is mine' was performed successfully, there is no longer any alternative path to political state formation and public law. This is because the successful performance of 'this is mine' has actualised the latent structure of the political 'power to' consisting in land grabbing and concrete ordering, and there is no other. This latent structure is the historical essence of political power. Philosophically speaking, it is merely the historicisation of metaphysical essence, and to that extent has exactly the same structure as Heidegger's *Seinsgeschick* ('destiny of being') that is inescapable and beyond human praxis, will formation and choice. For Schmitt, the pre-legal but already proto-legal—in *Political Theology* he calls it enigmatically 'juristic beyond legality'[24]—*nomos* is the original power that discloses once and forever the world of the political and, therefore, the first land grabbers' speech-act is a *seinsgeschichtliches Ereignis*: an 'occurrence in the history of Being'. *Nomos* in the political theory of the late Schmitt

[21] JJ Rousseau, *Second Discourse on Inequality*, part II, first sentence, quoted from Rousseau, *The Social Contract and Discourses* (London, Everyman, 1913) 192.

[22] See M Loughlin, 'Politonomy' in J Meierhenrich and O Simons (eds), *The Oxford Handbook of Carl Schmitt* (Oxford, Oxford University Press, 2017) 570–92. Rousseau and Kant are using the word 'usurpation' (illegal appropriation) to characterise the origin of the existing legal state of the 18th century (that is the pre-revolutionary states, where they lived, ie France and Prussia).

[23] In this point (and many other ones) Schmitt is completely in accordance with conservative fellow-travellers like Oakeshott and Strauß, see the brilliant analysis by P Anderson, 'The Intransigent Right at the End of the Century' (1992) 18 *London Review of Books* 7.

[24] C Schmitt, *Politische Theologie* (Berlin, Dunker & Humblot, 1990 [1922]) 19 (order '*im juristischen Sinne*' preceds the '*Rechtsordnung*').

thus becomes the constitution behind all written constitutions, the resolved 'riddle of all constitutions'.[25] If we follow Schmitt this far, then it becomes plausible that 'the core of all human order [is] the mutual relation of protection and obedience' ('*ewiger Zusammenhang von Schutz und Gehorsam*').[26] The power to establish a concrete ordering that emerged with the first land grabbing is therefore (in accordance with Schmitt's basic premise), already the first emergence of constituent power.

But this is only on the basis of Schmitt's highly implausible metaphysical assumptions. It is methodologically interesting to compare this with Marx's resolution of the riddle of all constitutions. For Marx, combining Hegelian dialectics with modern evolutionary social theory, the resolution is the respectively latest (and arguably highest) end point of a long constitutional evolution that (besides natural and social conditions) is due to cooperative labour and interactive praxis (class struggle). For Marx, democracy is the resolved riddle of all constitutions. This democratic resolution to the riddle of all constitutions did not exist before the French Revolution and could only be recognised after the French Revolution. Schmitt, on the other hand, thinks precisely the reverse, in an old-European and metaphysical way. The beginning of politics and public law, once disclosed by the first land grabbers, determines the resolution of the riddle, and whatever is written and defined as public law (legality) is a constitution if and only if it is grounded in a concrete ordering of mutual relations of protection and obedience.

Schmitt's argument, in consequence, is not only tied to a genealogy that relies on an untenable overgeneralisation and hypostatisation of a historically specific path of social evolution, but is crippled by extremely impoverished notions of 'power to' and political solidarity based on a supposedly eternal relation of protection and obedience. Schmitt, in this sense, makes just the same mistake that Rousseau had already criticised in Hobbes. According to Rousseau, Hobbes projected an advanced social state onto the state of nature, hence naturalising historically established societal relations—an argument that anticipates later Marxist critique of ideology.[27] Schmitt too conceals the historical and social conditions of *nomos* and *nemein*, which Rousseau had highlighted in his *Second Discourse*, anticipating Marx: The *nomos*-man is 'the first man who, having enclosed a piece of ground, bethought himself of saying this is mine'. However, Rousseau's point is that the land grabbing *nomos*-man not only 'found people [...] to believe him' (as quoted above and in accordance with Schmitt)—but found 'people *simple enough* to believe him' and only thus, Rousseau adds ironically, could he become 'the real founder of civil society'.[28] Indeed, as Rousseau argues, the *nomos*-man and his submissive believers must be identified neither with the natural man nor with the political animal. Identifying (with Hobbes and Schmitt) the origin of all possible formations of political 'power to' with land grabbing, agrarian production and social stratification beginning about 10,000 BCE, abstracts from the social fact that this was preceded by 100,000 years of segmentary, differentiated, egalitarian hunter- and gatherer

[25] K Marx, 'Kritik des Hegelschen Staatsrechts' §§ 261313 in *MEW* 1 (Berlin, Dietz, 1988) 201–333, at 231; see S Marks, *The Riddle of all Constitutions* (Oxford, Oxford University Press, 2000).

[26] C Schmitt, *The Nomos of the Earth* (New York, Telos Press, 2006) 318, see also 48; C Schmitt (n 20) 295.

[27] For an advanced version of this criticism, see CB MacPherson, *The Political Theory of Possessive Individualism—Hobbes to Locke* (Oxford, Oxford University Press, 2011). Loughlin rightly makes the same point with Rousseau against Hobbes (*Foundations* (n 1) 134–35, 137–38) and Montesquieu (*Politonomy* (n 22) 12) but not against Schmitt.

[28] Rousseau, *Second Discourse* (n 21) part II, first sentence.

societies (allowing only flat hierarchies). Moreover, it ignores the social fact that egalitarian societies were already socially integrated by a 'power to' that was 'rooted in the intersubjective generation of solidarity'.[29] Therefore, the evolutionary path of *nomos* and *nemein*—land grabbing and concrete ordering—is only one of many possible paths and to take it implied a political choice for hierarchy over egalitarianism. Rather than assenting to the *nomos*-man's claim, others could have resisted,

> pulling up the stakes, or filling up the ditch, and crying to his fellows, 'Beware of listening to this impostor; you are undone if you once forget that the fruits of the earth belong to us all, and the earth itself to nobody.'[30]

To conclude, the evolutionary path of land grabbing and class rule was neither a causal effect of natural laws nor an unavoidable and unchangeable 'destiny of being', but a process of social selection through a combination of accidents (due to the unavoidable complexity of interaction, especially 'double contingency'), already established structures of 'power to', and choice. Even if we (with Rousseau) take into account accident and the fact that the *nomos*-man might have had better weapons and well-armed allies, the people had the choice to assent to the *nomos*-man or not—they were not born 'so simple' (as Rousseau insists) that they had to believe the land grabbers.[31] Anyway, vis-à-vis the *nomos*-man the people already had the political power to accept or reject his speech-act 'this is mine'. Even if they used their power in the wrong way, they had the choice, and (more importantly) they still have it. They can, therefore, change their mind and revise their decision, especially after the negative experience of increasing injustice, 'how many crimes, wars and murders, (…) how many horrors and misfortunes' were effected by their tacit consent to the speech-act of the *nomos*-man.[32] At least Rousseau's path-breaking insight had liberated them (and us) in principle to try and try again, and to search for, construct and establish alternative paths of political power formation that are beyond political and social class rule. Rousseau's world-disclosing argument is that there are origins of the social evolution of 'power to' and the intersubjective generation of solidarity other than land grabbing and simple minds assenting without reflection to the speech-act 'this is mine'. Political action, in sum, is not predetermined to take the evolutionary path of reifying mutual relations of protection and obedience.

III. The Social Origin of Political Power

To overcome the conceptual regime of the *nomos*-man, Hannah Arendt provides an interesting alternative. In a first step, she traces political 'power to' back to the Greek polis and the Roman republic, and further back to *nomos*. However, Arendt's *nomos* is not the *nomos* of land grabbing and concrete ordering of domination (mutual relations of protection and

[29] *Fondations* (n 1) 169f.

[30] Rousseau, *Second Discourse* (n 21) part II, second sentence.

[31] As Rousseau writes realistically, 'there is great probability that things had then already come to such a pitch, that they could no longer continue as they were', but it is only a probability, not necessity that makes them believe (*Second Discourse* (n 21) part II, third sentence).

[32] Rousseau, *Second Discourse* (n 21) part II, first sentence.

obedience) but of reciprocal solidarity among citizens. Like Schmitt, she derives political solidarity from the Greek *nomia* but this time from *isonomia*. *Iso-nomia* marks an important break from *eco-nomia* and (Schmittian) *polito-nomia* but still is as Eurocentric, elitist and exclusive as the Schmittian genealogy, based on the same implicit social conditions of stratification, agrarian production, exclusion of the non-citizen, and slave labour. However, it is interesting to observe that in a second step, which she made in *The Human Condition*,[33] Arendt (without making it explicit) offers an alternative genealogy of the political that immediately avoids the pitfalls of Eurocentrism, elitism and exclusion. This alternative is announced with her famous idea that the ultimate evolutionary origin of political 'power to' is not *polis*, *res publica* or *isonomia* but 'natality'. *Polis*, *res publica* and *isonomia* thus only point to one possible path of constitutional evolution, whereas 'natality' keeps evolution open for alternative paths because of its connotations of creativity and universality.

In Arendt's anthropological reconstruction, natality is our 'second birth' that is co-original with the use of language. Therefore, political 'power to' is co-original with every performance of a new speech-act, or any unexpected symbolic act that is deviant or different, as compared with acting as always. Deviant use of language (symbols) includes forms of negation, and can be made explicit as negation ('this is different because it is not the same as usual'). Deviant and negating use of symbols is performed by everyone all the time in every society. Arendt's political anthropology therefore not only fits modern evolutionary theory (contradicting her own anti-evolutionist Heideggerian self-understanding), it also clearly opposes her own Eurocentric, elitist and exclusive genealogy of political 'power to' in the slaveholder society of the urban polis. When Arendt briefly turns to the Greek understanding of action in *The Human Condition*, she too quickly closes the path of political alternatives to the *nomos*- or *iso-nomos*-man. Such an alternative is, however, suggested by Arendt's own reconstruction of political 'power to' from a Christian understanding of natality as Augustinian *initium* (initiative, new beginning) and the egalitarian Christian hope that is related to the new beginning when a child is born.[34] In her political anthropology, not land grabbing but every unexpected negation or any other, more implicit expression of a normative expectation of a speech-act is political, the origin of (innovative) political power to, of communicative power and of public law.[35]

In Arendt's anthropological genealogy, the political is rooted in the *potentia* to begin something new, just by interrupting habitually settled interaction with an arbitrary act of negation, deviation or expectation. We are already political animals with these first acts, and not only after the polemical differentiation between citizens and idiots introduced by Aristotle at the beginning of his *Politics*.[36] Arbitrary action does not depend on the differentiation between urban centre and rural periphery, or between nobles, peoples and slaves. It is co-original with social evolution and the use of language. The origin of political 'power to' therefore is social 'power to'. It is only much later, after the emergence of a public

[33] H Arendt, *The Human Condition* (Chicago, University of Chicago Press, 1958).

[34] ibid 247; see already the last sentence of Arendt's *Origins of Totalitarianism* (San Diego, Harvest 1979).

[35] Arendt (n 33) 176–91, 246–47. On this point she is in accordance with Habermas and not Schmitt or Heidegger.

[36] Aristotle defines the *zoon politikon* as the essence of the human being which is realised only by perfect formations of human beings living in city-states as Athena, excluding metics (as Aristotle himself), women, passive homosexuals, slaves, peasants, and the colonised city-sates of the Athenian empire. See Aristotle, *Politics* (Oxford, Oxford University Press, 1995) 1252a–1255b, in particular 1253a–b.

sphere in urban societies of political class rule, that social power can (but need not) be transformed into the specifically political power of 'foundation'.[37] However, even then, communicative 'power to' (Arendt, Habermas) must be reproduced through private and non-political social spheres of intimate communication and life-long processes of socialisation, and the different domains of civil society where private and public spheres merge.[38]

IV. Secularisation, Sovereignty and Rationality

Once social power becomes political in the sense of being exercised within a differentiated political sphere of action, the power of action (or negation) is transformed into the 'constituent' (therefore potentially revolutionary) power that, in modern democratic constitutional regimes, is permanent, as Arendt, Böckenförde, and Habermas have argued.[39] As we can see from the ambivalent use of 'solidarity' in Durkheim, solidarity has a functional as well as a normative side. In modern societies, it binds together an ever-increasing number of conflicting differences, functionally through social division of professionalised labour (that) is the source of infrastructural discursive power (Mann, Foucault)—and normatively through collective consciousness (that is the source of political 'power to', the power of the people). But both sides are integral to the modern concept of law. To be sure, the *potentia* that originates in the social power to say 'no' and that can become the political power of foundation and permanent *pouvoir constituent*, need not develop in this way, as we have seen. It also can become an instrumental, technical and administrative power of control. 'Power to' can be instrumentalised from the *top-down* as 'power over', which is the technical and administrative power of control, discipline and surveillance (Duguit, Mann, Foucault, Gorski). Yet the possibility remains that it can still emerge from the *bottom-up* as public (Arendt) or communicative 'power to' (Habermas).[40] In other words, 'power over' can always be turned into 'power to' and vice versa.

Even though Loughlin is highly critical of administrative *potentia* (at least as far as it threatens the foundations of public law), in his defence of *Staatsrecht* against the normativism of *Rechtsstaat* he demonstrates a clearly state-supportive attitude that prioritises the top-down perspective. My contention is that Loughlin's polemical position in the discursive wars over the state is determined by a specific meta-narrative that supports it.[41] That is the meta-narrative of 'state-sovereignty'. The sovereign state is the result of the emancipation, first, of the mortal God that is a living person (the King) from the domination of the personalised, immortal God, and his religious foundation in the absolute truth of belief and the spiritual, and especially legal, power of the clerics. The next and final stage of this top-down process of emancipation of secular state-power consists in the 'absorption' of

[37] *Foundations* (n 1) 169.

[38] See J Habermas, *Structural Transformation of the Public Sphere* (Cambridge, Massachusetts, MIT Press, 1989).

[39] See H Arendt, *On Revolution* (New York, Viking, 1963); EW Böckenförde, *Verfassungsgebende Gewalt des Volkes: ein Grenzbegriff der Verfassungsrechts* (Frankfurt, Metzner, 1986); J Habermas, *Faktizität und Geltung* (Frankfurt, Suhrkampo, 1992).

[40] For a similar objection, see M Wilkinson, in chapter 12 of this volume.

[41] See C Thornhill's review of Loughlin, *Public Law* (2011) 651–57.

the personalised sovereign 'into the idea of the state' that is the abstract, de-personalised 'institutionalisation' of sovereign *potestas*, or public right, a position culminating with Hegel and German statutory positivism (*Staatswillenpositivismus*, in particular in the work of Georg Jellinek).[42]

There are two problematic features internal to this specific, one-sided genealogy which can be highlighted by comparing it with the story Max Weber tells about the process of religious disenchantment. First, the sovereign state retains from its religious origins the claim to omnipotence and sovereign authority achieved through the separation of state-power. This 'enables' an unprecedented augmentation of administrative power through establishing 'constraints'.[43] This enlargement of power through legally institutionalised differentiation was already prepared by the constitutional advances of the Papal Revolution of the eleventh, twelfth and thirteenth centuries.[44] Loughlin (like Hobbes, Protestantism, the Enlightenment, Hegel and many others) casually dismisses this as the 'dark ages', a cliché that seems to be constitutive for the meta-narrative of state-sovereignty. But this dismissal has been called into question considerably by medieval historians in the last decades of the twentieth century.[45] Moreover, as we will explore below, this genealogy elides an alternative, democratic narrative that can be traced back to the Marsilius of Padua in the thirteenth century. What the secularised state 'loses' in the turn from the (wrongly) so-called theocratic age to the age of confessionalisation (note: not secularisation) and the territorial and national state formation during the times of the Protestant Revolution (sixteenth and seventeenth centuries) is the claim to universal truth ('*auctoritas non veritas facit legem*'). The political result clearly is top-down: concrete-order-formation precedes public will-formation ('*der Staat als Verfassungsvoraussetzung*'). This provokes the emergence of a new and fundamental opposition of social groups ('classes') between wielders of state 'power over' and the rest, now describing themselves as a people or nation, and who bring truth-claims back to politics (culminating in the course of the Atlantic Revolution of the late eighteenth century).

Second, and closely related to the 'emancipation' of state-sovereignty from universal truth claims, is that the sovereign state retains from the 'dark ages' of clerical rule the idea of founding positive law on the will of the sovereign. However, distinct from the legislation through papal and imperial sovereignty, the new sovereign will of the secular ruler loses its foundation in rationality (or natural law). Therefore, the confessionalised (later secularised) sovereign state (or the prince) keeps *voluntas* and drops *ratio* (in this reading, the missing philosophical link between the 'dark ages' and the modern world is William of Ockham). The theory of the sovereign will that emerges from the time of the Reformation is then developed juristically by German statutory positivism and German *Staatsrecht* from Laband to Schmitt (albeit strongly opposed by Kelsen in his *Habilitationsschrift* in 1911 and his Viennese school of legal theory). The emancipation of absolute sovereignty and

[42] *Foundations* (n 1) 102.

[43] *Foundations* (n 1) 106, 167, 171, 177f, 231. That constraining, specialising and differentiating power augments and reinforces existing power instead of restricting and taming it is an old observation that has been periodically restated by such diverse thinkers as Machiavelli, Hegel, Spencer and Durkheim.

[44] See H Brunkhorst, *Critical Theory of Legal Revolutions. Evolutionary Perspectives* (New York, Bloomsbury 2014) 90–146.

[45] See, eg J Fried (ed), *Die abendländische Freiheit vom 10 zum 14 Jahrhundert* (Siegmaringen, Thorbecke, 1991); see also Brunkhorst, ibid 90–146 where I discuss more extensively the relevant literature.

the sovereign will of the functionally differentiated modern nation state (with the abstract state as the author/subject of *voluntas*) from universal claims to truth and rationality has rightly been described as the liberation of political organisation from the authoritarian truth-regime of a despotic cast of clerics. This liberation enabled the emergence of the modern public sphere that Loughlin identifies with the state. However, this is not the only story about religious truth and rationality that can be told.

V. Constituent Power, *Ratio* and *Voluntas*

Throughout the history of monotheism,[46] absolute truth-claims were also an important means of prophetic criticism of authoritarian rule and especially of the new and unprecedented social injustice of the socially stratified societies of political class-rule. The lower and under-classes of ancient societies were not just idiots (isolated, pre-political animals), as Aristotle and most philosophers who followed him have suggested over and again. The oppressed understood their social situation and the injustice of their oppressors, and therefore they had good reasons to follow the prophets (and not the philosophers). The anti-authoritarian Jesus gives one of these reasons, preaching to the poor: 'I am the truth, not the custom', hence you have to change custom if you want to constitute a better society.[47] If we now try to develop this other genealogy, we can tell the story of the evolutionary emergence of public law as a transformation and rationalisation of religious truth-claims. If we do so, the emergence of public law can be reconstructed as a bottom-up political learning process that is mediated through legal revolutions motivated by egalitarian and emancipatory goals which established a law to cope with the paradox that modern law is freedom, or in Hegel's famous phrase, '*Dasein des freien Willens*' (existence of the free will).

This (internally contradictory) law first emerged in the 100 years that followed the Papal Revolution.[48] At its core was the highly unlikely combination of Roman Civil Law and Cannon Law. Roman Law was an important advance of managerial *potentia* that stabilised the Roman Empire.[49] As all civil law, it worked primarily as a law of coordination of the ruling classes. But in contrast, and in dialectical opposition to Roman Law, Cannon Law was not only an instrument of oppression that stabilised and augmented the administrative power of the church-state and clerics. Canon Law was also an instrument of emancipation, as far as it was understood and designed as the embodiment of the egalitarian idea of universal salvation and equality of all men before God and his last judgment.[50] The concurrent activity of academic professionalisation led to the beginning of the functional differentiation of law and the transformation of the old Roman legal order into an autonomous legal system. The latter then was of great use for clerics and civil rulers to establish and improve

[46] One can probably generalise this to all religious worldviews that emerged during the axial-age all over the Eurasian continent.

[47] G Tellenbach, *Libertas* (Stuttgart, Kohlhammer, 1936) 195.

[48] H Berman, *Law and Revolution* (Cambridge Massachusetts, Harvard, 1982).

[49] T Parsons, *Societies* (Englewood Cliffs, Prentice Hall, 1966).

[50] Berman (n 48); Brunkhorst (n 44) 91ff.

their power over their subjects, and to increase the agrarian exploitation rates through the disciplinary advances of the first European Revolution.[51] However, the same law also could be used, and was used, over and over again, for the formation of bottom-up communicative power by the people. It could, in other words, 'strike back' (Friedrich Müller). It enabled, for example, the 'common man' (*Gemeiner Man*) in 1525, advised by Zwinglian jurists,[52] to justify their revolutionary claims with a fresh universalisable interpretation of the same medieval law books that had been used by the managerially minded, state-supportive lawyers to perpetuate their oppression.[53]

To reconstruct the emergence of the constituent power at the time of the 'common man' insurgencies of 1525, and later during the Protestant and the Atlantic revolutions, as a normative and political learning process, another concept of modern constituent power and public law is required. This descends from a different genealogy back to Ockham's radical decoupling of the sovereign will of God from its metaphysical foundation in objective rationality and natural law without thereby dropping truth and *ratio*. This genealogical narrative begins only a little earlier with a discourse initiated by Duns Scotus (1266–1308). If the sovereign God is real and absolutely free in his wants, he can start with an arbitrary decision. However, once he has first freely acted, he is then bound by the principle of consistency.[54] Such an alternative genealogy of the intellectual discourse (that is embedded in political and legal discourses and social class struggles) begins with the 'normative innovation' of the discovery of *voluntas* as the kernel of practical *ratio*.[55] This alternative story leads us, via the transplantation of the idea that *ratio* is *voluntas* into the idea of the political formation of the *general will* by the Marsilius of Padua,[56] to the discourse of rational will-formation elaborated by Rousseau, Madison, Sieyes, Kant and Fichte, and finally to Hegel's contradictory idea that law is the existence of the free will. This power of beginning is internal to modern law, at least as long as it remains a strange mix of oppressive facticity and emancipatory normativity. Furthermore, in this alternative genealogy of modern public law, rational will-formation precedes concrete order-formation and the written constitution that founds the state. On this account, the origin of modern public law is not the sovereign state/prince of the sixteenth and seventeenth centuries that dissociates power from truth-claims and legislative *voluntas* from *ratio*, but the Papal Revolution with its combination of law and religion and the idea of a *voluntas* that *is ratio*; hence, *veritas, non auctoritas facit legem*. Even if *voluntas* becomes utterly contingent in the evolution of public law and all law becomes positive law, this does not imply a new form of 'a-rational' and 'post-truth' public law. The resolution of the riddle of a contingent but rational legislative power is still democracy.[57]

[51] RI Moore, *The First European Revolution* (Melden, Ma, Blackwell, 2000).

[52] P Blickle, *Die Revolution von 1525* (Munich, Oldenburg 2004) 240, 243; P Blickle, *Von der Leibeigenschaft zu den Menschenrechten. Eine Geschichte der Freiheit in Deutschland* (Munich, Beck, 2003) 87.

[53] P Blickle, *Der Bauernkrieg* (München, Beck, 2006).

[54] L Honnefelder, *Duns Scotus* (München, Beck, 2005) 118ff.

[55] *Foundations* (n 1) 227

[56] J Habermas, *Versuch über Glauben und Wissen* [unpublished manuscript] (Starnberg, 2016) [on file with the author].

[57] This is the point of J Habermas, *Between Facts and Norms* (Cambridge, Polity Press, 1996).

VI. The Radical Democratic Reading of Constituent Power

Reading Loughlin's *Foundations*, I get the impression that he alternates between a dualistic construction of a Schmittian (substantial/ existential/ historical/ higher) constitution of *nomos* behind the written constitution and a dialectical construction of positive, changeable constitutional law that is internally related to popular will-formation within one and the same legal order. Like Hermann Heller, Loughlin uses Hobbes, Hegel and the whole branch of conservative state-theory (Schmitt, Oakeshott, etc) for his (probably empty) polemic against empty normativism. However, his allegiance to Schmitt is limited and these limits are interesting, as we have already seen above in section II. Loughlin parts from Schmitt, once Schmitt falls back to the dualism of political theology and explains the foundational relation between constitution (*nomos*) and constitutional law by drawing an ontological distinction between the constituting 'presence' of the substantial equality of the people and their 'representation' through different voices and interests articulated in constituted bodies such as parliaments and courts. Loughlin rejects Schmitt's 'mysterious prior substantial equality' of the 'people' in 'presence' that implies a fundamentalist 'opposition between representation and presence'.[58] Schmitt's 'concept of constitution in its substantive sense that is dealing with the *total situation* of the political unit', Loughlin writes, is of little value because it 'includes all natural and cultural conditions of the state unity without any worthwhile differentiation'.[59] However, if Schmitt's dualistic solution does not work, how can we 'move beyond this opposition between representation and presence?'[60] We first have to accept that there exists only a continuum of differences but no ontological distinction between 'legality and legitimacy'.[61] Therefore, we have to cope with the inbuilt 'tensions' 'between fact and norm',[62] between 'reason' and 'history', 'the rational and the empirical, the normative and the factual',[63] 'instrumental and communicative rationality',[64] 'an idea and the instantiation of that idea'.[65]

If *Foundations* is not based on a dualistic and transcendental relation between constituent and constituted power, then the relation must be—as Loughlin argues with Lindahl—'reflexive' and 'not causal',[66] and—as he argues with Heller—'dialectical',[67] hence circular or spiral and not linear. Therefore, Loughlin argues, although Schmitt was right in that constituent power, emerging in constitutional revolutions such as the French Revolution, 'interrupts representational practices',[68] he was wrong in that this 'rupture' through

[58] *Foundations* (n 1) 226. For the same reason he rightly rejects Rancière's dualism of the *political* and the *police*.
[59] *Foundations* (n 1) 236, quoting Hermann Heller.
[60] *Foundations* (n 1) 226.
[61] *Foundations* (n 1) 40.
[62] *Foundations* (n 1) 220, and see 171, 190, 204, 211, 235.
[63] *Foundations* (n 1) 85.
[64] *Foundations* (n 1) 170.
[65] *Foundations* (n 1) 208.
[66] *Foundations* (n 1) 228.
[67] *Foundations* (n 1) 226ff, 234ff.
[68] *Foundations* (n 1) 227 (quoted from Lindahl).

'normative innovation', 'is never a pure decision that 'emanates from nothingness'.[69] Because it does not emanate from nothing but emerges from something, the use of 'constituent power not only involves the exercise of power by a people; it simultaneously constitutes a people.' Consequently, 'constituent power cannot be understood without reference to constituted power'.[70] Emmanuel Josef Sieyès, for example, needed the constituted power of the assembly of Estates to constitute a completely new National Assembly, and to get rid of the old constitution of the French Monarchy. The 'existential and normative aspects of constituent power remain mutually dependent'.[71] Moreover, because the people are not static, status-like and statist but dynamic and in development, driven not only by relatively stable 'customs', but also by (sometimes rapidly) changing 'beliefs, and opinions', 'ie practices'—the 'political unity' they constitute 'comes not from a single constituent act but depends on continuous renewal of terms'.[72] The people's common will-formation matters exactly because constituent power is not just 'an idea founded *on* the people' but must be 'actively formed *by* the people'.[73] Thus, the 'content and validity of a norm are never determined merely by its text, and never solely by the standpoints and characteristics of its legislators, but above all by the characteristics of the norm addressees who observe them'.[74] This means that the constitution must enable the people to act as 'authors' of those legal norms that address them. The rule of law is not worth the paper it is (not) written on, unless it is author-ised *by* the people. Put in Habermasian terms, there is no *Rechtsstaat* without democracy and the norms that constrain state power presuppose the discursive articulation of the general will of the people through which the public or communicative power of citizens is ultimately exercised.

Once this point is accepted, the contradiction between Madison's republican idea of representation and the democratic idea of representation that emerged in conjunction with socialism in the twentieth century becomes evident. Whereas Madison, in Loughlin's quote, argues that constitutional checks and balances are designed to discipline the people ('enable the government to control the governed'),[75] and then to realise a strong executive power, Hermann Heller replaces this with an egalitarian and radical democratic interpretation of constitutional checks and balances:

> The whole system of the constitutional law of checks and balances, of reciprocal commitments and determinations as election, countersignature, parliamentary legislation, referenda, initiative, and of all the other provisions that determine the competences of presidents, governments, legislative bodies and so on—this whole constitutional apparatus has the one and only legal meaning to enable and guarantee that the power of the government factually originates in, stems from, and is performed by the people.[76]

[69] *Foundations* (n 1) 227 (quoted from Lindahl quoting Schmitt).

[70] *Foundations* (n 1) 227.

[71] *Foundations* (n 1) 236.

[72] *Foundations* (n 1) 233. Habermas (like Arendt) locates it in the 'anarchic' and 'untamable' character of public opinion and public will-formation that comes not from a single constituent act but from continuous renewal of terms. Public will-formation is, thus, the performance of communicative power that Habermas defines as a permanent revolution that is legal.

[73] *Foundations* (n 1) 224.

[74] *Foundations* (n 1) 233 (quoted from Herman Heller).

[75] *Foundations* (n 1) 284.

[76] H Heller, 'Souveränität' in *Gesammelte Schriften* 2 (translated by Poul Kjaer) (Leiden, Sijthoff, 1971) 39–40.

Here again, we are back to the dialectical idea that popular sovereignty precedes state sovereignty, and rational will-formation precedes concrete order-formation. Constituent power can reunite *ratio* and *voluntas* if recast as a democratic constitutional learning process based on the human potential for action and emancipation. At the very least, that path must neither be ignored in its concrete historical achievements nor foreclosed for the future.

7

Private Law, *Potentia* and the Ethical: On What Justification Does the State Coercively Tax its Subjects in Order to Build Bridges, Fund the BBC, and Subsidise Charities?

JAMES PENNER

I. Introduction

In this chapter I address the relation between private and public law, and how this might cast light on Loughlin's treatment of the latter in *Foundations of Public Law*.[1] In doing so I shall first examine the relation Kant finds between the enforcement of private right and the justification of the state, and then examine how Kant's vision of the state seems not to account for the form of state power known as '*potentia*', a form of state power that Loughlin discusses in detail. I will also offer a Razian justification of the state along the same lines, noting that his concern with autonomy may, suitably elaborated, provide a grounding for *potentia* that Kant lacks (though I shall find that, ultimately, this attempt fails). I shall then go on to frame the nature of *potentia* in terms of what I shall call the 'ethical' in politics and suggest that framing *potentia* in this way may resolve, or at least diminish, the antagonism Loughlin finds between *potentia* and the other power of the state, '*potestas*', the power to rule. But, towards the end, I shall also suggest a different way in which *potestas* and *potentia* may be antagonistically related.

Loughlin does not discuss in any sustained way Kant's *Metaphysics of Morals*,[2] the first part of which, the *Doctrine of Right*, more or less sets out Kant's theory of law and the state. I am not pointing this out as a criticism—Loughlin's book is long enough already and explores many other theorists with insight and verve. Nor do I want to mount a Kantian argument against anything Loughlin says. What I shall contend however is that there is an obvious absence in Kant's theory of the law and the state in failing to provide an account of

[1] M Loughlin, *Foundations of Public Law* (Oxford, Oxford University Press, 2010) [hereafter *Foundations*].

[2] I Kant, *The Metaphysics of Morals* (Cambridge, Cambridge University Press 1996) [hereafter *Metaphysics of Morals*].

potentia, which seems to be shared among many liberal theorists (in particular Rawls and Raz). More specifically, that failure lies in the absence of a clear justification for the state's having the power of *potentia*, given that Kant, Rawls and Raz all offer justificatory accounts of the state. Now let me say, again, that failing to address this question is not intended as a criticism of Loughlin. His project was not to justify the powers the state has, but to clarify our understanding of what those powers are, and wherein lie their conceptual foundations. My claim is that having laid the conceptual groundwork, Loughlin has provided us with better tools than we have had heretofore to consider what justifications there might be for the state's having the power of *potentia*. So this chapter can be regarded as a friendly enlargement of his project.

II. Loughlin on *Societas*, *Universitas*, *Potestas* and *Potentia*

In Chapter 6, entitled 'Political Jurisprudence', Loughlin treats us to a sustained meditation on two different conceptions of the way in which a polity can be considered as a mode of association between equal subjects. One mode, *societas*,

> is a mode of association that juristically 'was understood to be the product of a pact or agreement, not to act in concert but to acknowledge the authority of certain conditions of acting.' The tie is not that of engagement in a common enterprise or the pursuit of a common substantive purpose; it is 'a formal relationship in terms of rules, not a substantive relationship in terms of common action'. The members of the association each remain free to pursue their own interests or even to form other groups to promote common objectives and they relate to one another as *socii* simply 'in the common acknowledgement of the authority of rules of conduct indifferent to the pursuit of the achievement of any purpose.' Oakeshott argues that a *societas* expresses a moral relationship in which the conditions of association are specified by a system of law. There will therefore be judicial office-holders who settle disputes and there may be a ruler. But the office of the ruler, Oakeshott emphasises, is consonant with the nature of the association: '[T]he ruler of a state when it is understood as a *societas* is the custodian of the loyalties of the association and the guardian and administrator *of the conditions which constitute the relationship of socii*.[3]

As we shall see, this mode of association strongly resonates with Kant's characterisation of the state.[4]

The other mode, *universitas*, is a corporate mode of association established by its members to pursue some common, substantive, purpose.[5] Despite the prominence of the *societas* conception of the polity in political theory from the late sixteenth century onwards,[6] it was not a genuine reflection of state practice: *universitas*, the 'enterprise association', was found

[3] *Foundations* (n 1) 160 (emphasis added).

[4] A point adverted to by Loughlin via Oakeshott. See *Foundations* (n 1) 162, fn 12.

[5] *Foundations* (n 1) 161.

[6] To take a recent example, Rawls specifically denies that a democratic society is an association or community. J Rawls, *Political Liberalism* (expanded edition) (New York, Columbia University Press, 2005) 40–43.

everywhere in the state's managerial and 'tutorial' undertakings.[7] It is Loughlin's view that these modes are 'irreconcilably antagonistically aligned.'[8]

Each of these two modes of association can be elaborated to reveal distinctive modes of power by which they operate.[9] *Societas* operates by way of *potestas*, ie, 'the rightful power of rule'.[10] As the right to rule, it essentially involves the exercise of the coercive power to create standards binding the subjects of the realm. As Loughlin is careful to point out, this need not be understood in terms of domination; the exercise of *potestas* may be the rightful exercise of authority.[11]

Universitas, on the other hand, operates by way of *potentia*, ie, the governmental resources that a state requires to realise its substantive purposes. *Potentia* is more complicated than *potestas*. Drawing upon Spinoza, Oakeshott, Mann, Foucault, and the theory of civic republicanism, Loughlin weaves together a picture of *potentia* without giving a definition or explicit theory of it. But as I read him, Loughlin proposes four characteristics which in part define this particular sort of state power. First, *potentia* seems to arise in the modern world as a response to the state taking responsibility for the well-being of its population: it does not merely promulgate the relations of right as does *potestas*. Second, *potentia* realises the substantive purposes of the state by fulfilling various 'economic' functions, such as raising public resources through taxation,[12] issuing permits and licences and identity papers, controlling borders, and controlling the issue of money.[13] It thus arises at the same time as does the idea of 'political economy'.[14] Third, *potentia* is 'infrastructural' in the sense that it organises individuals using all the bureaucratic, statistic-gathering, power at its disposal to shape new social norms. Cast in a Foucauldian way, this can be thought of as a process of 'disciplining' the state's subjects to comply with these social norms.[15] Finally, and very importantly, it has a 'tutorial'[16] or 'moulding' function—that is, it shapes the 'character of the people'.[17]

The two modes of association, and their respective forms of power, are not only irreconcilably antagonistic towards each other:

> [t]he disjuncture they express can be neither eliminated nor reconciled, but only negotiated. This negotiation does not itself amount to the explication of right as such: it involves the exercise of prudential judgment. Rather than treating public law as the unfolding of some science of political right, then, public law should be understood to involve an exercise in political jurisprudence, whose task is to negotiate between the various conflicting accounts of political right that form part of its evolving discourse.[18]

Below I will explore whether this is necessarily the case.

[7] *Foundations* (n 1) 162.
[8] *Foundations* (n 1) 163.
[9] *Foundations* (n 1) 164–65.
[10] *Foundations* (n 1) 164.
[11] *Foundations* (n 1) 169.
[12] *Foundations* (n 1) 165.
[13] *Foundations* (n 1) 165.
[14] *Foundations* (n 1) 162, 167–68.
[15] *Foundations* (n 1) 165–68.
[16] *Foundations* (n 1) 162.
[17] *Foundations* (n 1) 176.
[18] *Foundations* (n 1) 164.

III. Kant on Private Right and the Foundations of the State

Kant begins with the thought that where people cannot avoid coming into contact, and therefore possible conflict, they must leave the state of nature where their rights vis-à-vis each other are only imperfect and provisional, and enter into a civil condition, which perhaps most importantly involves both creating an authority that, through legislation (including judicial law-making in systems where that occurs), crystallises laws, and creating an authority to adjudicate disputes. This is all in the way of ensuring the freedom of individuals conceived of as the independence from the choices of others with respect to a person's 'means'—that is, that person's body and appropriated property.[19]

On this account private law concerns both those forms of law that promulgate primary rules that make explicit each person's right to independence from the unilateral choices of others with respect to each person's means (such as tort, contract, property, unjust enrichment); and secondary, adjudicative rules that provide for the resolution of disputes between citizens. Criminal law concerns the application of the state's right to punish wrongdoing (the idea here being that the criminal law basically requires individuals to take their entry into the civil condition seriously—to enforce their commitment to it, as it were). Constitutional law is framed in terms of a hypothetical social contract: it imposes a kind of test on legislation so that the legislature cannot create a law which would violate the natural equality of individuals conceived of as embodied centres of freedom[20]—such as a law that would create an aristocratic class.[21]

As regards public law, this seems, as far as I can tell, for Kant to amount merely to variable rules which create the offices of the state and state prerogative law—such as the power to appoint individuals to offices and to declare war—all of which are directed to preserving the civil condition within the state's jurisdiction.[22] There is one very controversial addition to these, what Kant calls the 'state duty to support the poor'.[23] But his inclusion of this state power is so poorly justified within his general structure that to say this passage of the 'Doctrine of Right' is under-argued is to put it mildly. In any case, it is far from clear that a state duty to support the poor can be sustained as a justified application of state power on Kant's own premises.[24] But admissible or not, it is not a power which reflects what Loughlin refers to as *potentia*, the power of the modern state to marshal resources to address the 'needs' of its citizens through administrative action. Kantian arguments for the duty to support the poor seem either to be that the duty is structurally required under a just system of

[19] For a comprehensive modern elaboration of these ideas, see A Ripstein, *Force and Freedom: Kant's Legal and Political Philosophy* (Cambridge MA, Harvard University Press, 2009).

[20] *Metaphysics of Morals* (n 2) 92–93, [6: 315], 95, [6: 318–19]; see also I Kant, *On the Old Saw that Might be Right in Theory but it Won't Work in Practice* (Philadephia, University of Pennsylvania Press, 1974) [hereafter *On the Old Saw*] 65; Ripstein, ibid, 198–204. Kant's treatment of women, children, and dependent servants is a pretty significant blot on his conception of equality. See *Metaphysics of Morals* (n 2) 91–92, [6: 314–15], *On the Old Saw*, ibid, 62–64.

[21] See *On the Old Saw* (n 20) 65.

[22] *Metaphysics of Morals* (n 2) 89–113, [6:311]–[6:342].

[23] *Metaphysics of Morals* (n 2) 100–01, [6:325]–[6:326].

[24] For an extended discussion, see J Penner, 'The State Duty to Support the Poor in Kant's *Doctrine of Right*' (2010) 12 *British Journal of Politics and International Relations* 88.

property rights, or as a state-preserving power on the almost certainly untrue assumption that where a significant fraction of the society is in serious poverty the civil society itself is endangered.[25]

Everything here would appear to fit into the realm of *potestas*, the right to rule, which reflects the corresponding obligation of citizens to install an authority to protect their rights and then obey it. On the Kantian account, the ontology of rights is such that true right can only be achieved in a civil society with such a political authority. Although we can glimpse private right in the pre-civil condition, in the absence of a regime of enforcement to which all are committed, right as such does not exist.[26] If this is correct, then on Kant's account, all legislation that follows the initial institution of the state and the basic private law is essentially 'law reform'—that is, (1) refining or adjusting of the rules of private law, contract, tort, property and so on, for example to adapt to changing circumstances, in particular advances in technology; (2) doing the same for criminal law; and (3) constitutional reform, ie refining or adjusting the rules governing the executive, legislative, and adjudicative branches of government and the prerogative power.

IV. Raz on the Rights of Citizens and the Justification of the State

On the Razian account, there is no particular difficulty with the idea of pre-political right. Indeed, in virtue of Raz's 'dependence thesis',[27] Raz's account of state authority requires that the state only act for reasons which already apply to its subjects. To the extent these reasons are grounds for duties that (via the 'normal justification thesis')[28] the subjects of the law are more likely to comply with by following an authoritative directive, all else being equal the state has the authority—and the duty—to issue such a directive. Moreover, on what I would argue is the best version of the Razian 'service conception' of authority,[29] every individual comes under a positive obligation to institute and attorn to authorities in cases where only the coordination of action by an authority will discharge our moral obligations to ourselves and others in our community. So, for example, if people have a collective duty to deal with serious crime, and if the only way of doing so is to institute a public authority with a power of censure, then they have an obligation to do so. Similar reasons would arise, for example, in the case of whether or not there is an obligation to institute an authority to provide civil redress for wrongs.

I want now to emphasise one important similarity in Raz's and Kant's accounts that reflects a shared attitude to the relationship between private and public law, which significantly moves them away from the social contract tradition. For both Kant and Raz, one may

[25] See ibid, 268–86; E Weinrib, 'Poverty and Property in Kant's System of Rights' (2002–03) 78 *Notre Dame Law Review* 795.

[26] *Metaphysics of Morals* (n 2) 44–46, [6:255]–[6:257]; See also Ripstein (n 19) Ch 6.

[27] J Raz, *The Morality of Freedom* (Oxford, Clarendon Press, 1986) Ch 3.

[28] ibid Ch 4.

[29] ibid 56, 59, 67.

have an *obligation* to enter into agreement with others. Such obligations can be seen both in morality and law. For example, if I have a child, I will in most cases come under an obligation to enter into binding agreements with others, most obviously with the other parent of the child, to arrange for the care of the child. One of us has to feed the child, to look after her on this day rather than that, to collect her from school, whatever. I take this to be an untroubling example of an obligation to enter into an agreement. Likewise with the state: if I live in a community, then I have an obligation to enter into arrangements with others to deal, for example, with serious crime. Depending upon your views about punishment, this obligation might be discharged in various ways, but it seems natural to suppose that a community cannot just stand by when some of its members are victimised. Something must be done, though what that something is will be determined through a process of negotiation and agreement.

But now let me also point out a difference in their accounts. I have not yet addressed how, on Raz's theory as I have outlined it, there is room for the power of *potentia*, the power of the state to marshal resources so as to meet the needs of the states' citizens, and perhaps improve their life prospects in other ways, say by providing free universal education, or creating communication and transportation networks. I have already suggested that any real sense of *potentia* is absent in Kant's doctrine of right. Raz,[30] however, in reshaping Mill's harm principle, purports to overcome the libertarian objection to the state's use of resources raised by taxes to provide public goods, such as free education, and so on. Raz's claim is that we do not only have duties not to interfere with others causing them harm (which is itself framed as a blow to their autonomy, the ability to make significant life choices going forward), but we also have duties to enhance the ability of others to live autonomously. To re-frame the argument in a way in keeping with my presentation of Raz's position, we all have as individuals a 'pre-political' duty to secure the autonomy of our fellows, for otherwise they will lead lives of lower well-being than they are entitled to; to the extent this duty can only be effectively discharged, or is most likely to be effectively discharged, through the co-ordination of our resources through the mechanism of an authority, then the state is properly convened and empowered to discharge this obligation on our behalf. The form of the argument is no different from the one in which we have a pre-political obligation to institute an authority to deal with serious crime in our community.

Whether you find Raz's argument compelling is neither here nor there. I must say I am not particularly attracted to it, for reasons I shall raise below. Here, I only want to suggest one way in which the power of *potentia* might be harnessed on behalf of the state, that is, to use its resources to provide for the conditions of autonomy, in particular the provision of a range of meaningful life options for its subjects. But I want to suggest a different way of explaining, perhaps justifying, the realisation of the state's power of *potentia*.

V. *Potestas* and *Potentia*, and the Moral and the Ethical

I now want to raise a distinction between the 'moral' and the 'ethical' and see how it maps onto the two forms of state power under discussion, *potestas* and *potentia*. The distinction

[30] ibid Ch 15.

is largely intuitive, and cannot be perfectly sharp. It is sometimes framed as a distinction between the 'right' and the 'good' in morality generally, or in political morality specifically. Rawls famously argued that states should stand neutral as between different conceptions of the good, or 'the good life'.[31] More specifically, in virtue of his discussion of what individuals would choose behind a 'veil of ignorance'—that is, not knowing their own personal attributes—he argued that in providing for the rights of individuals in a just society, no recourse should be made to *particular* conceptions of the good life. What results is a distribution of *rights*, not *goods*.[32] In later work he either refined or elaborated his position to say that in a liberal democracy, the realm of political discourse—ie, 'public reason'—could not admit of reasons which drew upon comprehensive doctrines of the good.[33]

But regardless of whether or not the distinction is ultimately sound, and whether or not Rawl's own use of it stands up to scrutiny,[34] I want to proceed on the basis that there is something in it. I do however want to re-cast it in terms of the non-negotiable (the peremptory) and the negotiable. In terms of political theory, what distinguishes the two is that in the absence of the institutionalisation of norms that can be characterised as norms of the 'moral' or the 'right', individuals remain in a state of nature. This is the sense in which the moral is simply non-negotiable. I am not concerned about what particular norms fall within this class, about which there is obviously disagreement. It is that whatever view anyone takes, everyone takes the norms generated by their moral view as being 'non-negotiable'—as being *peremptorily* demanded by morality.

Most obviously, the basic norms of criminal law under which murder, assault, fraud and theft and so on are recognised as offences are the obvious sorts of candidates for this sort of non-negotiable norm, as would be the basic norms of private law, such as tort, property, contract, and so on, which more or less reflect the same underlying ideas. By contrast, the ethical is precisely that part of moral and political discourse which judges of norms that *are* negotiable, in the sense of not being peremptory. For liberals such as Rawls and Raz, there are many valuable ways of living a good—or ethical—life, and there is no single, true vantage point from which one life is to be chosen over any of the others. Nor is there a principle by which these various lives can be ranked. This need not, of course, be framed in terms of lives or life-plans. Ethics, in this sense, applies to evaluative judgements concerning all activities, for all activities realise values or disvalues in various ways. Nor is it claimed that there are no possible objective standards in these evaluations. The point is simply that the realm of the ethical *presupposes* adherence to a non-negotiable morality, the peremptory or non-negotiable sort of norms I have mentioned. In the absence of very particular circumstances, there could not be an ethical action or life-plan which was composed in part of immoral actions. I suppose Robin Hood would justify his stealing from the rich to give to

[31] J Rawls, *A Theory of Justice* (revised edn) (Cambridge MA, Belknap Press, 1999) [hereafter *Theory of Justice*] ss 50, 68.

[32] It is important to recognise that the 'difference principle' (ibid, s 13), under which differences in the allocation of resources between individuals can be justified only on the basis that the distribution provides more resources to the worst-off group in society than the available alternatives, does not concern a distribution of goods, but of rights. The rights in question are rights to economic resources, but not to any particular good or goods which the right-holder may use those resources to obtain.

[33] Rawls (n 6) xvi–xxi.

[34] For a critical discussion see Raz (n 27) 124–33.

the poor by making reference to his particular circumstances, as would those who plotted to murder Hitler. But I take it that the general point is uncontroversial.

If this is right, then it also seems right to say that the moral is the especial province of *potestas*. In the absence of a right to rule, by which I mean laying down the basic legal norms of interpersonal interaction, a state would be unable to be a state; that is, in the absence of *potestas*, there would not be a state, for the people would not be under a regime of law at all. From this perspective, as I have suggested, private law and criminal law go together as the basic non-negotiable foundations of any state, foundations which distinguish there being a state at all from the conditions of being in a state of nature.

Furthermore, if correct, this argument shows that in an important respect *postestas* and morality, the latter conceived of as the non-negotiable part of our evaluative judgements, are *prior* to the power of *potentia* and the ethical. However powerful *potentia* is in the modern state, it can only operate given that the state—and not a state of nature—actually obtains. This shows that the relationship between *societas* and *potestas*, and *universitas* and *potentia*, cannot be antagonistic all the way down as Loughlin has claimed, because the existence of the latter *depends* upon the existence of the former.

So I think their relationship must be framed more subtly. The antagonism seems to be this: for some theorists, in particular liberals such as Rawls[35] or Nozick,[36] the state should be seen as a *societas* full stop. For them, despite the facts on the ground, the state is illegitimate to the extent it reflects an association of the people conceived of as a *universitas*, for in pursuing the well-being of its people the state will necessarily have to make choices that are ethical and not simply moral; it will have to conceive of its people's well-being in one way rather than another. To put this in the terms I have been peddling, for liberals of this ilk the ethical is not a proper province for state authority or action. Their deepest disagreement lies with those who reject this austere notion of the realm of legitimate state action.

Before I proceed, in light of these considerations, to explore the nature of *potentia* further, the relationship between *potestas* and the moral/ethical distinction needs to be refined somewhat.

In the first place, the state, in exercising *potestas*, its right to rule, cannot do so by simply reading the 'non-negotiable' off some natural law book of morality, such that the ethical is not brought into play. The ethical permeates the private and criminal law in its every legal detail. By this I mean that it is straightforwardly not true that any modern private law is simply the realisation of a private ordering determined by basic moral principles, principles that can be spelt out more or less uncontroversially, whether on a state of nature model of pre-political right or on the basis of any other heuristic. The law of trusts, the law governing insolvency, security interests, wills, estates, and the law of probate, to say nothing of company law, and much more that would fall within private law conceived of as the law of private ordering, cannot be treated as directly reflective of natural rights. In particular, they are not the sorts of rights one could glean from a state-of-nature story. The long natural-law debates over what made a contract usurious and the particularities of the doctrine of the just price clearly make this point. In the view advanced here, these are controversies of ethics. They reflect all sorts of controversial evaluations about what sort of property laws

[35] Rawls (n 6) 40–43.

[36] R Nozick, *Anarchy, State, and Utopia* (reprint edn) (New York, Basic Books, 2013) 113–18.

we should have, how we understand the ethical behaviour of contracting parties, and so on. A more or less identical story could be told about the criminal law, in particular the criminal law power of punishment. To take but one example: I do not know whether capital punishment is immoral in all circumstances, in the sense that it is never justified for any crime however heinous, and I am not sure what the form of that argument would be. But I do understand what people mean when they say capital punishment is barbaric. Whether I agree with them or not, it seems to me that such a claim advances an evaluable *ethical* position, roughly along the lines that we as a society are degraded if we adopt this *form* of punishment, in the same way (though not to the same extent of course) we should be degraded if we used torture as a form of punishment.

The upshot of these considerations is that we cannot simply map the *potestas/potentia* distinction directly onto the moral/ethical distinction as I have described it. *Potestas* will invariably reflect both the moral and the ethical. However, it does seem right to say that *potentia*, on the other hand, reflects the ethical alone, and moreover, *potentia* seems to be the 'natural' province of the ethical.

If the preceding is right, it shows another way in which the relationship between *societas* and *potestas*, on the one hand, and *universitas* and *potentia*, on the other, need not be seen as antagonistic: the two powers can be seen along the lines of a division of labour. The power of *potestas* is there to set the non-negotiable terms of interaction of the subjects of the state, to give effect to what I have called the moral, though as stated this will involve ethical reasoning in determining the actual norms; whereas the power of *potentia*, which is devoted to the use of state resources to promote the well-being of its subjects, will be entirely about making ethical judgements about the nature of the good and what it is to have well-being.

VI. Justifying *Potentia* and the Ethical in Politics

As Loughlin pointed out, modern state practice reveals that the conception of the polity as *universitas*, and the corresponding exercise of *potentia* as a legitimate power of the state, appears in virtually every country where the European model of statehood has been adopted since the sixteenth century.

From the perspective of liberals such as Rawls and Nozick, this should come as rather disturbing news. If it is more or less universally accepted that the state may exercise *potentia*, then such liberals must be somewhat puzzled, since their 'from first principles' theory seems to render such acceptance deeply suspect. But leaving that to one side, this liberal perspective does raise a meaningful question: if the state can be conceived as *universitas*, with a power of *potentia*, on what basis is this kind of state power justified? More pointedly, the power of *potentia* seems to reflect a legitimacy on the part of the state to impose, coercively if necessary, controversial ethical positions on its subjects, or at least coercively tax them to pursue controversial ethical projects. This power seems prima facie illegitimate, for it forces people to participate in or support particular versions of conduct which they can reasonably, as individuals, reject. And note, this ethical state action cannot be justified in the way that the ethical rears its head in the exercise of *potestas*. In the course of determining, for example, the form of punishments for criminal offences or of remedies for breach of contract, one has no choice but to engage the ethical if one is going to institute the moral, the non-negotiable. For the reasons given above, the moral and the ethical necessarily cleave together in the creation of any actual system of criminal justice or private law.

One possible answer to the question of what justifies the state's power of *potentia* is a capacious notion of 'market failure'. Say it would be good for society to have modern medicine, and the only way to generate that good is through expensive scientific research. But given the non-rivalrousness of the good in question, a way of making penicillin for example, private ordering is unlikely to provide sufficient amounts of the good in question because of problems of free-riding and so on, which impinge upon the incentive structure of the would-be scientific researchers. So this could be addressed by the state publicly funding such research, or granting a state-enforced monopoly to researchers, or both. Both ways of addressing the problem clearly constitute an exercise of *potentia*.

But this argument does not work, because it hides a premise. The premise is that the good in question *is a good*. But determining that is precisely the sort of ethical evaluation which is the very thing to which the state is said not to have a right in the first place. The fact that the good in question, here modern medicine, is almost universally seen to be a good is not the question, or rather, does not meet the liberal's objection.

Perhaps Raz's liberal theory of autonomy can come to the rescue. Raz argues that individuals have not only 'negative duties' not to undermine the autonomy of others, but positive duties to advance the autonomy of others:

> There is more one can do to help another person have an autonomous life than stand off and refrain from coercing or manipulating him. There are two further categories of autonomy-based duties towards another person. One is to help in creating the inner capacities required for the conduct of an autonomous life. [...] The third type of autonomy-based duty towards another concerns the creation of an adequate range of options for him to choose from.[37]

Applying the normal justification thesis, if individuals are better able to meet these duties—and in particular the last two positive ones—with the support of state action—in particular, the state's exercise of its power of *potentia*—rather than trying individually to discharge these duties, then they should do so, and the state will incur a corresponding duty to exercise its power of *potentia* in appropriate ways:

> [A] government whose responsibility is to promote the autonomy of its citizens is entitled to redistribute resources, to provide public goods and to engage in the provision of other services on a compulsory basis, provided its laws merely reflect and make concrete autonomy-based duties of its citizens.[38]

Moreover, in complying with this duty, the state—just as in the case where the state must make ethical choices in promulgating the civil and criminal law—will, of necessity, have to make some ethical choices in the way it goes about instilling the inner capacities of its citizens to allow them to lead autonomous lives, say choices in providing for public education, or choices in creating an adequate range of options for its citizens to choose from:

> Autonomy-based duties, in conformity with the harm principle, require the use of public power to promote the conditions of autonomy, to secure an adequate range of options for the population. But [...] considerations of personal autonomy cannot dictate which options should be promoted.

[37] Raz (n 27) 407–08.
[38] Raz (n 27) 417.

> There are many possible options the provision of which can make the available options adequate. It is in deciding which options to encourage more than others that perfectionist considerations dominate. Here they are limited by the availability of resources mobilized in the above mentioned way. The harm principle is consistent with many perfectionist policies of the kind required by any moral theory which values autonomy highly.[39]

Another quotation enriches the picture:

> The conditions of autonomy [...] include the existence of a public culture which maintains and encourages the cultivation of certain tastes and the undertaking of certain pursuits. A public culture which inculcates respect for the environment, and for its transformation at the hands of past generations, and which cultivates agreeable design and good taste in landscaping and urban planning, while not positively required as a condition of autonomy, is consistent with it. Autonomy requires a public culture and is consistent with a tasteful rather than a vulgar and offensive environment. [...] [T]he Harm Principle is no obstacle to the pursuit of such a policy.[40]

So, if Raz is right about all of this, it would justify the state's exercise of *potentia*, necessarily making ethical evaluations in this exercise, because this would allow the citizens of that state to best meet their obligations to promote the autonomy of their fellows. Raz's claim, however, is subject to three objections.

In the first place, it is not clear whether Raz has justified the claim that individuals owe positive duties to enhance the autonomy of others, at least all others generally. This must be justified to justify the state's power of *potentia* because, remembering the dependence thesis, that state can only itself discharge duties which its citizens already have, but are less likely to discharge effectively by acting on their own. As far as I can tell, Raz's justification of these positive duties is found in this passage:

> Every reason of autonomy which leads to the duties of non-interference would lead to other duties as well, unless, of course, it is counteracted by conflicting reasons. Such countervailing reasons are likely to be sometimes present, but they are most unlikely to confine the duties of autonomy to non-interference only.[41]

The problem here is that Raz is, I think, missing a step in the argument. I take it that it is common ground between Raz and me that the reason for these duties is the interest people have in leading autonomous lives. In Raz's terminology, if the interest is sufficiently weighty, then that grounds a right in those people to the correlative duties in others to promote that interest.[42] But as I have argued elsewhere,[43] in order to justify such duties one must also explain why the correlative duty-ower is in the right sort of relationship to the right-bearer to justify the imposition of the duty. It is, I think, fairly straightforward to do so in the case of parents and their children. It seems perfectly plausible to say that a parent not only has a duty not to interfere with the ability of his child to develop a capacity for autonomy, but positively to instil such a capacity. But it is not clear to me what would justify my having such a positive duty to every other individual. Of course, I have *reason* to promote the autonomy of others, because by doing so I realise a value, the value of their

39 Raz (n 27) 418.
40 Raz (n 27) 421–22.
41 Raz (n 27) 408.
42 Raz (n 27) 170–72.
43 J Penner, 'The Analysis of Rights' (1997) 10 *Ratio Juris* 300.

leading autonomous lives. But that alone does not mean that I have a peremptory duty to attend to that reason.

In the second place, as we have seen, Raz says:

> A public culture which inculcates respect for the environment, and for its transformation at the hands of past generations, and which cultivates agreeable design and good taste in landscaping and urban planning, *while not positively required as a condition of autonomy, is consistent with it.*[44]

This suggests that Raz is not particularly concerned to meet the liberal objection to the exercise of *potentia*, even on the premises of his own theory. The story is supposed to be that the state is discharging *obligations* that it has inherited from its citizens by application of the normal justification theses. There is no justificatory basis in Raz's own theory for the state acting in a way that is merely consistent with the discharge of those obligations, but which it has no actual obligation to discharge.

Finally, however, there is the problem that describing the state's exercise of *potentia* in many plausible cases as the promotion of its subjects' autonomy seems fanciful. Building bridges and other infrastructure, such as sewage systems, roads, and much else would appear to make the lives of its subjects better in many ways without being justified or justifiable in terms of autonomy. It is not obvious to me that building bridges and sewage systems answers very directly to the goal of providing options to people so as to ensure their autonomy, as opposed to, say, the way that supporting public education appears to do. But states have historically done much more of the former than the latter. In fact, even public education appears to have been primarily brought into being, beginning in the nineteenth century in many countries, not as a way to promote individual autonomy, but simply to train the young so as to meet the interests of an industrial economy. What really enhanced the autonomy of the subjects in what are now regarded as 'developed' countries, from the nineteenth century going forward, with the programme being far from complete even today, was the dismantling of rigid class structures and making various forms of discrimination illegal. This thought is particularly relevant for two reasons.

The first is that this way of securing the availability of meaningful options for a state's subjects appears to mesh better with the kinds of options that Raz emphasises: options to choose one career over another and options for meaningful leisure activity.[45] The second is that this was all accomplished by the exercise of *potestas*.[46] This reveals a relation between autonomy and *potestas*: the first order of an autonomy-promoting state is to cleanse itself of illegitimate laws which require or permit the autonomy of some of its subjects to be restricted or diminished.

This seems to pose a difficulty for Raz's view. Raz frames our duties to others in terms of enhancing their autonomy. But there can be two distinct ways of doing this. The first is to use the power of *potestas* to more or less get out of its citizens' way, leaving the options to sort themselves out by way of private ordering. If, once various illegitimate barriers to participation are eliminated, and private ordering provides for a sufficient range of options in terms of both occupations and leisure activities, then there is no justification for the state to enter the field by coercively taxing its citizens using the resulting resources via *potentia*

[44] Raz (n 27) 421–22 (emphasis added).

[45] See J Raz, *Ethics in the Public Domain* (Oxford, Clarendon Press, 1994) 106–07.

[46] Indeed, for Rawls, the principle of 'equal opportunity' arises as a matter of basic right. See *Theory of Justice* (n 31) s 14.

to add more options. And it is far from obvious that private ordering has proved deficient in this regard.

There may, however, be other bases upon which the power of *potentia* might be engaged besides just adding more options. One might also justify the exercise of *potentia* to provide universal education and healthcare, on plausible assumptions about the debilitating effects of ignorance and illness, in their own right, on autonomy. The second way is actually to provide in some way for an array of options through the state's promotion of a 'culture of autonomy' (which is what Raz suggested above). But pursuing this latter cultural programme seems a *very* indirect way of discharging the duty in question.

A last difficulty is that Raz's outlook on this seems to suggest that 'autonomy' embraces all other goods which a state might, through the exercise of its power of *potentia*, bestow on its subjects. But this seems false. There are intrinsic values of health, education, and so on, which do not turn on their instrumental contribution to autonomy. I currently live in a state which, in the opinion of the author, is dedicated to its citizens being healthy, wealthy, and 'wise' (if 'wise' means educated). But to autonomy? Not so much if autonomy includes choosing options which depend upon a Western-like freedom of expression or assembly.

To take another example, I can think of many reasons for creating and funding the BBC that have nothing to do with autonomy. In my case the overwhelming reason for wanting the BBC is the lack of adverts. Watching US network television is, for me, an exercise in rage management. Of course, I also think the BBC produces some of the best content. But neither of these reasons for valuing the BBC has anything to do with my autonomy or, at least, I cannot see how it does. Similar thoughts might apply to the state's funding (through subsidies and tax reliefs of various kinds) of the legal activities we designate as charities. Some doubtless enhance the autonomy of some people—charities for the relief of poverty and for the advancement of education are obvious candidates, but in the case of others, again, the autonomy-enhancing effect is likely to be indirect if there at all.[47]

The upshot of these various considerations is that it seems unlikely that what the state does in its exercise of *potentia* can be justified simply as the promotion of its subjects' autonomy.

An alternative suggestion, promulgated by Loughlin himself, is that *potentia* is justified because the state is legitimately entitled to 'mould' the character of a people—that is, to mould its subjects into a particular people with some sort of shared identity.[48] There is no doubt that states often do engage in this sort of 'moulding', but the question is whether they should—ie, whether their doing so is justified. There is, I think, an obvious dark side, or a dark possibility, lurking in 'we the people' in so far as it embraces the 'character of a people'. That is, of course, nationalism: the bad version of patriotism (ie, uncritical patriotism). If patriotism means nothing more than a justified and measured respect or love for the admirable, local, features of one's place on the planet and the people found there, then it has nothing to be troubled about. This might be called 'critical' patriotism and Burke captured the thought well when he wrote '[t]o make us love our country, our country ought

[47] M Harding, *Charity Law and the Liberal State* (Cambridge, Cambridge University Press, 2014), advances a general theory of charity law which seeks to justify charity law as autonomy-enhancing on Razian lines. For critical discussion, see JE Penner, 'Autonomy, Religion and Politics: Reflections on Matthew Harding's *Charity Law and the Liberal State*' (2016) 41 *Australian Journal of Legal Philosophy* 126.

[48] *Cf* Raz (n 27) 321–22, who claims that the state should 'mould' the preferences of its subjects so that they prefer worthwhile pursuits to worthless or ignoble ones.

to be lovely'.[49] Thus, a state should do what it can to make its society and people admirable. But beyond this, it is not at all clear that this 'moulding' function is justified.

Let me make a final suggestion, which returns us to the antagonistic relationship Loughlin finds between *societas* and *universitas*. Above, I sought to defuse that tension, or at least reduce it, by proposing a division of labour between *potestas* and *potentia*. Now I want to suggest that, in certain circumstances, the tension will increase. Those circumstances arise when the operation of the rules promulgated by the exercise of *potestas*, reflecting a certain understanding of *societas*, lead systematically to results which are unethical—unethical in the sense that these results instantiate significant disvalues which detract from the good life.

Assume for the sake of argument that a particular outlook has shaped our notion of justice in the marketplace and in regard to private ordering or economic justice more generally. Such an outlook can span the 'left-right' spectrum in political terms. One version of this outlook is found in Rawls. For Rawls, once a 'basic structure' is put into place that is just, which as regards rights to economic resource is a structure that complies with the 'difference principle', any resultant economic distribution that arises from the interactions of citizens is itself just.[50] Another version, Nozick's, holds that any distribution resulting from initial just appropriations and subsequent fair transfers is also itself just.[51] Assume also that that outlook generates any number of outcomes, which from an ethical perspective seem problematic to say the least, such as a decline in equality of opportunity, the flourishing of mercenary marketplace behaviour, the degradation of the environment, or a large inequality in the distribution of resources. Also, assume that in this situation, the concept of *societas*, though always contestable in the sense that people will entertain and communicate very different beliefs about its nature, has been shaped by the sorts of outlook just mentioned so as to make it seem that *societas* just has embedded these outcomes as a matter of its own perspective or 'take' on justice—however unpalatable the results in its operation might seem on a more visceral level. One sort of thought along these lines would be that any resultant distribution of goods that arises through the unregulated working of the rules of private interaction just *is* just, however wrong or unsatisfying that distribution might appear at first glance.

Assuming that something like this story is plausible, the result is that there is a widely shared *misconceived* or *impoverished* conception of *societas*. In other words, though we have seen that the ethical is necessarily implicated in the exercise of *potestas*, the described liberal outlooks blind us to this fact: rather than reckoning on the role of the ethical in the exercise of *potestas*, particularly in the rules of private ordering in the market, we understand this realm as one in which self-interest—or worse, selfishness—is understood as the legitimate, operating motivation of all private activity. *Potestas* is, then, positively *deracinated*—its ethical dimension is torn out at the roots. To take but one sort of example, on this view legislation like the Unfair Contract Terms Act 1977 is an unjust legislative intervention by the state because it tips private ordering in favour of consumers, who on this austere understanding of *societas* must be taken to be self-responsible actors whose rights are not infringed unless someone else makes choices *for them* in respect of their means.

[49] E Burke, *Reflections on the Revolution in France* (edited by JGA Pocock) (Indianapolis, Hackett Publishing, 1987) 68.

[50] *Theory of Justice* (n 31) s 43. For critical discussion see G Cohen, *Rescuing Justice and Equality* (Cambridge MA, Harvard University Press, 2008) 27–86.

[51] Nozick (n 36) 149–231.

If this situation obtains, then the relation between *societas* and *universitas* will be antagonistic, and the exercise of their separate powers will generate conflict. For on this picture, rather than there being a division of labour within our evaluative outlook, eg, between the right and the good or between the moral and the ethical, there are two entirely different 'moralities' in conflictual operation. In these circumstances our conceptions of *societas* and *universitas* will be seen to 'reflect the existence *within human nature* of two equally powerful but contrary dispositions: the desire to be autonomous and the desire to be a participant in a common venture.'[52] In these circumstances such a tension or disjuncture 'can neither be eliminated nor reconciled, but only negotiated'.[53] The rather sad moral to such a story is that *potentia* is seen as a kind of ethical counterweight to deal with the worst results of our impoverished notion of freedom as the pursuit of our moral right to independence. *Potentia* does, therefore, find a justification in these circumstances: it undoes the ethically unconscionable or unbearable consequences of our misguided conception of *societas*.

VII. Conclusion

Let me conclude with two thoughts. The first is that I have obviously failed to provide a justificatory account of *potentia*, or at least one in which *societas* and *universitas* are not in conflict. The second is that this failure suggests a research programme that may take two different approaches.

One such approach would be to re-configure our conception of *societas*: integrating within it ethical dimensions which liberals like Rawls and Nozick do not think belong to it, but which overcome the liberal objection. Arguably, Raz attempted to do so by grounding his liberalism on the value of autonomy. But, as we have seen, I have found that approach wanting. So we might try to think about the ethical dimensions of *societas* in a different way.

The other, more interesting if not immediately more promising, approach that might be pursued is one in which a conception of *societas* is theorised such that it appropriately incorporates both moral and ethical dimensions. The liberals would then be right to argue that we no longer need think of our polity as a *universitas*—that conception of ourselves would be rendered unhelpful or misleading because it falsely suggests a conception of a polity of 'we the people' and the state as the promoter and manager of our common goals. Rather, once we get *societas* right, we will perceive a new understanding of and grounding for the *universitas* conception of the state to which *societas* stands in a relation of harmony (or at least co-operation), rather than in inveterate conflict.

In any event, let me conclude by adverting to the phrase I italicised in the last passage I quoted from Loughlin's book: that being his assertion that *societas* and *universitas* 'reflect the existence *within human nature* of two equally powerful but contrary dispositions: the desire to be autonomous and the desire to be a participant in a common venture.'[54] Whatever the truth of what I have expressed here about *societas* and *universitas*, I very much doubt that our self-understanding of either is rooted in human nature. I also very much hope that not to be the case.

[52] *Foundations* (n 1) 163 (emphasis added).
[53] *Foundations* (n 1) 164.
[54] *Foundations* (n 1) 163 (emphasis added).

8

A Conventional Narrative: The Rhetorical Shape of *Foundations of Public Law*

ANNA YEATMAN

I. Introduction: A Conventional Narrative

A particularly striking narrative concerning the trajectory of the modern state, as it appears to some important thinkers and those they have influenced, goes like this.[1] Over the course of the twentieth century the state became extraordinarily all-powerful. It fought 'total wars on an intercontinental scale', provided 'for its subjects in a previously undreamt of manner' so that they were no longer at the mercy of the vicissitudes of fate, but showed itself capable of controlling them 'in ways that were deeply troubling to liberals who valued above all the freedom of individuals to decide on the good for themselves'.[2] It is thus that '[t]he twentieth century may be said to have witnessed the apotheosis of the state'.[3]

If this narrative recalls a set of thematics that 'were staple topics of twentieth-century social and political thought,' it has also been suggested that the juridical dimensions of the topic have been rather neglected, even as from the turn of the twentieth century thinkers began to realise 'that the requirements of the modern state put increasing pressure on accepted understandings of law'.[4] How so? First, law became increasingly 'made or legislated', and in this way assumed a 'positive' as distinct from a 'natural' appearance. This development of state-made positive law 'threatened the connection that was previously assumed between the law and the basic values or mores of the community'.[5] On the older conception, law reflected custom. Now, not only custom but also 'other traditional forms of social cohesion' were 'losing their force', putting a premium on law 'being called upon to do more by way of legitimating the government apparatus'.[6] This intensification of the role of law in validating state authority compounded the expansion of state-made law driven

[1] D Dyzenhaus and T Poole, 'Introduction' in D Dyzenhaus and T Poole (eds), *Law, Liberty and State: Oakeshott, Hayek and Schmitt on the Rule of Law* (Cambridge, Cambridge University Press, 2015).
[2] ibid 1.
[3] ibid.
[4] ibid.
[5] ibid 1–2.
[6] ibid.

by the extension of state regulation over social life. Here is the crescendo that brings this set of claims together:

> This sense of juristic disorientation was heightened by the specificity of the new functional rule making. As law seemed to become regulation, increasingly a matter of detail and of technique, it became unclear what space remained for the image of law as anchor of basic principles and brake on overweening or arbitrary political action. If the *Rechtsstaat* is meant to embody general liberal principles, how can it abide a particularistic core?[7]

How one evaluates the processes of state formation in the twentieth century and from what standpoint is more complex than the conventional narrative just sketched suggests. Is the alleged apotheosis of the state referable to all or only some of: Nazi Germany, the Stalinist Soviet Union, George W Bush's USA before or after the invasion of Iraq, to all or only some of the liberal democratic European welfare states? And, at what precise point in their development?

Yet, in broad terms this argument characterises the narrative arc of Loughlin's *Foundations of Public Law*.[8] At least by the last two parts of this compendious text we get something very similar in character to this argument. Loughlin makes it seem that the 'rise of the social' must imply such an apotheosis of the state. Since it is difficult to argue against the historical trajectory of the 'rise of the social' without invoking an impossibly nostalgic standpoint, this seems like a form of negative historicism, namely the proposition that an historical development as complex and as politically contested as the rise of the social must inevitably lead in a certain direction, one that undermines the juristic autonomy and integrity of the state.

In what follows, my stance is that of a political and social theorist, and my focus is on ideas, especially on rival ideas. In good part I am calling into question any historicist narrative that masks its doctrinal commitments through the appearance of a history that rolls out over time. In particular, this historicism masks the normative significance of public law as an achievement of the early modern state, which embodies the subjective freedom of the citizen. Loughlin loses sight of this achievement because, whether by default or design, he permits a liberal constitutional understanding of negative liberty to overwhelm the immanent relation between state and freedom.

II. The Early Modern Discovery of the Idea of the State

Loughlin begins his account of the foundations of public law in the early modern era, presenting public law as the legal dimension of 'a set of institutional arrangements' that constitutes the state, or the office of the sovereign.[9] Bodin is key for Loughlin in this regard, representing the shift in focus promoted by early modern juristic and political thinkers from the idea of the prince as a single individual ruler of a domain, a seigneurial conception,

[7] ibid 2.
[8] M Loughlin, *Foundations of Public Law* (Oxford, Oxford University Press, 2010) [hereafter *Foundations*].
[9] ibid 91.

to the idea of the prince as a system of public office.[10] Seigneurial government implied that the prince could treat crown land and jurisdictional rights 'as part of his private patrimony, subject to ordinary legal rules of inheritance, succession, seisin, and sale, a doctrine that later jurists such as Grotius, Pufendorf, and Vattel would call patrimonial kingship'.[11] As Daniel Lee highlights, Bodin's juristic-political thought was trenchantly anti-seigneurial or anti-feudal, rejecting 'the idea that the sovereign ruler of a state was also its ruler [Fr. *seigneur*, L. *dominus*] and, therefore, was legally entitled to govern the state just as if it were an object of private property held *in patrimonio*'.[12]

In arguing that the prince does not have 'the proprietie of the publike demaines', and that 'propertie of the crowne lands [demesne] is not the princes,' but instead, 'belong[s] unto the commonweale',[13] Bodin presents a public domain that is something other than patrimonial private property, a public domain in other words that is not to be thought of as analogous to a household (*oikos*). Where a household requires management, a public domain is constructed in terms of the immanent requirements of sovereign rule.[14] To rule this public domain, then, the prince has to assume an entirely different role to that of a private owner who can do with it as he pleases. While for Bodin seigneurial government was government by the sovereign's arbitrary will, rule of a public domain required lawful government: 'What made lawful government possible on this analysis was the use of law, rather than one's arbitrary will, in discharging the functions and powers of government.'[15] It is in this conception of lawful government that we find the *idea* of law. It refers to the construction in law of the state as a system of public office. This is law understood as the structuring principle of this system, or as Bodin put it:

> To change the laws which concern the estate, is as dangerous, as to remove the foundation or corner stones which uphold the whole weight or burden of the buildings; in which doing the whole fabric is to be sore shaken, and beside the danger of falling, receiveth more hurt by the shaking thereof, than it doth good by the new reparation, especially if be now old and ruinous.[16]

In order to ensure that the prince or sovereign power is something other than arbitrary will, that this power is bound by fundamental law understood in the sense just given, Bodin argued that in 'ordinary matters of government and administration of state',

[10] As D Lee, '"Office is a Thing Borrowed": Jean Bodin on Offices and Seigneurial Government' (2013) 41 *Political Theory* 409 points out.

[11] ibid 413.

[12] ibid 412.

[13] Bodin cited in Lee, ibid 413.

[14] A public domain that is constructed in terms of the immanent requirements of sovereign rule *must* have a functional aspect concerning how this domain is resourced, a point that Loughlin appears to understand when he speaks of crown privileges and rights as required to meet the costs of governing (see below). However, later in *Foundations*, Loughlin allows himself to be converted by Oakeshott's wholesale view of the prince's domain as the 'unpurged relic of "lordship"'. The full passage reads: 'Here, the "unpurged relic of 'lordship' hidden in the office of modern monarchs and which the successors to kings inherited and have shown no inclination to relinquish" has been exploited and the modern European state recognised as a domain, its territory an estate, its government a form of estate-management, and its laws as rules that are instrumentally orientated to the success of this enterprise' (*Foundations* (n 8) 162). This view also enables Loughlin to interpret modern state prerogative powers as a relic of patrimonial monarchical power.

[15] Lee (n 10) 416.

[16] Bodin cited in Lee (n 10) 417–18.

'public power must be delegated to others, acting as agents or 'keepers in trust' of the sovereign power'.[17] It is this 'legal scheme of delegation and agency' that constitutes a system of public office.[18]

Loughlin's use of Bodin in *Foundations* is conceptually consistent with Lee's account, but the normative aspect goes missing. Fundamental law for Bodin is not as the medieval meaning had it, customary law, but rather refers to 'the rules that define the nature of the office' of the sovereign.[19] Loughlin continues: 'Bodin seeks to establish the office of the sovereign as a permanent and perpetual institution', which being so means that the sovereign 'is not free, as under patrimonial kingships, to bestow the crown on whomever he desires', nor free to sell off the royal estate.[20] Instead, crown privileges or rights—'rights to public lands, rents, fines, tolls and such like—exist to meet the costs of governing, and if that endowment were depleted the future authority of the office would be diminished.'[21] Accordingly, Loughlin emphasises, 'the fundamental rules are constitutive of the office and exist to ensure that absolute authority is continuously and permanently established'.[22]

Loughlin recognises, then, that in this account of sovereign power we have something other than a conception of patrimonial kingship. But he does not emphasise, as Lee does, the *normative* significance of Bodin's rejection of seigneurial authority, and of his insistence on its alternative—sovereignty conceived as the state or as public authority. What is this normative significance? In her account of the era of French juristic thought to which Bodin belongs, Blandine Kriegel argues that these anti-feudal thinkers are rejecting the condition of slavery or servitude in which feudal authority places those who find themselves in subjection to the patrimonial ruler. Kriegel argues these thinkers give a resounding 'no' to three questions: must subjects be treated as slaves? Must human beings be treated as things? Do political relationships derive from property relationships?[23] Thus, Bodin rejects seigneurial rule because in such a condition the subject cannot be free:

> Whatever goods or chattels a subject held, in fact, really belonged by right, to the princely seigneur who permitted the subject to make use of it, 'so long as it shall please' him. In this way, then, the material well-being of the subject in a seigneurial regime was fully dependent upon the sovereign's permissive will—literally, the sovereign's 'benevolence'.[24]

It is this condition of being dependent on the arbitrary will of another that Quentin Skinner, in reference to the Roman doctrine of *patria potestas*, and following the usage of Roman moralists and historians, calls *obnoxius*, namely 'the predicament of anyone who depends on the will—or, as we say, on the goodwill—of someone else'.[25] In their normative rejection of this relational mode of being human, the early modern juristic and political thinkers reconstitute the status of the human subject as a free being, and, thus, as the kind of being for whom authority has to be other than patrimonial mastery or feudal rule.

[17] Bodin cited in Lee (n 10) 419.
[18] Bodin cited in Lee (n 10) 419.
[19] *Foundations* (n 8) 67.
[20] *Foundations* (n 8) 67.
[21] *Foundations* (n 8) 67.
[22] *Foundations* (n 8) 67.
[23] B Kriegel, *The State and the Rule of Law* (Princeton, Princeton University Press, 1995) 25–26.
[24] Lee (n 10) 414.
[25] Q Skinner, *Liberty before Liberalism* (Cambridge, Cambridge University Press, 1998) 42.

Authority, in short, has to assume the features of a system of rule that orders relationships between human beings in such a way that they can be free, both in relation to one another, and in relation to their inner being (which at this time centres on confessional freedom).

The rationale for sovereign power thought of as an anti-seigneurial form of rule, a system of public office that is constituted in public law, resides in how it provides for a human mode of being that can be termed free. Such a mode is inherently relational so that, in institutionally securing and enabling freedom, this system of rule is oriented to the freedom of each on an equal basis. The public good then has a precise meaning that is not adequately conveyed by Loughlin's repeated use of Cicero's phrase *salus populi*, which refers to the health or good of the people. Rather, the public good denotes a shared condition of being free that is given positive expression both in the institutional order of the state and in the political body or association that those individuals who share this condition of being free comprise. 'Society' in this conception is 'political society'. Political society represents a distinctive order of artifice that is coeval and co-extensive with the artifice that is involved in the institutionalisation of sovereign power. Thus 'society' does not pre-exist the state, but is constituted as a jurisdiction of free persons through the state. At the same time, political society denotes a mode of being and acting as a free subject that is structured by an obligation to obey the sovereign authority. In this way, it might be said that political society *produces* sovereign authority.

The idea of the state, in this account, takes on both institutional and subjective-phenomenological dimensions. This is what Hegel means by the state as ethical life. This same understanding extends to the meaning of 'law'. Law is irreducible to its formal expression and extends to an ethos of law, thus permitting a two-way dynamic relationship between formal law and this ethos. Such an approach calls into question Loughlin's view of the juridical and the regulative aspects of governing as mutually exclusive. Loughlin does refer to the early modern rationale for sovereign power, but in doing so converts it into a standard dogma rather than carefully investigating it as a set of rich ideas. His reference to the doctrine of *salus populi* or the good of the people as the normative referent for the early modern idea of rule is, as I have said, insufficiently precise. In contrast, when discussing Spinoza, he does relate this idea of public good to the proposition that the true aim of government is liberty:

> A slave 'is one who is bound to obey his master's orders, though they are given solely in the master's interest', whereas a subject 'obeys the orders of the sovereign power, given for the common interest, wherein he is included'. The object of government 'is not to change men from rational beings into beasts or puppets, but to enable them to develop their minds and bodies in security, and to employ their reason unshackled'. The 'true aim of government is liberty'.[26]

The early modern juristic and political thinkers view the state and public law as the necessary condition of freedom understood as a relational or social condition. To be sure, Hobbes insists that the right of nature, namely, 'the Liberty each man hath, to use his own power, as he will himself, for the preservation of his own Nature' can never be surrendered.[27] The individual retains her right to personal security even when she finds herself a subject of

[26] *Foundations* (n 8) 105, internal quotations referring to Spinoza's *Tractatus Politicus*.
[27] T Hobbes, *Leviathan* (Cambridge, Cambridge University Press, 1991) 91.

sovereign power. For personal security (Blandine Kriegel's apt rephrasing of the right to self-preservation) is 'the ground' of sovereign power, which means that sovereign power cancels its own rationale should it threaten personal security.[28] Of how Hobbes constructs natural right, Kriegel says: 'Personal security is the end and object of all social transactions' and it cannot be surrendered.[29] Thus, if the state should act in such a way as to threaten personal security, Hobbesian individuals have the right to resist it.

Outside the artifice of the state/political society, as Hobbes insisted, natural right is merely virtual. Blandine Kriegel's commentary makes the point clearly:

> The right to personal security, then, has pride of place among all individual rights. It is the only one that is nonnegotiable. More importantly, it is the only civil right. In the state of nature, personal security is merely the object of a desire, an aspiration of the individual, but never a reality. *Homo homini lupus*: the anarchical and collective law of force poses a constant threat to each person's physical safety. In the civil state, by contrast, the sovereign's confiscation of all acts of war, his monopoly on the sword of justice, brings about individual security by means of the rule of law. The civil state confers reality on a right that remained virtual in the state of nature.[30]

Freedom does not precede the state and public law, and therefore it makes no sense to propose, as many liberal-constitutionalist thinkers do,[31] that the rationale for the state and public law resides in protection of an individual's inherent right to freedom *against* the tendency of public power to exceed its remit. Such a tendency can be conceded but it should be thought of differently, not as the violation of an already existing individual freedom but rather as the corruption of public authority, and as some kind of reversion to seigneurial power, that is, the assertion of power as a form of private rather than public right. We can make these points a little more carefully with reference to Hobbes, a thinker who followed and elaborated Bodin's conception of sovereign power, and is drawn on by Loughlin to establish the early modern territory of public law.

Hobbes, to reiterate, posits freedom in terms of an early modern idea of natural law, this being 'the right of nature' or

> Liberty each man hath to use his own power, as he will himself, for the preservation of his own Nature; that is to say, of his own Life; and consequently, of doing any thing, which in his own Judgement, and Reason, hee shall conceive to be the aptest means thereunto.[32]

This, it seems to me, is a fundamentally anti-feudal posit: it is the idea that, as an individual, each human being has her own integrity, and should be free to use her 'own power' to express, and serve, this integrity. This is the meaning of the 'individualism' that we associate with Hobbes's thought. It is decidedly not the monadic individualism of the Robinson Crusoe kind, for which liberal thinkers are often criticised. Hobbes (as Samantha

[28] Here I work with Malpas's understanding of 'ground': 'The point can be made quite generally, in a way not restricted to Kant: to determine that in which the possibility of something rests, is, at one and the same time, to determine what is possible for it—to determine ground, is also to determine limit' J Malpas, 'Ground, Unity, Limit' in J Malpas, *Heidegger and the Thinking of Place: Explorations in the Topology of Being* (Cambridge, Massachusetts, England, MIT Press, 2012) 83.

[29] Kriegel (n 23) 40.

[30] Kriegel (n 23) 40.

[31] See *Foundations* (n 8) Ch 12.

[32] Hobbes (n 27) 91.

Frost brilliantly analyses) is quite clear: the human condition is one of interdependence.[33] Put another way: in using our own power and translating it into action, we constitute each other's environment. Hobbes's argument concerns how this environment is structured. If it is privately ordered, that is directed by private arbitrary will, then we find ourselves in an *obnoxius* condition—we are either subjected to the will of the presently stronger party, or we manage temporarily at least to be this stronger party, thereby subjecting the will of others to our own. On the other hand, if this environment is publicly ordered, then it is possible for each to enjoy security for their existence as a free being, at least as far as institutional authority can provide for such.

It is Hobbes's genius to show how a feudal private ordering of relationships appears from the standpoint of an early modern conception of freedom. It appears as a condition of chronic fear and insecurity for all, where it is impossible for arts and industry to flourish. But Hobbes emphasises that this state of affairs suits those whose sense of honour requires that they engage in war.[34] The ethical problem that feudalism poses is thus disclosed only from the standpoint of the principle of subjective freedom.

Having demonstrated that a private ordering of the human condition vitiates the right of nature, Hobbes is able to argue that only a public ordering of the same can enable the right of nature to be something other than a virtual right, that is, to become real. This means that freedom is immanent within the public ordering of social life, a point that Loughlin takes from Spinoza. The passages of *Foundations* I have in mind read as follows:

> Given that individuals in their natural state are marked by inequalities, some type of institutional framework is required before relations of equality can be formulated [...] Spinoza is critical of scholastic expressions of right, whether objective, as the expression of a prior, divinely inspired order, or subjective, as the expression of a universal human characteristic of autonomy. An individual's right is simultaneously an expression of power. Individuals live in a relation of mutual independence, in that one is able 'in general to live after his own mind', and dependence, in that he is 'rightfully dependent on another' [...] Given this mutuality, we can see why Spinoza does not regard sovereign power and individual right as inherently antagonistic, especially since 'if two come together and unite in their strength, they have jointly more power [...] and the more there are that have so joined in alliance, the more right they all collectively will possess'. The individual is to be seen 'not as an obstacle to the sovereign's power (*potestas*) but an active, constituent element of the power (*potentia*) of the state'. The immanent relations of sovereignty evolve as the dynamic of dependence-independence generates 'real' power, a power generated from limitations and functional differentiations intrinsic to the process.[35]

[33] S Frost, *Lessons from a Materialist Thinker: Hobbesian Reflections on Ethics and Politics* (Stanford, Stanford University Press, 2008).

[34] V Sullivan, *Machiavelli, Hobbes and the Formation of a Liberal Republicanism in England* (Cambridge, Cambridge University Press, 2004) 98, discusses how the aristocratic families that supported Europe's monarchies were a problem for Hobbes: 'Trained to seek honor on the battlefield, they are likely to advocate for war abroad; disposed to view themselves as superior in strength and resolve, they are likely to defend their honor vigorously, even violently from insults and slights, and are, as a result, a source of disturbance within the realm. Their way of life, their passions, and their virtues are obstacles to Hobbes's goals of peace and stability.' Sullivan continues: 'As much as the aristocratic few pose formidable obstacles to Hobbes's purposes, he does not so much attack them as a class as condemn proud individuals. Because these proud individuals are likely to be conscious of their status, wealth, and education, ready proponents of war, and eager for rule, Hobbes leaves no doubt from which class the most troublesome are drawn'.

[35] *Foundations* (n 8) 105, internal quotations referring to Spinoza.

Here, Loughlin affirms the insight that *potestas* and *potentia* are reciprocally constitutive. The state that conforms to the idea of a constitutive condition of a free mode of being is a legitimate state: sovereign power or *potestas* can be granted its full majesty. At the same time, in their manner of obeying sovereign power, free individuals turn this majesty into effective power. As Hobbes puts it: 'in the act of our Submission consisteth both our Obligation and our Liberty'.[36]

Hobbes argues that in the construction of a common power that imposes a civil peace each gives up their natural rights, and specifically their natural right to govern themselves in matters bearing on their security. Thus in establishing a public collective entity to which each belongs, individuals transform the nature of their being from 'natural' to 'civil'. In Hobbes's words,

> [t]his is more than Consent or Concord; it is a reall Unitie of them all, in one and the same Person, made by Covenant of every man with every man, in such manner, as if every man should say to every man, *I Authorise and give up my Right of Governing my selfe, to this Man, or to this Assembly of men, on this condition, that thou give up thy Right to him, and Authorise all his Actions in like manner.*

Hobbes continues: 'the Multitude so united in one Person, is called a COMMON-WEALTH, in latine CIVITAS'.[37] The remarkable clarity of this passage demonstrates a thoroughly anti-patrimonial politics. To suggest that, in becoming part of a public collectivity that acquires lawful agency in the form of sovereign power, the individual must surrender the private right of self-government rejects not just the feudal conception of authority in terms of private power but also the liberal understanding of freedom in terms of a pre-existing right of self-government. Quentin Skinner suggests that in this conception of 'liberty before liberalism' we find something quite other than the 'liberal analysis of negative liberty'.[38] Indeed so. As he suggests, these two distinct conceptions of liberty lead to quite different conceptions of the state, and it must follow, of public law.[39]

Liberal thought justifies state authority in terms of liberty understood as an already-constituted mode of being. State authority, then, is limited to formal recognition and protection of a pre-existing state of affairs. In this framework, any elaboration of state authority, as occurs especially with the historical transition from a patriarchal household society to a modern differentiated society, must appear problematic. For instance, when the employment relationship is no longer contained within a patrimonial household economy, but is placed within the relationships of civil society, now understood in its modern, rather than early modern sense, as a sphere of private associational action, the question of how the employment relationship is to be constituted appears as something that has to be dealt with. For the social liberal thinker, it makes sense for the state to consider the employment contract as something other than a purely contractual or privately transacted relationship, as a relationship that needs to be situated within political society in the early modern sense of the word.[40] For the liberal thinker, the employment contract as a privately transacted

[36] Hobbes (n 27) 150.
[37] Hobbes (n 27) 120.
[38] Skinner (n 25) 112.
[39] Skinner (n 25) 119.
[40] This is how TH Green argues in his 'Lecture on "Liberal Legislation and Freedom of Contract"' in *Lectures on the Principles of Political Obligation and Other Writings* (Cambridge, Cambridge University Press, 1986) 194–213. It also relates to Durkheim's argument concerning the 'non-contractual' elements of contract in *The Division of Labor in Society* (New York, The Free Press, 1964).

relationship should be respected by the state, and the bias is against state interference in this relationship.

The liberal thinker's suspicion of 'state intervention' in private transactional relationships makes it inevitable that s/he will be suspicious of state power, seeing it as inherently likely to exceed and undermine state *potestas*. Yet, as indicated, the terms of the early modern conception of the reciprocal constitution of *potestas* and *potentia* can be carried over into 'the rise of the social' and how this affects our understanding of the state and political society. The question becomes how the extension and intensification of the idea of freedom requires a more elaborate understanding of the state/political society ensemble of relationships under post-patrimonial conditions. In this conception, the test of state authority (considered as both *potestas* and *potentia)* is how it is or continues to be constitutive of freedom, understood as a shared and relational mode of being. Thus, what I called at the start the conventional account of the development of the state in the epoch of the rise of the social is driven essentially by a liberal, if not a liberal-patrimonial, point of view or value orientation. The only point I need to make here is that there can be an alternative account that develops the early modern conception of the state and freedom. What we find in Loughlin's narrative in *Foundations* is a refusal to see such an alternative account and to investigate its implications for a conception of public law. The problem, in short, is that Loughlin's own insights (especially but not only via Spinoza's thought) into the immanent relationship between freedom and the state are eclipsed over the course of *Foundations* as a liberal idea of the state and its constitution begins to take hold.

III. The Liberal Idea of the State

Precisely because the early modern anti-feudal thinkers are so profoundly aware that a state of non-liberty is the historical condition their thinking is designed to problematise, their claim that liberty is a right of nature (as Hobbes has it) is strongly ethical in import. It is not a claim about human nature, but a claim about the potential of human beings for living a free life. Since this claim comes into being as an ethical response to an already existing historical state of affairs that denies liberty, its character is historical rather than ontological. Hegel follows this line of thinking in associating the development of the principle of subjective freedom with the historical phenomenology of Christianity.[41]

On this matter there is a profound equivocation in liberalism. Liberal thinkers tend to ontologise freedom or liberty by making it a characteristic of the human as such.[42] Arguably this follows from their privileging an already existent freedom, which in relation to a derivative public authority that is established in order to recognise this pre-existing freedom, retains its private, and thus on Hobbes's terms, its 'natural' character. In this way, freedom as an ethical claim cedes place to freedom as a naturally given condition.

[41] See GFW Hegel, *Elements of the Philosophy of Right* (Cambridge, Cambridge University Press, 1991) [hereafter *Philosophy of Right*] eg §124, 151–52.

[42] Thus Loughlin (*Foundations* (n 8) 163) invokes Oakeshott's idea of 'the existence within human nature of two equally powerful but contrary dispositions: the desire to be autonomous and the desire to be a participant in a common venture.'

Instead of being thought of as immanent to a politically constituted mode of association, freedom becomes immanent to a civil society now understood in the modern sense of a transactional sphere of individual conduct, that is, as a set of relations that are structured in terms of their instrumental value for natural persons. As Loughlin makes clear in his account of Thomas Paine's idea of inherent rights, this sphere is given to and precedes the state.[43]

Liberals accept that this private ordering of relationships is not self-sufficient. It has to be completed or overlaid by 'the rule of law' understood as legally enforceable rules that concern 'the propriety of conduct'.[44] These rules concern, as Oakeshott puts it, adverbial conditions of conduct, adding to conduct the quality of conformity to law.[45] And yet liberal thinkers abandon any idea of a public collectivity. They are deeply suspicious of attributing substantive features to the public or political association (the state) that supposedly enable the freedom of those who come under its jurisdiction. Instead, liberal thinkers attempt to give the rules or conditions of such association a formal and substantively empty character (this is political association thought of as *societas*, a term that Loughlin borrows from Oakeshott). Otherwise they fear that they run the risk of prescribing the content of free action, or more precisely, the logic of the situation is that someone will have to decide the content of free action, which must necessarily represent the return of the arbitrary will.

Liberals are thus compelled to offer a formulation that posits the rules or conditions of free conduct as distinct from the exercise or practice of free conduct. This then leaves the liberal thinker in a quandary. Even if he is clear that free conduct is not possible except as it enjoys such conditions or rules, he has to make free conduct appear to precede or reside outside these conditions or rules, whereas, on the early modern conception, an understanding (both political and juridical) of the status of being a free person has to inform the exercise of freedom.[46] For the liberal way of thinking, the idea that the state might act on behalf of personal security understood as a condition of holding the status of a free person must lead in an illiberal direction. Thus, if state action on behalf of personal security is inherently problematic, it is because such action will be driven by considerations other than those which bear on the question of subjective right. This is precisely how Loughlin's argument unfolds.

In his chapter on constitutional rights (Chapter 12) Loughlin thus comes to adopt a liberal frame of reference. The early modern conception of sovereign power is reinterpreted from a liberal point of view, the effect of which is to problematise natural right as the 'ground' of the state. As I understand it, his argument goes like this. If, he says, natural right

[43] *Foundations* (n 8) 346–49.

[44] M Oakeshott, 'The Rule of Law' in *On History and Other Essays* (Indianapolis, Liberty Fund, 1999) 139.

[45] I agree with Dyzenhaus's suggestion that Oakeshott, a subtle thinker, offers a 'Hobbesian' account of freedom which, on the terms of my argument, brings Oakeshott closer to the early modern conception perhaps than the designation of him as a liberal thinker suggests (see D Dyzenhaus, 'Dreaming the Rule of Law' in D Dyzenhaus and T Poole (eds), *Law, Liberty and State: Oakeshott, Hayek and Schmitt on the Rule of Law* (Cambridge, Cambridge University Press, 2015) 234–61). Nevertheless, I think Oakeshott understood himself as a liberal thinker, and he certainly embraced the antinomies of liberal thought.

[46] This is the argument that I can practice freedom only if I understand at least on some level what it means to be a free being. This is obviously something quite other than ownership of private property, even as the idea of private property is different depending on whether it is framed by a seigneurial, liberal, or 'early modern' understanding of the subject.

is understood in liberal fashion, as inherent 'subjective' rights, preceding the construction of the authority of the state, determining whether state action is legitimate or not, and limiting state authority, then we have an account of state legitimacy and power that preserves a private sphere of freedom for the individual, 'a zone of private autonomy'.[47] For Loughlin this is not without problems. First, such rights, if they are enshrined in constitutional law, must be interpreted, and there can be no ultimate criterion for determining the basis of such interpretation.[48] Second, Loughlin argues that the classical liberal conception of 'the society/government relationship has nowhere come close to existing in a stable form'.[49] Society is not self-regulating in the way that liberals suggest it is, and the constitutive rules 'that establish and regulate governmental power' by no means exhaust the scope of state action, which, over time, becomes more regulatory than juridical.[50]

If, on the other hand, natural right is understood as realised 'only through the constitutional order that authorises the office of government', then rights 'are no longer conceived as defining a zone of individual autonomy freed from governmental interest'.[51] The full passage reads:

> In modern constitutional settlements, the basis of rights theories has dramatically shifted. Rights are no longer conceived as defining a zone of individual autonomy freed from governmental interest. Rights are now conceived to be part of the objective organisational principles of the constitutional order that has been instituted. Rather than being treated as pre-political rights that specify the limits of government, constitutional rights emerge from and obtain their realisation only through the constitutional order that authorises the office of government [...] Instead of being treated as a natural condition—the product of pre-political social processes—liberty becomes a political condition that is itself institutionally shaped and normatively ordered.[52]

Loughlin argues that the logic of this situation is one in which rights become conditional 'on a perception of their utility in ensuring the realisation of the public aspirations of the political nation (which aspiration must, of course, remain highly contestable).'[53] Not only that, he goes on to say, but 'their existence and exercise increasingly appears to depend on positive action by government'.[54] Essentially, government is positioned as the arbiter of rights, and this must lead in the direction of functionalising rights, that is, making them subservient to the government's interpretation of electoral, social and/or economic utility.

Loughlin is in no doubt that the historical trend is for functionalism to overwhelm the first, liberal, possibility: 'With the emergence of modern regimes of government, the concept of subjective rights, strictly conceived, has been superseded.'[55] Loughlin thus evaluates the development of the late modern and especially the administrative state of the twentieth century using the liberal conception of rights. The early modern conception of

[47] *Foundations* (n 8) 368.
[48] However, Loughlin argues, if this is openly acknowledged, then the door is open for 'the practical necessities', for 'the methods of *droit politique*' to become the reference point for decision (*Foundations* (n 8) 365–66).
[49] *Foundations* (n 8) 369.
[50] *Foundations* (n 8) 339.
[51] *Foundations* (n 8) 369.
[52] *Foundations* (n 8) 369.
[53] *Foundations* (n 8) 369–70.
[54] *Foundations* (n 8) 370.
[55] *Foundations* (n 8) 369.

right recedes, or rather it is made over in the image of the idea of 'objective law' where constitutional rights become both conditional and functionalised.[56]

IV. The Twentieth Century State—The Narrative of 'the Triumph of the Social' and the Displacement of Political Right by Regulatory Power

Liberal thinkers consider themselves anti-feudal because of their attempt to find a mode of ordering relationships that is free from the domination of the arbitrary will. This mode is the transactional relationship that is oriented in terms of how individuals themselves decide what it is they want and value, and the transactional relationship acquires a legal quality through the rule of law, thus ensuring its propriety.[57] As we have seen, within this frame of thinking, any substantive determination on the part of the public authority of what enables individual freedom comes under suspicion. In Loughlin's narrative it is either the relic of lordship from the feudal era, which he sees as underlying the prerogative powers of the state, or it is the expression of the disciplinary-pastoral conception of the state, which originates in Calvinism, or it is an inherently metaphysical conception of the substance of freedom, which being so is in the modern secular era contestable, arbitrary, and subjective. The difficulty with liberal thought is that it cannot accommodate the rise of the social, as becomes evident in Loughlin's account of the implications of the rise of the social for public law. But on the terms of my account of the early modern conception of freedom, an alternative exists: here the rise of the social requires of the state/political society ensemble of relationships that the status of the free being be further considered and elaborated.

In its reliance on formally ordered transactional relationships, liberalism is unable to show how personal security (the early modern conception of freedom) is possible within privately ordered and asymmetrical relationships of power (eg between employer and employee). In the private domain of an individual, action is structured either as formal norm (such as the formal legal rules that constitute freedom of contract) or as decision. From this vantage point any substantive use of public authority to constitute the status of a free being comes under suspicion. In this frame of reference, we also lose sight of the early modern idea of sovereign power as a system of public office. The nature of public office cannot be thought of in terms of the conjunction of formal constitutive rules and private decision. This is so for two reasons: first, the nature of things public has substantive ethical features that bind those who serve in public office; second, it is the nature of such service to require the public official to assume an ethical persona whose field of action is quite distinct from that of a private individual.

[56] Loughlin reads Hegel as a theorist of this idea of objective law rather than as I see him (in *Philosophy of Right* (n 41)) as the last great thinker in the early modern tradition of political right.

[57] In Part I of *Philosophy of Right* (n 41) Hegel criticises this expression of freedom as 'abstract' precisely because it presupposes an opposition between the universal aspect of right (the rule of contract) and the particular, arbitrary will.

Let me take these two points in turn. On the first, we need to consider further the significance of Kriegel's account of early modern juristic-political thought as an anti-feudal ethics. I interpret Kriegel to be saying that if individuals are not to be left in thrall to the vicissitudes of privately ordered power, then their status as free beings has to be constituted by means of public authority or sovereign power. This status is an artificial construct. Thus, the citizen as a 'free subject' in Bodin's words can be regarded as a type of office, and when the individual conducts herself as a citizen she is assuming an official persona.[58] This persona is just that, one aspect of individual conduct that obtains in relation to two situations: the issue of the standing or status of the individual in relation to other individuals and the issue of the standing or status of the individual in relation to public authority. In both cases, the persona requires of the individual that she assume the obligation to obey both the letter and the ethos of the law in requiring her to know what it is to be a free being who is capable of recognising others as free beings too.

On the second point, the nature of the ethics of public office as a specialised vocation, Paul du Gay's work is helpful. As the early moderns insisted, office cannot be the private property of those who hold it. By the same token these individuals have to bracket their personal or private feelings, value commitments, and relationships, when they serve in public office. They have to assume a specific ethical comportment where they are 'willing and able to live up to the ethical demands placed upon them within their location within particular life-orders', in this case the life order of public office, where their conduct combines 'practical rationality with ethical seriousness'.[59] It is clear that this account of office cannot be reconciled with the liberal assumption that decision is inherently subjectivist, an assertion of the arbitrary will.

Public office as a specialised vocation is a term that covers a range of distinct offices: the bureaucracy, the judiciary, the elected official, and the military. Each of these types brings with it a specific persona that the official is to assume, a specific ethical comportment the official is to live up to. What they have in common is an ethos which du Gay (owing a debt to Max Weber) characterises as 'strict adherence to procedure, commitment to the purposes of the office, abnegation of personal moral enthusiasms', and separation of the conduct of public office from the private interest of the official.[60] I would go further here. Since the reason for this system of public office is the constitution of the status of persons as free beings, the purpose of the office has to be oriented accordingly.

The conception of the status of the person as a free being is historically and contextually specific. As I have said, it is entirely different when a patrimonial household economy is operative than when 'the economy' has become socialised in the sense of being placed outside the household and in the domain of civil society. Moreover, the conception of the

[58] For Bodin it is the relationship between prince/system of public office and the subject that constitutes both the obligation of the subject to obey the prince and the status of the citizen: 'It is therefore the submission and obedience of a free subject to his prince, and the tuition, protection, and jurisdiction exercised by the prince over his subject that makes the citizen' J Bodin, *On Sovereignty: Six Books of the Commonwealth* (Lexington, Seven Treasures Publications, 2009) 42.

[59] P Du Gay, 'Is Office a Vocation in "Post-Bureaucratic" Public Management?' in A Yeatman (ed), *Neoliberalism and the Crisis of Public Institutions, Working Papers in the Human Rights and Public Life Program* (Sydney, Whitlam Institute 2015) 41.

[60] ibid 42–43.

status of the person must always be interpreted in relation to the practicalities of a system of relationships between free persons as it operates at any one time. The idea of the status of the person as a free being belongs thus within this system. It concerns how to enable and to protect the personal security of individuals, to ensure that their condition is not *obnoxius*. Such considerations have justified ideas of, for example, compulsory universal schooling,[61] a minimum wage, a public corrections system in which prisoners are also treated as 'clients',[62] refuges for victims of domestic violence, and of publicly funded services for men who are perpetrators of domestic violence, and obliging disability service providers to adopt a practical ethic of respect for the 'voice' of their clients even if this requires positive action in enabling or facilitating the voice of people whose disability is such as to make it impossible for them to assume a voice on their own. On this approach, policy and regulation do not substitute for law but complement it.[63] Policy and regulation are understood to belong to the domain of the ethos of law, thus enabling law to be developed in relation to the practical exigencies of this domain, while ensuring that policy and regulation are developed in an open, transparent, politically as well as legally accountable way.

To reiterate, this idea of the status of a free being finds specification in law and public policy (understood not just in their formal aspect, but also in the ethos out of which this formal aspect grows and to which it returns) and concerns the world of public office. In other words, it reaches to and no further than a public ordering of conduct. Just as the ethic of public office requires those who serve it to leave their personal and private preferences and attachments at the door, the public aspect of conduct concerns the standing of individuals both in relation to one another and the state, but not their entire personality, nor other kinds of ethical commitment, whether to family, religion, business, and so on. A practical ethic of freedom, in other words, goes along with an ethical pluralism, as well as a clearly made differentiation between public and private life. Not only is such an ethic entirely irreconcilable with the twentieth century totalitarianisms, it is also irreconcilable with any exercise of state power that denies the standing of those subject to it as free beings. Finally, the account I offer of how the early modern idea of sovereign power can be further developed to accommodate and respond to the rise of the social returns us to the idea of the public domain that is not to be thought of as analogous to a household, but is constructed in terms of the immanent requirements of sovereign rule. This domain obviously has to be resourced, and it is here we find the case for both public ownership and a progressive taxation system.

[61] Here it is important to remember that this discussion is one of *ideas*. In historical practice, the case for public education that found its way into public policy was an uneasy coming together of different arguments, only one of which concerns how education is necessary if people are to enjoy the status of a free being.

[62] 'The fact of being positioned in an involuntary relationship to a human service does not disqualify the individual from being considered a client of this service', see D Gursansky and A Yeatman, 'Are Prisoners Clients? The Individualisation of Public Correctional Services' in A Yeatman with G Dowsett, M Fine, and D Gursansky *Individualisation and the Delivery of Welfare Services: Contestation and Complexity* (Basingstoke, Palgrave Macmillan, 2009) 235.

[63] John Braithwaite's regulation pyramid is a good example. He and his team developed this in considering how to bring nursing home operators within the spirit as well as the letter of the policy and the legislation that governed nursing homes in Australia. Clearly how nursing home clients are treated by the staff is an excellent example of whether the status of a free being is sustained in a context where the former are deeply dependent on the latter for not just their quality of life but their survival. For this approach, see J Braithwaite 'The Essence of Responsive Regulation' (2011) 475 44 *University of British Columbia Law Review* 475.

If I understand his argument correctly, Loughlin's *riposte* to this alternative account of the rise of the social and its implications for the juridical conception of the state would go something like this: Indeed it is true that the rise of the social means that a legally constituted sphere of private transactional conduct cannot be thought of as self-regulating. Instead its many inadequacies place demands on government, but these are demands for government regulation. Regulation is an inherently administrative rather than juridical activity:

> [T]he rise of civil society does not lead to the decline of government. Since the workings of markets and individual action possess the power to destroy as well as create, such operations stand in need of regulation by government. For government to realise these responsibilities, an extensive administrative apparatus is needed: the modern state becomes an administrative state.[64]

From this point of view, Loughlin might say, it does not really matter whether the conception of political right is more liberal than early modern. The essential point is that the idea of political right as the ethical foundation of public law has as its ground some notion of what it is to live as a free being, and in a community or society of free beings. The idea of liberty before *or* after liberalism is implicated in the conception of law as the modality of rule. To this conception belongs the entire 'constitutionalist' family of concepts: separation of powers, representative and responsible government, judicial review, and a clear public/private distinction. His argument is that this juridical conception of the state as the embodiment of political right has been overtaken by an entirely different conception of the state thought of as the management of the social, which returns in force the idea of the state as a public version of the *oikos*/household economy.[65]

Loughlin traces this alternative conception of the state to eighteenth century Cameralist thought and its science of police.[66] Here the state is thought of in terms of a household economy where the task is good economic management on behalf of the members of the household. State administration then is thought of in terms of the functional requirements of such management. The protection of the economic interests of the state is inseparable from the tasks of maintaining social order, regulating the national population, and socialising the subjects of the state into normalised behaviour of a kind that a well-ordered and prosperous state depends on. In this frame of reference, state administration is expressed as the power of regulation, and with the extension of governmental power understood in the eighteenth century sense as police power, regulatory power extends its tentacles over social life. The *potentia* of the state grows and has very little to do now with the *potestas* of the state, for the justificatory criteria for the exercise of state power are functional in nature and reference is made to liberty or freedom only to the extent this is required within a functionalist conception of social order and wealth generation. In other words, a socio-economic functionalism displaces the idea of political right.

Loughlin's real concern is late twentieth century extensions of the regulatory power of the state and of this functionalist approach to state power. It is from this perspective that Loughlin discusses 'bureaucracy' as the bearer of regulatory administrative power. He does

[64] *Foundations* (n 8) 435.

[65] In Oakeshott's binary conception of the state as either *societas* or *universitas*, this is the state as *universitas*, as a community of purpose.

[66] *Foundations* (n 8) Ch 14.

not consider the ethical nature of bureaucratic public office framed in terms of the idea of political right. Instead he generalises the term 'bureaucracy' to cover what du Gay would call post-bureaucratic as well as classical-bureaucratic phenomena.[67] A more nuanced and historically specific account of the trajectory of modern state bureaucracy is lost. We also lose the possibility that the administrative state may be made adequate to a juridical perspective as intended by various approaches to 'administrative reform' in the twentieth century.[68]

Loughlin argues that 'the disciplinary mechanisms of police' now extend to the central questions of government:

> fiscal rules devised in the regulatory framework discipline ministers, monetary policies laid down by central banks constrain governments, audit regulations structure the programmes of public bodies, and performance targets established through these arrangements structure the ways in which they undertake their responsibilities.[69]

An entire new army of public and private, national and international regulatory agencies and consultants to such agencies are involved in the administration of these disciplinary mechanisms. In this context, law is reconceived as 'a set of techniques—signalled through statutes, regulations, and enforcement policies—which are designed to realise certain practical objectives'.[70] The essential criterion of legal instruments is their functional value. Loughlin gloomily concludes:

> All governing bodies now claim their authority not from some original conferral of jurisdiction but from their ability effectively to discharge public (ie social) tasks. This undermines the public/private distinction: if government is conceived as forming an elaborate network geared to the realisation of social objectives, then once those objectives are adequately specified the mode of delivery is determined by the metric of efficiency and effectiveness, and this is likely to involve a mix of private and public agencies. The public/private distinction ceases to be one of clear institutional specification. It is the concept of the social that now seems to determine regulatory objectives and to shape the variety of techniques (some public, some private) required to ensure their realisation. Once the network metaphor is set in place, the foundational elements of public law need to be reconsidered. The triumph of objective social law would signal an overcoming of the tensions between *potestas* and *potentia*, and mark the destruction of the modern edifice of public law.[71]

Moreover, those who determine the substance of what counts as social objectives can do so as though the early modern political settlement never happened. They do not have to be aware that their determination is necessarily driven by their subjective valuation or belief,

[67] Du Gay (n 59).

[68] For example, in the Australian context, P Wilenski 'Administrative Reform—General Principles and the Australian Experience' (1986) 64 *Public Administration* 3, 257–76; G Hawker, *Who's Master, Who's Servant? Reforming Bureaucracy* (Sydney, George Allen & Unwin, 1981). More generally, A Yeatman, 'Democratisation and the Administrative State' in *Bureaucrats, Technocrats, Femocrats: Essays on the Contemporary Australian State* (Sydney, Allen & Unwin, 1990) 36–61; and W Wirth, 'Responding to Citizens' Needs: From Bureaucratic Accountability to Individual Coproduction in the Public Sector' in FX Kaufmann (ed), *The Public Sector: Challenge for Coordination and Learning* (Berlin, Walter de Gruyter, 1991) 69–87.

[69] *Foundations* (n 8) 452.

[70] *Foundations* (n 8) 457.

[71] *Foundations* (n 8) 462.

nor that public law was 'founded not only on the drawing of a distinction between the political and the social, but also between the discourses of public reason and religious truth':

> As its early-modern founders fully appreciated the most basic purpose of public law was that of maintaining the civil peace against a backcloth of (often violent) competing truths. Public law is born of a compromise effected between antagonists who cannot defeat one another and it is in this sense that it becomes 'the organising schema of a de jure fragmented public space assuring unresolvable confrontation'.[72]

V. Conclusion

Loughlin's melancholic and pessimistic conclusion as to the current fate of public law sustains the conventional narrative to which I referred at the beginning of this article. I have argued that this narrative is driven by essentially liberal-conservative presuppositions where it is impossible to reconcile the rise of the social with the idea of law. Since the rise of the social is inexorable, this position requires us to adopt a view that is generally biased against the state in its late-modern incarnation(s). I have argued also that this view is not just insufficiently nuanced, but that it represses the knowledge that Loughlin most certainly has of a conception of freedom as the ground of political-juridical authority that is not liberal, but early modern. It is this early modern idea of freedom as immanent within sovereign power that permits an alternative account of the challenges that the rise of the social poses for the state thought of in Hegelian terms as ethical life: as both the system of public office *and* political society. In the suggestions I have offered as to how this alternative approach might work, I have sought to suggest an evaluative criterion by which we can distinguish when the state's responses to the rise of the social are congruent with the early modern understanding of the conditions of being free and when they are not. I have suggested that on this approach, regulation and juridical modes of state agency do not have to be thought of as in opposition but that on the contrary they can be thought of as complementary approaches, where one is able to do what the other cannot. Human rights, understood on this approach as the most recent iteration of the idea of the status of a free being, can be viewed as a late modern expression of political right to which both regulation and juridical modes of agency are to be held to account.[73]

[72] *Foundations* (n 8) 465 citing M Gauchet, *The Disenchantment of the World: A Political History of Religion* (Princeton, Princeton University Press, 1997) 192.

[73] For a suggestive discussion of New Zealand Chief Justice Sian Elias's view of this set of relationships, see G Cartier, 'A Simple Common Lawyer: Essays in Honour of Michael Taggart' (edited by D Dyzenhaus, M Hunt, and G Huscroft) (2014) 64 *University of Toronto Law Journal* 301–02.

9

Foundations of Public Law and Postnational Constitutionalism

NEIL WALKER

I. Introduction

Both in *Foundations of Public Law*[1] and at greater length in subsequent writings,[2] Martin Loughlin makes no secret of his scepticism towards a strain of thinking that understands fundamental legal and political authority as having shifted away from the state towards postnational sites and mechanisms. Loughlin is far from being in denial about the increasing density of regulatory structures that cross state boundaries, whether in the classic historical medium of public international law, or along the many and varied other private, public and hybrid channels of transnational and global law.[3] Yet he resists efforts to view these developments as sounding at the deepest level of legal and political authority, and so as implying a new 'pluralism of foundations'[4] in which other independent sources and containers of authority join the state in a new global multiverse.

In a nutshell, Loughlin's objection to this new strain of thinking is two-fold. On the one hand, he claims that the postnationalists do not supply the evidence to substantiate their perception of a new or emerging diversity of foundations. On the other hand, Loughlin claims that although the burden should lie on the postnationalists, as self-appointed heralds of 'the new', to build upon their diagnosis of deep structural change by offering a coherent or developed account of a 'sustainable future state'[5] of globally extended political forms and relations, they fail to discharge that burden. These are large claims. They are developed in a typically rigorous fashion, but also with a degree of confident assertion that both reflects the continuing polarisation of views on these questions between statists and

[1] M Loughlin, *Foundations of Public Law* (Oxford, Oxford University Press, 2010) [hereafter Foundations] especially Ch 15.

[2] See, eg his 'Constitutional Pluralism: An Oxymoron? (2014) 3 *Global Constitutionalism* 1–30; see also 'A-legality or *Jus Politicum?* A Critical Appraisal of Lindahl's 'Fault lines of Globalisation' (2014) 2 *Ethics and Politics* 965–72.

[3] For an extended discussion, see, eg N Walker, *Intimations of Global Law* (Cambridge, Cambridge University Press, 2015) especially Ch 3.

[4] Loughlin, 'Constitutional Pluralism' (n 2) 29.

[5] Loughlin, 'Constitutional Pluralism' (n 2) 29.

postnationalists, and, because Loughlin himself is such an influential and persuasive voice in contemporary constitutional theory, in some measure reinforces that polarisation.

The matters at stake here are large and important, and I cannot hope to do anything like full justice to them in a short chapter. I do however, want to uncover and, in turn, question some of the deep and often hardly articulated assumptions that lie behind the claims and arguments of Loughlin, and of others who walk in his path. My purpose in so doing, even though we *do* disagree on these matters, is certainly not to try to 'prove' Loughlin wrong. That ambition, indeed, would rather defeat a different and more modest purpose. For in signaling my disagreement, I want instead to stress that there are no certainties in this debate *on either side*, no unquestionable (as opposed to unquestioned) axioms or undeniable premises, and I venture to suggest that a little more acknowledgment of that all-round might fuel a more constructive exchange. I seek, if you like, to be somewhat sceptical of the security of the premises and deep argumentative structure that sustain Loughlin's own postnational constitutional scepticism, and in so doing encourage a more ecumenical perspective to a set of questions that surely challenges all faiths.

II. What Would Count as Evidence of an Underlying Shift?

In his formulation of the idea of *droit politique* or 'political jurisprudence',[6] Loughlin paints a memorably rich picture of the *épistème* or social imaginary through which the idea and practice of the modern state is formed and sustained. For Loughlin, the modern state is neither the agent of some distinct and higher authority, whether this authority be religious or otherwise metaphysical, or capital 'C' Constitutional in the positive doctrinal (and typically also Constitutional-documentary) sense, nor is it merely the expression and fruit of a prior cultural achievement—an accomplishment of national solidarity which supplies the 'battery of power'[7] necessary to run the constitutional machine effectively. Rather, the modern state embraces 'a scheme of intelligibility […] a comprehensive way of seeing, understanding and acting in the world'[8] through which peoplehood and positive law are mutually and reflexively constructed and reconstructed over time.

But why, according to Loughlin, does the state thus conceived nevertheless remain a distinctively *juristic* idea? It does so because and inasmuch as (1) its sovereign authority can only ever be expressed and secured in legal-institutional form, through the vesting of a superordinate legal power in the state and its offices of government, and (2) the medium of everyday governmental power is primarily one of legal authority. There can, in other words, be no positive law that stands above and prior to the state and the realm of the political, but equally, there can be no articulation and no operationalisation of the state and of the political *qua* political other than through and in the form of positive law. (Public) law in this deeper, pre-positive sense of *droit politique*, then, is neither the master nor the servant of politics. That is a false choice, albeit a common one that we find reflected in and re-fuelled

[6] See ch 1, by Michael A Wilkinson and Michael W Dowdle, of this volume.

[7] M Canovan, *Nationhood and Political Theory* (Cheltenham, Edward Elgar, 1996) 80.

[8] See M Loughlin, 'In Defence of *Staatslehre*' (2009) 48 *Der Staat* 1–28, 8.

by the incessant debate in constitutional theory between law-favouring 'normativists' and politics-favouring 'decisionists'.[9] Rather, for Loughlin, public law *is* politics, at least politics as understood in its generative rather than its everyday programmatic mode; or, if you prefer, politics conceived of as *le politique* rather than *la politique*.[10]

Vitally, this notion of a pre-positive and pre-programmatic-political modality of *droit politique* is necessary to frame and grasp the basic idea of a domain of practice that is autonomously and generally political, and, indeed, a domain that may be considered political in the full and distinctively modern sense only and precisely *because* it is autonomous of other social forces and is general and open-ended in its purported remit. This domain, which is independent of any pre-given belief system or metaphysical claim, or of the unmediated direction of any particular person, group of persons or even of 'the people' understood as a non-disaggregable whole, is constitutive of rather than constituted through positive constitutional law—limited only by and in its own terms. For Loughlin, it is through the notion of the autonomy and generality of the political, thus secured, that we come to understand the distinctive contribution of the modern state, considered as a system of secular self-rule involving an exclusive relationship of territory, ruling authority and people. Furthermore, it is only through that notion of the autonomy and generality of the political that we can appreciate the distinctive contribution of politics (now also incorporating its everyday programmatic sense as the means of negotiating and preserving 'civil peace' in the face of competing truths) as the energising current of that system.

There is much here that is persuasive, and much that I am persuaded by. In particular, if our focus is the state, as, understandably enough, it has been for much constitutional theory of the extended modern age, then Loughlin does offer an insightful way of avoiding many of the repetitive sterilities of the normativism *versus* decisionism—law *versus* politics debate. Yet just as Loughlin's framework serves well this one large and largely historically-directed purpose, it may do a disservice to another. For all its suggestiveness and insight into the conditions of possibility and consolidation of the Western conception of the polity over the expanse of political modernity, such a holistic understanding of the trinity of state-law-political is also stacked against any attempt to come fully to terms with the emergence of postnational forms of authority which might challenge its dominant standing. This is so because, while Loughlin—not surprisingly and apparently not unreasonably—asks us to demonstrate rather than simply to assert any deep postnational shift, it remains unclear how, in his own theoretically self-contained terms, any such demonstration would ever be possible.

In part, the problem is an epistemological one. The very way in which Loughlin conceives of the modern political realm seems to preclude or discount evidence of any emergent alternatives or supplements. If positive legal-institutional forms and developments are understood only as surface phenomena, dependent upon and developed in accordance with an underlying way of political knowing and being, then changes at this legal-institutional

[9] This is a distinction developed by Loughlin in 'The Concept of Constituent Power' (2014) 13 *European Journal of Political Theory* 218–37; see further, N Walker, 'The Return of Constituent Power: A Reply to Matthias Kumm' (2016) 14 *International Journal of Constitutional Law* 906–13.

[10] A distinction closely associated with the work of Claude Lefort; for illuminating discussion, see D Steinmetz-Jenkins, 'Claude Lefort and the Illegitimacy of Modernity' (2009) 10 *Journal for Cultural and Religious Theory* 102–17.

level, however densely registered, can never offer direct evidence of an underlying transformation. At best they can offer hints, marks and traces,[11] but to the extent that this might indicate a shift at the deeper level of the social and political imaginary, just because any such deeper shift occurs in our *pre-empirical* 'scheme of intelligibility'—in the very *framing* of the social and political world, and not just in the institutional picture so *framed* and revealed—evidence of it will remain elusive and indirect. Instead, there is a kind of 'settlement bias' in favour of the established frame and its familiar manifestations, even when we are confronted with new types of legal-institutional evidence. If, for example, we are looking at the European Union, or the World Trade Organisation, or the international human rights system, or any other significant international or postnational regulatory form, the temptation is to treat its emergence and evolution as continuous with and interwoven with the already available deep frame and narrative of state-centred *droit politique*, and so by reference to tried and tested notions internal to that deep state-centred frame and narrative, rather than to understand it as the mark of an incipient new imaginary. These tried and tested state-centred notions would include the *delegation* of state governmental functions, or the *demarcation* and separation of matters of expertise of technical administration from state-centred political prerogatives, or the domestic *incorporation* of transnational or international norms and their reduction to national norms.[12]

Reflecting on his own work, Loughlin is not unaware of the kind of epistemological challenge his kind of approach poses.[13] He tells us that he is engaged neither in ideal theory—seeking to elaborate 'the structure of some ideal constitution',[14] nor in a closely observed comparative historical and contemporary inquiry into 'the detailed arrangements of particular regimes'.[15] Instead, his method offers a kind of stylised reconstruction, a simultaneously deep and encompassing account of a dominant conception of state-building and state-maintaining that allows us better 'to understand the ways in which existing constitutional arrangements can be said to work'.[16] Loughlin, therefore, acknowledges the difficulty of accessing the kind of deep interpretive understanding he is interested in, and turns to a form of 'ideal type' approach in which the abstract and the concrete—the deep and the surface—operate through a process of mutual corroboration. That is to say, the extensive range of application of the deep statist template he seeks to depict is certified by the reiterated expression of what he posits as its various stylised general characteristics—Governing, Politics, Representation, Sovereignty, Constituent Power, Rights, etc[17] in various particular

[11] The idea of the 'marks' of sovereignty is famously developed by J Bodin, *The Six Books of a Commonweale* [1576: translated by R Knolles 1606] (Cambridge, Harvard University Press, 1962) Book 1, Ch 1. See further D Baranger, 'The Apparition of Sovereignty' in H Kalmo and Q Skinner (eds), *Sovereignty in Fragments: The Past, Present and Future of a Contested Concept* (Cambridge, Cambridge University Press, 2010) 47–63; N Walker, 'Sovereignty Frames and Sovereignty Claims in R Rawlings, P Leyland and A Young (eds), *Sovereignty and the Law: Domestic, European and International Perspectives* (Oxford, Oxford University Press, 2013) 18–33.

[12] For discussion see, eg N Walker, 'Surface and Depth: The EU's Resilient Sovereignty Question' in J Neyer and A Wiener (eds), *Political Theory and the European Union* (Oxford, Oxford University Press, 2010) 91–110.

[13] M Loughlin, 'Reflection on *The Idea of Public Law*' in E Christodoulidis and S Tierney (eds), *Public Law and Politics: The Scope and Limits of Constitutionalism* (London, Ashgate, 2008) 47–65.

[14] ibid 50.

[15] ibid 49.

[16] ibid 49.

[17] These six themes being the headings of chapters 2–7 of Loughlin's, *The Idea of Public Law* (Oxford, Oxford University Press, 2004).

forms in many state locations over the significant timescale of high modernity, which in its impressively dense and expansive record of reiteration in turn reinforces the notion of a resilient common general template behind such diverse expressions.

But it is precisely this kind of mutual corroboration and reinforcement that feeds the settlement bias. Absent a deeply embedded reinforcing pattern of deep imaginary and surface form, of abstract and concrete, of framing and framed, in the form exemplified by Loughlin's understanding of the elements of a state-centred political modernity, then the methodology of discovery he adheres to cannot work. There is no way, in other words, to capture any emergent rather than embedded framing template which might be more adequate to novel surface legal-institutional forms, precisely because it *is* only emergent, and there is no pre-established genus of the political imaginary to which it can refer and through which the cycle of mutual corroboration can 'take off'. To illustrate this point, we need only revisit the example of the European Union. We may note, and find telling, the still widespread tendency to characterise the EU either—as already indicated—as a state-emanated delegation or confederation at one extreme, or as a kind of state-in-waiting at the other, and so in either case as still conforming to a state-centred template, and to criticise attempts at a 'third way' analysis as simply unimaginable, or as inadequately imagined.[18]

Behind the epistemological and methodological problem of relevant forms of knowledge, and of access to these, lies the deeper question of the nature of Loughlin's ontological claims, and how these further militate against serious contemplation of alternatives. For it is not just the historically resilient dominance of the state-centred paradigm of *droit politique* within its own terms of reference that screens out alternative ways of knowing in Loughlin's perspective, but the expansive range and shape of these very terms of reference. According to Loughlin, the framing of the autonomy of the political through the mechanism of a pre-positive public law inherits and adapts through a process of 'secularisation, historicisation and positivisation',[19] some of the core assumptions of earlier conceptions of natural law. In particular, it retains and sustains from religious and non-religious imaginings of a natural order of things the very idea of a level and genus of law that is framing rather than framed, and that supplies an irreducible basis and encompassing framework for the organisation of social life.

To put it (too) bluntly, just as the state may be understood as having filled a 'God-shaped hole' in modern life, so Loughlin cannot take seriously any reading of the contemporary age that is alternative or supplementary to his own unless it can fill or repair a 'state-shaped hole'. That is to say, if the state's claimed achievement has been to provide a general self-norming framework within which both the terms and the extent to which we put things publicly and politically in common are secured and generated, then it is difficult if not impossible to see how any alternative or additional frame can contribute, *since that claim is by its very nature monopolistic.* Either any specific state-shaped hole is filled by a new state order—the authority of any particular species of the state genus dependent upon and vulnerable before 'a set of beliefs held by its subjects about that government's authority to rule',[20] or the specific state order in question continues. There is no scope, in other words,

[18] For a particularly robust recent critique of 'third way' analysis of the EU, see R Schütze, *European Constitutional Law*, 2nd edn (Cambridge, Cambridge University Press, 2015).

[19] Loughlin (n 8) 5.

[20] Loughlin, 'Constitutional Pluralism' (n 2) 19.

for a form of authority, by its nature monopolistic and categorical, to be supplemented from the outside (rather than ran on its own terms) by some quite different genus of authority.

III. On Whom Lies the Burden to Imagine and Chart the Future?

If Loughlin's analysis of the past and present is strongly conditioned by his ontological claims about the nature of modernity and his accompanying epistemological lens and methodological approach, what of the future?

In an insightful essay, Mattias Kumm has divided the world of constitutional theory in contemplation of globalisation into those who are 'nostalgic' about a disappearing state-centred past or present, and those who are 'triumphalist' about the spread of constitutional mechanisms and values into a previously anarchic international society.[21] He counsels against both attitudes. The nostalgists are guilty either of fatalistic resignation if they believe the eleventh hour has come and gone, or of complacency or wishful thinking if they believe that a state-centred political architecture remains fully or largely adequate to contemporary circumstances. Equally, the triumphalists are guilty of naivety, and, indeed, of hubris, if they believe that the mere spread of constitutional and similarly dignifying labels to transnational contexts can ensure that the hard-won goods of the state-centred polity can be seamlessly transferred to postnational sites and contexts.

I tend to agree with this double-edged warning.[22] There is surely no room for complacency or wishful thinking, or their opposites, on either side. Equally unproductive, and insidious, is an accompanying, and mutually inciting and reinforcing, intellectual politics of rhetorical deflection. The postnationalists can stray into the territory of lampooning the statists for their obdurate belief in the centrality of the state, in so doing deflecting attention from their own unanswered questions. Equally, the statists can caricature the postnationalists for their excessive and imprudent enthusiasm for 'spreading the word' beyond the state, in so doing deflecting attention from their own unanswered questions. And often accompanying these rhetorical deflections one finds quasi-empirical diagnostic claims. These tend to be presented as self-evident on either side, but they cannot both be right. For they involve sharp and significant disagreement about the present condition of the world, and in particular, how far and how reversibly political power and authority has migrated beyond the state.

We are all offenders in this regard, and Loughlin is far from being the worst, but he does sometime fall into the trap of rhetorical deflection. On the one hand, in line with his general scepticism about the credentials of any existing counter-currents to a state-centred understanding of political right, he is critical of the more projective efforts to re-think public law

[21] M Kumm, 'The Best of Times and the Worst of Times: Between Constitutional Triumphalism and Nostalgia' in P Dobner and M Loughlin (eds), *The Twilight of Constitutionalism* (Oxford, Oxford University Press, 2010) 201–19.

[22] For a developed view, see N Walker, *Intimations of Global Law* (Cambridge, Cambridge University Press, 2015) Ch 6.

beyond the state. In particular, he is wary of the universalising or epistocratic tendencies in global constitutional law, global administrative law, global human rights and other such discourses that encourage us further 'down the path of total liberal individualism or of total legalisation'.[23] On the other hand, he chastises constitutional pluralists and others for 'pretend(ing) that we have already reached … a condition in which the collective association [ie the state] which possesses ultimate political authority no longer presents itself as a unitary entity able to take extreme collective action whenever its way of life is threatened'; and criticises them for, thereby, 'refus(ing) to engage in serious political or legal action'.[24]

Just as no site has a monopoly of political authority, it seems to me that no one has a monopoly of 'seriousness' on these matters. The world today is faced with collective action problems and opportunities which are typically both the (at least partial) product of state actions in aggregation and incapable of appropriate address and pursuit unless through deeper form of concert. Whether we are dealing with climate change, or global pandemics, or transnational security, or the conduct of trade, or the alleviation of poverty, or water shortage, or the operation of the internet, our optimal means of deciding these matters in common will not necessarily always involve individual states retaining veto rights, or states alone having rights of decisional input, but may also involve other regional or global bodies. This proviso may well still be compatible with a sovereign state's right to defend its collective way of life in the last analysis, as Loughlin requires, but it will nevertheless involve some adaptive work of political imagination as well as institutional design. For such a defence of sovereign right should mean neither that the ruling elite of any state can assert a right of non-intervention against external forces simply because they *claim* to defend a collective way of life in their state if in fact they are subjecting their own people to humanitarian distress;[25] nor, more broadly, that other forms and modes of political authority should not prevail (a) when the defence of a collective way of life of one state would ultimately undermine the collective way of life of *all* states, and so involves a performative contradiction (as eg in climate change acceleration), or (b) in those many other spheres of transnational collective action where existential state interests are *not* at stake.

My point is a simple one. The idea of the state, as Martin Loughlin's historical work often brilliantly reveals, remains one of the imaginative achievements of the modern age—albeit always a mixed blessing. Loughlin is right to castigate those who, in witnessing some seepage of legal and political authority away from the state, would encourage or allow the baby to be thrown out with the bathwater without any clear sense of what should be put in its place and how. By the same token, the onus rests on all serious analysts, from either side of the debate and regardless of their orientating preferences, to engage with the pressing question of the imagination and justification of authority in ways that supplement the authority of states conceived of merely discretely and aggregately.[26] That others sometimes fail to take the state seriously enough as a key continuing actor in global politics, and therefore do not frame that question as soberly or acutely as they should, does not exempt any of us from that wider task.

[23] Loughlin, 'Constitutional Pluralism' (n 2) 29; see further *Foundations* (n 1) 461–65.

[24] Loughlin, 'Constitutional Pluralism' (n 2) 30.

[25] See, eg R Dworkin, 'A New Philosophy for International Law' (2013) 41 *Philosophy and Public Affairs* 2–30.

[26] For my own recent attempt along these lines, see N Walker, 'Constitutional Pluralism Revisited' (2016) 23 *European Law Journal* 333–55.

Part IV

The Material Critique

10

Putting Public Law in its Place: State-Theoretical Comments on *Foundations of Public Law*

BOB JESSOP

I. Introduction

The German nihilist philosopher, Friedrich Nietzsche, declared that '[a]ll concepts in which an entire process is semiotically concentrated defy definition; only something which has no history can be defined'.[1] This certainly holds for the moving target comprised by states, the interstate system, and public law.[2] The problem is compounded when the moving target or shifting referent is essentially contested, ie raises important theoretical and normative questions that divide scholars and social and political agents. This calls for a comparative, historical and dynamic analysis of the state and state power that is sensitive to its contested nature. Martin Loughlin offers such an analysis in his magnum opus on sovereignty, the modern state, and state power when he takes the foundational nature of public law as the reference point, unifying discourse, and integrative practice of the state.[3] As Wilkinson and Dowdle explain: *Foundations* 'offers a thorough reworking of the study of public law, converting it into a wide-ranging, interdisciplinary investigation into the foundational elements and evolutionary character of the modern state'.[4] This is the aspect of this intensely rich and provocative text that I will explore in the present contribution.

Continuing changes in state forms and functions explain the many alternative definitions of the modern state, often qualified by different adjectival descriptors: administrative state, constitutional state, cooperative state, democratic state, national state, nation-state, network state, patriarchal state, security state, tax state, transnational state, welfare state, and so on. These semantic and substantive issues arise even before we consider other ways of periodising or classifying states and political regimes than the simplistic traditional-modern distinction.

[1] FW Nietzsche, *The Genealogy of Morals: A Polemic* (Cambridge, Cambridge University Press, 1994) 53.

[2] G Duso, *La logica del potere. Storia dei concetti come filosofia politica* (Monza, Polimetrica International Scientific Publisher, 2007) 20–25.

[3] M Loughlin, *Foundations of Public Law* (Oxford, Oxford University Press, 2010) [hereafter *Foundations*].

[4] See 'Introduction', in Ch 1 of this volume.

In commenting on Martin Loughlin's work, I proceed in five steps. First, I identify seven significant analytical approaches to the state and identify the mix of five such approaches that Loughlin uses to develop his argument. This invites the questions whether these are combined in a consistent way or, at least, are complementary, illuminating their respective blind-spots, and whether the missing approaches are significant (section II). Second, I evaluate the role of conceptual history in his approach, compare it with pragmatic conceptual history and historical semantics, and ask how Loughlin accounts for the genealogy, reception, and effectivity of theological, political, and legal theory—three themes that run throughout his book. This invites us to consider the broader limitations of a conceptual historical approach (section III). Third, I problematise the 'three-element' tradition of *allgemeine Staatslehre* (general state theory) and show how *Foundations* extends this by effectively introducing a fourth element, namely, the state idea, with all four combining to produce a 'state effect' through practices of governmentality (section IV). Fourth, I consider whether public law is *the* foundation of the sovereign state as opposed to one among several self-descriptions of the political system and whether public law as such can provide the unifying principle or material foundation of state action or is just one factor among several around which struggles for such unity occur. Answering these questions requires putting public law in its place alongside other aspects or dimensions of the state and in particular alongside the substantive crisis mechanisms of the state (section V). The chapter ends with some general comments and direct questions on Loughlin's work that suggest a research agenda rather than offer firm conclusions (section VI).

II. Seven Approaches to the Analysis of the State

The state is a polymorphous institutional ensemble and different approaches are better positioned to reveal different aspects. Accordingly, I outline seven approaches to states and state power that, if combined to exploit their respective strengths, might offer a powerful heuristic for addressing these complexities. Each perspective has its specific blind-spot, which prevents us from seeing what we cannot see with it. This supports a non-eclectic pluralism in analysing the state and requires a careful choice of entry-points and standpoints for specific theoretical and/or practical purposes.

First, some study the 'historical constitution' of states in terms of path-dependent histories or genealogies of individual parts of states in different periods. This approach bears comparison to the historical analysis of the 'material constitution' in legal theory, where constitution refers to juridico-political institutions rather than to state-building processes. The two perspectives share interests in genealogy and the links of their respective analytical objects (state, constitution) to wider social orders. Moving beyond genealogy, historical constitution also offers useful insights into the eventual structural couplings and co-evolution of key elements of the modern state, like a standing army, modern tax system, rational bureaucracy, rule of law, parliament, universal suffrage, citizenship rights, and recognition by other states. Building on this approach to coupling and co-evolution, one might ask what, if anything, unifies these elements. Loughlin, for one, suggests that public law can provide such a unifying and integrating principle in state formation.

Second, one can investigate the state's 'formal constitution', that is, its nature as a distinctive form of social relations that is differentiated from other social forms. Whereas analysing the historical constitution involves a diachronic approach, a more synchronic one is used for the formal constitution. The key issue here is the complementarity (sometimes even isomorphism) among the various features of a given state form or political regime. This approach is more suited to the modern state in so far as it is institutionally differentiated rather than embedded in, or intertwined with, a more complex societal order. It offers accounts, for example, of how the modern state gets formally separated (disembedded) from other spheres of society (notably, as Loughlin shows, religion and the church), how it gains its own political rationale (*raison d'état*) and *modus operandi* (framed, for Loughlin, by public law) and how it lays claim to a distinctive constitutional legitimation based on adherence to its own political procedures rather than on values such as divine right or natural law.

Third, diverse 'institutionalist analyses' argue that 'institutions matter'. Institution here sometimes refers to social institutions in a general sociological sense (eg, family, language, law, money, and statehood); sometimes it denotes specific organisations or social bodies that have major significance for the wider society and can act in a quasi-corporate manner—and may, indeed, be established by the constitution or public law. The latter usage applies to institutions such as the executive, legislative, and judicial branches of government or central banks, the armed forces, or established religious faiths. A key issue, especially for Loughlin's text, is the relevance of constructivist, discursive, or ideational institutionalism alongside an interest in the path-dependent history of legal institutions and the scope for path-shaping or even revolutionary breaks in specific periods or conjunctures.

Fourth, 'agent-centred institutionalism' studies how social forces make history—their own and that of others—in specific institutional contexts and whether this occurs in a top-down, bottom-up or hybrid fashion. Such work explores specific institutional arrangements in terms of the asymmetrical opportunities they offer to various kinds of complex actors (rather than some abstract individual) to make a difference to social development. They focus on actors' interests, identities, dispositions, and resources in specific conjunctures and on different kinds of interaction (eg, negotiation, multi-level decision-making, or hierarchical command). They consider the emergent logics and dynamics of different institutional orders or social fields, including multi-level, multi-site interactions, or multi-spatial arenas.

Fifth, 'figurational studies' focus on 'state-civil society' relations broadly interpreted and locate state formation within wider historical developments such as bureaucratic empires,[5] the *longue durée* dynamics of state and civilisation,[6] European state formation over half a century,[7] the history of government,[8] and state formation seen in terms of the changing weight of four sources of social power.[9]

[5] S Eisenstadt, *The Political Systems of Empires: The Rise and Fall of Bureaucratic Societies* (New York, Free Press, 1963).

[6] N Elias, *The Civilizing Process: State Formation and Civilization* [1939] (Oxford, Blackwell, 1982).

[7] P Flora (ed), *State-Formation, Nation-Building And Mass Politics in Europe: The Theory of Stein Rokkan* (Oxford, Oxford University Press, 1999).

[8] S Finer, *The History of Government 3 Volumes* (Oxford, Oxford University Press, 1997).

[9] M Mann, *The Social Sources of Power* (Cambridge, Cambridge University Press, 1986).

Sixth, inspired by Michel Foucault, his followers, and more general critical governance studies, there are diverse studies of the production of the 'state effect' through various practices oriented to governmentality, governance, and meta-governance. Foucauldian scholarship examines the state in terms of dispositives (apparatuses) and discourses and their role in the strategic codification of power relations. This is reflected in important studies of specific governmental discourses, technologies, and disciplines such as cameralistics, public administration, public law, public security, statistics, and diverse policy sciences.[10]

Seventh, 'historical semantics' (including conceptual history and critical discourse analysis) is used to analyse the emergence of the 'state idea', including state doctrines, the consolidation of the state concept (and cognate terminology) in the early modern period, the spread of the state idea from Western Europe, and the diverse political imaginaries, state projects, and hegemonic visions that shape the contest for state power within and beyond the state.[11] Broad economic and political visions as well as specific policy paradigms are relevant here and are linked to the wide diversity of state forms.

Viewing this list, we can see that Loughlin focuses on five of the seven approaches in his analysis of the foundations of public law, albeit to different extents and, as expected, for different purposes: historical constitution; formal constitution (oriented to the role of public law in providing an overarching unity to the three components of the state identified in *allgemeine Staatslehre*); institutional analysis (regarding the constitutional and institutional architecture of the modern state); figurational studies, for the pre-modern as well as modern period; and historical semantics (especially conceptual historical, history of ideas, and political and legal theory). This raises issues about the overall consistency of the resulting analysis, as well as the marginalised perspectives of agent-centred institutionalism and critical Foucauldian studies of power relations and governmentality. But I first address the issue of conceptual history (*Begriffsgeschichte*) and its adequacy as an entry-point into the study of public law and state power.

III. Conceptual History and its Limitations

The histories of states and state systems are closely connected to those of political philosophy, normative political theory, accounts of geopolitics and/or geo-economics, and theoretical inquiries into actual (inter-)state systems. All of these modes of intellection, with their different rationales and rationalities, constitute contested terrains and the results of these intellectual (and sometimes real) battles figure strongly in state formation and

[10] See, eg D Campesi, *A Genealogy of Public Security: The Theory and History of Police Powers* (London, Routledge, 2016); M Dean, *The Constitution of Poverty: Towards a Genealogy of Liberal Governance* (London, Routledge, 1990); M Foucault, *Security, Territory, Population. Lectures at the College de France* (Basingstoke, Palgrave, 2008); P Miller and N Rose, *Governing the Present: Administering Economic, Social and Personal Life* (Cambridge, Polity Press, 2008); M Neocleous, *Administering Civil Society: Towards a Theory of State Power* (Basingstoke, Macmillan, 1996); B Jessop, *State Power: A Strategic-Relational Approach* (Cambridge, Polity Press, 2007).

[11] J Bartelson, *A Genealogy of Sovereignty* (Cambridge, Cambridge University Press, 1995); M Neocleous, *Imagining the State* (Maidenhead, Open University Press, 2003); Q Skinner, 'State' in T Ball, J Farr and R Hanson (eds), *Political Innovation and Conceptual Change* (Cambridge University Press, 1989); P Steinberger, *The Idea of the State* (Cambridge, Cambridge University Press, 2004).

transformation. Indeed, state authorities are rarely, if ever, indifferent to political philosophies, political theories, and state theories, or their organic intellectuals, other supporters, and institutional bases of support. They encourage strategy- and policy-based normative and theoretical legitimations and evidence and seek to marginalise, oppress, or eliminate unwanted voices. Conversely, changes in state forms and functions and inter-state relations have prompted shifts in the leading forms and styles of philosophical, normative, and theoretical reflection on the state. Thus, one might analyse the history of the state via its co-evolution (sometimes leading, sometimes lagging) with ideational change.

This line of inquiry is an important aspect of Loughlin's text. To show what is at stake here and how Loughlin proceeds, I distinguish *pragmatic* conceptual history (the Cambridge School), the historical *semantics* of basic concepts (German *Begriffsgeschichte*, or conceptual history, and its offshoots), and Luhmannian semantics.

The Cambridge School explores the intertextuality (or interweaving and cross-referencing) of political texts in developing political lexicons and puts them in their changing intellectual and societal context. While John Pocock focuses on the pragmatics of language use as key figures articulate a political world view within a community of language-users,[12] Quentin Skinner is more philosophical in approach, inquiring into the rules and conventions that govern rhetoric, argumentation, and discourse.[13]

On my reading of his text, Loughlin goes well beyond pragmatic conceptual history. This is one of the more exciting, if unsignalled, aspects of his work. He offers many reflections on the historical semantics of the modern state, that is, the emergence and consolidation of a specialised lexicon to describe the state. He not only traces the genealogy of specific concepts or semantic frames, but also considers their immediate reception and long-term politico-social impact.[14] He carefully explores how this semantic framework helps to constitute, consolidate, reproduce, and guide various juridico-political institutions, modes of calculation, practices, and imaginaries, whether in high politics or everyday life. In short, he examines the links between semantic change and societal transformation and their mediation through struggles over state projects. This is a key contribution of the text.

In this sense, Loughlin's work is closer to German conceptual history than Cambridge pragmatic conceptual history. The former studies the co-evolution of semantics and social structure.[15] Reinhart Koselleck, its leading figure, argued that, without concepts, there can be no society and no political field of action.[16] This approach aims to put words and concepts in their place historically as well as discursively and to show that only some

[12] JGA Pocock, 'Concepts and Discourses: A Difference in Culture' in H Lehmann and M Richter (eds), *The Meaning of Historical Terms and Concepts* (Washington DC, German Historical Institute, 1996) and *Politics, Language and Time: Essays on Political Thought and History* (New York, Atheneum, 1973).

[13] Q Skinner, *Visions of History, Vol 1: Regarding Method* (Cambridge, Cambridge University Press, 2002).

[14] *Cf* N-L Sum and B Jessop, *Towards a Cultural Political Economy: Putting Culture in its Place in Political Economy* (Cheltenham, Edward Elgar, 2013) 136–37.

[15] R Koselleck, '*Begriffsgeschichte* and Social History' (1982) 11 *Economy and Society* 409; N Luhmann, *Gesellschaftsstruktur und Semantik. Band 1* (Frankfurt, Suhrkamp, 1980); *Ideenevolution: Beiträge zur Wissenssoziologie* (Frankfurt, Suhrkamp, 2008); M Richter, 'Reconstructing the History of Political Languages: Pocock, Skinner and the *Geschichtliche Grundbegriffe*' (1990) 19 *History and Theory* 38; on differences within as well as between the two schools, see S Chignola, 'History of Political Thought and the History of Political Concepts': Koselleck's Proposal and Italian Research' (2002) 33 *History of Political Thought* 517.

[16] Koselleck, ibid 410.

concepts become foundational and what this implies for social organisation. Some concepts have strong path-shaping effects on social life and societal organisation and significantly influence collective experience, collective memory, and collective utopias. These are called *Grundbegriffe* (basic concepts) and are usually linked to *Nebenbegriffe* (neighbour, or linked, concepts) and, often, to *Gegenbegriffe* (counter-concepts). Together, these constitute contested semantic fields in which:

> all concepts have two aspects. On the one hand, they point to something external to them, to the context in which they are used. On the other hand, this reality is perceived in terms of categories provided by language. Therefore, concepts are both indicators of and factors in political and social life. Put metaphorically, concepts are like joints linking language and the extralinguistic world.[17]

Koselleck analyses this in what one might call strategic-relational terms.[18] For he interprets the process of concept formation as a shifting, discursively-mediated condensation of a changing balance of forces that are engaged in struggle on a semantic battlefield over the past, present, and future meaning of concepts, linked concepts, and counter-concepts and their interrelations. He argues that, in semantic struggles, positions must be won linguistically before specific social forces can occupy them—with different forces attempting to identify themselves with the privileged side of asymmetric concepts or else to reverse the asymmetries.[19] In short, he posits a war of semantic positioning guided by polemical concepts.[20] It follows that current semantic fields are path-dependent products of past conceptual struggles and, even when sedimented, remain open to contestation.

Fundamental concepts cannot be distinguished from other concepts in purely linguistic terms, whether lexical or semantic. They are fundamental because of their central role in organising social, especially political, discourse. They provide the minimum shared lexicon to facilitate consensus and to order conflict and do so by simplifying complex realities as a basis for 'going on' in the social world. Indeed, Koselleck notes that 'our concepts are founded in politico-social systems that are far more complex than would be indicated by treating them simply as linguistic communities organised around specific key concepts'.[21] This comment has two implications for exploring the semantic foundations of social (dis)order. First, society is not reducible to the concepts in play in one period or political conjuncture and, hence, that society cannot be modelled, or explained, purely in conceptual terms.[22] Second, there is scope for disjunctions between what can be thought and said and the complex extra-discursive realities of societal development. Accordingly, Koselleck argues that societal evolution (with all its continuities and discontinuities) occurs via the uneven, mutual constitution of conceptual and institutional development.[23]

[17] R Koselleck, 'A Response' in H Lehmann and M Richter (eds), *The Meaning of Historical Terms and Concepts: New Studies on Begriffsgeschichte* (Washington DC, German Historical Institute, 1996) 64–67, 61.

[18] On which, see Jessop (n 10).

[19] Koselleck (n 15) 413–14; *cf* R Koselleck, *Futures Past. On the Semantics of Historical Time* (Cambridge, MIT, 1985) 155–91.

[20] On wars of position, see A Gramsci, *Selections from the Prison Notebooks* (London, Lawrence and Wishart, 1971).

[21] Koselleck, *Futures Past* (n 19) 74.

[22] This claim is implicit in the work of E Laclau and C Mouffe, *Hegemony and Socialist Strategy* (London, NLB, 1985).

[23] Koselleck, *Futures Past* (n 19).

Niklas Luhmann develops this argument by referring to the three general mechanisms of evolution: variation, selection, and retention. These apply both to semantic development and structural development but also operate through different vectors and produce different effects. Moreover, just as there are limits to compossible and reproducible structural configurations, there are limits to *resonant* and *plausible* arguments in semiosis. This said, Luhmann identifies greater scope for variation in semantics than structures—suggesting that constraints on discourse are looser than those in structural fields. Semantics and structures also co-evolve in a spiral relation. While ideational changes facilitate changes in structure, structural changes open possibilities for new ideas. There is no one-to-one correlation between semantics and social structure: indeed, too tight a connection would block innovation in both. Sense- and meaning-making tend to unfold within the limits of combinability of structural and semantic evolution.[24] As societal complexity increases, greater variation and variety are required in both semantics and in structures—more specialised codes and programmes develop on the one side, more specialised functional systems and institutional orders develop on the other.

This is reflected in Loughlin's analysis of the historical semantics of the state and the increasing internal differentiation of the legal system, especially public law, which reflects a growing internal differentiation of the state and wider political system. Much of this narrative is familiar to historians of theological, political and legal theory and/or state formation. What *Foundations of Public Law* does not explain, however, is why, of the many variations of juridico-political discourse and resulting conceptual innovations, only some are reflected in (and thereby help to co-constitute) institutional innovations that help to consolidate the modern state. This is an important limitation of the analysis that Loughlin provides.

To overcome this limitation requires not only descriptions of specific theological, political, and legal theories or of constitutional and legal theory (Parts I and II of *Foundations*) but also explanations for why these specific theories were chosen (beyond their place in the relevant canon) and why, of these theories, only some proved influential in one or another historical context. Beside the genealogy of specific theories or theoretical traditions (*Entstehungsgeschichte*), which requires a focus on authorial intention and pragmatics as well as lexical and historical legacies, an adequate explanation must also address questions of the short-term reception of texts (*Rezeptionsgeschichte*). On the second requirement, as Gareth Stedman Jones notes, any good historian of ideas must go beyond an author's aims to 'give equal or greater attention to questions of intended constituency, to the different forms of appropriation of specific texts—what meanings were actually conveyed, how they were understood and interpreted?'.[25] A third issue is the long-term effectiveness of lexical and semantic innovation (*Wirkungsgeschichte*). To explain this requires attention to an even wider set of causal mechanisms and mediations. Thus, beyond pragmatic (in the linguistic sense), semantic, and other discursive factors, long-term effects are mediated via structural asymmetries, technological biases, and agential capacities.

This approach would have similarities to Foucault's archaeology of discourse and discursive formations, covering the 'general system of the formation and transformation of

[24] Luhmann (n 15) 60.

[25] GS Jones, 'The Determinist Fix: Some Obstacles to the Further Development of the Linguistic Approach to History (1996) 42 *History Workshop Journal* 19–35.

statements',[26] its role in writing 'critical and effective histories', and its analysis of discourse and dispositifs.[27] Foucault's work on governmentality is mentioned in Parts II, III, and V of *Foundations* but is not fully integrated into the overall analysis. Yet the links between discourse and dispositif should be central to an analysis of public law, the modern state, the institutions of sovereignty, and the institutional architecture of the state.[28]

As Loughlin notes early on in *Foundations*,[29] there are many disputes over the theoretical value and descriptive validity of the concept of the state.[30] Critics have therefore opted to focus their inquiries on political institutions and their performance and/or on the micro-physics of power. Neither solution to this theoretical conundrum is satisfactory. A consistent interest in politics requires attention, explicitly or implicitly, to the polity, politics, and policy.[31] The polity is the institutional matrix that creates a distinctive terrain, realm, domain, field or region of specifically political actions.[32] This is equivalent to statehood *in its inclusive sense* as explored by Antonio Gramsci in terms of 'political society + civil society' or 'hegemony protected by the armour of coercion'.[33] It has affinities with Michel Foucault's analyses of statecraft and state effects.[34] And key elements in the stability of this institutional matrix are an effective constitution and consistent body of public law.[35] Nonetheless, equally important for research on constitutions, public law, state power, and statecraft is a recognition that, whereas the *polity* provides a relatively stable institutional framework, *politics* is inherently dynamic, open-ended, and heterogeneous. It is a field of contention over the constitutional and institutional architecture of the state and the nature of the political sphere—including, of course, the public law aspects of both—and it also involves struggles 'outside' the state that, intentionally or not, modify political calculation and/or views on the nature and purposes of state power. Politics in turn constrains the set of feasible policies, ie policy-making, as an art of the possible. Thus, if politics refers to the overall strategic direction of the state and its division of 'policy labour', policy denotes specific fields of state intervention and abstention, decisions and non-decisions, etc. Influences and causation can also run, of course, in the opposite direction. For example, the implementation of new public management policies change the framework for political action and redraws the constitutional boundaries between the polity and other sets of social relations in a given social order.

[26] M Foucault, *Archaeology of Knowledge* (London, Tavistock, 1972) 130.

[27] *Cf* NÅ Andersen, *Discourse Analytical Strategies: Foucault, Koselleck, Laclau, Luhmann* (Bristol, Policy Press, 2003); Sum and Jessop (n 14).

[28] Neocleous (n 10); Jessop (n 10); B Golder (ed), *Re-Reading Foucault: On Law, Power and Rights* (London, Routledge, 2013).

[29] *Foundations* (n 3) 183ff.

[30] See also P Abrams, 'Notes on the Difficulty of Studying the State' (1988) 1 *Journal of Historical Sociology* 58; B Jessop, *The State: Past, Present, Future* (Cambridge, Polity Press, 2015).

[31] AJ Heidenheimer, 'Politics, Policy and Policy as Concepts in English and Continental Languages' (1986) 48 *Review of Politics*, 1.

[32] M Weber, *Economy and Society* (New York, Bedminster Press, 1968); K Palonen, 'Two Concepts of Politics, Two Histories of a Concept? Conceptual History and Present Controversies' (2006) 7 *Distinktion: Scandinavian Journal of Social Theory* 11.

[33] Gramsci (n 20) 261–62.

[34] Foucault (n 10).

[35] *Cf Foundations* (n 3). See also M Goldoni and M Wilkinson, 'The Material Constitution' (2016) *LSE Working Paper Series*.

IV. Beyond *Allgemeine Staatslehre*

Like many other commentators, myself included, Loughlin believes that legal and political theorists need to operate with the concept of the state. The challenge is to conceptualise the state in historically relevant, theoretically productive, and juridico-politically pertinent ways. What conception, if any, can capture the distinctiveness of the state (or, at least, the modern state) as a form of political organisation and support analyses of its institutional and spatio-temporal variability? After the important detour through juridico-political theory in Parts I and II of *Foundations*, Loughlin presents the historical semantic argument that the conception of the state emerges from amongst competing conceptions because it captures the impersonal character of the state (distinct from the person of the ruler or the occupants of high political office) and its separation from the people over whom its exercises sovereign authority.[36] In this context, he refers to the Continental European tradition of state theory, which highlights three core elements of the modern state: territory (*Staatsgebiet*), an authoritative apparatus (*Staatsgewalt*—also known as *Staatshoheit* and *Staatsapparat*), and a stable population subject to state authority (*Staatsvolk*).[37] Table 1 presents these elements and provides brief comments on each, including the effects of a one-sided treatment of any one at the expense of the two other elements. Loughlin then suggests that the state denotes the *unity* of these three elements rather than any one considered in isolation and that public law has a crucial role in securing this unity.

Based on his analysis, one could well add a fourth element, ie the juridical and/or political imaginary, vision, or project that defines the nature and purposes of the state (*Staatsidee*). This element encompasses the historical semantics of state formation and the variability of political imaginaries and state projects. The *Staatsidee* invokes higher goal(s) than the self-preservation of the state and its officials' self-interest, thereby distinguishing it from mafia-like bodies. It legitimates the state and its exercise of power and provides more general criteria for legitimacy crises and state failure. State projects provide a reference point for the always problematic operational unity and coherence of a state that is internally differentiated along institutional and functional lines and in terms of its spatio-temporal location and horizons of action. Indeed, whatever the precise origins of different components of the modern state (such as the army, bureaucracy, taxation, legal system, legislative assemblies), their existence as a relatively coherent institutional ensemble depends crucially on the emergence of the state idea and its instantiation in public law.

These four elements are constituted, reproduced, and transformed by practices of government, governance and/or governmentality, which combine to produce a coherent 'state effect'. They will now be reviewed in turn.

[36] *Cf* Skinner (n 11).

[37] See also, explicitly, M Loughlin, 'In Defence of Staatslehre' (2009) 48 *Der Staat* 1.

A. State Territory

A large literature examines the practices that enable the territorialisation of political power and create new territorial matrices that frame the polity, politics, and policies.[38] The territorial organisation of political authority is regarded by many theorists as the essential feature of the state, *pre*-modern as well as modern.[39] It certainly gives a common form to all effective states in the modern interstate system and provides an important criterion of the de-statisation of authority and, in other contexts, state failure. It also provides a basis for distinguishing politics in general (eg, office politics) from politics that is oriented to the exercise of state power.[40]

Territorialisation denotes the division of the earth into more or less clearly demarcated areas that are governed by a political authority empowered to make decisions binding on the residents of these areas.[41] Territory in this sense should not be confused with the more generic notion of *terra* or the terrestrial (which encompasses 'land' in its broadest sense, ie land and the subterranean, the sea, its depths and seabed, the air above and outer space), which provides a variable, technologically conditioned, and relational 'raw material' of territorialisation as a specific political process. Land without centralised political authority is sometimes declared to be *terra nullius*, ie land without a sovereign (the Antarctic land mass is a current example); its maritime parallel is 'the high seas'. An important moment in the rise of the modern Westphalian state was the papal declaration that Europe would be governed by independent, sovereign, and Christian national states, that war would only be conducted between states (ruling out civil wars), and that the New World, viewed as *terra nullius*, would be divided between Portugal and Spain to colonise as their rulers saw fit in line with European natural law traditions. These principles were often ignored, especially the last one.[42]

The nature of this terrestrial raw material shapes claims to sovereignty (contrast, for example, continental and archipelagic states) and is reflected in cartographic practices as states map the earth and territories as part of their state projects or for wider purposes.[43] This prompts different kinds of territorial dispute (eg rights of navigation through straits). Further, as maritime technologies have changed and aviation technologies evolve, so does the scope of territorialisation (eg, 'territorial waters', exclusive maritime economic zones, continental shelves, and high seas). This is the stuff of geopolitics, customary law, and international law and leads to shifting principles of territorialisation. One example is the

[38] N Brenner, B Jessop, MR Jones, and DJ McLeod (eds), *STATE/SPACE: A Reader* (Oxford, Blackwell, 2003); D Delaney, *Territory: A Short Introduction* (Oxford, Blackwell, 2005); SJ Elden, 'How to Do the History of Territory' (2013) 1 *Territory, Politics, Governance* 5.

[39] See, eg N Luhmann, Staat und Staatsräson im Überang von traditionaler Herrschaft zu moderner Politik. In *Gesellschaftstruktur und Semantik 3* (Frankfurt, Suhrkamp, 1989); C Schmitt, *The Nomos of the Earth in the Public Law of the Jus Publicum Europaaeum* (New York, Telos Press, 2003 [1950]).

[40] M Weber, *Political Writings* (Cambridge, Cambridge University Press, 1994).

[41] Delaney (n 38).

[42] Schmitt (n 39).

[43] M Escolar, 'Exploration, Cartography and the Modernisation of State Power' (1997) 151 *International Social Science Journal* 55; M Biggs, 'Putting the State on the Map: Cartography, Territory and European State Formation' (1999) 41 *Comparative Studies in Society and History* 374; SJ Elden, 'Land, Terrain, Territory' (2010) 36 *Progress in Human Geography* 799; J Barkan, 'Law and the Geographic Analysis of Economic Globalisation' (2011) 35 *Progress in Human Geography* 589.

changing priority that individual states give to 'freedom of the high seas' and 'sovereignty over territorial waters' (eg, the current dispute between the USA and China over the South China Sea). Another is the arms race for 'full spectrum dominance' to include outer space and cyberspace as well as land, sea and air.[44] While one might think of territory as fixed, ships and aircraft not only have *national* identities but can also have *sovereign territorial* status and so gain immunity from uninvited intervention.[45]

Westphalian territorial principles are the main reference point in modern political struggles, including their division into domestic and international affairs. Some scholars suggest that the Westphalian state is dissolving into, or reverting towards, earlier forms of territorial organisation, exemplified in debates over neo-medievalism.[46] Others highlight the variable coincidence or disjunction between different boundaries, borders or frontiers of action and the changing primacy of different tiers or scales of political action. The latter involves multi-level or multi-spatial government and governance arrangements.[47] More generally, these principles—or at least their repetition as founding myths—also provide the symbolic, institutional and organisational basis for geopolitical interactions up to the global scale—interactions that would prove anarchic were they not governed by enforceable rules or practices.[48]

B. State Apparatus

This refers to a politically organised coercive, administrative, *and symbolic* apparatus with sovereign authority vis-à-vis its own population and other states. This does not limit state power to coercion, whether deployed for internal purposes or external defence, and invites attention to the many modalities, including micro- as well as macro-political practices, in and through which state power is exercised.[49] Much attention has gone to the difference between normal and exceptional states in terms of the intermittent and legal use of coercion and the open, often unconstrained, use of force in emergencies. Indeed, massive reliance on domestic coercion is often a sign of state crisis or even state failure. The importance of

[44] *Cf* R Bernhardt (ed), *Encyclopedia of Public International Law, vol. 11. Law of the Sea, Air and, Space* (Amsterdam, Elsevier, 1989); FW Engdahl, *Full Spectrum Dominance: Totalitarian Democracy in the New World Order* (Wiesbaden, Edition Engdahl, 2009).

[45] Bernhardt (n 44).

[46] On neo-medievalism, see J Anderson, 'The Shifting Stage of Politics: New Medieval and Postmodern Territorialities?' (1996) 14 *Environment and Planning D: Society and Space*, 133 and J Friedrichs, 'The Meaning of New Medievalism' (2001) 7 *European Journal of International Relations*, 475.

[47] B Jessop, 'Territory, Politics, Governance and Multispatial Metagovernance' (2016) 4 *Territory, Politics, Governance* 8.

[48] On the Westphalian state, see F Kratochwil, 'Of Systems, Boundaries and Territoriality: An Inquiry into the Formation of the State System' (1986) 34 *World Politics* 27; J Ruggie, 'Territoriality and Beyond' (1993) 47 *International Organisation* 139; H Spruyt, *The Sovereign State and its Competitors: An Analysis of Systems Change* (Princeton, Princeton University Press, 1993); and B Teschke, *The Myth of 1648: Class, Geopolitics, and the Making of Modern International Relations* (London, Verso, 2003).

[49] *Cf* M Foucault, *Power/Knowledge: Selected Interviews and Other Writings 1972–1977* (Pantheon, New York, 1980); P Bourdieu, 'Rethinking the State: Genesis and Structure of the Bureaucratic Field' (1994) 12 *Sociological Theory* 1; P Bourdieu, *On The State. Lectures at the College de France, 1989–1992* (Cambridge, Polity, 2014); P Bratsis, *Everyday Life and the State* (London, Anthem, 2006); Gramsci (n 20); P Miller and N Rose, *Governing the Present. Administering Economic, Social and Personal Life* (Cambridge, Polity, 2008); TJ Mitchell, 'The Limits of the State: Beyond Statist Approaches and Their Critics (1991) 85 *American Political Science Review* 77.

non-violent bases of authority is clear even in the earliest states, where bureaucratic forms [or at least a hierarchy of offices and associated personnel] emerged and were linked to ritual authority as well as military power.[50]

This said, many state authorities routinely infringe their own legality, whether openly or beneath the cloak of official secrecy, whether at home or abroad, relying on a mix of terror, force, fraud, and corruption to exercise power.[51] Individual state agents may also abuse state power for fraudulent enrichment on a petty or grand scale. This suggests limits to the role of the formal constitution and public law in unifying the state apparatus. Furthermore, all states regarded as legal subjects reserve the right—or claim the need—to suspend the constitution or specific legal provisions in exceptional conditions. Carl Schmitt even proposed that 'Sovereign is he who decides on the exception'.[52] The resulting 'states of emergency' are, in principle at least, temporary and tied to specific threats or challenges—initially around security issues, more recently extending to economic emergencies.[53] In normal conditions, states of emergency are also subject to prior or post hoc constitutional or parliamentary approval. In some cases, however, the state of emergency may be declared permanent and this is used to justify an enduring rather than temporary dictatorship.[54]

C. State Population

Originally, populate and population denoted the 'populating' of a place or space.[55] Only later did population signify an object (the households, families, or persons who populated a place or space) to be enumerated and governed. Populating its territory (in the 'right ways') has long been a major concern of state-building, reflected in the biopolitics of population density, demographic qualities of the population, its generational profile, people's rights and obligations, loyalty and disloyalty, and so on.[56] Conversely, states may engage

[50] S Breuer, *Der Charismatische Staat: Ursprunge and Fruhfomen staatlicher Herrschaft* (Darmstadt, WBG, 2014).

[51] On state criminality, see G Barak, *Crimes by the Capitalist State: An Introduction to State Criminality* (New York, SUNY Press, 1991); Q Reno, *Warlord Politics and African States* (Boulder, Lyme Regis, 1998); P Green and T Ward, *State Crime. Governments, Violence and Corruption* (London, Pluto, 2004); DL Rothe, *State Criminality: The Crime of All Crimes* (Lanham, MD: Lexington, 2009); E Wilson (ed), *Government of the Shadows. Parapolitcs and Criminal Sovereignty* (London, Pluto Press, 2009); on corruption, see JP Dobel, 'The Corruption of a State' (1978) 72 *American Political Science Review* 958; D Satter, *Darkness at Dawn. The Rise of the Russian Criminal State* (New Haven, Yale University Press, 2003); N Kofele-Kala, *The International Law of Responsibility for Economic Crimes. Golding State Officials Individually Liable for Fraudulent Enrichment* (Aldershot, Ashgate, 2006).

[52] C Schmitt, *Political Theology: Four Chapters on the Concept of Sovereignty* (Cambridge Massachusetts, MIT Press, 1985) 5; *cf* W Scheuerman, *The Rule of Law Under Siege: Selected Essays of Franz Neumann and Otto Kirchheimer* (Berkeley, University of California Press, 1994); G Agamben, *State of Exception* (Chicago, Chicago University Press, 2005); C Boukalas, 'No Exceptions: Authoritarian Statism, Agamben, Poulantzas and Homeland Security' (2014) 7 *Critical Studies on Terrorism* 112.

[53] W Scheuerman, 'The Economic State of Emergency' (2000) 21 *Cardozo Law Review*, 1869.

[54] On these complexities, see J Ferejohn and P Pasquino, 'The Law of Exception: A Typology of Emergency Powers' (2004) 210 *International Journal of Constitutional Law* 333; C Schmitt, *Dictatorship. From the Origin of the Modern Concept of Sovereignty to Proletarian Class Struggle* (Cambridge, Polity Press, 2014 [1921]).

[55] G McNicoll, 'Population' in P Demeny and G McNichol (eds), *Encyclopedia of Population* (New York, MacMillan, 2003).

[56] P Biller, *The Measure of the Multitude: Population in Medieval Thought* (Oxford, Oxford University Press, 2000); B Curtis, 'Foucault on Governmentality and Population: The Impossible Discovery' (2002) 27 *Canadian Journal of Sociology* 505; V Petit, *Counting Populations, Understanding Societies: Towards an Interpretive Approach* (Dordrecht, Springer, 2013).

in struggles to occupy land and secure the resources deemed necessary to support a large population; or, again, to displace populations, which can lead to ethnic cleansing or genocide, whether this occurs for economic and political advantage, as a form of punishment, due to racism, or as a perverse mode of ethnic nation-building in a multi-ethnic society.[57]

As Michel Foucault observed, population is an object of both anatomo-politics and biopolitics—of disciplining individual bodies and governing populations respectively. In other words, the population of the state is not just the aggregate of the individuals residing in or passing through a state's territory but is construed, constituted, and governed as a complex object of state policy that varies across types of state, historical periods, and political regimes. The rise of population as an object of governance involves 'the creation of new orders of knowledge, new objects of intervention, new forms of subjectivity and [...] new state forms'.[58] Further, in governing population, policy-makers in modern states consider issues like migration, taxation, family policy, education and vocational training, health care, housing policy, and spatial planning. Finally, interest in population and bio-political practices extends beyond city-states and territorial states to colonial rule and, from the 1930s onwards, if not earlier, also emerged at the level of global policy.[59]

Five issues related to population in the modern era are: (1) the right to national self-determination; (2) the relation between population and nationhood (however understood); (3) the relation between population and citizenship (including issues of social inclusion and exclusion as well as legal and political rights); (4) the international legal question of formal rights to belong to and receive protection from a state and, conversely, the rights of stateless persons; and (5) the right of states to engage in humanitarian intervention in other states under the right to protection. Each of these is an important aspect of domestic or international public law.

Table 1: Towards a Four-Element State Theory

	State Territory (Staatsgebiet)	**State Apparatus (Staatsapparat)**	**State People (Staatsvolk)**	**State Idea (Staatsidee)**
Defining features	A bordered territory subject to control by a de facto state authority	Special staff with an internal division of labour and specific state capacities	Population resident in or beyond state territory and subject to state authority	Defines nature and purposes of state as an orientation point and for legitimation
Similar Concepts	Border, frontier, *limes*, domain, realm, region	Apparatus, Dispositive State sovereignty	Residents, denizens Sojourners Constituent power	Types of legitimation Political imaginary Myths of the state

(continued)

[57] M Levene, *Genocide in the Age of the Nation-State. Volumes 1 and 2* (London, IB Tuarus, 2005); M Mann, *Incoherent Empire* (London, Verso, 2005).

[58] B Curtis, 'Foucault on Governmentality and Population: The Impossible Discovery' (2002) 27 *Canadian Journal of Sociology* 505, 507; *cf* M Dean, *The Constitution of Poverty* (London, Routledge, 1990); Petit (n 56).

[59] O Kaasch and K Martens (eds), *Actors and Agency in Global Social Governance* (Oxford, Oxford University Press, 2015).

Table 1: (*Continued*)

	State Territory (Staatsgebiet)	**State Apparatus (Staatsapparat)**	**State People (Staatsvolk)**	**State Idea (Staatsidee)**
External dimension	Exclaves, colonies, protectorates, dependencies Claims to extra-territoriality	Recognition of state sovereignty and/or of legitimate authority of the government by other states	Aliens, refugees, asylum seekers, stateless persons	Role in the inter-state system (eg, non-aligned nations, the defender of free world, a proletarian nation)
State Crisis	Insecure borders, occupation	Failure of state capacity Government-in-exile	Demographic decline	Crisis of institutional integration Authority crisis
State Failure	Military defeat Loss of territorial sovereignty	Administrative failure, loss of legitimacy	Forcible removal, genocide, civil war, divided loyalties	Constitutional crisis Dual power
One-sided analysis	Neglect of space of flows and relevance of place, scale, and network relations	Failure to distinguish the state from mafia-like organisations or terrorist groups	Methodological nationalism Ethnocentrism	Idealism State embodies the general will
Remarks	Does not need to be contiguous (eg, enclaves, exclaves) Includes island, city and micro-states	Can be unitary or federal, multi-level or multi-tiered May not involve a constitution	Differs from a nation, community of feeling and citizenship Subjects not limited to individuals	Not to be confused with hegemony (a broader concept) General will is a political construct

Source: Revised and significantly expanded version of Table 2.2 (B Jessop, *The State: Past, Present, Future* (Cambridge, Polity, 2015) 35).

D. The State Idea

State discourses have played a key role in the separation of the political sphere from other institutional orders and, whether as mystification, self-motivation, or self-description, still shape the state as a complex ensemble of political relations linked to their respective social formations.[60] The discursive as well as material constitution of the state/civil

[60] See *Foundations* (n 3) Parts I–III; for other studies of how this separation has been conceived, see, eg J Keane, *Democracy and Civil Society* (London, Verso, 1988); TJ Mitchell, 'The Limits of the State: Beyond Statist Approaches and Their Critics (1991) 85 *American Political Science Review* 77; PM Nickel, 'Network Governance and the New Constitutionalism' (2007) 29 *Administrative Theory and Praxis* 198; M Foucault, *Security, Territory and Population. Lectures at the College de France, 1977–78* (Basingstoke, Palgrave, 2008); N Luhmann, *Law as a Social System* (Oxford, Oxford University Press, 2004).

society boundary enables state managers to deploy that movable boundary in the exercise of state power—and may in turn provoke counter-proposals or resistance from social forces. This line of demarcation also shapes how other actors on the political scene orient their actions towards the 'state', acting *as if* it existed. And struggles over dominant or hegemonic political and state imaginaries can be decisive in shaping the nature, purposes, and stakes of government.[61]

Concern with the state idea suggests that existing state formations appear as polyvalent, polymorphous crystallisations of rival principles of societal organisation. Hegemonic or dominant principles vary across long periods (eg industrialisation, nation-building, revolutionary transformation) and their sub-periods or phases (eg rise of monopoly capitalism, popular struggles for universal suffrage, consolidating mass support) and with specific responses to acute crises or other urgent situations (eg financial crisis, threats to national security, counter-revolutionary insurgency). State power may also become ineffective because state projects reflect inconsistent societalisation principles. This would make 'state effects' even more incoherent than usual. Looking at competing principles of societalisation reveals the limits of taking public law as the entry-point into the theme of the unity of the state—for this would seem to imply the primacy of juridification over other principles. The conditions of possibility of this primary role of public law remain to be established.

V. Public Law, the Multi-Dimensionality of the State and Substantive Crisis Mechanisms

To further develop the four elements approach, it is useful to explore six analytically distinct, empirically overlapping, and potentially disjointed dimensions of the state that can be studied from the most basic state forms to specific regimes at different scales of political organisation (see Table 2). Three dimensions mainly concern formal institutional aspects of the state apparatus. They are modes of political representation and their articulation; the vertical, horizontal, and transversal articulation of the state as an institutional ensemble and its demarcation from, and relation to, other states; and diverse mechanisms and modes of state intervention. The other three concern more discursive and action-oriented aspects of state power and give substance and strategic meaning to the three formal dimensions. They are the social bases that provide a stable core of support for the state and are its major material and/or symbolic beneficiaries; the 'state projects' that shape its internal unity and *modus operandi* (modes of policy-making, etc); and the 'hegemonic visions' that define the nature and purposes of the state for the wider society/world.

The last two dimensions relate to the paradox that the state is just one institutional order (with its own problematic unity, to be secured through a coherent state project) among many in a social formation but is held responsible (in the last instance, if not sooner) for securing the overall integration and cohesion of this formation. If I read Loughlin's comments on Spinoza correctly, the distinction between formal and material constitution of the state is relevant here. Similar distinctions occur in other discussions of political jurisprudence.

[61] Gramsci (n 20); Mitchell (n 60); Bartelson (n 11); Neocleous (n 10).

For example, Marco Goldoni and Michael Wilkinson discuss material constitution as 'a field of juristic knowledge [...] whose content is both dynamic and continually contested in its internal relation to the formal constitution'.[62] The key point here is the need to supplement formal analysis (whether simply juridical or juridico-statal) with analysis of material factors that shape the substance of a constitutional or statal order.

The six dimensions offer an initial framework to analyse major aspects of the state, compare 'normal' and 'exceptional' forms, and describe the hybrid character of particular states and their strategic selectivities. Indeed the internal organisation of the state system has a key role in maintaining the hierarchies among forms of representation and intervention. Incongruence among these forms can lead to crisis within the state. A well-known example, studied in the 1920s and 1930s, is the crisis of liberal parliamentarism that followed the rise of mass politics and the expansion of state economic intervention.[63] More generally, this matrix helps to identify aspects of state crisis that point beyond the three elements approach of *allgemeine Staatslehre*, because they identify substantive crisis mechanisms rather than the formal crisis possibilities. Corresponding to the six dimensions of the state we can mention the following substantive possibilities: representational, institutional, rationality, legitimacy, authority, and hegemonic crises of the state and, from the viewpoint of the wider social formation, organic crises.[64]

Public law is relevant to all three formal aspects of the state and not just to questions of its constitutional or institutional architecture. The latter dimension concerns, of course, the internal vertical, horizontal, and transversal organisation of the state system as expressed through the distribution of powers among its parts considered territorially and/or functionally. Obvious issues here are the relative weight of the legislative and executive branches of government, whether formally specified or simply reproduced in routine interaction(s), and the extent to which there is at least formal scope for oversight and veto of executive actions by an external authority (judiciary, church, or mob). We should also consider the weight of various parts of the administrative apparatus, the role of law, money, and knowledge in its internal organisation, mechanisms of recruitment of state officials and to what extent they own their offices and means of administration, and the form and extent of its administrative unity. Too rigid a prescription of these arrangements and rules can limit institutional innovation and adaptability to unexpected shocks. Increasingly important here are the relations between national territorial states and emergent trans- and supranational state forms as well as among central, local, regional, and parastatal forms of rule. How well this institutional structure is designed and its capacity for relatively unified action is the secret of durable governments.[65] Finally, the state's constitutional and institutional architecture selectively and asymmetrically shapes the possibilities for the substantive form of the state.

[62] Goldoni and Wilkinson (n 35) 5.

[63] C Schmitt, *The Crisis of Parliamentary Democracy* (Cambridge Massachusetts, MIT Press, 1988); Scheuerman (n 52); M Wilkinson, in chapter 12 of this volume.

[64] The concepts of representational crisis, crisis of hegemony, and organic crisis derive from Gramsci (n 20); 'rationality crisis' and 'legitimacy crisis' from J Habermas, *Legitimation Crisis* (London, Hutchinson, 1976); and institutional crisis from N Poulantzas, 'The Political Crisis and the Crisis of the State' in JW Freiburg (ed), *Critical Sociology* (New York, Halstead Press, 1979).

[65] Finer (n 8).

Ignoring this dimension would lead to the state being treated as a 'black box' inside which external demands and support somehow get translated in unknowable ways into specific policies that are then directed outwards. A 'black box' view rigidly separates 'inputs' from 'outputs', neglects the 'withinputs' that transform the former into the latter, and ignores the organisational routines and statecraft concerned with maintaining the state system as a mode of political domination. Public law has key roles in all these respects: it shapes the inputs and outputs, has a major impact on the forms of their treatment inside the state system, and is essential in reproducing the state system itself. These activities are reflected in specialised fields and guidance in areas such as statecraft, state science, mercantilism, cameralistics (or public finance), public administration, new public management, and so on. Securing the unity of the state apparatus as an institutional ensemble and an organ of societal domination requires not only the mobilisation of resources for the state's continued operations (such as finance,personnel, information, means of administration) but also the formal and substantive coordination of its different branches and activities. Balancing competing forces and interests is crucial here not only in terms of constitutional checks and balances, but also in terms of securing what can at best only be a *relatively* unstable equilibrium of compromise among them.[66]

Table 2: Six Dimensions of the State

Dimension	Substantive Definition	Substantive Significance	Substantive Crisis Aspects
Three Formal Dimensions			
Modes of Representation	These give social forces direct and/or indirect access to the state apparatus	Unequal access to state and unequal ability to resist at distance from state	Crises of political representation Enduring political exclusion
Modes of Articulation	Institutional design and functioning of branches and levels of the state	Unequal capacity of state managers to shape, make, and execute decisions	Crisis of vertical and horizontal institutional integration of the state apparatus
Modes of Intervention	Internal 'withinputs' and intervention in wider social order	Different sites and mechanisms of intervention	Series of major policy failures Rationality crisis
Three Substantive Dimensions			
Social Basis of State	Institutionalised social compromise between social classes and/or other politically vital social categories of the state population	Uneven distribution of concessions to the 'population' to secure support for state projects and policy approaches	Crisis within the power bloc (bloc of elites) Disaffection with parties and the state Civil unrest, civil war, revolution

(continued)

[66] On 'equilibrium of compromise', its inherent fragility, and the risks of catastrophic equilibria, see Gramsci (n 20) 175–76, 182–85, 216–18, 221–23, 245, 256–57; for further discussion, Buci-Glucksmann, *Gramsci and the State* (London, Lawrence and Wishart, 1980) 91–110.

Table 2: (*Continued*)

Dimension	Substantive Definition	Substantive Significance	Substantive Crisis Aspects
State Project	Secures apparatus unity of the state and orients capacities for state intervention	Secures unlikely unity of the state system by setting common goals to orient state actors	Legitimacy crisis based on rejection of state project and state authority
Hegemonic Vision	Relates role of the state and state power to a wider concept of the general interest	Provides legitimacy for state, defined in terms of promoting general interest, etc	Crisis of hegemony of the power bloc (elites) over the population Organic crisis

Source: Substantially revised version of Table 3.1 (Jessop, ibid 59).

The state's *formal* institutional unity is typically related to its hierarchical organisation as a sovereign state with a unified executive body at its peak empowered to make authoritative decisions and to bureaucratisation that provides the means to implement these decisions *sine ire et studio*. Bureaucratisation involves the formation of a special category of career officials separated from ownership of the means of administration and their subordination to formal rules of legal and financial accountability within a hierarchical chain of command linking different levels and branches of the state. The growth of bureaucracy involves an increasingly specialised division of tasks and more layers of command and execution. Yet the extent to which this formal unity is also substantive depends on the unity of the political executive at the top of the command chain and can be circumscribed or undermined through the resistance or non-compliance of officials on other levels and/or in other branches of the state system.

However, although bureaucratic forms are appropriate to the execution of general laws or policies in accordance with the rule of law, they are less suited to *ad hoc*, discretionary forms of intervention, big one-off projects, or responsiveness to participatory forms of decision-making and implementation.[67] Indeed, the bureaucratic preconditions for the formal unity of the state system may limit the substantive efficacy of policies oriented to accumulation, legitimacy, and social cohesion. This is reflected in the co-existence of formal bureaucracy governed by clear procedures and more informal, flexible, or ad hoc modes of intervention. These contribute to the material constitution of the state and its capacities for action. The development of corporatism, public-private partnerships, contracting out, regulated self-regulation, and so forth are different examples of these hybrid mechanisms that straddle the public-private divide. However, they also generate interesting problems in defining the formal boundaries of the state *qua* institutional ensemble and also threaten the substantive unity of the state through their potential for clientelistic degeneration and the pursuit of particular 'economic-corporate' demands. This suggests, once again, the need for control over such mechanisms by an overarching political executive authority and/or cross-cutting networks that can secure relative unity of state action.

[67] *Cf* C Offe, 'The Theory of the Capitalist State and the Problem of Policy Formation' in LN Lindberg, R Alford, C Crouch and C Offe (eds), *Stress and Contradiction in Modern Capitalism* (Lexington K, DC Heath, 1975).

The articulation of the branches and departments of the state system (including quasi-non-governmental organisations and similar bodies) helps to structure power relations. The relative dominance of departments or ministries can underwrite the hegemony of specific material and ideal interests. The internal structure of the state is also crucial in considering 'normal' and 'exceptional' regimes. For, whereas normal states can be categorised in the first instance in terms of the relative dominance of different channels of 'democratic' representation (eg, clientelist, corporatist, parliamentary, and pluralist), exceptional states can be differentiated in the first instance in terms of the relative dominance of different parts of the administrative state apparatus (such as the military, bureaucracy, political police, security branch, fascist party, religious police, or economic ministries). For normal states, the hierarchy of state apparatuses provides a further means of distinguishing political regimes and their various selectivities; and, for exceptional regimes, we need to examine the relative primacy of different channels of representation, especially to the dominant state apparatus. Combining forms of representation and the internal architecture of the state indicates the *potential* for the state to exercise 'despotic power' but its actual extent will also depend on the social bases of the state, the character of state projects and political imaginaries, and the extent to which state power involves hegemony as well as coercion.[68]

VI. Concluding Comments and Direct Questions

I have provided a state-theoretical gloss to the public-law focused political jurisprudence presented in Martin Loughlin's analysis and have suggested some of the limitations inherent in his. Now I turn to some more direct comments and questions inspired by the text.

Let me begin by noting that Loughlin provides awesome detail in Parts I and II of *Foundations* on the medieval origins, birth of public law, and development of different aspects of public law and draws on an impressive range of theological, political, and legal sources and languages. But this poses four questions related to the cliché about woods and trees. First, what is the basis for selecting the texts and debates to be covered—does this reflect their place in a theoretical canon, their influence in the process of constitution-making and state building, or their contemporary significance in the fields of public law and the state? Second, given the wide range of concepts and positions adopted in these debates, what factors influenced the reception and eventual influence of some rather than others? Third, can this be explained in terms of discursive factors alone and, if not, do historical semantics provide a sufficient explanation for the eventual consolidation of the modern lexicon of the state, sovereignty, and the public law? And, fourth, could this be tested by looking at the complementarity or co-evolution of the history of state formation in different historical contexts within Europe and/or Europe abroad (USA, Canada, Australia, Latin America, settler states, etc)?

Next, each of the three elements that *allgemeine Staatslehre* posits as foundational for the state is problematic because of their internal heterogeneity and the scope for disjunctions

[68] Mann (n 9) (*cf* the notion of *potestas* as opposed to *potentia*, which would seem relevant to Mann's infrastructural power).

between them, the importance of their changing constitutive outsides, and the propensities for failure or crisis in each component. This raises the question whether the notion of the state, state sovereignty, or the constitutionalisation of state authority can provide the point of unification so that they can be analysed in terms of separation-in-unity? This is the provocative claim advanced in *Foundations of Public Law*. But in what sense, if any, does the state as a concept that is irreducible to any single component subsume (and, presumably, organise) all three components, giving them a unity and coherence that they would not otherwise have? Niklas Luhmann suggests that the state (like the 'market' in relation to the economy) is a simplifying self-description of an otherwise inordinately complex political system.[69] As such it is polycontextural, having different meanings depending both on context and the form of contexture (ie the interweaving of components into a whole).

Perhaps the relativisation and historicisation of the notion of the state, in all its polymorphic and polycontextural complexity, can be avoided through a decisive role for public law as the organisational as well as semantic matrix of the state. In other words, the potential unity of the state can inhere in the coherence of public law and the implementation of public law. But then how is this affected by the increasing internal differentiation of public law and its supranational or international elaboration as well as in the decreasing significance of national territorial boundaries to the operation of the state in an allegedly post-sovereign world?[70] Particularly interesting in this regard are: first, questions of the constitutional and institutional architecture of multi-level government practices that operate with different scales and scope;[71] second, the strengthening of the 'new constitutionalism' under which the disciplines and practices of neo-liberal governmentality are enshrined in international treaties;[72] and the public law implications of recently aborted (but potentially zombie-like) proposals such as the Transpacific Partnership, the Transatlantic Trade and Investment Partnership, and a future Trade in International Services Agreement.

Regarding my proposed fourth component of the state, the *Staatsidee*, can this be subsumed under the other three components as interpreted by Loughlin, or does it add intellectual value and heuristic power to the analysis? Loughlin's comments on Peter Steinberger's book *The Idea of the State* are pertinent here.[73] Against Steinberger's claim that the key to state analysis is the idea of the state and that institutions are secondary, even accidental, Loughlin argues that state ideas become effective when they 'animate, guide and give meaning to the workings of the component material entities'.[74] The state is both an idea and the instantiation of that idea and, thus viewed, the state idea provides a scheme of intelligibility for ideational and institutional ensemble.[75] Loughlin adds that the state idea is controversial and ambivalent.[76] We can go further by noting that stepping outside the unifying

[69] See N Luhmann, 'Staat und Politik: Zur Semantik der Selbstbeschreibung politischer Systeme', *Politische Vierteljahresschrift* (1994) 15 *Sonderheft* 99–125; and 'Der Markt als innere Umwelt des Wirtschaftssystems', in idem, *Die Wirtschaft der Gesellschaft* (Frankfurt, Suhrkamp) 91–130.

[70] See Walker's contribution to the present volume in chapter 9.

[71] A theme that I prefer to explore in terms of multi-spatial metagovernance, Jessop (n 47).

[72] See, especially, S Gill, *Power and Resistance in the New World Order* (Basingstoke, Palgrave MacMillan, 2008) especially chs 7, 9, and 12.

[73] P Steinberger, *The Idea of the State* (Cambridge, Cambridge University Press, 2004).

[74] *Foundations* (n 3) 207.

[75] *Foundations* (n 3) 208.

[76] *Foundations* (n 3) 208.

frame of public law opens a far wider space for contestation and conflict. His discussion of Rousseau on the 'general will' versus the 'will of all' is particularly provocative in this regard,[77] but, for present purposes, should be linked to the historical materialist position, developed inter alia by Marx, Engels, and Gramsci, that the claim to represent the national interest, general will, or common good is always selective and may exclude significant social categories, identities, and interests.[78] This theme can also be related to Luhmann's commentaries on the paradox of the constitution—how to deparadoxify the historical fact that constitutions govern the state and the transfer of power within it through a constitutional settlement that was established extra-constitutionally, often through a violent, extra-constitutional rupture with earlier statal or governmental forms?[79] It also relates to the interest of Loughlin and Walker in another paradox of the constitution: whether the moment when a constitution is founded is the last moment when the constituent power can shape the development of that constitution.[80] Carl Schmitt's work is justifiably famous in this regard but also poses difficult questions about the nature of constitutions, commissarial and sovereign dictatorships, and states of emergency. Many of Schmitt's ideas are elegantly integrated in *Foundations* but, in certain respects, the thrust of Schmitt's work from the late 1920s through to the 1950s runs counter to the overall theme of Martin Loughlin's text. This is when Schmitt casts negative light on politics and the rule of law and became an apologist for the exceptional state, which fundamentally modifies many of the key themes of public law.[81] A similar concern arises regarding the Foucauldian concept of governmentality. This was cited in relation to *allgemeine Staatslehre* (with Foucault's triplet of *Security, Territory, Population* being treated as equivalent to the three components), in relation to the state as a scheme or grid of intelligibility, and in relation to forms of disciplinary power. But can it be fully integrated into the analysis in this text? Or do Foucault's efforts to put law in its place decentre public law as a unifying principle of juridical and statal organisation?

The historical semantics of the state also pose questions about the Eurocentric nature of state theory and, on this basis, the relevance of (Eurocentric) state theory to territorially organised forms of political authority beyond the centres of European state formation, especially before their rulers and subjects encountered the representatives of European states, as plunderers, traders, explorers, missionaries, diplomats, conquerors, or in some other guise. Such reflections can help reveal the historical specificity of different forms of political organisation and types of state and/or political regime.[82]

A final issue, prominent in the theoretical traditions within which I normally work (plain Marxism as defined by C Wright Mills,[83] German rather than American readings of Max Weber, the Gramscian tradition with its interest in the state in its inclusive sense of 'political society + civil society' or 'hegemony protected by the armour of coercion',

[77] *Foundations* (n 3) Ch 4, section ii.

[78] See J Rehmann, *Theories of Ideology: The Powers of Alienation and Subjection* (Leiden, Brill, 2013) chs 2 and 5; Jessop (n 30) 51–52, 112–13, 248.

[79] See Luhmann (n 60), and A Febbrajo and G Corsi (eds), *Sociology of Constitutions: A Paradoxical Perspective* (London, Routledge, 2016).

[80] M Loughlin and N Walker (eds), *The Paradox of Constitutionalism: Constituent Poser and Constitutional Form* (Oxford, Oxford University Press, 2007).

[81] M Loughlin, *Swords and Scales* (Oxford, Hart Publishing, 2000) 12, 80, 92, 128.

[82] *Cf* Halpin, in chapter 3 of this volume.

[83] *Cf* CW Mills, *The Marxists* (New York, Dell, 1962) 98–99.

and Foucauldian rather than Anglo-Foucauldian studies of governmentality) is the interest in the state as a key foundation for social domination. In a work on the foundations of public law one might have expected some discussion, if only to consider and then dismiss, the suggestions that the state is a form of domination and that public law should be subjected to *Ideologiekritik*. Ideology is mentioned on occasion in the text but, compared with the precision of the analysis of the state, it is underspecified and loosely used.[84] Yet, if we reject views of law and the state as neutral instruments or benevolent agents, state-theoretical inquiry demands critical engagement with the asymmetries of authority and domination inscribed in law, the state and political regimes and their structural and strategic roles in reproducing wider patterns of exploitation, oppression, and domination in specific times and places. Indeed, the separation between constitutional law and the state can have its own role in this regard.[85] More importantly, critique should not be limited to rogue, pariah, predatory, violent, totalitarian, or authoritarian states but extend to those conventionally described as benevolent liberal democratic regimes. This is even more urgent nowadays as we observe the Eurozone crisis unfolding, the resurgence of authoritarian populism, the drift towards a permanent state of exception, whether in the name of war on terror or as a means to maintain an enduring austerity state, and the growing extent to which states (or state officials) engage in extra-constitutional, extra-legal action that infringes public law principles. In short, while it is important to identify the importance of public law in the operation of normal states and to consider how it may serve to limit the exercise of power in exceptional states, it is also important to consider whether other mechanisms can be developed to provide at least a semblance of unity to the operation of the state, to facilitate its pursuit of a democratically-determined account of the general interest, and to protect a rule of law that is more than a means to consolidate private interests.

[84] For an excellent analysis of the complexities of *Ideologiekritik*, see Rehmann (n 78).

[85] See, for example, N Luhmann, *Politische Soziologie* (Berlin, Surhkamp, 2010); C Möllers, 'Les Gardiennes d'une Separation. Les Constitutions Comme Instruments de Protection des Differences Entre le Droit et la Politique' (2012) 7 *Jus Politicum* 1.

11

The Materiality of Political Jurisprudence

MARCO GOLDONI

I. Introduction

The contribution *Foundations of Public Law* makes to the development of contemporary constitutional thought is open to multiple interpretations.[1] Its core concerns cover different layers of current constitutional discourse. In fact, it is clear that *Foundations* is simultaneously a work of constitutional history, theory, doctrine and comparative law. One might easily adapt its theoretical insights for comparative analysis or its historical parts for an analysis of the evolution of contemporary constitutionalism. Overall, it is practically impossible to disentangle each layer without missing many of its nuances. So, even when discussing the key methodology of political jurisprudence, it is difficult to separate it from the rest of the book and its impressive breadth.[2] This preliminary qualification is necessary in order to flag that the criticism of political jurisprudence advanced here will have to be tested against the background of Loughlin's numerous engagements with different constitutional experiences and theories.

This chapter's aim is two-fold. First, to read political jurisprudence as a way of remedying the deficiencies of existing scholarship within the tradition of political constitutionalism. Political jurisprudence offers a *political* approach to constitutional studies which is distinctive.[3] Second, to suggest that in privileging formal right ordering over processes of subjectivation, Loughlin's analysis prioritises the symbolic over the material dimension of constitutional development. A material critique of political jurisprudence will then be sketched out, but with the *caveat* that there are many resources within *Foundations* itself which actually hint at a material conception of public law. In fact, (a reformulated?) political jurisprudence can accommodate a material reading of the modern constitution.

[1] M Loughlin, *Foundations of Public Law* (Oxford, Oxford University Press, 2010) [hereafter *Foundations*].

[2] The same can be said about other works by Loughlin. In general, a discussion of political jurisprudence cannot be separated from the idea of political right and from the conception of key tenets of the constitutional discourse such as state, constitution, power, authority, freedom, and government. Some of them will be highlighted below in other footnotes.

[3] As it will become apparent in the following analysis, political jurisprudence offers a leverage point also to comparative constitutional studies.

II. Methodology: The Prudential Rationality of Political Jurisprudence

Political jurisprudence offers an understanding of the relation between politics and public law with a specific history (mostly modern) and a clear jurisdiction (discourses of political right around the constitution of the state). The core of its approach to the study of public law is discussed in Chapter 6 of *Foundations*, as the concluding section of Part II of the book entitled 'Formation [of public law]'. Its genesis is contextual and genetically tied to the idea of political right or *droit politique*. Its field of knowledge is not (only) positive law, but the undergirding governmental order and its political space.[4] More specifically, the discourse of political right 'takes shape as a set of rules, principles, canons, maxims, customs, usages and manners that condition, sustain, and regulate the activity of governing the state'.[5]

As an approach, the study of political jurisprudence is not therefore a subgenre of legal positivism and Loughlin makes this clear on several occasions.[6] Legal positivism expels questions of concrete order and symbolic representation underlying the legal system. It leaves the so-called 'laws of governmental ordering' (as Loughlin calls them) to another domain of knowledge, outside of juristic inquiry. In contrast, political jurisprudence calls for a prudential and holistic analysis of constitutional orders. This is demanding for the constitutional scholar. As a prudential method, political jurisprudence is a historical and practical reflection on the ordering functions of public law, that is, its *autonomous* governing capacity. Both dimensions (historical and practical) are necessary because the emergence of an autonomous sphere of public law is the outcome of a series of historical conditions: 1) the end of a transcendental form of *auctoritas* which implied that what previously was an external or transcendental source of authority is now socially internalised through self-actualisation; 2) the state becomes, between the sixteenth and the seventeenth centuries, the place of sovereignty (hence: 'the concept of the state is nothing less than the *sine qua non* of public law');[7] 3) but since the paths to the formation of an autonomous public law are context-dependent, giving rise to a plurality of discourses of political right, public law is local knowledge. In fact, as chapters 4 and 5 of *Foundations* show, many different accounts of the science of political right have been offered in the history of modern political philosophy. What that dense excursus reveals is that any definitive and objective interpretation of political right is vain and, in practice, impossible. The knowledge of political jurisprudence is practical because it is always an internal reflection on (to stick to Loughlin's terminology) the 'grammar' and the 'architecture' of the practice itself and on the presumptions which anchor them. It is also an unstable form of knowledge, because it has to negotiate between the polarities of a bifurcated discourse.

Again, the political jurisprudent faces a situation of deep ambiguity. On the one hand, public law is a juristic enterprise requiring, at the very least, a theory of the source of the

[4] See P Bourdieu, *The Logic of Practice* (Stanford, Stanford University Press, 1990) 59.

[5] *Foundations* (n 1) 10.

[6] For eg 'if the objective is to apprehend the legal order as something inherently rational, then legal positivist methods are altogether inadequate' *Foundations* (n 1) 159.

[7] *Foundations* (n 1) 183.

authority of the laws that establish the state and the institutions of its self-actualisation; on the other hand there is no Archimedean point 'from which objective authority can be determined'.[8] To cope with this tension (potentially fatal for the scientific status of the discipline), political jurisprudence strikes a cautionary note. It reminds us, first, that 'the relationship between theory and practice is [...] of such complexity as to render any general account of the emergence of modern public law both partial and provisional'.[9] Second, political jurisprudence begins with the recognition that there are multiple, partial accounts of political right. This means that the task of political jurisprudence is *not* to provide a general theory of public law. On the contrary, the task of political jurisprudence is 'to negotiate between the various conflicting accounts of political right that form part of its evolving discourse'.[10] Loughlin's extension of the scope of public law to encompass the negotiation of competing conceptions of political right is not to deprive public law of its juristic quality or transform it into an exercise in moral or political reasoning.[11] The idea of public law germane to political jurisprudence is that of 'an immanent practice that conditions and sustains the activity of governing' and which 'incorporates no transcendental or metaphysical ideas of justice and goodness: it is concerned solely with those precepts of conduct that have evolved through political practice to ensure the maintenance of the public realm as an autonomous entity'.[12]

Public law has a distinctive role in generating and sustaining institutional authority in an autonomous political realm and its nature makes it essential to engage with political jurisprudence. Understanding the foundations of public law is critical because public law is a discourse where concepts such as 'governing', 'sovereignty' and 'representation' are organised and combined in order to establish the autonomous sphere in which public power can effectively operate.[13]

It is crucial to remember that this conception of public law is not meant to convert it into the pursuit of a (impossible) science of political right.[14] The rationality of political jurisprudence is grounded in prudential considerations, so that it is more about 'negotiating' than reconciling or eliminating tensions between the polarities of public law. The negotiation itself, we are told, is the exercise rather than the explanation of prudential judgement.[15] In this respect, the core of Loughlin's methodology is *hermeneutical*. Rather than seeking to separate facts and values, Loughlin adopts an interpretative method to develop his approach. Once a field of investigation is identified, the task for the political jurisprudent is to reconstruct the discourse of its subjects with 'a search for coherence' which derives from 'a common pattern of meaning shared amongst these subjects'.[16] When looking for

[8] *Foundations* (n 1) 159.

[9] *Foundations* (n 1) 158.

[10] *Foundations* (n 1) 164.

[11] This idea might actually leave open a space for more consideration of the role of political and social conflict in political jurisprudence (see below section V).

[12] *Foundations* (n 1) 163.

[13] See M Walters, 'Is Public Law Ordinary?' (2012) 75 *Modern Law Review* 894, 912 for a critique of the claim that public law is autonomous.

[14] *Cf* Minkkinen in chapter 4 of this volume.

[15] eg the remark that public law is 'a form of political reasoning driven by prudential considerations', see M Loughlin, *The Idea Of Public Law* (Oxford, Oxford University Press, 2003) 163.

[16] M Loughlin, 'Theory and Values in Public Law: An Interpretation' (2005) *Public Law* 61.

the content of public law, the 'assumption that there are indisputable facts in this field that can be acquired by objective empirical investigation is erroneous: we are constantly seeking to fit this evidence to our pre-existing assumptions about the subject'.[17] The core of this approach is interpretation: indeed, when we are concerned about meaning 'we are always interpreting'.[18] If hermeneutics is its epistemology, the legal philosophy of political jurisprudence is a form of institutionalism capable of finessing the relation between normativity and facticity.[19] As we shall see below, this is functional to the reconstruction of modern public law based on the distinction between *potentia* and *potestas*. In light of the previous remarks, it should be evident that Loughlin's institutionalism does not share the normative assumptions undergirding Neil MacCormick's type of institutionalism.[20] On the contrary, it retrieves an understanding of legal institutionalism indebted to Schmitt's turn to concrete order thinking,[21] and to an LSE tradition heavily influenced by French legal institutionalism.[22] In particular, Loughlin's reading of the LSE functionalists (Laski, Robson, Jennings) emphasises their institutionalist background and is rather original because it downplays their legal positivism in favour of the juristic qualities of their constitutional thought.[23] The argument will now be made that political jurisprudence is a new chapter in this history of constitutional thought.

III. Trajectory: From a Functional to a Reflexive Political Jurisprudence

The previous remarks on Loughlin's institutionalism can help trace the trajectory of his approach. Political jurisprudence is a way of framing the knowledge of public law and as such it addresses a concern already present in the work of John Griffith. Griffith is rarely invoked in *Foundations* and his dismissal of the state as metaphysical nonsense is firmly rejected by Loughlin at the outset of the book.[24] Yet, *Foundations* is dedicated to Griffith and, on closer inspection, it seems indebted to his tradition of thought in two ways. The first is that political jurisprudence is a way to respond to Griffith's appeal for a renewal of

[17] ibid 63.

[18] ibid.

[19] See Loughlin's 'Nomos' in D Dyzenhaus and T Poole (eds), *Law, Liberty and the State: Hayek, Oakeshott and Schmitt on the Rule of Law* (Cambridge, Cambridge University Press, 2015) 65–95.

[20] *Cf* N MacCormick, *Institutions of Law* (Oxford, Oxford University Press, 2007).

[21] C Schmitt, *On the Three Types of Juristic Thought* (Westport CT, Praeger, 2004).

[22] A classic example of this influence is visible in the collection *Modern Theories of Law* (Oxford, Oxford University Press, 1933) where a chapter by HJ Laski is devoted to Maurice Hauriou and one by WI Jennings to Duguit. It is also important to note that Laski translated Duguit's classic *Les transformations du droit public* (1913).

[23] For an intriguing attempt at reconciling political jurisprudence with one particular version of legal positivism (normative positivism), see M Gordon, 'A Basis for Positivist and Political Public Law: Reconciling Loughlin's Public Law with (Normative) Legal Positivism (2015) 6 *Jurisprudence* 1. Gordon makes an interesting point based on the normative concept of law endorsed by J Waldron and T Campbell, stating that this is compatible with political jurisprudence.

[24] In a recent article, Loughlin proposes to read the famous article on the political constitution as the swan song of functionalism, that is, the eulogy of a constitution that was no longer: 'Modernism in British Public Law: 1919–1979' (2014) *Public Law* 56.

constitutional scholarship advanced as early as the 1960s in an article entitled 'Why We Need a Revolution'.[25] Political jurisprudence as the prudential science of political right is offered as a more solid and refined approach to constitutional studies. Actually, one might read political jurisprudence as a vindication of the necessity to understand the constitution beyond its formal appearance as suggested by Griffith.[26] Except that, contrary to Griffith, Loughlin's concrete order thinking does not dismiss the state as a metaphysical construct. Bringing back state sovereignty into the picture is a way of going *against* Griffith *with* Griffith.

The consequences of such a renewal of constitutional scholarship are multiple and varied. This brings us to the second rather clear link to Griffith's work and, more generally, to the recently debated tradition of the political constitution. Loughlin gives a particular reading of the idea of the political constitution by enlarging the scope of the inquiry to include the continental traditions of constitutional thought and by placing the reflection on the British constitution within the dynamics of the development of European states.[27] This time one might say that political jurisprudence interprets public law in a manner that avoids the pitfalls of the previous conceptions of the political constitution, but at the same time redeems some of the intuitions of its first functionalist phase. In other words, to adopt Loughlin's register, political jurisprudence can be read as an attempt at remedying the shortcomings of the first two waves of functional and then normative political constitutionalism.[28] In fact, political jurisprudence offers a new take on public law studies and is at the forefront of an incipient 'third wave' of political constitutionalist scholarship.[29]

At this point, some clarification is necessary. A first wave of political constitutionalist studies can be traced back to an arch spanning, roughly, from Jennings' major works in the 1930s to Griffith's famous *Chorley Lecture*.[30] The main thrust of this trend is to reject the classic liberal normativism of the Diceyan school, based on individualism and on the necessity of constraining an increasingly invasive government. The functionalists reverted to utilitarianism and adopted an instrumental conception of public law, that is, they viewed public law as a tool through which one might effect social change. From the perspective of political jurisprudence, the relationship between political power and law is trivialised because the idea of legal ordering is bypassed in favour of a conception of law as the transmission belt of political will.

From the 1990s to the present, a second 'wave' of political constitutionalists has tried to overcome the limits of the functionalist approach by resorting to a normative conception of constitutional law and constitutionalism. That enquiry has become highly idealised

[25] J Griffith, 'Why We Need a Revolution' (1969) 40 *Political Quarterly* 383.

[26] The iconic reference is J Griffith, 'The Political Constitution' (1979) 42 *Modern Law Review* 1. On this influential piece see, at least, G Gee, 'The Political Constitutionalism of John Griffith' (2008) 28 *Legal Studies* 20 and T Poole, 'Tilting at Windmills?' (2007) 70 *Modern Law Review* 250.

[27] This plan is stated clearly at the outset of the book: 'In order to address these foundational questions, the British are obliged to re-connect with the mainstream of the European tradition of public law' *Foundations* (n 1) 6.

[28] For a reconstruction of functional political constitutionalism, see M Loughlin, *Public Law and Political Theory* (Oxford, Clarendon, 1992) Ch 6.

[29] For a similar project, see G Gee and G Webber, 'Rationalism in Public Law' (2013) 76 *Modern Law Review* 708.

[30] WI Jennings, *Cabinet Government* (Cambridge, Cambridge University Press, 1936); id, *Parliament* (Cambridge, Cambridge University Press, 1938).

and often abstracts from the concrete relations of power between political subjects. It is also not surprising that the legal theory undergirding this second wave has been normative positivism.[31] The concrete politicality of the constitution is lost because the state is collapsed into government, and parliamentary politics is abstracted from the dynamics of parliamentary systems and political conflict. The basic intuition underlying the second wave is that parliamentary sovereignty needs a stronger normative (rather than functional) justification and in order to provide for that, political constitutionalists accept the basic premise of liberal normativism: the individual as the main unit of constitutional analysis.[32]

The premises upon which this second wave is built are famously known as the two circumstances of politics: that human beings disagree (Hannah Arendt would say that the human condition is marked by plurality) and that they need to reach a decision on common problems.[33] Reasonable disagreement is the originating phenomenon to which the political constitution is supposed to respond. The resilience of parliamentary sovereignty is supposed to accommodate this type of disagreement. The political constitution offers

> a site for discussion and debate, and the reconciliation of conflict. It is a recognition that everyone matters, that there is no monopoly of wisdom on ideas, and that differences can be reconciled in a deliberative assembly. It can accommodate the politics of both post-war socialism and modern-day neo-liberalism.[34]

As a result, in this normative version, political constitutionalism takes the formal approach of recognising individual disagreement and channelling it either through political accountability (Tomkins) or representative law-making (Bellamy, Waldron, Ewing and Campbell).

But this stream of political constitutionalism is in danger of surrendering to empty abstractions (parliament, government, accountability) and remaining blind to the layers of material complexity throughout the political constitution.[35] Most importantly, this normative wave of political constitutionalism does not draw any analytical distinction between the state and the government. As a result, the question of the generation and preservation of political power is blurred and questions of the protection of individual rights take precedence.

Political jurisprudence offers precious insights to overcome the drawbacks of these normative efforts and to redeem some important functionalist arguments. A first crucial difference is that the politics/law nexus is seen through an analysis of the political formation of the modern state. Applied to parliamentary sovereignty, for example, this means an inquiry into the historical and factual conditions undergirding it. In the case of the UK Constitution (usually singled out as the classic example of the political constitution), the reason why Parliament occupies such a central place in the constitutional imagination is because it has represented the institutionalisation of the political unity of England (then extended

[31] See, eg J Waldron, *Law and Disagreement* (Oxford, Oxford University Press, 1999); T Campbell, *The Legal Theory of Ethical Positivism* (Aldershot, Ashgate, 1996); R Bellamy, 'Political Constitutionalism and the Human Rights Act' (2011) 9 *International Journal of Constitutional Law* 86.

[32] This is one of the main accusations made by Jennings to Dicey, see his *The Law and the Constitution* (London, University of London Press, 1963).

[33] Waldron (n 31) 102.

[34] K Ewing, 'The Resilience of the Political Constitution' (2013) 13 *German Law Journal* 2111.

[35] For a similar criticism, this time concerning the use of constitutional language, G Gee and G Webber, 'A Grammar of Public Law' (2013) 14 *German Law Journal* 2137.

to the other nations). Loughlin calls this process the formation of the 'parliamentary state'. The reason it endured is that it represented, through a series of reforms (financial, military and administrative), the most powerful state-building force.[36] The conclusion is that parliamentary sovereignty cannot be explained away by reference to normative arguments, but has to be analysed and understood as the outcome of a concrete process of organising the constitutional imagination within a specific jurisdiction. The state provides the spatial and temporal matrix for the organisation of the legal order, but its form is determined by different prudential factors.

This last point introduces a second crucial difference, which is that the state and the government are not conflated or confused in political jurisprudence. The state is presented as a scheme of intelligibility,[37] which makes it possible to identify the relevant relations between the state and governmental apparatus. The political constitution is not therefore reduced to a single relation between government and the individual or to institutional questions of the protection of rights. Political jurisprudence avoids these narrow concerns precisely because it does not sever law from politics. Indeed, one of the greatest insights of political jurisprudence is its retrieval of juristic knowledge of state-building and state transformation. This type of juristic knowledge demands a step back from the exclusive focus on government and the 'restoration' of fundamental laws as its main concern.[38] From the perspective of political jurisprudence, the critical flaw of the legal positivism that informs the second wave of political constitutionalism is that it abstracts from juristic inquiry those aspects of political right which are manifest in the operation of constitutional orders. The influence of this kind of legal positivism has been such that 'by foregrounding the question of validity (is this or is this not a rule of an extant legal order?), modern jurisprudence has tended to push issues of authority to its periphery'.[39] All the foundational concepts of public law enabling the activity of governing are marginalised in this line of thought.

Public law as political jurisprudence is crafted by employing a methodology rooted in the assumption that the object of the discipline can 'have meaning only within a field (that is, in relation to other things)'.[40] Applied to political jurisprudence, the 'assumption that there are indisputable facts in this field that can be acquired by objective empirical investigation is erroneous: we are constantly seeking to fit this evidence to our pre-existing assumptions about the subject'.[41] In fact, understood from the perspective of juristic knowledge, public law can only be conceived as local knowledge: 'the relationship between theory and practice is, in short, of such complexity as to render any general account of the emergence of modern public law both partial and provisional'.[42] In other words, mapping the knowledge of

[36] M Loughlin, *The British Constitution* (Oxford, Oxford University Press, 2013).

[37] P Steinberger, *The Idea of the State* (Cambridge, Cambridge University Press, 2004) 25.

[38] Loughlin is very clear about the difference with classic legal positivism: 'a clean break cannot be effected between the ancient and modern ideas of the constitution and [...] the modern attempt to focus purely on the constitution of the office of government provides no substitute for reflection on the constitution of the state [...] Only by restoring a public law perspective, by viewing the constitution as an exercise in statecraft that functions according to the precepts of *droit politique*, will it be possible adequately to address the fundamental issue' *Foundations* (n 1) 310–11.

[39] *Foundations* (n 1) 10.

[40] Loughlin (n 16) 61.

[41] Loughlin (n 16) 63.

[42] *Foundations* (n 1) 158.

public law entails, at most, only historical *a priori* (the modern state being the main reference for modern constitutions) whose texture is given by family resemblances.[43]

Once brought into this debate, political jurisprudence provides added value, which is later characterised by Loughlin in terms of the reflexivity of constitutionalism.[44] One of the goods offered by political jurisprudence is epistemic:

> by placing modern constitutions within the frame of *droit politique*, the critical dynamic between the constitution (the text) and constitutionality (the process whereby the text comes to play an increasingly important role in the regulation of the political sphere) is revealed.[45]

Political jurisprudence unveils several aspects of the relational nature of public law: the conditional authority of the constitution, the moment of foundation as a post-hoc rationalisation, the relational nature of constituent power,[46] and the symbolic role played by constitutions as forces of stability in the shaping of political and national identity, to name just a few.

And yet, despite all the emphasis on the *process* rather than the *event* within the institutional configuration of authority, there is one aspect that remains neglected in *Foundations*: the role of subjects and their subjectivation in the formation and development of modern constitutions. Before examining this point, a brief detour on the idea of right ordering is necessary to understand the reasons for this neglect.

IV. Object: Right Ordering and its Grammar

As remarked above, what is missing completely from the perspective of the second, normative wave of political constitutionalism is the idea of ordering, and the distinction between *droit politique* and the positive law that accompanies it. The second wave of political constitutionalism ends up adopting a normative positivist view of the constitution, reducing it to a system of norms. In contrast, the main objects of analysis in political jurisprudence inhabit three distinct layers: the state, the constitution and the government. These terms also provide the entry point for understanding the forms of power generated by public law (*potestas* and *potentia*). Loughlin assumes that the point of an autonomous public law is, in modern times, to generate power and freedom.[47] The task for political jurisprudence is to explain how, despite competing accounts of political right, public law can manage and govern the ambiguous relation between the sovereign state and the freedom of the subject or, in other words, between power and liberty. In short, and at risk of oversimplification, both terms ought to be understood as 'correlative'.[48] Power is defined as two-fold: structural

[43] The classic reference here is M Foucault, *The Archaeology of Knowledge* (London, Routledge, 2004) 126–28.
[44] *Foundations* (n 1) 310–11.
[45] *Foundations* (n 1) 311.
[46] *Cf* M Loughlin, 'Constituent Power' (2014) 13 *European Journal of Political Theory* 218.
[47] While they strongly disagree on the scope of public law's autonomy and, obviously, on methodology, Loughlin and Thornhill both agree that modern public law generated (and not just limited) huge amount of political power.
[48] *Foundations* (n 1) 178.

and infrastructural, *potentia* and *potestas*. Liberty, far from being negative freedom, is also an ambivalent notion, fully inscribed within the operations of political power.[49]

In terms of constitutional theory, the main insight offered by these observations is that power and liberty are not pre-political, but created by public law itself: more precisely, 'power and liberty are created through the operation of the practices of public law'.[50] Within the field of public law, one cannot exist without the other, but also, critically, one cannot become synonymous with the other. The efficient core of public law lies precisely in the maintenance of a productive tension between these polarities. Political jurisprudence, by managing these tensions, is meant to rationalise the 'art of governing', developing a prudential discourse that does not dissolve or blur the distinctions.

At this level of discourse, a critical point for the deployment of political jurisprudence is reached; it is a point where the methodological difference between the normative and the reflexive understanding of constitutionalism is at its greatest. As already noted, the issue of the generation of power is not registered by normative constitutionalists. Political jurisprudence makes an astute move here because it commits to the ambiguity of political power: once political power is understood as emerging internally from society and then necessarily managed without any reference to a transcendental source, public law (as the architecture of political power) can absorb society and condition citizens' freedoms. Here lies also the immanent ambiguity of public law: public law is constitutive of power and freedom but the art of governing can potentially absorb society and become a dangerous activity.

As already noted, the main concern behind the enterprise of political jurisprudence is to secure the protection (and intelligibility) of the constitutional order through prudential judgement. Endorsing Meinecke's analysis of the reasons of state, Loughlin argues that for political jurisprudence the main value is represented by the well-being of the state because 'power, maintenance of power, extension of power, is the indispensable means which must [...] be procured'.[51] Right ordering, as the coupling of the power to rule and the right of rule, is an essential tenet of this process of power formation.[52] Political jurisprudence provides the *grammar* for understanding it *qua* practice.

Despite his many claims that the edifice of public law is based on prudential grounds, there seems to be a lot left unstated in Loughlin's use of metaphorical terms such as 'architecture',[53] 'framework', 'grammar', 'code'—all concepts suggesting structure and stability. Much less attention is devoted to subjectivity. Once one might have said: organisation has the upper hand, subjectivity is marginal.[54] In fact, political jurisprudence greatly emphasises the grammar of the practice of public law. Focusing on the grammar of public law allows us to unveil the double dimension of constitutive rules: 'they are the rules that we have devised [...] for the correct use of certain terms' and they are based on certain

[49] A key reference here is Hannah Arendt, *The Human Condition* (Chicago, Chicago University Press, 1958) Ch V.

[50] *Foundations* (n 1) 178.

[51] *Foundations* (n 1) 87 (quoting from F Meinecke, *Machiavellism: The Doctrine of Raison d'Etat and its Place in Modern History* (New Haven, Yale University Press, 1962).

[52] On this point there are many affinities between Loughlin's account of right ordering and Hans Lindahl's. Loughlin himself has noted these similarities: 'A-legality or Jus Politicum: A Critical Appraisal of Hans Lindhal's Fault Line of Globalisation' (2014) 2 *Ethics and Politics* 965.

[53] For eg Chapter 3 of *Foundations* (n 1) is titled 'The Architecture of Public Law'.

[54] M Tronti, *Operai e capitale* (Roma, Derive e Approdi, 2004) 23.

background assumptions.[55] This means that they operate both as enabling and limiting rules. The meaning of the latter is conditioned by their peculiar grammar.

The grammar of public law reminds us that public law is local knowledge, not universal. Alternative grammars are always conceivable and available. Language itself is in constant evolution and no sovereign stands outside it.[56] In fact, Loughlin notes that 'we acquire knowledge of the words and symbols of the language in conjunction with an understanding of the appropriate circumstances in which to use them'.[57] Intriguingly, he adds that the reconstruction of the practice of public law 'must be seen to be context-dependent and purpose-relative'.[58] The meaning of a constitutional rule can be grasped only if one understands the relevant constitutional language. Crucially, in order to understand the latter, one has to be able to imagine the form of life which undergirds it.

The added value of political jurisprudence is therefore to offer a more accurate understanding of public law: 'by studying the grammar we become more skilled at extending the language to cover unusual cases or situations that appear exceptional'.[59] The grammar of public law opens juristic knowledge to a wider array of concerns, exceptions and political decisions.[60] No wonder, then, that to speak of public law is equivalent to imagining a form of life that inhabits it. This configures political jurisprudence always as an *internal* enterprise. The fact that it is exercised from within does not mean that it will demand constitutional reform.[61]

However, because its form is conventional, grammar does not fully capture a particular constitutional reality. The scrutiny of political jurisprudence based on conventional rules alone does not have the capacity to represent the whole constitutional reality. Indeed, the criterion of appropriateness is linked to logical ordering rather than a substantive representation.

One might therefore ask whether grammar operates as an excessively rigid structure and, in the end, actually represents a reductive approach. After all, 'we turn to grammar for an explanation of the structural features of a language'.[62] But is the grammar generative of constitutional meaning analogous to the relation between language (*langue*) and speech (*parole*)? Loughlin discards the idea of a generative grammar (or Ur-grammar) and defends the virtue of having competing grammars as a way to maintain the ambiguity of public law. Yet, such a recognition is not enough to avoid the pitfalls of constitutional structuralism. The questions of how the grammar is shaped and what is its impact upon its subjects remain open. Are the identity and the role of subjects completely determined by the language of public law? It is doubtful that the study of the grammar of public law can capture all its constituent and dynamic components. If taken literally, the analogy of grammar implies

[55] *Foundations* (n 1) 178.

[56] It is not clear from the text whether language is used as language or *langue*. The impression is that grammar and the specific instantiation of a language (how the language is spoken) are conflated by Loughlin.

[57] *Foundations* (n 1) 179.

[58] *Foundations* (n 1) 179.

[59] *Foundations* (n 1) 179.

[60] Mortati had already identified the juridical relevance of the exception, as M Croce and A Salvatore reminded in *The Legal Theory of Carl Schmitt* (Abingdon, Routledge, 2012) 187.

[61] A similar approach, but more attentive to a cultural understanding of constitutional theory, is put forward by P Kahn, *The Cultural Study of Law* (Chicago, Chicago University Press, 1999).

[62] *Foundations* (n 1) 178.

the study of public law as an examination of its constitutive and performative aspects. For a theory whose idea of power is fully relational (political power is not to be found in one place, but rather it 'ultimately inheres in the form which the political relationship takes'),[63] the analogy of grammar might then come across as a straitjacket rather than an enabling perspective. After all, how and where political unity is obtained are constitutional questions which cannot be wished away by postulating the epistemic necessity of sovereignty and they cannot be addressed through the perspective of grammar. The risk is that the subjects of public law are described as an *effect* of its grammar and all the political nuances related to their formation and development are lost.

Processes of subjectivation are far from being exhausted by constitutive and regulative rules; they are obtained through immersion in a series of relations which cannot be accessed exclusively through grammar and syntax.[64] For example, the political force of the main agents behind a constitutional order does not derive (at least not entirely) from the grammatical structure of public law. A grammar of public law cannot account for the non-linguistic element of political agency. It is to this material level of the determination of subjectivity that we now turn.

V. Subjectivity: The Material Constitution

The partial lack of focus on subjectivity betrays a residue of formalism which, or so it seems from the text, is not intended by the author. It is also quite striking that the *processes* of subjectivation are not taken into account given that the reconstruction of the power/liberty nexus advanced by Loughlin is much indebted to the analysis of—among others—Michel Foucault, for whom subjectivation was intrinsic to the dynamics of molecular power, in particular through various forms of resistance.[65]

The point made here, however, concerns a different level of engagement and argues that the marginal treatment of the role of subjects and subjectivation generates a 'material deficit', that is, a lack of materiality, in Loughlin's analysis of both the state and its constitution. One has to be careful in order to avoid misunderstandings. This is not to argue that the lack of treatment of subjectivation can be easily remedied by resorting to the work of political philosophers such as Jacques Rancière or Alain Badiou. The advocates of a 'politics of rupture' are not interested 'in the question of the forms of organisation of political collectives' and they do not take into consideration 'the alterations produced by acts of political subjectivation'.[66] Rancière (whose work provides a powerful conception of constituent

[63] Loughlin (n 15) 83.

[64] *Cf* M Bakhtin, *Speech Genres* (Austin, University of Texas, 1986).

[65] M Foucault, 'The Subject and Power' in H Dreyfus and P Rabinow (eds), *Michel Foucault. Beyond Hermeneutics and Structuralism* (Chicago, University of Chicago Press, 1983) 327–48. At the same time, Foucault would ground subjectivation on an ethics of the government of the self: 'Government of self and others'. I doubt that Loughlin would allow any kind of ethics slipping into political jurisprudence.

[66] J Rancière, 'La méthode de l'égalité' in *La philosophie déplacée: autour de Jacques Rancière* (Paris, Horlieu Editions, 2006) 514. Rancière refuses to examine 'the forms of consistency of the groups that produce them'.

power) is rather adamant in adopting a 'formalist' understanding of the political. Politics is above all a question of form, a formalism of equality:

> what makes an action political is not its object or the place where it is carried out, but solely its form, the form in which confirmation of equality is inscribed in the setting up of a dispute, of a community existing solely through being divided.[67]

The point made here is rather that the role of subjects (in particular, political subjectivities) ought to be taken into account by political jurisprudence because political action forges the material constitution. In particular, juristic knowledge should not ignore the material conditioning of subjectivities within a constitutional state and, from this perspective, their contribution to right ordering (usually through political conflict, bargaining, negotiations and, last but not least, the creation of a hegemonic bloc). The issue flagged up here, then, is not that political jurisprudence does not take into account disruptive politics; this is a misplaced criticism because the main concern of political jurisprudence is right ordering. It is, rather, that every concrete legal order is supported by particular subjects or, in constitutional jargon, political and social forces. To repeat what was stated in the previous section, the particular strength of hegemonic political forces is not the result of grammatical rules.

Loughlin himself concedes that there is no single exemplary model of the modern constitutional state but multiple experiences of it. The state exists only in its instantiations and those instantiations cannot be explained nor described by the grammar of public law. Nonetheless, it should be remembered that political jurisprudence begins from the recognition of the primacy of the material over the formal constitution. This points to five consequences affecting the study of public law: 1) the validity of the formal constitution is determined by an act of political will;[68] 2) the validity of the formal constitution does not rest on its correctness; 3) the formal constitution is not a codification; 4) the state of exception is legitimate when it preserves the material constitution; 5) amendability of the constitution is limited by the main tenets of the material constitution.[69] These insights are precious for public law and for comparative constitutional law. Yet, the potential dividends of these points are not fully cashed out in *Foundations*.

In fact, the consequences of the political economy that undergirds the material constitution are not explored at all. The analysis of Sieyès' conception of the constitution illustrates this point. His famous political treatise on the Third Estate is rightly recognised as a work of political jurisprudence. But Loughlin reads too much into Sieyès' emphasis on the nation as the only authentic source of the constitution and, in the language of political jurisprudence, as the guarantor of political unity. What is missing from the analysis is the link between the material dimension of the nation and the artificial construction of the political unity (the abbé, in order to stress its artificial nature, called the latter process *adunation*).[70]

While it is correct to highlight that Sieyès distinguishes between state and government, nation and positive law, it cannot be assumed that Sieyès' statement—'The nation exists prior to everything: it is the origin of everything. Its will is always legal. It is the law

[67] J Rancière, *Disagreement* (Minneapolis, University of Minnesota Press, 1999) 32.
[68] *Cf* P Kahn, *Putting Liberalism in its Place* (Princeton, Princeton University Press, 2005) 303.
[69] *Foundations* (n 1) 215.
[70] See P Pasquino, *Sieyes et l'invention de la constitution* (Paris, Edile Jacob, 1998) 33–35.

itself'[71]—is tantamount to a recognition of the juristic distinction between constitution and constitutional law. In fact, Sieyès adds a few lines below that 'A nation is formed solely by *natural* law'.[72] Many commentators have noted that when Sieyes speaks of natural law he means the organisation of society according to its political economy.[73] The nation, in fact, is far from being an existential unity. On the contrary, the nation is the organisation of functions and services, as is clearly stated at the beginning of that famous tract. These public and private functions ensure the constitution and reproduction of society around certain political principles, which in the case of Sieyès' constitutional thought are the division of labour and representation. While it remains clear that Sieyès' thought operates within certain coordinates (dictated by the modern state), it is impossible, on the other hand, to understand why the constitutional order ought to take a certain form without considering the subjects that make up the Third Estate.

Enlarging the scope of juristic knowledge to the study of the material constitution enlarges the field of public law and illuminates the concrete nature of legal orders in their different configurations. The study of the material dimension of modern constitutional orders can illustrate their specificities and peculiarities in a way that is precluded in grammatical analysis.[74] Political unity is shaped according to a concrete political trajectory and supported through the creation of hegemonic blocs, usually united around the pursuit of basic political aims. As Nicos Poulantzas brilliantly reminded us, there must be a reason why the contemporary liberal state gave itself that distinctive type of political constitution rather than another one.[75] Following his advice, the materiality of states and constitutions ought to be reconstructed through analysing the concrete spatial-temporal matrix that establishes the conditions of visibility and relevance of political subjects in a particular time and place. Moreover, it demands analysis of why political forces gather together and converge around certain objectives.

The material constitution has an object and a function. Its function is the production of political unity, while its object is the political trajectory of the state.[76] Both 'operations' impact on the organisation of society and its political system. The material constitution is always organised around the pursuit of specific objectives and the struggle to reach those objectives is strengthened by the formation of a hegemonic bloc whose concrete political power is supposed to leave an imprint upon society. Hence, the determination of the political trajectory of the state becomes an autonomous and peculiar trait of the modern art of governing societies.[77] In other words, the materiality of the constitution is the

[71] E Sieyès, *What Is the Third Estate?* in *Political Writings* (Indianapolis, Hackett, 2003) 128.

[72] ibid 136–37.

[73] *Cf* O Beaud, *La puissance de l'Etat* (Paris, Puf, 1994) 338; C Larrère, 'Sieyès lecteur des physiocrates: Droit naturel ou économie?' in PY Quiviger, V Denis and J Salem (eds), *Figures de Sieyès* (Paris, Publications de la Sorbonne, 2008) 195–212.

[74] A fruitful example of this type of analysis, applied to the EU, is M Wilkinson, 'Political Constitutionalism and the European Union' (2013) 76 *Modern Law Review* 191.

[75] N Poulantzas, *State, Power, Socialism* (London, Verso, 2004) 104.

[76] I use the expression 'political trajectory' to translate what Italian constitutional realists defined as 'indirizzo politico'. See V Crisafulli, 'Per una teoria giuridica dell'indirizzo politico' (1939) in his *Prima e dopo la costituzione* (Naples, ESI, 2015) 35–113.

[77] Costantino Mortati identified first the governing function as the Ur-function of every state in his 1931 *L'ordinamento del governo nel nuovo diritto pubblico italiano* (Milan, Giuffré, 2000).

'condensation' of social and political forces around determined objectives.[78] The condensation of specific forces around fixed political aims entails the creation of an institutional structure functional to the pursuit of those aims; nonetheless, the edification of this structure cannot be identified strictly with the realisation of those aims. The discrepancy between structure and function opens up a space for a relative political autonomy. Clearly, the political unity of a society is not granted once and for all, but is constantly subject to internal and external pressures. Unlike the classic understanding of the state as external to society and as a static institution, the material constitution shows the internally relational and dynamic nature of the state/society nexus.[79]

This is clearly relevant for juristic knowledge, for two reasons: it provides a more accurate picture of the evolution of political constitutions and regimes,[80] and, from the perspective of public law, it unveils the imprint behind the legal order, revealing the point of its rules from the perspective of the state's political trajectory and its governing function.[81]

Loughlin's understanding of the materiality of institutions and political subjects is riddled with ambiguity. He recognises that institutions (and the state as institution of institutions) are based on ideas, which confer meaning on the component parts of an institution. Ideas are not only regulative, but also constitutive. But to perform the latter function they cannot remain purely abstract. Loughlin here follows Peter Steinberger's reconstruction of the idea of the state: constituting ideas 'work through the principle of necessary embodiment'.[82] What kind of embodiment is this? At this point, political jurisprudence is in danger of leaving the domain of concrete order and landing in the field of political theology. The embodiment could be read as requiring that ideas are literally inscribed upon the citizen's body, which would work here as the material substratum of the constitutional imagination. It is not clear whether *Foundations* endorses this reading of embodiment, which would resonate with Schmitt's concept of the political.[83] A different possible reading of embodiment, suggested by the previous remarks, would focus on its materiality as an instrument to shape and reproduce social order and organisation through the exercise of political power.

Foundations of Public Law hints at this material dimension,[84] but never develops the thread of subjectivity. In his *Chorley Lecture*, Loughlin notes that the problem with the tradition of the material constitution is 'the assumption that economic forces act on ideas in a purely causal fashion'.[85] While this remark might apply to certain forms of

[78] Poulantzas (n 75) 186–87.

[79] See the criticisms of the state as a thing or as a subject in Poulantzas (n 75) 190–204.

[80] Some of the same concerns are shared by the American School of Constitutional Development: *cf* S Skowronek, *The Politics Presidents Make* (Cambridge Massachusetts, Harvard University Press, 1993).

[81] The same set of rules (say, the same formal constitution), applied in two different material contexts, has different points. This is a common insight of classic legal institutionalism, either in the version of the directive idea (*idée directrice*) by Hauriou or, more recently, in terms of commitment by R Cover, 'Nomos and Narrative' (1983) 67 *Harvard Law Review* 4, 34–35.

[82] *Foundations* (n 1) 207.

[83] It should be noted that Steinberger refers to the objectification of institutions, that is, the fact that they need to take a form in the material world: Steinberger (n 37) 25.

[84] At page 208, Loughlin notes that 'the material setting in which the idea of the state is set to work—the extent, location, and resources of the territory, and the customs and cultures of the peoples who comprise its members—not only have a significant impact on the ways in which the idea can be explicated, but will also re-shape the meaning of the idea itself' *Foundations* (n 1) 208.

[85] M Loughlin, 'The Constitutional Imagination' (2015) 78 *Modern Law Review* 1, 12.

economic reductionism as presented, for example, in the works of Ferdinand Lassalle or Charles Beard,[86] for whom the constitutional structure is just a reflex of undergirding economic power relations, it is certainly not applicable to more recent scholarship according to which the material constitution is a *political* construction whose requirements enable a relative autonomy of the political and are often confronted with a number of contradictions.[87]

A possible explanation for the relative absence of the role of subjects and their material conflicts in *Foundations* might be found in its historical reconstruction of the rise of the state's sovereignty. The lineage adopted by Loughlin is clear and privileges the type of modern political thought expressed in the philosophies of Bodin, Hobbes, Spinoza, Rousseau, and Hegel. The role of conflicts in right ordering is nonetheless present in the works attentive to questions linked to the *salus rei publicae*. One outstanding example is represented by Machiavelli, according to whom (and contrary to Hegel's influential interpretation of his work), at the origin of every order lies not a principle of political unity but always an inexhaustible conflict between antagonists.[88] Machiavelli sees a constitutive relation between order and conflict because the latter is immanent and it is intrinsic to reality. When he promises to follow '*la verità effettuale delle cose*' (the effective reality of things), he refers to the immanent space of conflict which saturates the space of reality.[89] In Machiavelli's constitutional thought, collective subjects ('*I grandi*' and '*il populo*') and political forces are a quintessential staple in structuring the political constitution. It would be possible to trace the same methodological position through other modern political philosophers, although, in most cases, they would not belong to the tradition on which Loughlin builds.[90]

By avoiding the material dimension of the constitution, the risk is that the autonomy of the political will not be able to maintain the productive tension between polarities but will sever its internal relation with the social in favour of a transcendental relation. Only by focusing on the conflictual processes of subjectivation in the formation and maintenance of political unity is it possible, for political jurisprudence, to maintain the material dimension of public law as both visible and relevant. By including a material dimension, political jurisprudence would shed an additional and different light on the governing art.

[86] See F Lassalle, *Qu'est-ce qu'une constitution?* (Paris, Dulliver, 1999) and C Beard, *An Economic Interpretation of the Constitution* (New York, Free Press, 1986).

[87] Beyond Mortati and Poulantzas, an obvious example is represented by Antonio Gramsci, *Prison Notebooks* (New York, Columbia University Press, 2011) and, more recently, A Negri, 'Towards a Critique of the Material Constitution' in *Books For Burning* (London, Verso, 2005) 180–229; id 'On the Constitution and Financial Capital' (2015) 32 *Theory, Culture & Society* (2015) 25.

[88] N Machiavelli, *Discourses* (London, Penguin, 1983). *Cf* F del Lucchese, 'Machiavelli and Constituent Power' (2016) *European Journal of Political Theory* 3–23.

[89] N Machiavelli, *Il principe* (Turin, Einaudi, 2002) 37. For analysis along these terms, see M Vatter, *Between Form and Event. Machiavelli's Theory of Political Freedom* (Dordrecht, Kluwer, 2000); *cf* R Esposito, *Living Thought: The Origins and Actuality of Italian Thought* (Stanford, Stanford University Press, 2012) 41–54.

[90] For example, the young Marx wrote a draft of a strong criticism of Hegel's doctrine of public law which contains many important considerations for the critique developed in this article: K Marx, 'Critique of Hegel's Doctrine of the State' in *Early Writings* (London, Penguin, 2005) 67–221; *cf* G della Volpe, *Rousseau and Marx* (London, Lawrence & Wishart, 1978).

12

Public Law and the Autonomy of the Political: *A Material Critique*

MICHAEL A WILKINSON

I. Introduction

The conceptual history outlined in *Foundations of Public Law*[1] depends for its concrete success on the modern European state of the 'long nineteenth century' (the period from the French Revolution to the First World War). Central to this reconstruction is the idea of the 'autonomy of the political realm'. This is largely accounted for by an orthodox secularisation thesis of modernity, claiming the autonomy of the political from the theological domain. Loughlin advances his own account of the foundations of public law by insisting, persuasively, that secularisation does not mean sheer legal positivisation. Public law does not become freestanding or self-executing through its modernisation: it depends upon a political order to sustain it. This political order, or better, the process of political ordering (to convey its dynamic quality) is conceptualised in the language of *droit politique* (political right) or, as in the opening chapter to this collection, 'political jurisprudence'. Political ordering stands in an internal relation to the positive law; this is by no means a straightforward coupling; it is a complex and potentially fraught relation. But secularisation does clear the way for a prudential *science* of political right, a 'pure theory' of public law, and all the difficulties that come with reconciling the claim to prudential and scientific logics.[2]

But what does the autonomy of the political look like if viewed in relation to the economic, rather than the religious worldview? How does the political ordering of public law stand in relation to the material reproduction of society? It might be said that political jurisprudence supposes a relative autonomy from this realm too. There is no autonomy of the political if, for example, political power is determined by economic power or specific class interests; if the political is a mere super-structural reflection of a material base, to adopt the Marxian metaphor. The autonomy of the political requires that the governing relationship in the modern state does *not* rest on the explicit fusion of political and economic power: it is the autonomy of the political from the economy that sustains the

[1] M Loughlin, *Foundations of Public Law* (Oxford, Oxford University Press, 2010) (hereinafter '*Foundations*').
[2] See also Panu Minkkinen, in chapter 4 of this volume.

authority and legitimacy of the ruling relationship, and distinguishes modern statehood from prior political forms.[3]

Loughlin is occasionally explicit about this, if less in *Foundations* than elsewhere in his work. Political relationships, he notes, cannot be reduced to socio-economic relations, political power is not reducible to economic power, political office is not based on property rights, subjects are to be considered 'citizens' rather than 'labourers, capitalists, or bourgeosie', and so on.[4]

But what *kind* of claims are these? This autonomy, even 'primacy', of the political over the economic is asserted by way of conceptual *stipulation*, rather than explained through any historical reconstruction. Unlike the autonomy of the political from the theological realm, Loughlin does not offer even a brief narrative of their relation; he gives no account, for example, of how political power is separated from economic power or how this is sustained in the modern state. Just as significantly, there is no sense of how the political might be threatened, subsumed or transformed by—from the other side—an autonomous 'economic realm' working on the basis of a distinct market logic. The autonomy of the political from the economic is instead *presupposed*; the basic relation between political ordering and the reproduction of material social relations is essentially implicit in *Foundations*.[5] All, that is, until its closing stages, a point to which we shall shortly return.

A more direct way of putting this is to say that the *capitalist state*, unlike the secular state, the state which distinguishes itself from market (rather than clerical) power receives little, if any, attention. The bearing of material questions on the process of political ordering take a back stage: relations between capital and labour, debtors and creditors, core and peripheral nations, the role of political economic strategies, mercantilism and colonial expansion, the role of taxation and control of the money supply—are all avoided. Processes of commodification, and the dynamic relation between public political power and private economic power, between public goods and private ownership, solidarity and competition, community and individualism, are under-examined. Relations of material equality and inequality, domestically, and in the uneven and combined development of global and regional economic systems, play little or no role in explaining the constitution of the modern state and the modern state-system.

The foundations of public law as presented by Loughlin indeed flatten or screen out material social relations, informal hierarchies, and more generally the persistence of socio-economic inequalities and class divisions, through the employment of terms such as 'political unity', 'the people' and 'popular sovereignty', however symbolic or reflexive their reprisal.[6] Material relations are also flattened out *geo-politically*, in a world order sustained through the sovereign equality of states, rather than through imperialism, colonialism, or other forms of domination within and between states or regional organisations. The state

[3] For extended discussion, see E Wood, *From Lords to Citizens: A Social History of Western Political Thought* (London, Verso, 2011).

[4] See M Loughlin, 'Political Jurisprudence', in chapter 2 of this volume, and earlier, eg 'Ten Tenets of Sovereignty' in N Walker (ed), *Sovereignty in Transition* (Oxford, Hart Publishing, 2003).

[5] These dual stories of differentiation of the political from the theological on the one hand, and the economic on the other, might of course themselves be inter-connected, in the relationship between secularisation and capitalism from the Reformation through the protestant work ethic, as outlined by Max Weber. But there is nothing to suggest that Loughlin endorses this Weberian story and Weber does not feature heavily in *Foundations*.

[6] See Loughlin, 'Political Jurisprudence' in chapter 2 of this volume.

is the unity of an undifferentiated multitude in this vision; political ordering is the process of achieving this (symbolic) juristic unity.

This absence gives political jurisprudence a formalistic character, despite the extraordinarily rich array of sources drawn on. There are, we are told, always 'rulers and ruled'; but we are never told how relative positions of ruling power are obtained, contested, or change, and what the role of public law is in establishing, maintaining or contesting them. We are told that public law provides a rule-based guide to the management of conflict; and that conflict will never be fully or finally resolved. But the account of underlying conflict is essentially Hobbesian—abstract rather than historicised, based on irreconcilable contest intrinsic to human nature rather than material inequalities, social hierarchies, class divisions, inter-state domination or imperial rivalries.[7]

In other words, the political economy of the modern state and state-system, unlike its political secularity, is irrelevant or only marginally relevant for framing political jurisprudence, a kind of irritant which can be kept external to political ordering. Although Loughlin hints at an exception to this elision—beginning with the Rousseauvian imperative to avoid 'extreme inequality of fortunes',[8] and continued in Hegel's concern with the inequalities produced by the workings of natural law in civil society,[9] the theme of inequality remains marginal in *Foundations* and is certainly not structural.

But why might this be considered theoretically problematic rather than merely a choice of emphasis? After all, even within the Marxist tradition, the juridico-political life of the capitalist state has come to be recognised as relatively autonomous, if in the last instance determined by the material base.[10] Another way of putting the question is to ask, what does the *presupposition* of the (relative) autonomy of the political from the economic *conceal*?

Two, related, responses to this question can be given at the outset because they inform the chapter as a whole. The first goes to the dynamic quality of the ruling relationship, a relationship that is central to Loughlin's juristic point of view. If material social relations can be marginalised in a political order which is characterised by and depends on the accepted idea of a particular ruling class or fixed arrangement of political power (eg aristocracy), they are problematised in an order which claims to be democratic in form, which aspires, one might say, to the complete interchangeability of rulers and ruled, or to some notion of *political equality*.[11] Claude Lefort's conception of the autonomy of the political, which Loughlin leans on, is nothing without the democratic impetus, beginning with the bourgeoisie revolutions of popular sovereignty at the end of the eighteenth century but continuing through the struggles for universal suffrage, and in its broader distinction with modern totalitarianism into the twentieth century. This is because Lefort's autonomy of the political, the 'empty place of power', is underpinned not just by secularisation but by the move from absolutism to democracy; it is through democracy as a *social regime* that political indeterminacy is maintained.[12]

[7] *Cf* Anna Yeatman, in chapter 8 of this volume.

[8] See *Foundations* (n 1) 119, 428.

[9] See *Foundations* (n 1) 349–50.

[10] See, especially, N Poulantzas, *State, Power, Socialism* (London, Verso, 1980).

[11] Loughlin doesn't spell out what political equality means, but it clearly plays a central conceptual role for him. As Andrew Halpin notes, in chapter 3 of this volume, the 'equality premise' is problematic, rich and complex, yet under-theorised by Loughlin.

[12] See C Lefort, 'The Question of Democracy', *Democracy and Political Theory* (translated by D Macey) (Cambridge, Polity Press, 1988) 9–20.

But does Lefort—and following him, Loughlin—underestimate the role of economic power in the material constitution of a society which is not just democratic but also *capitalist* in form, where the empty place of power is in danger of being 'filled'? The suggestion here is that the autonomy of the political on which public law rests should be approached less as a one-off rupture, and more as a continuous democratic, political struggle for the place of power to remain 'empty'—one that is fully material in nature because it has to contend with the dynamics of economic (and geo-economic) systems and the inequalities they generate. This has only become more pressing in the struggle against the increasingly conspicuous inequalities of advanced capitalism in the twenty-first century and new regimes of 'total market thinking' that threaten to erode the autonomy of the political.[13]

The second, related, point speaks to the episodic crises of legitimacy of the modern state and state-system. That this might be problematic is evident from within *Foundations* itself, Loughlin briefly recognising towards the end that public law comes under severe strain in the late twentieth century with the 'triumph of the social'.[14] But what is this a crisis *of*? Because of the insistence on secularism at the start, Loughlin is tempted into claiming that the crisis reflects a return of claims to religious truth but now in the form of objective social law; it is this that disrupts the interplay of political jurisprudence, threatening the distinctions on which public law rests, between state and society, private and public, inside and outside the sovereign state.[15] Since *Foundations* is built on the displacement of the theological, it is natural to suppose that crisis coincides with its resurfacing.[16] But is it plausible to suggest that modern crises can be made sense of predominantly in terms of the collapse of the dichotomy between public reason and religious truth? Is 'the social' really just a stand-in for 'the religious'?

From a material perspective, the strains on political jurisprudence instead arise from the destabilisation of the relation between the political and the economic realms, from crises of *democratic capitalism*. This destabilisation changes, or threatens to change, the material constitution of social relations in a way that undermines the relative autonomy of the political. Although heightened in critical moments, this reflects a general tension, or 'disequilibrium', between the logics of democracy and capitalism, community and individualism, solidarity and competition.[17] This set of material dynamics is central to the process of political ordering that political jurisprudence reconstructs. Or so it will be argued.

The chapter proceeds as follows. First, by asking what grounds the autonomy of the political, I will explore the issue of the material foundation of *Foundations*. This is elided by a focus on the secularisation thesis, but is thrown into sharper relief by Loughlin's later turn to Schmitt's reading of *nomos* (section II). Second, I explore the possibility—suggested in the threefold order of *nomos* itself—that the autonomy of the political stands in complex

[13] See E Christodoulidis, 'Total Market Thinking' (2015) *German Law Journal*. See also Panu Minkkinen, in chapter 4 of this volume, on the 'totalitarianism' of modern capitalism.

[14] *Foundations* (n 1) 461–65.

[15] *Foundations* (n 1) 462.

[16] The decisive theoretical figures, again, are Gauchet and Lefort, see *Foundations* (n 1) 48, 465.

[17] See, eg W Streeck, 'Taking Capitalism Seriously: Towards an Institutionalist Approach to Contemporary Political Economy' (2011) 9 *Socio-Economic Review* 137–67. Loughlin tentatively explores a variation of this dynamic through the anthropological work of Christopher Boehm, but this naturalises hierarchy and domination and presents the state as essentially egalitarian, *Foundations* (n 1) 196–98.

but internal relation to material social reproduction, dependent on but also threatened by the *relative autonomy of the economic*. Opening up this relation exposes the material dynamic of political ordering; revolving around social and political struggles for the relative autonomy of the political from the economic (section III). Then, moving to a more diachronic register, I suggest that this relation can also provide a cogent account of the periodic crises of public law and of the dynamic transformation, not only of government, but also of the state itself. This can only be touched on here, by examining first a critical period, the interwar breakdown of political order (section IV) and then, a major realignment of the political-economic relation, the post-war reconstitution of the European state in the project of European integration, which now again enters a critical phase (section V).

II. What Grounds the Autonomy of the Political?

The conceptual building blocks of *Foundations* coincide with the consolidation of the nation-state as a sovereign entity in a two-fold manner. Internally, it acquires the monopoly of legitimate force, based on secular foundations; in constitutional language, 'we, the people do solemnly ordain' our political and legal order. Externally, the nation-state is recognised as the only legitimate subject of international relations, with the right to decide on matters of war and peace, subject to conventions regarding civilised warfare, with a European 'balance of power' consolidated over a longer period, from the early modern nomos in the age of absolutism through to the 'golden age of the classical interstate system'.[18]

This is of course a simplification of a long and uneven historical process, but it crystallises a series of key conceptual distinctions: between international and domestic, public and private, state and society, the political and the social realms.[19] It culminates in a distinct field of juristic thought, the German tradition of *Staatslehre* at the turn of the century, where the constitution of the state is based on a trinity of territory, ruling authority, and people.[20] This begins its decline with the First World War and is radically problematised with the interwar breakdown of liberal constitutionalism and the collapse of the inter-state system, an interregnum that will be explored later in more detail.

But what are the material conditions for the grounding of these conceptual distinctions, as well as their eventual effacement? How do they appear in 'social-historical' perspective? On this, Loughlin appears ambiguous, particularly when *Foundations* is viewed alongside his other work.

Foundations itself suggests that the crucial rupture on which public law is built is immaterial: it is the autonomy—and primacy—of the political from the theological-spiritual domain that opens the space for the development of its key elements. This move is justified on the basis of Marcel Gauchet's 'secularisation thesis'—where modernity is characterised

[18] See B Teschke, 'Fatal Attraction: A Critique of Carl Schmitt's International Legal and Political Theory' (2011) 3 *International Theory* 179–227. Accordingly, the *jus publicum europaeum* implied a decisive rupture not only with divine right, but also with medieval just war theories, grounded in the moral universalism of the *respublica christiana*.

[19] For Loughlin's own statement see, eg 'Ten Tenets of Sovereignty' (n 4) above.

[20] See *Foundations* (n 1) 190–96.

as a process of religious disenchantment and the rupture is signaled by the secularisation of the grounds of political authority. This is identified and embraced by Loughlin at the very outset of *Foundations* as essential to the project of public law understood as *droit politique*.[21] It is the rational, symbolic and ideal that plays the lead role in generating the modern constitutional dialectic presented in *Foundations*, albeit without any Hegelian terminus.

But on the character of the state itself, more than a merely symbolic reading is required in order to explain how the concept of the people 'can incorporate some sense of a collective *body*, conscious of its political existence and with the capacity for action'.[22] Loughlin equivocates on the nature of this embodiment, drawing on Hans Lindahl's account of reflexive identity, and concluding that secular constitutional ordering is dynamic, never static.[23] An existential unity, which 'presupposes a mysterious prior substantial equality of the people', is thus replaced with a less reductionist and more 'relational' reading of the normative power of the factual.[24] His purpose is not to offer a new 'anti-normativism' but rather to capture the dialectic of fact and norm in the course of constitutional development.[25] This even leads the way to a (half-hearted) substitution of the Habermasian notion of the 'public sphere' for the concept of 'the state'.[26] Power then can be understood in fairly orthodox liberal fashion as based on allegiance, or consent, and generated by open, responsible government, and even—although Loughlin is careful not to endorse it as such—the notion of discourse ethics and the aim (if never the realisation) of something approximating rational consensus.[27]

The Habermasian reading clearly leads where Loughlin is reluctant to follow, to an embrace of a liberal normativism, where the political project of constitution-building is a stepping stone to the constitution of a world society, albeit based on a multi-level configuration: domestic, regional, international.[28] At a very basic level, the Habermasian notion of rational consensus would sit uncomfortably with Loughlin's insistence on the stubborn persistence of conflict in the human condition. But the broader problem, as I perceive it, is that reflexivity on its own does not and cannot account for the historical *unity* of the state, for its existence as a concrete political entity. It cannot account for 'the foundations of *Foundations*' at least not in anything other than a purely formal sense. In Lindahl's analytically informed enquiry, the state is reduced to just one more formal mode of collective association (or self-representation), subject to the same paradoxical modalities as any other, rather than representing the dominant instantiation of modern political ordering.[29] But the modern state for Loughlin is central to the foundations of public law.

[21] *Foundations* (n 1) 6–7.

[22] *Foundations* (n 1) 224. Italics added.

[23] *Foundations* (n 1) 226–27.

[24] *Foundations* (n 1) 220 (Jellinek's phrase). See also, 'Constituent Power' in M Dowdle and M Wilkinson (eds), *Constitutionalism Beyond Liberalism* (Cambridge, Cambridge University Press, 2017).

[25] *Foundations* (n 1) 220–21.

[26] *Foundations* (n 1) 228–31.

[27] *Foundations* (n 1) 171, describing Habermas's route as 'contentious' but noting that 'by maintaining a distinction between the generative and distributive aspects of power and between the forms of power exhibited in *potestas* and *potentia*, his achievement is to have established an intellectual framework that is able to incorporate the specificities of political power'.

[28] See J Habermas, *The Postnational Constellation* (Cambridge, Polity, 2001).

[29] See H Lindahl, *Fault-Lines of Globalisation* (Oxford, Oxford University Press, 2014).

Loughlin's later employment of the figure of *nomos* as developed by Carl Schmitt represents an attempt to firm up this ground. From this quite distinct perspective, public law is not founded primarily on the symbolic or the ideal, but on a *nomos* understood in its ancient, spatial, sense as a three-fold 'concrete order', based on an original appropriation (*nehmen*), then distribution (or division) and finally production (or pasturage) of land.[30] Together, this signifies the origins and source of the material constitution of political authority, sketched diachronically across three large-scale historical epochs.[31] The *jus publicum Europaeum* is specifically grounded on the second phase of the *nomos of the earth*, coinciding with the maritime 'discoveries' made by European peoples and the overcoming of civil war internally. This early modern *nomos*, based on land appropriation, accrual of the monopoly of legitimate violence, and a claim to radical title overseas, underwrites the foundations of modern public law. It provides nothing less than the social historical conditions for the relative 'autonomy of the political', 'an expression of the constituent power to establish order'.[32]

Loughlin is candid about this process that begins with a 'land-grab'; the 'original sin' of constitutional ordering remains at the foundations of public law.[33] But, again following Lindahl, Loughlin gives it a reflexive twist: only in hindsight, once the second and third orders of *nomos* (of distribution and production) are established, can the original act be identified as having succeeded in laying foundations. Again, reflexivity on its own might be a philosophically intriguing way out of a conceptual conundrum, but is substantively empty, flattening all instances of political ordering as if there were no specific form of the modern state in terms of the material organisation of distribution and production of resources in the economy.

The relation between the symbolic representation of the state inaugurated by the rupture of secularisation and the concrete form of the *nomos* in its material development is unclear. To complicate matters, there is in fact a trio of foundational elements that Loughlin develops, once we add in the significance of the concept of sovereignty and of the marks of sovereign power.[34] Sovereignty stands as the representation of the autonomy of the political, which requires the state as its scheme of intelligibility and sovereign powers to effectuate any right to rule; but sovereignty is not integrated into the narrative arc of *Foundations*. Neither is the relation between the marks of sovereignty and concrete order explained in Loughlin's turn to *nomos*.

[30] See M Loughlin, 'Nomos' in T Poole and D Dyzenhaus (eds), *Theorists of Constitutional Crisis: Oakeshott, Hayek and Schmitt on Law, Liberty and State* (Cambridge, Cambridge University Press, 2015) and M Loughlin, 'Politonomy' in J Meierhenrich and O Simons (eds), *The Oxford Handbook of Carl Schmitt* (Oxford, Oxford University Press, 2017) 570–92.

[31] It is interesting to note, as Schmitt does, commenting on its use in classical Greece, that *nomoi* and the Aristotelian notion of *politiea* could be created not only by land division but also by the liquidation of *debt*, see *The Nomos of the Earth in the Public Law of the Jus Publicum Europeaum* (New York, Telos Press, 2003 [1950]) 68.

[32] See Loughlin, 'Nomos' (n 30) above.

[33] Loughlin, 'Nomos' (n 30). The connection of *nomos* with violence is one reason for Arendt's ambivalence about the concept, and ultimate preference for the Roman *lex*, which is suggestive of a more dynamic, relational and less absolutist conception of origins. For discussion, see M Wilkinson, 'Between Freedom and Law: Hannah Arendt on the Burden of the Tradition' in Goldoni and MacCorkindale (eds), *Hannah Arendt and the Law* (Oxford, Hart Publishing, 2012).

[34] See, eg M Loughlin, 'Sovereignty' in *The idea of Public Law* (Oxford, Oxford University Press, 2003) Ch 5.

Nomos does, however, intriguingly, suggest a new avenue of conceptual-historical exploration for the adventures of the dialectic of political ordering—the material relation among its various orders: appropriation, distribution and production. To put it differently, it throws open the dynamic of state origin and state transformation from the perspective of the evolution of political economy and material social relations, to which we can now directly turn.

III. The Relation between the Political and the Economic in the Material Ordering of the *Nomos*

The three-fold concrete order of *nomos* suggests the autonomy of the political does not (only) depend on the symbolic process of religious disenchantment. It also suggests a more complex and dynamic ground than the act of territorial appropriation alone; a process that integrates the material organisation of distributive and productive forces and social relations, the second and third orders of *nomos*.

But appropriation, distribution and production operate within a capitalist economy according to an internal logic of their own and one that exists in an uneasy relation with the autonomy of the political realm. This relation between political and economic logics as a feature of *nomos* is captured by an extension of Rosa Luxemburg's characterisation of imperialist *Land-nahme* as signifying not only literal 'land-grabbing' ('simple robbery' as Arendt calls it) but also metaphorical market expansion, integrating spatial accumulation with increasing *commodification*.

Luxemburg's insight suggests a political-economic reconstruction of the three-fold order of *nomos*, as well as a related but distinct periodisation in contrast to Schmitt's.[35] The changing character of *nomos* reflects the transformation of the state from a *feudal* to a *capitalist and later to an imperial* organisation of political and economic power;[36] and even to postmodern types of state power such as those emerging in the more recent period of informal American empire and economic neo-liberalism.[37]

The process of political ordering and state development can then be internally related (but not reduced) to the logic of capitalist social relations. Political ordering operates not just on the initial—or subsequent—forceful accumulation, concentration and protection of land (or property), but on a *continual transformation* of social relations, setting 'in train distinctive imperatives of competition, profit-maximisation, the compulsion to

[35] See R Luxemburg, *The Accumulation of Capital* (London, Routledge, 2013 [1913]).

[36] Arendt's endorsement of Rosa Luxemburg's 'brilliant insight into the political structure of imperialism' (*Origins of Totalitarianism* (San Diego, Harvest, 1979 [1951]) 148) is interesting because Arendt, like Schmitt, tries to retrieve the Greek idea of *nomos*. Although Schmitt omits discussion of Luxemburg's updating of Marxism for the imperial age, he does, briefly, address Marx's idea of original appropriation in *Nomos of the Earth* (n 31) 333–34. He adds, 'if the essence of imperialism lies in the precedence of appropriation before distribution and production, then a doctrine such as expropriation of the expropriators is obviously the strongest imperialism, because it is the most modern' 334.

[37] See L Panitch and S Gindin, *The Making of Global Capitalism: The Political Economy of American Empire* (London, Verso, 2012). For an exploration of the recent continuation of capitalist land-grabbing, see, eg F Jamieson, 'Aesthetics of Singularity' (2015) *New Left Review*.

reinvest surpluses, and the need to improve labour productivity by developing the forces of production'.[38] It is not only original or 'primitive' accumulation (or 'appropriation') that sets up the economic and social conditions for the market, as Smith, Marx and Weber noted,[39] but also the periodical re-constitution of these conditions through 'accumulation by dispossession' (through re-distribution and re-production of resources by political means).[40] Social relations are transformed through direct and indirect forms of intervention which function to commodify and marketise, impose competitiveness, austerity or privatization, or shift private into public debt, and so on. The extent to which these processes can still usefully be categorised on the basis of traditional class analysis is moot, but the class pedigree of *nomos* can hardly be doubted. As Brunkhorst bluntly puts it, 'no nomos without class rule',[41] a feature of *nomos* also noted right at its root, by Aristotle.[42]

The autonomy of the political from the economic is thus a dynamic, two-sided affair, rather than the one-off rupture from religion sealed by the event of secularisation.[43] To keep both sides in sight has the advantage of thrusting into view the consequences for political ordering of the *relative autonomy of the economic*, which contemporaneously evolves in the modern state. This reveals the state 'from the other side', as it were. These are not parallel developments but interlinked; the state might be said to encompass the 'unity in difference' of these two faces of the political *and* the economic, public and private. In other words, the state, if viewed not only as a secular but as a capitalist formation is one in which the *economy* (comprising taking, distributing and producing) *is relatively autonomous from the political*, paradigmatically expressed in classical as well as newer forms of liberalism in the idea of the self-regulating market, the myth of the invisible hand, the sanctity of debt, conditions of perfect competition, etc. This develops its own set of legal couplings, with property rights, contractual obligations, formal equality of status, emerging in the constitution of the modern state and state-system. As a dynamic, it tracks the transformation of social relations of reciprocity and solidarity into what Hayek would later call 'catallactic relations': relations of exchange, based on competition and self-interest. Within this realm, *inequality* is legitimated, justified, or naturalised. It is, in any case, 'privatised' and de-politicised.[44]

It is notable that it is not only Marxist and critical theories that are missing from Loughlin's account of the dynamic of political ordering. *Foundations*' own conceptual categories are never placed in relation with the traditions of classical, neo-classical, ordo-liberal or neo-liberal thought that insist on naturalising or insulating the 'laws' of the

[38] E Wood, 'Logics of Power: A Conversation with David Harvey' (2006) *Historical Materialism* 19–20.

[39] The identification of coercive forms of appropriation—whether through domestic corruption, war, or in forms of global imperialism ('political capitalism')—as central to the formation of the modern state is stressed by Max Weber. See, eg R Swedberg, *Max Weber and the Idea of Economic Sociology* (Princeton, Princeton University Press, 1998) 46–53.

[40] See D Harvey, *The New Imperialism* (Oxford, Oxford University Press, 2003) 36.

[41] See Hauke Brunkhorst, in chapter 6 of this volume.

[42] For Aristotle, 'the rule of nomos means the rule of the middle classes as opposed to the rule of the very rich, on the one hand, and the rule of the masses or the poor, on the other', cited in Schmitt, above, *Nomos of the Earth* (n 31).

[43] Whether or not this is in fact such a neat and singular rupture is debatable, but need not be explored here. See Jacco Bomhoff, in chapter 5 of this volume, for some doubts.

[44] According to Wood, 'Capitalism alone has created an autonomously economic form of domination', in 'Logics of Power' (n 38) 13.

private, market sphere, beginning with Locke, Smith and Paine but continuing in prominence in the post-war era with the group associated with the Mont Pelerin Society.[45] The figure of John Locke, who arguably grounds this more substantive material account of the modern state but from a classical liberal perspective, based on individual property rights, and a labour theory of ownership, is conspicuous by his absence in *Foundations*, featuring only in regard to his influence on modern understandings of the prerogative power.[46]

Loughlin, unlike Schmitt (or in different ways Hayek or Oakeshott) does not aim to defend a liberal (bourgeois) *Rechtsstaat* against the perceived encroachments of political social democracy.[47] Political jurisprudence is thus resistant to the Marxist critique (as well as the liberal defence) of political economy to the extent that its aim is not to defend an illusive bourgeois order, but to account for political order as such, which only contingently depends on the workings of a liberal rule of law. And the politically disruptive potential of an autonomous civil society is alluded to by Loughlin, albeit rather in passing, when taking note of Hegel's reconstruction, where the market, if left to its own devices, would paradoxically tend to increase the need for government, as it would exacerbate existing inequalities that would then need to be tempered through political means.[48] Hegel's concern for the tendency of bourgeoisie society towards inequality and therefore instability due to its tendency towards over-accumulation at one end and deprivation at the other is captured in his notion of the 'rabble', a problem of the dispossessed (as well as the ultra-wealthy) that is produced by industrial capitalism.[49] Although it is one to which Hegel offers no satisfactory solution, he captured the nature of the problem, unlike many later liberals.

And yet, for Loughlin, as for Hegel, this problem of inequality—to the limited degree it is addressed—is presented entirely from the 'top-down'. It is presented in terms of governing *potentia* (capacity to rule) rather than in its dynamic with *potestas* (right to rule). *Potentia* emerges as a managerial, top-down activity of government rather than a bottom-up struggle for equal rights taking place in civil society through social movements and political parties, mediating the balance between public goods and private interests.[50] Material relations are relegated to a technical, administrative machinery of governing in the interest of the *salus populi*—a term which itself flattens out material inequalities, and the continuous oscillation between public and private power. The dynamic of *potentia* is not rejoined to its roots as collective *power to* but restricted to a question of capacity

[45] See P Mirowski, *The Road from Mont Pelerin: The Making of the Neo-Liberal Thought Collective* (Harvard University Press, 2009).

[46] *Foundations* (n 1) 383–87.

[47] Perry Anderson, in a masterful essay, groups Schmitt, Hayek and Oakeshott, along with Strauss, as the 'Intransigent Right' of the twentieth century, see P Anderson, 'The Intransigent Right at the End of the Century' (1992) *London Review of Books*.

[48] *Foundations* (n 1) 349–50.

[49] See F Ruda, *Hegel's Rabble: An Investigation into Hegel's Philosophy of Right* (London, Bloomsbury, 2011).

[50] Although Loughlin makes brief reference to Mortati's emphasis on political parties (*Foundations* (n 1) 397), as Brunkhorst puts it: 'the alternative version of *potentia* that he had distinguished in Chapter 6 on "Political Jurisprudence" … characterised … as "power to" (with Arendt and Habermas), as distinct from "power over" (Mann, Foucault) and which is "rooted in the intersubjective generation of solidarity" is gradually lost in later chapters' (Hauke Brunkhorst, in chapter 6 of this volume).

in a mechanical sense, despite Loughlin having the resources to reunite it with the more emancipatory traditions that draw from Spinoza.[51]

The dialectic of capacity and right to rule (the 'capacity-right nexus', as Loughlin now calls it) tracks the relation between the political and the economic not only as a question of governmental power but also of state (and inter-state) formation.[52] This is because the constitution of political power—in its relation to the economy and vice versa—goes to the question of the governing relationship and the set of beliefs on which it rests. In Loughlin's own terminology, material relations go to the question of *potestas* and the relation between *potestas* and *potentia*.

This is not to deny of course, that material relations are, to a large extent, 'managed' through governmentality, as Loughlin argues, but this view alone misses the significance of social movements, political parties, geo-political currents and interpersonal social relations in the dynamic of political ordering and disordering. These are material forces which constitute and reconstitute beliefs about the ruling relationship and about the nature of the *demos* itself. The idea of equal political liberty, a principle apparently central to but insufficiently articulated in 'political jurisprudence', does not transpire as a moment of symbolic or normative revelation, but unfolds over time; it attracts a different *meaning* over time through democratic movements of solidarity and emancipation as well as capitalist movements of competition and domination.

The Enlightenment trinity of 'liberty, equality and fraternity' rather loses its third component for the major part of *Foundations*—until it re-appears through the work of Duguit and his functionalist notion of 'social solidarity'. But it is disarmed of any radical potential. Solidarity is merely a fact of social life in this account, divorced from any class or other struggle against injustice, domination or exploitation. The project of egalitarian solidarity, as Brunkhorst puts it, which emerges from the bottom-up as communicative 'power to' (as a feature of the dialectic of *potentia*/*potestas*), is elided in *Foundations*. These struggles may well have a functional element, but it is hard to see how functionality would *guarantee* the necessary equilibrium, short of a strong, and perhaps improbable, social-biological evolutionary thesis.[53]

By marginalising the problem of inequality or delegating it to a discrete domain of anthropological enquiry, and by *presupposing* the relative autonomy of the political from the economic, rather than reconstructing it and problematising its social-historical development, Loughlin's account is deprived of a crucial aspect if not *the key* to conceptualising the material tensions inherent in the actual dynamic of political ordering and—crucially, of *disordering*.

The broader point is that the political is only relatively autonomous from the material composition of society. Material inequalities are not hermetically sealed off or fully separated from the political. They pose a challenge not just to the necessary stability of the governing arrangements but to the maintenance of the idea of political equality on which the

[51] See, eg M Hardt and A Negri, *Empire* (Cambridge, Massachusetts, Harvard University Press, 2000).

[52] See now M Loughlin, 'Erosion of Sovereignty' (2017) *Netherlands Journal of Legal Philosophy*.

[53] For Loughlin, according to his brief anthropological reconstruction, the egalitarian impulse comes, if at all, from the state, in contrast to the natural inequalities of man. See *Foundations* (n 1) 197–98.

autonomy of the political depends, not least because of the potential of a hegemonic bloc to dominate or even determine the activity and structure of political ordering, or erode it altogether. The empty place of power, recall, depends on a political indeterminacy that can only be guaranteed by the praxis of democratic struggle. It is achieved or rather is achievable (since it must be viewed as ongoing) through contesting the heteronomy of the market, the alienation of class rule, the domination of cultural hierarchy, the subjugation of imperialist coercion. These struggles are abstract tussles over the meaning of concepts such as freedom and equality as well as material contests over power and resources, involving persuasion, solidarity and force.

Loughlin's metaphor of 'grammar', like the concept of 'reflexivity', is too formal a notion to account for these dynamics and the emergence of competing and collective subjects in conditions of inequality.[54] This deficiency is common to the line of thinking that is so central in Loughlin's reconstruction of political order, from Hobbes through to Schmitt. The Hobbesian-Schmittian foregrounding of a ruling relation of 'protection and obedience' (despite their differences) elides social relations of domination as well as those acts of resistance against them that shape the quality of political order. Both aim to overcome a supposedly natural hierarchy, in Hobbes case by supposing rough equality between persons, in Schmitt's account by employing the concept of homogeneity. But in so doing they naturalise social hierarchies and inequalities of wealth and resources, by projecting as a state of nature or as the basic political binary (friend/enemy) what is in fact a *social* state of conflict.

Political jurisprudence makes a similar move, flattening out social relations with the concept of 'political unity', however reflexive a twist this is given. Without any account of the material struggle *for and over* the autonomy of the political—from a dominant economic class, geo-political formations or from 'economism' more generally—the autonomy of the political becomes substantively less rich, and, if secularisation is considered to be a fait accompli, ultimately empty.

At this point, we can bring the democratic character of the modern state more sharply into view. This is not merely a normative issue. The relevant problem posed by modern democracy is primarily *material* in nature. It is that the democratic dynamic historically (naturally?) expands and extends the demand for material goods, and for relative material equality, calling for redistribution or changes in the conditions of production. As individuals, groups and classes strive for political emancipation in the struggle for universal franchise, for basic political equality (workers movements, women's movements, post-colonial movements, etc) their demands place exacting material burdens on the governing arrangements of the state as well changing the basic ideas of collective autonomy. These are not only political struggles narrowly conceived, but struggles for the transformation of material social relations, for 'effective autonomy', or for us to will the means to our collective autonomy, as Castoriadis puts it.[55]

These struggles face obstacles, first, to be pursued in a way which respects other constitutional principles associated with the advance of liberal ideas of good government,

[54] See also Marco Goldoni, in chapter 11 of this volume.

[55] See C Castoriadis, *Philosophy, Politics, Autonomy: Essays in Political Philosophy* (translated by D Ames) (Oxford, Oxford University Press, 1991). *Cf* James Penner in chapter 7 of this volume.

historically with the liberal rule of law (or *bourgeois Rechtsstaat*). The political-economic relation exposes how positive public law can come into conflict with various imperatives of governmentality, which are themselves directed and conditioned by social and political contest. The relationship between state and society, the political and the economic, is thus mediated not only by governmental policy but by a liberal order which guarantees the conditions for market autonomy in an apparently 'neutral' manner; private property relations, intellectual property guarantees, freedom of contract, conditions of free competition and so on.

Over the course of the 'short twentieth century', as democracy increasingly makes its mark as a material force, the relationship is also mediated by the imperatives of the *sozial Rechtsstaat*, regulating matters such as welfare, social rights and industrial relations, in an attempt to balance or remedy the harsh and potential disruptive consequences of the market society.

But these democratic material demands are not placed within a vacuum, but face the counter-pressure of a capitalist dynamic (whether framed as a hegemonic class or bloc or as a representation of 'market justice'), through the ability of a capitalist class to affect the political process, to threaten to transfer wealth, withhold or avoid tax, utilise the conservative machinery of the very same liberal legal system to refuse or obstruct structural change to the political-economic order. As Wolfgang Streeck puts it, the modern state has to maintain equilibrium between the *Staatsvolk* and the *Marktvolk* that is increasingly in tension.[56] This is explainable on the basis of the contradictory tendencies of democratic capitalism itself—but this explanation is not open to Loughlin because of his focus on the imaginary on the one side, and the managerial on the other. At root it is because of his avoidance of any investigation into the modern state *as* a democratic and/or capitalist state, which is the material form that the political-economic relation takes in modernity.

IV. The Interwar Breakdown of Public Law: A Crisis of the State

From a material perspective, the autonomy of the political is a fragile, ambiguous and even illusive achievement, rather than a one-off creation of the modern world, 'born of the deepest ever fracture in history'.[57] Once the autonomy of the political is placed in dialectical relation with the autonomy of the economic, the political state with the market state, the material constitution of order and disorder can be explored and with it the fragility of public law. This cannot be passed off or bracketed as vulnerable only in the exceptional situation when 'extreme inequality' or a tumultuous rabble makes its presence felt as a political irritant; it is intrinsic to the ebb and flow of state transformation, if making its mark most clearly in conjunctural moments.

This precarious situation of political order reaches breaking point in the interwar years, and now returns if not (yet) with quite the same intensity in the current crises of

[56] See W Streeck, *Buying Time: The Delayed Crisis of Democratic Capitalism* (London, Verso, 2014).
[57] *Foundations* (n 1) 7, citing Gauchet.

democratic capitalism, presented acutely in the recent Euro-crisis, but reflected elsewhere. The later set of events of course largely post-dates *Foundations*. But it will be suggested here that a diachronic analysis of interwar Europe and post-war reconstruction offers an account of the heightened tension and collapse followed by a basic re-ordering of the political-economic relation crucial to the transformation of public law in the twentieth century.

It is curious that neither the interwar breakdown of political ordering nor its post-war reconstruction is given much attention in *Foundations*, or indeed in Loughlin's later turn to explore the concept of *nomos*. And it is a disconcerting feature of the narrative of *Foundations* that recent developments such as those associated with the 'triumph of the social' get blurred into Duguit's work from the 1920s, skipping the 'short twentieth century' in between.

In the interwar period, the key distinctions on which *Foundations* builds are put under severe stress—between interstate and domestic, between state and society, the political and the economic, public and private, *potestas* and *potentia*. The myth of the state of the 'long nineteenth century' and the order it represented faced extreme pressures, an order in crisis if not in terminal decline.[58] The problem for an approach to political ordering which prioritises *nomos* as land appropriation in this context is apparent; Schmitt himself considered the modern *jus publicum Europaeum* to have been displaced, because land was no longer the 'clear-cut ground for political and economic organisation', even though political and legal thinking remained mired in the 'older elemental presuppositions'.[59]

The second phase of the *nomos* of the *jus publicum Europeaum* had reached its end game with the First World War. Schmitt would later speculate that the chaos brought about with the end of the British Empire and the disintegration of the inter-state Westphalian order it loosely underwrote could only properly be resolved if the world was reorganised into continental blocks underpinned by large-scale transnational economic orders. When German hegemony failed to materialise, Schmitt turned his attention to the emerging American empire with its liberal universalist ideology and the technical means to extend its global influence, with control of air power. As Loughlin himself puts it: 'in place of European powers determining the spatial order of the world, during the 20th century the world determined the spatial order of Europe', a reversal that signals a new stage in the evolution of the *nomos* of the Earth.[60]

But rather than merely signifying geo-elemental or geo-political shifts, the interwar breakdown of political order and its post-war resettlement must be reconstructed on the basis of the political-economic order, and the tension between democracy and capitalism. Without discounting the importance of regional and global re-orientations, it is the threat posed by democracy and capitalism as domestic social forces to disrupt the political-economic relation that is salient for political jurisprudence.

All that can be offered here is a brief and stylised reconstruction of this interregnum. There is of course a much longer background dynamic involved. The conservative fear of popular emancipation is presaged in an earlier epoch; evident from Marx's critique of Hegel's *Philosophy of Right* and the 'democratic revolutions' of 1871, and 1848, and even

58 Teschke (n 18) 187.
59 G Balakrishnan, 'Geopolitics of Separation' (2012) *New Left Review* 68.
60 Loughlin, 'Nomos' (n 30).

earlier with the Rousseauian influence on the Jacobins.[61] But for interwar conservative liberals, such as Schmitt, the question of how the process of democratisation could be made safe for liberal economics had become immediately pressing for domestic political reasons (heightened by the threat posed by the Bolshevik revolution).

Interwar pressure on the established political-economic relation of classical liberalism comes from two directions—from unfettered market power leading to monopoly capitalism and ultimately Fascist dictatorship on the one hand, and from unfettered democracy leading to socialism, common ownership of the means of production and the loss of the relative autonomy of the economic on the other. Both threaten the normal workings of distribution and production in the liberal market economy of the 'long nineteenth century'. The threat to the old political order emerged, in other words, in relation to *internal* as much as external 'enemies' of the existing state and state-system of the *jus publicum Europeaum*.

Political equality—hitherto merely a formal presupposition of liberal social contract theory—becomes materially significant in the interwar period both as a force of social and economic change, and as a new basis for claims of legitimate authority. This is a general phenomenon, but a focus on Weimar Germany sharpens the issues. As a social force, democracy is liberated and strengthened through the grant of universal suffrage (guaranteed for the first time in German history by the Weimar constitution itself), and by intense party politics and parliamentary democracy, the rise of local and regional claims to autonomy, including worker's councils and other movements of economic democracy.

For Schmitt, the welfare state, the 'quantitatively total state', colonised by interest groups and associations, would be a deformation of the classical liberal 'neutral state' of the nineteenth century.[62] Actually existing pluralism, seen through Hobbesian eyes, was one step away from a condition of civil war within which there would be no judge to determine 'mine' and 'thine', threatening the disintegration of bourgeois society.[63]

The emancipatory potential of class-consciousness combined with universal suffrage raised the possibility for full political control over the economy—threatening the balance between the political and the economic and precipitating a crisis of political ordering and of public law itself. As an ideological matter, democracy becomes increasingly central to constitutional theory through the linking of legitimate authority with democratic procedure (coincident with the associated rise of legal positivism).[64]

All were subject to Schmitt's fierce polemic. But above all, it was social democracy that threatened his position because it called into question not only how socio-economic conflicts should be mediated through structures of 'government' (*potentia*) but the basic

[61] See, eg M Goldoni, 'Rousseau's Radical Constitutionalism and its Legacy' in Dowdle and Wilkinson (n 24).

[62] See K Tribe, *Strategies of Economic Order: German Economic Discourse 1750–1950* (Cambridge, Cambridge University Press, 1995) 179–80.

[63] G Balakrishnan, *The Enemy: An Intellectual Portrait of Carl Schmitt* (London, Verso, 2002) 124. 'In Schmitt's view' Balakrishnan notes, 'the polycratic, corporatist, welfare state threatened the existence of the state as a higher power standing above society, or even as a neutral power standing impartially between the major social classes' (at 104).

[64] Schmitt thus considered authoritarianism a necessary antidote both to the fragmentary processes of democratization and pluralisation, which were weakening the German state and endangering its Constitution, and to the relativism of a legal positivism without substance, personified in the figure of Hans Kelsen and his *Pure Theory of Law*.

relationship between state and society, the political and the economic, central to the established category of the right to rule (*potestas*). The very idea of the General Will—which eliminates the right of resistance in classical social contract thought—became threatening with the politically active population no longer a discreet and homogenous male bourgeoisie. The problem that democratic emancipation and class struggle posed for the politically conservative and economically liberal Schmitt was apparent: 'in a democratic age it was entirely possible that a legislature based on universal suffrage could chip away at the rules of property and contract which regulate the intercourse of bourgeoisie society.'[65] It threatened the governing relationship, the remodeling of the idea of the political order of the state and of the people who constituted it. What for Sieyes was the 'third estate', which was nothing and shall become everything, potentially becomes the working class. This was Schmitt's fear.

> Now the proletariat becomes the people, because it is the bearer of this negativity. It is the part of the population which does not have property, does not participate in the productive majority, and finds no place in the existing order … Democracy becomes a proletarian democracy, and eliminates the liberalism of the propertied and educated bourgeoisie.[66]

How could the normal political-economic relation be protected or reinvented in the political turbulence of late Weimar? For Schmitt, as for many other conservatives (with the notable exception of Austrian economic liberals), it was impossible to envisage any straightforward return to laissez-faire, a 'nightwatchman state' in the vein of Hayek and other conservative liberals and later libertarians across the Atlantic; the restoration of the relationship between the political and economic could be achieved only with a temporary (or more permanent) suspension of legal order by commissarial dictatorship, violating the separation between politics and economics in order to restore it. If the movement of the autonomy of the political threatened the capitalist state (viz. *the relative autonomy of the economic*), then militant protection was required to defeat it. What was required was, in his view, an authoritarian state.

The significance of this new authoritarianism is apparent in Schmitt's address in November 1932 to an association of German industrialists, the *Langnam Verein*: 'Strong state, free economy',[67] in which he advocates a robust autonomous economic order, as a third category in addition to and separate from the state and the individual entrepreneur (or 'private sphere').[68] In this model, economics must become neither totally politicised, as recommended by social democrats, nor totally privatised, as urged in classical liberalism. But above all, it must not be subject to the forces of democracy.

Hermann Heller, Schmitt's social democratic protagonist in late Weimar, saw with great clarity the authoritarian nature of the political formation that Schmitt was defending. To grasp its full significance, a reaction to the inherent instability of political order in a society

[65] Balakrishnan (n 63) 98.

[66] C Schmitt, *Constitutional Theory* (translated by J Seitzer) (Durham, NC, Duke University Press, 2008) 271–72.

[67] See R Cristi, *Carl Schmitt and Authoritarian Liberalism: Strong State, Free Economy* (University of Wales Press, 1998). Schmitt permitted its reprinting at least twice, suggesting for W Scheuerman that it was a text that was of some significance to him, see *Carl Schmitt and the End of Law* (Rowman and Littlefield, 1999) 288.

[68] The demand for *autonomous economic administration* would complement and overlap the third form of institutional juristic thought he was concurrently developing, based on concrete order, influenced by French jurist, Hauriou. See K Jayasuriya, 'Globalisation, Sovereignty and the Rule of Law: From Political to Economic Constitutionalism' (2001) 8 *Constellations* 442–60.

that is both democratic and capitalist, Heller takes a longer view of the ebbs and flows of nineteenth and early twentieth century liberalism, and its strange mutation into a form of 'conservative liberalism'.[69] In the nineteenth century, the conservative, reactionary forces protecting the feudal order had put up fierce if uneven resistance to the pressures of liberalism and capitalist modernisation. Although largely unsuccessful, not all their efforts went unrewarded, as conservatives managed to inculcate into the bourgeoisie political sensibilities that produced a 'peculiar feudal capitalist inter-breeding', labeled 'national liberalism'. The reverse process was now taking place, in Heller's view, as the forces of conservatism are marshaled in *defence* of liberal capitalism and against any forms of solidarity. 'Matching this sociological transformation, the "authoritarian" state represents a further development of national liberalism. Most appropriately it is' Heller concludes, 'to be addressed as *authoritarian liberalism*'.[70]

This designation is justified in Heller's view because of its position vis-à-vis the 'cardinal problem' of the present, 'the question of the economic order', prescribing, as it does, a strict *separation* of politics and the economy. Mutual bonds, rather than being urged to resist the pressures of liberal modernisation, must now be 'loosened', at least regarding socio-economic matters.[71] The primary object of the authoritarian liberals was the elimination of social democracy from politics and the defence of an autonomous economic sphere, not through laissez-faire, but through intervention.

Loughlin's insistence on neutralising Heller, suggesting that he adopted a 'highly abstract' conception of constituent power, is puzzling.[72] It is not only that this elides Heller's active part in the German Social Democratic Party as antagonist of Schmitt, which is clearly at the surface of his political writings in Weimar; it is that these commitments are essential in Heller's view for stabilising the constitutional dialectic itself. In an era of actual democracy, with full participation, the material prospect of socio-economic equality in addition to the symbolic integration of society is required for the constitutional state to function, to obtain enduring political legitimacy; in its absence, the tendency will be to turn to authoritarian alternatives, whether of Left or Right.

For the process of political ordering in a democracy there must be some prospect of substantive equality 'between rulers and ruled', even though Heller doubts that this can ever be truly and finally achieved, because the social structure is 'necessarily antagonistic'.[73] This antagonism, for Heller, is fully material in nature due to the dynamics of a capitalist economy. But in Heller's vision, material inequality may ultimately be fatal to political order: the prospect at least of relative socio-economic equality is required for the stability of the

[69] H Heller, 'Authoritarian Liberalism' (translated from 1932) (2015) *European Law Journal.*

[70] ibid.

[71] ibid.

[72] See M Loughlin, 'On Constituent Power' in Dowdle and Wilkinson (n 24) 170. Loughlin is not alone in marginalising Heller's substantive commitments. Dyzenhaus makes the same move in his book on Heller, Schmitt and Kelsen, underplaying both Schmitt's economic liberalism and Heller's democratic socialism, see D Dyzenhaus, *Legality and Legitimacy: Carl Schmitt, Hans Kelsen and Hermman Heller in Weimar* (Oxford, Oxford University Press, 1997). The problem with this move has been noted elsewhere, see, eg C Thornhill, 'Carl Schmitt after the Deluge' (2000) *History of European Ideas* 225–64. It is at the same time a great strength, and a weakness, of *Foundations* that it so strenuously avoids questions of *politics*.

[73] H Heller, 'Political Democracy and Social Homogeneity' from A Jacobson and B Schlink (eds), *Weimar: A Jurisprudence of Crisis* (University of California Press, 2002) 257. The dialectic of fact and norm is, in a democracy more than elsewhere, dependent on and shaped by 'social equalisation', Heller, ibid, 261.

governing relation. It is for political democracy to work this through peacefully, with the aid of political parties, which are able to unite a multitude of wills into a singular voice.

To refocus political ordering with a view to its broader reintegration with political economy and the issue of inequality, and over a longer durée, we can turn to the work of Karl Polanyi, whose account of *The Great Transformation* of industrial capitalism, and the resulting political and social reaction to its dis-embedding of social relations mirrors Heller's own reflections. In Polanyi's account, the modern nation-state exists and evolves in dialectical relation with the modern market economy.[74] If the modern nation-state operates according to a logic of political equality and solidarity, the modern market economy functions on the basis of material inequality and competition.

These two distinct logics exist in a perpetual tension, captured by the Polanyian figure of the 'market society'. The commodification of the 'fictitious commodities' of land, money and labour (disembedding that which must remain embedded in society) thus produces a reaction, when society tries to protect itself from the harsh consequences of marketisation, a reaction which may be spontaneous as well as organised. The form this response takes varies greatly depending on the strength of the democratic culture of the society—where this has been hollowed out by forms of authoritarianism, and where spontaneous reaction has been obstructed by political power, society may be too weak to prevent an eventual extreme response. This explains the interwar breakdown of liberal constitutionalism, when forced economic liberalisation and rigid adherence to austerity ultimately produces a 'double movement' of dramatic social and ultimately political reaction.

Polanyi notes how this dialectic plays out in geopolitical as well as domestic relations; politics could be made submissive to the economy by external constraints on the democratic process. Particularly significant in Polanyi's account, is the attempt in the 1920s to restore the Gold Standard, submitting politics to an overwhelming 'economic rationality', in an attempt to protect currency stability.[75] It was no coincidence, for Polanyi, that those countries which extricated themselves from Gold, regaining monetary control, and their status as 'masters not servants of the currency',[76] were better able to respond to economic circumstances, to rebalance social relations without departing from the essence of liberal democratic politics.[77]

To return to Loughlin's *nomos*, there is a suggestive analogy between Polanyi's three 'fictitious commodities'—land, money and labour—and the three-fold ordering of *nomos*: appropriation, distribution and production. It suggests that the autonomy of the political depends on maintaining democratic control over these 'non-commodities', or at least the political capacity to condition society against market forces and the capitalist economic logic of accumulation, distribution and production that acts upon them. The interwar interregnum specifically shows that the process of political ordering hinges on a political-economic relation that is in a delicate balance between the antagonist material forces of

[74] K Polanyi, *The Great Transformation: The Political and Economic Origins of Our Time* (Boston, Beacon Press, 2001 (1944)).

[75] ibid, at 236.

[76] ibid, 242.

[77] According to Polanyi, the political dispossession of Wall Street by going off Gold (Roosevelt did so almost immediately on gaining power in 1933) was the key to preventing the occurrence in the US of a 'social catastrophe of the continental type', ibid, 238.

capitalism and democracy and that public law is subject to the vagaries of this conflict as well as marking its shifting boundaries.

V. The Post-War Constitutional Imagination: A Transformation of the State

But could the *democratic capitalist state*—the relative autonomy of the political and of the economic—be restored in the post-war period if instead of democratisation, institutions were turned towards ensuring the economic sphere functioned on the basis of free competition? If the focus of public law shifted to securing equality in the marketplace, preventing monopolies and cartels, and ensuring economic freedom, might Heller's and Polanyi's lessons, and the democratic struggles for material equality, be forgotten?

Schmitt's motto of the 'free economy' requiring the 'strong state'—the maintenance of the material conditions of the bourgeois *Rechtsstaat*—would be taken up and reformulated by the Freiberg ordo-liberals. They, unlike Schmitt, *were* concerned as much with the perceived dangers of monopoly capitalism as with socialism,[78] fearing the impact of monopolisation and cartelisation on economic freedom as much as the 'irrationality' of social democracy. The ordo-liberals were more consistent than Schmitt, taking note of the threat to political order from the other side, as it were, from the dysfunctionality of capitalist logic in a relatively autonomous economy. From their perspective, the strong state had to be equipped with independent institutions capable of intervening if necessary to ensure the conditions of fair competition and a free market. The ordo-liberals made a new attempt at a differentiation of politics and economics based on the political decision for a liberal economic order, backed by constitutional guarantees and institutional protections. Once it gets started, the free market machine does not run itself; it requires constant oiling through the supervisory mechanisms of the state.

But this was not a vision of a vibrant democratic state. In the jargon of post-war European reconstruction, it was 'restrained democracy' (a post-war reflection of the inappositely named 'militant democracy'),[79] and encapsulated in the story of West German constitutional development: 'we are (afraid of) the people'.[80]

This view of restrained democracy goes not only to the functional question of governmental powers but to the very idea of the governing relationship, of the nature and limits of the right to rule over the economy. Indeed, the ideological and constitutional significance of ordo-liberalism is identified as early as 1955, Carl Joachim Friedrich noting how it

[78] On the links between authoritarian liberalism, Carl Schmitt, and ordo-liberalism, see W Bonefeld, 'Freedom and the Strong State: On Ordo-Liberalism (2012) *New Political Economy* 633–656. It was Franz Neumann's classic text on National Socialism, *Behemoth*, published in 1941, that described National Socialism as 'Totalitarian Monopoly Capitalism' and Neumann who, long before ordo-liberalism, had already doubted whether the legal institutions of the capitalist economy can perform their functions where the market is subordinated to the power of monopolists, developing the idea of an 'Economic Constitution' to counter this. For discussion, see Tribe (n 62) 174.

[79] JW Müller, *Contesting Democracy* (Princeton University Press, 2012).

[80] See C Möllers, 'We are (afraid of) the People: Constituent Power in German Constitutional Thought' in M Loughlin and N Walker (eds), *The Paradox of Constitutionalism: Constituent Power and Constitutional Form* (Oxford, Oxford University Press, 2007).

signals a fundamental re-ordering of the basic ideas underpinning constitutional theory.[81] As Friedrich understood, and as Foucault would later explore in his lectures on neo-liberal governmentality in 1979, the decisive theoretical turn triggered by ordo-liberalism had been to replace constituent power (or popular sovereignty) with individual economic freedom—a freedom to participate in the market—as the legitimating device for the whole constitutional order.[82]

If to put the law above man, as Rousseau quipped, 'il faudrait des dieux' (one would need Gods), the ordo-liberals answered the call for a new set of elites, who, confounding Rousseau, could, like Gods, finally 'give laws to men'.[83] The means to achieve this was a new understanding of economic constitutionalism, protecting the free market against democratic as well as capitalist interference. This was not just a departure but a reversal of its original intent, the idea of an economic constitution prefigured by Frankfurt school theorists Franz Neumann and Hugo Sinzheimer had signified democratic control of the economic structures of society; it was a labour constitution.[84]

The new economic constitutionalism, based on formal equality and individual economic rights, would mean the complete abolition of class conflict from the political domain.[85] The class-conscious democratic struggles of the interwar period would be repressed in order to secure political and economic *stability*.

Although it was far from straightforwardly applied, ordo-liberalism's particular constitutional prescriptions represented a reconfiguration of the constitutional imagination, specifically regarding the political-economic relation. Its ideological linkage of neoclassical market economics and liberal constitutionalism would become a key conceptual plank in the process of European constitutionalisation.[86] The ordo-liberal legacy could be seen, for example, in how the self-understandings of constitutional actors in Europe (in particular the European Court of Justice and the European Commission) became increasingly conditioned by ideologies and interests that correspond to the pressures of economic rationality and the logic of market competition. These trends become more acute over time, particularly after the Treaty of Maastricht, and of course extend far beyond the EU. The economic neo-liberalism that is captured in the literature on the 'new constitutionalism' can be understood as a direct descendent of ordo-liberalism's critique of the dangers of democratic constituent power.[87]

Foundations addresses neither ordo-liberalism nor European integration in any detail. But this is entirely *consistent* with Loughlin's avoidance of *any* political-economic conceptualisation of the dynamic of state development, from Locke through to Polanyi.

[81] CJ Friedrich, 'The Political Thought of Neo-Liberalism' (1955) 49 *American Political Science Review*; M Foucault, *The Birth of Biopolitics—Lectures at the College de France 1978–1979* (New York, Palgrave MacMillan, 2008).

[82] Friedrich, ibid.

[83] *Cf* H Arendt, *On Revolution* (London, Penguin, 1958) 184.

[84] See R Dukes, *The Labour Constitution* (Oxford, Oxford University Press, 2012).

[85] See EV Bonn, *Standard Texts on Social Market Economy: Two Centuries of Discussion* (edited by H Friedrich Wunsche and translated by D Rutter) (Stuttgart, Gustav Fisher Verlag, 1982) ix.

[86] S Dullien and U Guérot, 'The Long Shadow of Ordoliberalism: Germany's Approach to the Euro-Crisis' (2012) *European Council of Foreign Relations* 49.

[87] See K Jayasuriya, 'Globalisation, Sovereignty and the Rule of Law: From Political to Economic Constitutionalism' (2001) 8 *Constellations* 442.

European integration thus features only in the very closing part of *Foundations* and is there presented as affecting only the category of *potentia* in the limited sense of governmentality. The final chapter of *Foundations* entitled 'The New Architecture of Public Law' examines the growth of the administrative state, and this includes the impact of the EU, but only in so far as it modifies our understanding of 'government', and not of 'State' or 'Constitution'.[88]

Loughlin's reluctance to extend his dialectical approach to political ordering to the project of European integration leads him to suggest that the changes reflected by it are merely super-structural and, elsewhere, to insist that the formal right to leave means that *potestas* is basically untouched.[89] In the vernacular of public law, sovereignty can entail membership of the EU or exit from it, now in accordance with a Treaty to which each Member State is bound (Article 50 Treaty of the European Union (TEU)). Just as the constituent power to change the constitutional direction from ordo-liberalism towards socialism theoretically remains, the governmental powers that are channeled through European institutions can be reclaimed. The channeling of authority occurs in accordance with a constitution that can itself be changed by the constituent power of the nation. There is thus a way to reconcile ordo-liberalism, as well as European integration, with the autonomy of the political realm. For both, strictly speaking, it remains a political decision that is the basis for the economic or supranational constitutional arrangements.

But once *politics* is reduced to a single political-economic logic, and the possibility of genuine renewal comes down to the possibility of exercising the constituent power, the autonomy of the political is reduced to a bare formality or the prospect of a revolutionary rupture. Constituent power might even be absorbed into a new regime of constituted power, based on constitutional rights, protected by constitutional courts, or managed by other institutions. This reversal is captured in the discourse of 'de-politicisation', where issues of appropriation, distribution and production are increasingly taken out of the public political sphere of contestation, and determined by market logic, or the technocratic bodies which are supposed to replicate it. The process of de-politicisation (which would better be termed 'de-democratisation') can be constitutionalised, as in the Eurozone, with the structural and institutional prescriptions of Economic and Monetary Union in the Treaty of Maastricht, and defended by the European Central Bank and Court of Justice. But it can also be channeled through political ideology, such as in the refrain that 'There is no alternative' to neoliberal structural reform (so-called TINA).

The post-war shifting of boundaries between the political and the economic is especially evident in public law's constitutionalist variant, where not only a private micro-economic sphere, but increasingly a macro-economic sphere is insulated from politics through legal-institutional means—with constitutional courts, central banks and supranational institutions increasingly determining political principles and conditioning political outcomes.[90] And what must be captured is not only formal channeling but constitutionalism's framing

[88] *Foundations* (n 1) 435–67.

[89] See, eg M Loughlin, 'Why Sovereignty' in R Rawlings, P Leyland, and A Young (eds), *Sovereignty and the Law* (Oxford, Hart Publishing, 2013).

[90] See, eg K Tuori and K Tuori, *The Eurocrisis: A Constitutional Analysis* (Cambridge, Cambridge University Press, 2013).

function, the way a constitution (understood broadly) establishes not just how political debate is to be organised, but what its limits are.[91]

Potestas is not captured by formal possibilities alone; it integrates an element of subjective belief about the right to rule, in combination with the perceived capacity to govern. Ordo-liberalism and European integration do not only set in motion a series of new institutions and governmental arrangements. Contrary to what *Foundations* suggests, these reflect and in turn reconstitute a deeper set of beliefs about the governing relationship. There has been not only a 'quantitative' change in governing activities, an increase in delegation and pooling of governmental powers, but a 'qualitative' shift in the political constitution of the state, a transformation of the basic idea of the right to rule itself.

It is, in other words, in relation to *potestas* as much as *potentia* that the post-war constitutional imagination is reborn, a structural reconfiguration of the state, as a new ideal type of political-economic community, albeit one whose lineages can be traced back to ideas associated with classical liberalism. According to Giandomineco Majone:

> The possibility of separating economics and politics was a key, if implicit, assumption of the founders of the EEC. It was not a new idea but rather a return to a classical liberal tenet which in the nineteenth century and up to World War I had made it possible for the world economy to develop in such a fashion that 'between national and international economic integration there was only a difference in degree but not in kind'.[92]

To fully capture integration as part of this process of state transformation, Chris Bickerton's analysis is useful, not least since he builds on Loughlin's own schema as outlined in *Foundations*. Drawing on integration studies and work in critical political economy, Bickerton conceptualises the transformation of the 'nation-state' into a 'member state' as a feature of membership of the EU.[93] He argues that European integration, in a second phase (after the post-war *trentes glorieuses*) beginning in the mid-late 1970s, has transformed the state by transforming, or more specifically, opposing (rather than uniting) state–society relations, separating the state and its sovereign power from the popular will. This is because, regarding the limiting of national power—central to the modern constitutional imagination—European integration 'is different from the acts of self-binding by the modern state: '[t]he active subject, namely the people, is not doing the binding'.[94] This reflects not just a superficial change to the 'architecture of public law' or to the category of *potentia* but a dismantling of the social contract or the right to rule:

> Constraints upon the exercise of national power are based not upon a political ideal or principle but rather on an institutional and bureaucratic understanding of such limits. The picture

[91] As Gavin Anderson puts it, 'constitutional discourse is always more than the rules it generates or legitimates ..., setting the parameters not just for how politics is contested, but what is deemed politically contestable'. See G Anderson, 'Constitutionalism as Critical Project: The Epistemological Challenge to Politics' in S Gill and A Cutler (eds), *New Constitutionalism and World Order* (Cambridge, Cambridge University Press, 2014) 283, quoting Christodoulidis.

[92] G Majone, *Rethinking the Union of Europe Post-Crisis* (Oxford, Oxford University Press, 2014) 149, citing Röpke.

[93] C Bickerton, *European Integration: From Nation-State to Member State* (Oxford, Oxford University Press, 2012).

[94] ibid, 67.

> we thus have of the member state … is one of administrative machine rather than a political community. We are in the realm of what Engels called 'the administration of things'.[95]

The constitutional implications of this are wide-ranging. Political and social identity is fragmented, and increasingly commodified and quantified as merely consisting of a particular collection of individualist tastes and preferences—replacing the citizen with a simple consumer of economic benefits. And in terms of the political responsiveness of the new 'debt state' and its institutions in this period, the constituency that matters is no longer the *Statsvolk* but the *Marktsvolk*, 'inaugurating a new stage in the relationship between democracy and capitalism'.[96] The dominant means for the state to collect resources shifts from reliance on its citizens through direct taxation, to reliance on financial investors in the global marketplace. These changes, of course, were only fully realised in the context of momentous geopolitical, political and ideological shifts that hit Europe at the end of the 'short twentieth century', marked with the collapse of the Soviet Union.

But this neo-liberal phase, on the view offered here, represents an exaggeration of post-war trends rather than a departure from them. European integration, *right from its initial formation*, is properly conceived as a response to the series of interwar dynamics sketched above, both reflecting and helping to set in train a process of state transformation based on restrained democracy (and tempered by restrained capitalism). To be sure, this is a complex and uneven process, and each country stands in a different material relation with the project of integration, making conceptual generalisation problematic. Thus, the British relationship to the project is quite different from the 'founding six' (Germany, Italy, France and Benelux), as well as the post-Fascist Mediterranean accessions and post-Communist entries, not only geo—politically, institutionally and culturally, but also temporally—joining at the end of the Golden Age of Keynesian governmentality rather than at the beginning of post-war reconstruction or the end of the Cold War.

But abstracting from these significant differences, and to adopt Loughlin's own conceptual dichotomy, the changes inaugurated by the project of restrained democracy go not only to the question of *potentia*, but also to the question of *potestas* (and to the dynamic relation between *potestas* and *potentia*). It reflects a change in this basic dynamic not because of any return of the religious as a threat to the autonomy of the political but because the right to rule is no longer extended to those who would fundamentally question the differentiation of the political and the economic as demanded in the new post-war order of liberal political economy, and in which European integration plays a central and increasingly prominent role.

To put it (too) bluntly, in the post-war constitutional settlement the Communist Party of Germany does not have the right to rule, at least not according to the German Constitutional Court.[97] But neither can the right to rule include the right to relinquish a commitment to the project of European integration, now updated to exclude any questioning of the single currency as representing the fate of the continent ('if the Euro fails, Europe fails').

[95] ibid, 69.

[96] See, eg Streeck (n 56) 79–88.

[97] See D Kommers and R Miller, *The Constitutional Jurisprudence of the Federal Republic of Germany* (Durham, NC, Duke University Press, 2012) 291. A more informal bargain might be identified in the earlier commitment of the British Labour party to the parliamentary route to socialism or with the Eurocommunism of continental European communist parties.

On the other hand, nor can the Government 'surrender' the right to rule over 'essential state tasks' to the EU, as the Lisbon ruling of the German Constitutional Court would later insist, precluding the development of a European federal state.[98]

The post-war reconstitution of the modern state is not just an attempt to tame the passions unleashed in the interwar period through various regimes of governmentality. It reflects a basic re-orientation of the constitutional imagination and a new ground of legitimate authority, an inversion even of the relation between the political and the economic, based on *the primacy of the economic*. Although this is far from an irreversible formation—and it will come to generate new sets of tensions between the political and the economic, democracy and capitalism, that continue to reverberate—it does mark a transformation in the constitution of the state and state-system.

The European project is integral to this resetting of the political-economic relation. But its political form is ambiguous. To this day, it remains in limbo: not a mere international organisation but neither a fully-fledged federal super-state. In fact it bears a strong resemblance to Schmitt's notion of a federation or *Bund*, a form that is inherently unstable in Schmitt's view.[99]

The formal right to leave the EU of course exists, marking it as distinct from the normal federation, but leaving would represent a material re-constitution of the state, particularly for those in the Eurozone. To be sure, sovereignty, held in abeyance, suspended in the post-war European federal construct, may now be back on the agenda. Is there a better expression not only of the relative autonomy of the political, but of the desire for a reclaiming of politics vis-à-vis the economic than the event of 'Brexit'?

This cannot be more fully developed here, but the point should be clear enough: the crisis of the contemporary state and the regional state-system in Europe is fully material in nature, and revolves around the political-economic struggles between democracy and capitalism, as much within as between states, in a reprisal, albeit in different conditions, of the interwar interregnum.[100] This is why the fragility of public law returns in plain sight.

VI. Conclusion

If Hegel represents the last standard-bearer of an idealist political jurisprudence, Schmitt marks its twilight, providing the clearest sense that the manner in which the dialectic of *potestas* and *potentia* has concretely emerged in modernity is marked by significant discontinuities, and even rupture. This emerges forcefully in the interwar era but reverberates beyond, into the post-war reconstruction of the European state and state-system. It is far

[98] See M Wilkinson, 'Political Constitutionalism and the European Union' (2013) *Modern Law Review* 191–222.

[99] Schmitt (n 66). See also O Beaud, *Théorie de la* Fédération (Paris, PUF, 2007); C Schönberger, 'Die Europäische Union als Bund' (March 2004)129 (1) *Archiv des öffentlichen Rechts*; R Schütze, 'Federalism as Constitutional Pluralism: "Letters from America"' in Avbelj and Komarek (eds), *Constitutional Pluralism in the European Union and Beyond* (Oxford, Hart Publishing, 2012); M Avbelj, 'Theory of European Union' (2011) *European Law Review* 2011.

[100] For a fuller account, see M Wilkinson, 'The Reconstitution of Postwar Europe: Liberal Excesses, Democratic Deficiencies' in Dowdle and Wilkinson (n 24).

from being resolved, as that reconstruction now comes under sustained pressure in the recent period of crises.

Loughlin's turn to *nomos* in order to provide firmer ground for the foundations of public law is indicative of a renewed period of tension in the contemporary state form—when, again, its ability to maintain political order is in question. This turn is material but in a quite specific and limited way, maintaining public law's distance from any reconnection with the tradition of political eco-nomy (either classical liberal or critical-Marxist). Without any account of the political-economy and geo-politics of the three-fold ordering of *nomos*, land appropriation simply becomes a material mirror-image of the Kelsenian presupposition, a *Grund-nomos*. For Loughlin, gesturing towards a more reflexive account than Schmitt, *nomos* continues to evolve, because the state expresses 'the dynamic emergence of political unity, of the process of constantly renewed formation and emergence of this unity from a fundamental or ultimately effective power or energy'.[101] Energy, of course, cannot be created or destroyed, but only transformed. But from what, and into what? And what opposing material forces does *political* energy encounter?

According to Loughlin, the most basic purpose of the practices of early modern public law was that of 'maintaining the civil peace against a backcloth of (often violent) competing truths.'[102] *Auctoritas non veritas facet legem*, as Hobbes taught. But what were these truths *about*?

It is not only 'truths' that are competing, but also real and ideological interests, and in constant motion. Reflexivity cannot do the necessary work of capturing this dynamic. The meaning of the political equality that is required to generate reflexivity in practice is never elaborated by Loughlin, nor are the material reasons for its fragility in a market society explored. The key conceptual-historical argument advanced here is that the dynamic of political ordering is conditioned by the material relation between democracy and capitalism as real social forces. The advantage of foregrounding this political-economic relation as a matter of state formation is that it brings us closer to what public law actually *does*, closer to how this relation is materially constituted and regulated, as well as how public law can be threatened by it, from capitalism on the one side, and democracy on the other.

Processes of political and economic ordering take place across two spheres, which are only relatively autonomous from one another. To maintain the relative autonomy and primacy of the political requires a degree of democratic political control *over* the economy and our material social relations. It is the autonomy of the political realm that allows *politics* to occur, to permit political contest between different economic models or substantive social goals, for example, or to reorganise or recondition the taking, distribution and production of land and resources. But this control can be lost, eroded or at least marginalised through the hegemony of particular political-economic structures, ideas and interests in a capitalist society and state-system. It can also be regained by struggles for the relative autonomy of the political realm, through movements that build on and generate solidarity and co-operation in a democratic manner. Would it not be imprudent to reduce struggles for equal liberty to a matter of functional or scientific logic alone?

[101] Loughlin, 'Politonomy' (n 30).
[102] *Foundations* (n 1) 465.

Part V

The Comparative Critique

13

Foundations of Public Law: A View from the United States

MARK TUSHNET

I. Introduction

No US-based scholar with a chair in public law could have written *Foundations of Public Law*, and not simply because it operates on a level of erudition well beyond the reach of any such person. The book could not be written from a US perspective because—to use a metaphor from American pragmatism—it scratches an itch that we don't currently feel. This may of course suggest some limitations on the value of pragmatism, but it may also help us see Loughlin's work from an external point of view.

Two indications of this possibility come early in the book. Loughlin writes that

> [t]he hegemonic account of the status of ordinary law in the British system rests on foundations of right, foundations that were hidden from view only while the authority of British constitutional arrangements remained unquestioned. *During the latter half of the twentieth century, those arrangements have become subjected to more searching inquiry.*[1]

The itch here is something about the status of law in Great Britain today. Further, he argues that his approach brings the 'power-generating' role of public law into view and 'opens up a novel [...] way of looking at the relationship between government and law'.[2] For a US-based scholar of US public law,[3] the power-generating role of public law has always been in view. Loughlin's formulation distinguishes between but also connects 'ordinary law' and 'constitutional law' in a way that makes sense from the British point of view, but is different from the way in which US law distinguishes between those terms (and connects them only quite indirectly). British constitutional law has been developed by the courts in a way not readily distinguishable from the way in which they develop the common law.

[1] M Loughlin, *Foundations of Public Law* (Oxford, Oxford University Press, 2010) [hereafter *Foundations*] 5, emphasis added.

[2] ibid, 12.

[3] Throughout, I use Loughlin's term *public law*, although US usage of the term is somewhat different. In US usage, the term refers to three bodies of law: constitutional law, administrative law understood as the law dealing with judicial supervision of actions taken by executive officials and administrative agencies, and the substantive law applied and developed by administrative agencies. The best 'translation' of Loughlin's term into US usage is probably 'constitutional law.'

In contrast, US constitutional law has always been grounded in a canonical text, 'interpreted' by the courts.[4]

Suppose a US-based scholar were asked, 'What are the foundations of public law in the United States?' The scholar would not agonise at all. Her immediate response would be, 'The US Constitution'. And, one consequence of giving that answer would be that the power-generating role of the US Constitution would be apparent, because a great deal of the discussion around the time the Constitution was adopted dealt precisely with the question of whether the new Constitution gave the national government too much power—that is, it was implicit in the discussion that the Constitution was a power-generating document, and the only question was how much power it should produce. To some extent, contemporary constitutional scholarship in the United States, with its focus on constitutional rights—and therefore on constitutional limitations on public power—obscures the fact that the national Constitution is *primarily* about creating a national government empowered to do what the more feeble government under the Articles of Confederation could not.[5]

An additional indication of the distance between the problems that appear to motivate Loughlin's inquiry and the way US-based scholars think about constitutional foundations is his reference to the 'relatively recent' 'divergence' between 'the English system of governance' and 'the modern practice of constitution-making'.[6] For US-based scholars, associating the term 'recent' with the practice of constitution-making would seem odd except in so far as the practice referred to is something like the post-Second World War wave of constitution-making. Loughlin's formulation suggests that *his* inquiry into the foundations of public law scratches an itch associated with recent British experience—and it should not be surprising that US-based scholars do not feel that particular itch.

II. US Constitutionalism: No Itch to Scratch?

I understand that this is a naïve way of addressing the deep questions Loughlin's inquiry seeks to answer, but again I stress that my aim is to explain why his inquiry is not one US-based scholars of public law would pursue. Of course, US-based scholars occasionally ask themselves, 'But why is the Constitution foundational?' That is, sometimes we ask, 'Why should we comply with the Constitution?'[7] Here such scholars offer several convergent answers, all of which are simplified versions of accounts Loughlin offers. Two answers sound in political theory, the other in something like historical sociology.

[4] In addition, the common law in the United States is almost entirely a matter of 'state' (that is, subnational) law, connected only in the most indirect ways to the law of the US Constitution.

[5] In addition, the US federal structure is one in which the subnational ('state') governments are assumed, as a matter of national constitutional law, to have plenary power, restricted, again as a matter of national constitutional law, only by rights laid out in the national Constitution. As a result, the constitutional law dealing with subnational governments is a law dealing solely with restrictions on power, not on power-creation. That too can distort one's view of the Constitution's power-creating effects.

[6] *Foundations* (n 1) 239.

[7] For a recent example, see L Michael Seidman, *On Constitutional Disobedience* (Oxford, Oxford University Press, 2013).

The political theory answer, put telegraphically, is this. Humans find themselves in a Hobbesian state of nature, from whose terrors we escape by agreeing to create a sovereign. But, the Hobbesian sovereign poses a risk of depredation severe enough for us to want to place some limits on its power. We do so by writing a constitution identifying with some precision the sovereign's powers (and thereby protecting our [natural] rights by excluding rights-violations from the scope of the powers thereby created). But, the written constitution is not self-enforcing. We have to design institutions that make the constitution enforceable. We do so by creating political arrangements—a legislature (Congress) and an executive (the Presidency). Notice that, in the US-based account, these institutions are *creations*, not something already given to us (as a matter of political theory—but also as a matter of historical experience with respect to the national institutions).[8] Occupants of positions in those institutions pursue their self-interest, and in doing so they effectively check—that is, limit—the power each exercises.[9] But, concerned that the political process might be insufficient to limit the exercise of power, we also use the judiciary—an institution that (conceptually) precedes the creation of a US-style constitution because something like courts are needed to ensure that disputes over private rights are resolved peacefully—to enforce the written constitution's limits on public power. That, however, leads to another conceptual problem, which is the central topic in US-based constitutional theory: How do we keep the courts from becoming the Hobbesian unlimited sovereign?

This is obviously a highly truncated sketch. It is not dramatically different from the more complete version presented in much of Loughlin's Chapter 10 on 'The Constitutional Contract'.[10] So, for example, Loughlin writes,

> First, the constitution is recognised as a type of fundamental law. Second, the judiciary presents itself as interpreters and enforcers of this fundamental law. Finally the judiciary asserts its claim to be the supreme guardian of the constitution. With these developments, the meaning of fundamental law in the modern context is significantly altered. As modern republican constitutions evolve and acquire authority, the claim that the constitution has the status of fundamental law not only expresses a formal hierarchical relationship within the structure of positive law; it also takes on a broader meaning. This ambiguity comes from the tendency of modern regimes to blur the distinction between the constitution of government (regulated by positive law) and the constitution of the state (regulated by *droit publique*).[11]

The second political theory answer a US-based scholar would offer is much more pragmatic. The Constitution is simply a means for coordinating action and, importantly, for settling disagreements among a population holding widely varying views about good public policy and about the content (if any) of 'natural' rights. It has no deep foundations. All that matters is that it be 'good enough' to get us through our disagreements.

[8] The government created by the Articles of Confederation lacked an executive, for example, and the judicial power under the Articles was quite narrow. Even the national Congress was substantially different from—more powerful than—the Congress under the Articles, and its structure was so different that it was in central respects a new institution. Of course the Constitution's authors were familiar with the Montesquiean idea that government had three functions, but the institutions they created to implement those functions were novel to a substantial degree.

[9] This is, of course, Madison's idea of 'ambition counteracting ambition'.

[10] Perhaps this should not be surprising because *Foundations* (n 1) Ch 10 is the first place in the book where Loughlin offers an extended discussion of the United States.

[11] *Foundations* (n 1) 288–89.

As I read Loughlin, he would treat these sketches as incomplete (not merely sketchy), because they offer institutional accounts of the foundations of public law without providing a conceptual account of what 'the People' are that stand behind the law's authority. Loughlin's discussion of Carl Schmitt, in Chapter 9, 'The Constitution of the State', provides, as I take the argument, such an account—and it is hardly an accident that the discussion of 'The Constitution of the State' precedes that of 'The Constitutional Contract'. As Loughlin writes, summarising a position Schmitt criticises,

> Once the state is thus reconceptualised, the relationship between state, sovereignty, constitution, and law can be reworked: the constitution is the state, the state is the legal order, the constitution is the basic norm of that legal order, and sovereignty expresses the totality of norms in that autonomous legal order.[12]

Loughlin presents, I believe sympathetically, Schmitt's critique of this position, which is that it presupposes the existence of a prior 'will', an active people.[13] For this reason, the US-based scholar's approach fails because 'the modern attempt to focus purely on the constitution of the office of government provides no substitute for reflection on the constitution of the state'.[14]

At this point, the US-based scholar might revert to what I called the historical-sociological account, which provides an account of how the people of the United States are constituted. Here too I offer a sketch. To adopt and generalise a term used by scholars of federal systems, the United States was and is a 'coming-together' nation. The constituent states (there is no way to avoid the term here, though it refers to something other than 'the State' in Loughlin's terminology) that were theretofore joined together in a confederation came together to create the new nation. The Constitution was the act that did so. Simultaneously (conceptually), the people of the new nation came together to constitute themselves as a nation, and there too the Constitution was the means. The 'We the People' of the United States constitutes itself through its orientation toward the Constitution as the foundation not only of the government but also of the State.[15] As was understood early in the history of the United States, to be an American (to use the term from the period) was to be committed to the Constitution's principles, nothing more and nothing less.[16]

Loughlin's presentation of the Habermasian idea of 'constitutional patriotism', in which a nation's people is constituted not in ethno-national terms but rather through commitments to national constitutions that satisfy basic conditions of rights-protection, is at least consistent with this understanding. Loughlin's discussion comes near the conclusion of his chapter on the 'Constitutional Contract', which as I have noted deals primarily with US constitutional theory, and it is immediately preceded by a discussion of the educative role of the US Constitution and the correspondingly important role lawyers have in sustaining

[12] *Foundations* (n 1) 212.

[13] *Foundations* (n 1) 212–13.

[14] *Foundations* (n 1) 310.

[15] In my work I limit the claim to one about orientation toward what I call the 'thin' constitution, the basic ideas of the Declaration of Independence and the Constitution's Preamble.

[16] Of course there are competing strands in the actual sociology and history of the United States, and particularly a strand of nativist exclusionary thinking. In my view, though, that strand, and others, are clearly subordinated to the primary narrative of US citizenship as constituted by adherence to the Constitution.

the people's commitment to the Constitution (and so to the United States as both government and nation). For Habermas, and perhaps for Loughlin, 'constitutional patriotism' deals with a state's place in a world in which ethno-nationalist commitments have been (somewhat) discredited, which weakens the state's foundations in ethno-nationalism, and in which each state is tied in increasingly complex ways to other states, which weakens each state's distinctiveness. Or, more pointedly, Habermas (and perhaps Loughlin) are concerned with the place of previously strong states such as Germany and Great Britain within the modern European context. Constitutional scholars based in the United States do not face anything like that problem. For such scholars, 'constitutional patriotism' is not a solution but is rather constitutive of the United States as a nation[17]—though the Habermasian idea might help us address *other* questions we do face.

So, for the US-based scholar, the Constitution—the written thing as assimilated into the political imagination of US citizens/long-term residents[18]—is the foundation of public law, and it is also the foundation of the State as the mode in which the nation's people are organised. I take it that Loughlin questions the cogency of these (or similar) claims. My point, though, is that they are not questioned by US-based scholars engaged in the enterprise of constitutional theory.[19]

III. The UK's Position in a Changing World

All this raises the question for me of why Loughlin—and, as the response to his work represented in this collection indicates, others as well—feels an itch he needs to scratch. It seems to me that the answer is reasonably clear, and lies in the political/constitutional conditions of the contemporary (sort of) United Kingdom. The United Kingdom finds itself as (sort of) lacking a written constitution in a constitutional universe where almost everyone else has one. With the Human Rights Act 1998 (HRA), the United Kingdom acquired something resembling part of a written constitution, though as Loughlin emphasises, not the important parts that are power-creating instead of power-restricting. But, the legal status of the HRA is uncertain because of its incorporation by reference of parts of the European Convention on Human Rights, which makes it a mixture of a domestic enactment and an international one that is difficult to theorise in a constitutional system nominally committed to parliamentary supremacy. And, of course, the HRA's political status is highly contested. Under these constitutional and political circumstances, it is not surprising that a constitutional theorist like Loughlin would think that the British legal order needs to be placed on stable constitutional foundations.

[17] 'Constitutional patriotism', understood in certain ways, might offer a solution to *other* problems in the United States, particularly those arising from racial diversity within the United States.

[18] I include the latter because the United States is self-consciously a nation of immigration, even if that characterisation is sometimes forgotten and contested, and long-term residents are generally understood by themselves and by others as on the way to becoming citizens.

[19] A modest qualification: Some political scientists occasionally address some of Loughlin's concerns, but their work has not been deeply assimilated into the general body of US constitutional scholarship (indeed, I would guess that I am one of fewer than a handful of scholars located in the US legal academy who are even aware of the existence of that strand of political science).

In addition, the United Kingdom finds itself in a world that is facing centralising and de-centralising pressures simultaneously. Something is going on in Europe in connection with the organisation of and relations among Westphalian states. For the moment Scotland remains part of the United Kingdom, for example, but its relation to that entity is surely going to be the subject of repeated negotiation over the next decades. And similarly, for the moment the United Kingdom is committed to leaving the European Union, but again what 'leaving' means is likely to be negotiated repeatedly because of the complex economic and social ties between the United Kingdom and Europe. These are examples of de-centralising pressures. Over the past decades, the centralising ones, especially in connection with the European Union, have been quite strong, and the economic conditions that generated those pressures and led to centralisation—in particular, the place of European economies in the world economic system—seem to me likely to persist even when (or if) the formal legal arrangements regulating relations between the United Kingdom and Europe change.

As with most of my comments in this chapter, these observations are quite off-handed and casual. Even so, I am reasonably confident that, even when developed and qualified as they should be, they help identify the itch. To quote Bob Dylan, 'Something is happening *here*, but you don't know what it is, do you Mr. Jones?' I emphasise 'here' to suggest that Loughlin's itch is localised to the conditions of British constitutional theory. The United States has not been immune from the economic and social pressures I have described, as the rise of an ethno-nationalist movement—the Tea Party and the campaign of Donald Trump for President—shows. At this writing, that movement has not reached the point where the prospects of substantial success have generated a felt need to think about constitutional foundations in the United States. The movement and a broader political polarisation, which has produced phenomena such as 'gridlock' in the US Congress, are seen as, and might even be, aberrations. Only if they come to be seen as products of how the basic institutions of the US Constitution are designed will US-based constitutional scholars begin to think about constitutional foundations.[20] And even then, we will have to overcome the near-sacred place the Constitution holds in the US political imagination. Yet, constitutional theorists based in the United States do not feel the itch for a combination of reasons.

One set of reasons is political/constitutional. We have a written Constitution; we have had it for a long time; even though the concrete content of the Constitution has changed substantially over time, both through amendment and, more importantly, through judicial interpretation, 'the Constitution' remains a single entity in the US political imagination; there are no serious pressures to redesign the Constitution, and especially no serious pressure in favour of separating some geographic parts of the United States from other parts; and US political identity is organised around the written Constitution. US-based constitutional theorists simply do not (now) see a problem for which an examination of the foundations of public law is a solution. The political circumstances of the contemporary United Kingdom are quite different.

Similar differences attend the political/economic circumstances of the two nations. Of course the United States does not face difficulties in negotiating its relationship to

[20] Almost uniquely among such scholars, Sanford Levinson has been arguing for many years that the current state of affairs is a pathology rooted in constitutional design. See, for example, S Levinson, *Framed: America's 51 Constitutions and the Crisis of Governance* (Oxford, Oxford University Press, 2012).

some supranational entity with which it has relations as institutionalised as the United Kingdom's with the European Union. In addition, even taking the Great Recession into account, the United States has maintained a dominant position in the world economy. So, US-based scholars do not need to explore the foundations of public law for the purpose of figuring out how to understand complex institutional interactions among national economies.[21]

To revert in conclusion to the American pragmatist tradition, US-based scholars see nothing at stake in examining the foundations of public law—whereas European-based ones, and especially ones based in the United Kingdom, do see something at stake. And, the condition of (sensible, non-neurotic) inquiry, pragmatists tell us, is that there be something at stake. No itch, no need to scratch. Loughlin might remind us, though, that decay may be occurring so far below the surface that we don't feel an itch now, but might experience crisis when the decay bursts through. So, he might sensibly urge us, we ought to be thinking right now about the foundations of public law.

[21] Such scholars can use ordinary tools of mundane political and economic analysis, rather than a deep account of foundations, to understand those interactions.

14

The Elusive Quest for Community: The Making of Political Identity in Modern Indian Constitutionalism

MATHEW JOHN

I. Introduction

Martin Loughlin's masterly overview of the modern Euro-American public law tradition attempts to unseat the ascendance of conceptions of public law founded primarily on the internal coherence of positive legal norms. Accordingly, and in contrast to strictly normative accounts of law, his inquiry is framed as a politico-legal enquiry into the prior source of authority that undergirds the ongoing practice of positive public law in North Atlantic democracies. In his own words, his study of public law is intended to be an 'investigation [...] relating to the conferral of authority and legitimacy on modern governmental ordering'.[1]

In disciplinary terms this implies, for Loughlin, that the true foundation of public law is tied to inquiries in a whole range of the social sciences that uncover the manner in which a political system produces and enforces conformity with legal norms. To get these inquiries off the ground, a key historical moment in Loughlin's account is the emergence of secular political systems in modern European societies, which dislocated the transcendent or divine foundations of public authority. And, flowing from this point of origin, the overarching task that Loughlin sets for himself is to explain the manner in which secular configurations of knowledge and practice have generated and sustained the authority of law once the divine foundations of law are no longer available. There are various dimensions to Loughlin's scheme of public law, including its underpinnings as a legal science or template to manage the challenges of modern politics; the forms through which it pragmatically negotiates competing individual and collective claims; as well as the techniques through which it effectively limits as well as augments political power. Each of these lines of enquiry examines different aspects salient to the organisation of the modern state.

The present article critically examines this scheme of public law. However, the task of the article is undertaken more by way of comparative juxtaposition than as an examination of

[1] M Loughlin, *Foundations of Public Law* (Oxford, Oxford University Press, 2010) [hereafter *Foundations*] 2.

the internal coherence of Loughlin's argument. In particular, the article will examine the central role Loughlin assigns to the political will of a consenting people in authorising the modern European public law tradition embodied in the state. And, it does so by showing that that idea of such a will is of limited social intelligibility in the context of the development of the Indian constitutional state.

However, the Indian state and the constitutional practices flowing from it have been built on a pedagogic reliance on the European public law tradition and has, for well over a 100 years, attempted to engender its own version of a political will. Even so, to think of political community in India in terms of a unified political will stretches the limits of its social and cultural intelligibility to breaking point. This article is therefore organised as an exploration of this aspect of Loughlin's public law framework and the limits of the socio-cultural resonance of its building blocks when exported beyond the Euro-American context.

II. The Authority of Community in Public Law

In Loughlin's analytical framework, the public will authorises the voice of an unlimited sovereign state which is the form in which modern European polities have come to actualise themselves. In its modern form, this sovereign public will is the product of what Loughlin terms a 'political jurisprudence' or a 'science of political right'.[2] That is, an abstracted form of rationalisation in the study of politics that ties the foundation of state or legal authority to the notion of a 'people' understood largely as a rationally motivated association of free and equal individuals.

As Loughlin rightly observes, the real world of practical politics would not allow this abstract conceptual foundation of legal and political authority to function as a mould from which copies of political association could be cast off. That is, there would necessarily be multiple accounts of the political right that could fit the requirements of a rational association of free and equal individuals. Even so, drawing on Michael Oakeshott, Loughlin observes that there are two recurring themes in European reflections on the state that capture broad patterns through which states have embodied the public will. Following Oakeshott, he classifies these themes as the state understood as a *societas* and as a *universitas* respectively.

As an idea drawn from Roman law, a *universitas* signifies a state imagined as a corporation established to pursue a common end.[3] A *universitas* is accordingly 'telocratic' in its orientation, such that it may facilitate the management of its common concerns. Oakeshott contrasts the *universitas* with the state understood as a *societas*, a condition defined by laws, where 'government is a nomocracy whose laws are to be understood as conditions of conduct, not devices instrumental to the satisfaction of preferred wants'.[4] A ruler in a *societas* is therefore merely a 'custodian of the loyalties and the guardian administrator […] his concern is to keep the conversation going'.[5]

[2] ibid, chs 2, 4, 5 and 6.
[3] M Oakeshott, *On Human Conduct* (Oxford, Clarendon Press, 1975) 205–06.
[4] ibid, 202–03.
[5] ibid.

The *societas* and the *universitas* are not, however, meant as theories explicating the nature of the public will but conceptual categories that reflect contrary and mutually present dispositions in human nature to be autonomous as well as to be part of a common venture respectively. Loughlin argues that this 'polarised consciousness', containing within itself different contingently possible forms of state association, supplies the pragmatic motivations for the manner in which political jurisprudence secures the assent of a people in specific contexts within and across states.

For the purposes of this article it is sufficient to note that across the *societas* and *universitas* the authority of the state is constitutively tied to the voice or the consent of a 'people'. This conception of the state is further clarified in Loughlin's discussion of the *Staatslehre* tradition, wherein the sovereign state power is characterised not merely as an apparatus of rule but as also embodying the spirit of a people or community.[6] More importantly it is significant to note that even when the state is conceived as a *societas*, legitimate state authority seems inextricably tied to some conception of a public will or a 'people'. It is in this respect that the emergence of constitutionalism in modern India offers a significant contrasting case that illustrates the limits of the contours of the public law tradition that Loughlin so exhaustively maps.

III. Constitutionalism as the Search for Community in Colonial and Post-Colonial India

A defining problem of Indian constitutionalism as it emerged in colonial conditions has been the British perception that there was an absence of a political community or, in Loughlin's framework, 'political will' in India. Accordingly, colonial government was structured as a pedagogic project that sought to impart to Indian society, as pedagogues, the virtues of forging a unified political community that could in turn serve as the foundation for stable state and constitutional government. This goal of a unified political community, or nation, to express the political will of the Indian people has been the unwavering object of Indian government ever since, and the post-independent state has only deepened this presumption.

Thus, from the moment of its introduction by the British, constitutionalism in India has been articulated as a state-led project of education to overcome the divisions of Indian society that hamper the formation of a unified nation. The only question mark surrounding this project was British scepticism as to whether these constitutional goals would be internalised by Indian society. As we will see, the resulting constitutionalist nationalism has institutionally flattened and bypassed alternative ways of identification and belonging, although it is uncertain whether it has been able to secure a deeper social acquiescence for its pedagogic demands.

A good vantage point from which to examine the halting ambition to forge a national political community in India is through the doctrinal prism of 'minority rights', as it has evolved in Indian constitutional history over the last 100 years. The choice of minority

[6] *Foundations* (n 1) 190–96.

rights to discuss constitutional development in India draws on the observation that colonial government regarded the introduction and institutionalisation of minority rights as a critical axis for its pedagogical-constitutionalising mission. The granting of minority rights to India's supposedly divided social body were foundational to the way in which constitutionalism in India was conceived, and this has continued to be the case even as parts of the intellectual framework of justifying minority rights were marginally altered at independence.

The principal legislative milestones that mark British colonial attempts to introduce, as pedagogues, ordered constitutional politics to what they viewed to be the feuding races, classes, and castes of India are the constitutional settlements of 1909, 1919, and 1935.[7] These colonial regulations of supposed divisions in the Indian social body formed the basis for native participation in British colonial-constitutional government in India.

Of India's various communities, Muslims were initially considered particularly important, and through the Indian Councils Act of 1909, Indian Muslims were granted the privilege of having places reserved to them in colonial legislatures and, eventually, in public employment.[8] Similar representational allotments were then extended to other special groups—or 'minorities' as they came to be called—via the Government of India Acts of 1919 and 1935. Such representational allotments in both political institutions and in government jobs became the principal gateway both for local political participation and for the management of India's cultural diversity in British government.[9]

This conception of a divided society was also inherited by the makers of India's post-independence constitution. However, shedding British pessimism about Indian nationhood and the capacity to generate a political will, the constitutional framers of what would be independent India viewed the justification for colonial constitutionalism as a contrivance aimed at dividing and preventing the realisation of what they felt was a nation in waiting. For instance, in 1947 Govind Ballabh Pant, speaking before the Constituent Assembly that had been established to draft a post-independence constitution for India, sought to highlight the 'minority question' in the following manner:

> [T]he question of minorities everywhere looms large in constitutional discussions. Many a constitution has foundered on this rock [...] *It has been used so far for creating strife, distrust and cleavage between the different sections of the Indian nation. Imperialism thrives on such strife.* It is interested in fomenting such tendencies. So far, the minorities have been incited and have been influenced in a manner which has hampered the growth of cohesion and unity.[10]

Thus, in Pant's account, social divisions are produced by the mischievous designs and descriptions of imperial government. However, despite disagreements regarding the

[7] See The India Councils Act of 1909, the Government of India Act of 1919, and the Government of India Act of 1935. See also R Coupland, *Report on the Constitutional Problem in India: The Indian Problem, 1833–1935* (Oxford, Oxford University Press, 1943). *Cf* US Mehta, 'Constitutionalism' in NG Jayal and PB Mehta (eds), *The Oxford Companion to Politics in India* (Oxford, Oxford University Press, 2010).

[8] See East India (Advisory and Legislative Councils, &c.) *Vol. I: Proposals of the Government of India and Despatch of the Secretary of State* (London, His Majesty's Stationery Office, 1908) 8. See also Coupland, ibid, 25–27.

[9] See also S Pathan, 'A Historical and Theoretical Investigation into Communalism' (Manipal, India, Manipal University PhD thesis, 2009).

[10] BS Rao et al, *The Framing of India's Constitution* (Dehli, Indian Institute of Public Administration, 1966) Vol 2, 61 (emphasis added).

sources of social division, the only real difference between the earlier colonial account of these divisions and a later nationalist account like that of Pant was the latter's belief that the constitutional-pedagogical goals of national unity and universal citizenship were now within reach. But the goal of a unified political community continued to define the debate for the nationalist anti-colonial movement just as it did for the earlier colonial administration.

Therefore, when deliberating the new constitution, the wishes of nationalists like Pant notwithstanding, the framers could not escape the epistemic and practical challenges left behind by the idea of social fragmentation that founded British constitutionalism. The new Constituent Assembly, which as we saw above had been called to draft India's post-independence constitution, had inherited a model of constitutional government built around the idea that India's social divisions could only be constitutionally negotiated via an entrenched scheme of privileges granted to assorted scheduled minorities. This was a model that was now so embedded in colonial constitutionalism that it seemed unavoidable for any post-independence constitutional framework. Therefore, the nationalist mission to sweep away the framework of differentiated citizenship in post-independence India simply could not and would not easily overcome entrenched sectional or minority interests.

Thus, in relation to the existing framework of minority rights, the question as it initially arose before the Constituent Assembly was not whether the framework of differentiated and fragmented citizenship would continue, but what shape it would assume in Independent India. In fact, during the early debates, the Constituent Assembly adopted a report by the Advisory Committee on Fundamental Rights granting minorities a set of rights similar to those they had hitherto enjoyed under the colonial state—the only significant difference being the case of separate electorates, which many minorities enjoyed in British India but were explicitly excluded from the Advisory Committee's report.[11]

But the partition of India, while the proceedings of the Constituent Assembly were still ongoing, into a largely Hindu India and a predominantly Muslim Pakistan removed the Muslim League as a force in Indian constitutional politics; it allowed the Indian National Congress, the political party controlling the Assembly, to push towards a position of universal equal citizenship quite like the position envisioned by Pant and other leading nationalist voices of the Assembly.[12] Accordingly, the leadership of the Constituent Assembly was able to get ratified a revised proposal on minority rights, also drafted by the Advisory Committee on Fundamental Rights, that recommended 'that the system of reservation for minorities other than Scheduled Castes in Legislatures be abolished'.[13] 'Scheduled Castes' referred to caste groups that had been identified during the colonial era as eligible for reserved allotments in legislatures and jobs due to social discrimination stemming from traditional Hindu caste hierarchies. Other 'minorities' that had enjoyed similar minority rights under colonial India but who were not classified as scheduled castes—Muslims being the most prominent—were only entitled under the new constitution to a limited set of educational and cultural rights. Importantly, the term 'minority' was now used to describe a category that was clearly distinct from that described by the term 'Scheduled Castes'.

[11] See Part XIV of the Draft Constitution of February 1948.

[12] *Cf* R Bajpai, *Debating Difference: Group Rights and Liberal Democracy in India* (Oxford, Oxford University Press, 2011). See also I Ansari, 'Minorities and the Politics of Constitution Making in India' in D Sheth and G Mahajan (eds), *Minority Identities and the Nation-State* (Oxford, Oxford University Press, 1999) 111–23.

[13] *Constituent Assembly Debates: Official Report*, vol 4 (New Delhi, Lok Sabha Secretariat, 1999) 601.

This new constitutional formulation was clearly set within a nationalist imagination that denied the colonial pessimism about the divisions of Indian society to express itself as a unified political community. Even so, it continued to recognise specific 'minority' identities to which attached a now much more limited band of special rights, and continued to grant to the Scheduled Castes special rights analogous to those enjoyed by the 'minorities' of colonial India. This was of course in recognition of the practical needs to politically accommodate different social groups in Indian society. In post-partition India, the overwhelming political dominance of the Indian National Congress permitted the constitution makers to fend off the demands for special rights by groups like the Muslims and the Sikhs. However, as a vehicle of social reform and justice, the new Indian republic could not afford to be as dismissive to the Scheduled Castes, whose political identities were largely defined by the historical injustices of caste society in India, and which had already been recognised by the Poona Pact of 1932.[14] (The constitutional settlement also included special political rights for 'Scheduled Tribes', but whose constitutional import is not directly relevant to the focus of this chapter.)

Thus, as the Constituent Assembly was able to whittle down the rights of the non-caste minorities, it nevertheless continued to defend special rights for the Scheduled Castes. In the new context of post-colonial independence, this required a new justificatory language. Accordingly, the new framework of special rights, for minorities as well as castes, was now justified in the name of 'social transformation'—meaning, the need to alleviate the injustices of contemporary Indian society and thus allowing the identities of castes and minorities to be braided together into a common citizenship through a granting of a universal justice, if not through the immediate universalist articulation of citizenship rights.

Commenting on constitutionalism as social transformation—or even as social revolution—Uday Mehta notes insightfully that it was the assertion of this new transformational form of politics that shed the colonial pessimism about the possibility of a unified national polity. That is, social revolution was framed as an assertion of the supremacy of political claims channelled through the new national-constitutional order over those of the social order that it sought to subject to its control. Within this now unified field of politics, different constitutionally recognised identities like castes and minorities could be treated differently from the 'majority' and from each other, as it could be argued that these castes and minorities needed to be differently prepared for the transformations that a unified politics demanded.[15] Furthermore, the special rights granted to castes were seen as temporary.[16] And this meant that these rights did not seriously dent the idea of a universal citizenship, but merely functioned as preconditions for a future society with full freedom and equality for all.

On the other hand, the rights granted to minorities by the new constitution were not considered temporary. But these were not political rights and therefore were not regarded as being as threatening to the idea of national unity as were the rights granted to the

[14] See SV Desika Char (ed), *Readings in the Constitutional History of India 1757–1947* (Oxford, Oxford University Press, 1983) 561–63.

[15] See, eg *Narasu Appa Mali v State of Bombay AIR*, 1952 Bom 84.

[16] See Constitution of India, Art 334.

Scheduled Castes and Tribes. It was in this manner that the revolutionary or transformative approach to constitutionalism could accommodate the differentiated grant of rights both to Scheduled Castes (and Tribes) and to (other) minorities, and yet present this as simply a part of an integrated journey towards a unified political community and universal citizenship.

It could therefore be said that the nationalist resolution of the problem of political community as represented in the Constitution institutionally incorporated the pedagogic lessons set in motion by the colonial state with some success, even overcoming the pessimism that India would not be able to rise beyond its entrenched differences. However, it is far from certain if Indian *society* would be as successfully incorporated by this new nationalist vision. That is, it is far from obvious that the nationalist coalition has been able to represent the diversity of India any more successfully than the colonial state.

Evaluating the ability of nationalist politics to credibly represent the divisions of Indian society as constituents of a unified nation or political community requires training the spotlight of enquiry onto the particular constitutional practices that have been used to incorporate those distinct social identities into a broader national community. Consequently, focusing on constitutional debates on the 'minorities' of independent India, we shall see that the framework of a unified nation which accommodates special privileges for different social interests have also been not entirely successful in conceptually representing Indian forms of identification and belonging.[17]

IV. Adjudicating Minority Rights in the Indian Constitution

A. The Constitutional Framework

The Indian Constitution grants the groups recognised as 'minorities' special rights which captures its vision of the distinct composition and needs of these groups as set against those of the broader national community. Unlike the right to political representation granted by the colonial regime that preceded it, the present-day Constitution grants both 'minorities' and other distinct cultural groupings special rights grouped under the heading 'cultural and educational rights', which are elaborated in Articles 29 and 30 of the Indian Constitution. Article 29 grants '*any section of the citizens* [...] having a distinct language, script or culture of its own [...] the right to conserve the same.' Article 30 grants '*minorities*, whether based on religion or language, the right to establish and administer educational institutions of their choice'. (Emphasis added.)

It is important to note that only Article 30 mentions the word 'minority', and it grants to them a special right to establish and administer educational institutions. Article 29, on the other hand, simply refers to any 'section' of citizens having distinct language, script or

[17] M John, 'Identity and the Social Revolution: On the Political Sociology of Constitutionalism in Contemporary India', *Jawaharlal Nehru University Centre for the Study of Law and Governance Working Paper* No CSLG/WP/18 (New Delhi, Jawaharlal Nehru University, 2012).

culture, and it merely grants to these sections rights to preserve the same. Despite these differences, the rights granted by these two provisions are organised under a common heading, and must therefore be understood as drawing from a common inspiration. Further, to the extent that legislative history is relevant to understanding the structure of these rights, B R Ambedkar, the Chairman of the drafting committee of India's Constitution and independent India's first Minister of Law, asserted in the Constituent Assembly when discussing a draft version of Article 29 that the phrase 'any section of citizens' also referred to 'minorities', although in a more loosely defined sense.[18] This raises the question of the definitional framework that both constitutional understanding and constitutional practice have brought to bear on the term 'minority', whether loosely defined or more firmly tethered to conceptual and definitional parameters. And, in the context of our present enquiry, it also raises the question of how this definitional framework comports which conceptions of social and political identification in Indian society.

As to the constitutional identification of a minority under Article 30, one commonsense approach would identify its essence in terms of cultural distinctness from the 'Hindu' majority. Thus, in an archetypically nationalist portrayal considering India's constitutional future, the Nehru Report of 1928 identified the idea of political community, and by implication a 'minority', in the following way:

> The communal problem in India is essentially the Hindu-Muslim problem. Other communities have however latterly taken up an aggressive attitude and have demanded special rights and privileges. The Sikhs in the Punjab are an important and well knit community which cannot be ignored. Amongst the Hindus themselves there is occasional friction especially in the south, between non-Brahmans and Brahmans. But essentially the problem is how to adjust the differences between Hindus and Muslims.[19]

In other words, political community in India was pegged to a majority 'Hindu' community and to other minorities of whom the Muslims were the most significant. This position is also supported by judicial decisions, although these decisions seldom represented this foundational characterisation of political community in India with such clarity.

At the same time, however, this conception of political community ran and continues to run against fundamental social intuitions about identification and belonging. We examine this mismatch between state led identification of political community and its disjuncture from social intuitions about identity by examining some important cases in which the Supreme Court of India had to address the issue of defining minorities.

B. Two Conceptualisations of 'Minorities'

The challenge of defining minorities within a larger representative framework of Indian nationhood has been posed most sharply by particular 'Hindu' groups whose claims to minority status possess the least credibility. However, in practice, the claims made by these groups display a conceptual coherence that has caused considerable problems for courts seeking to defend the nationalist demarcation of political community. The cases

[18] See *Constituent Assembly Debates: Official Report*, vol 7 (New Delhi, Lok Sabha Secretariat, 1999) 922–23.
[19] *The Nehru Report: An Anti-Separatist Manifesto* (New Delhi, Michiko & Panjathan, 1975) 27.

involving 'Hindu' groups have brought to a head two very different conceptions of political community in addressing the challenge of identifying minorities. On the one hand, the constitutionalist and nationalist conception of minority refers to a distinct community that is numerically smaller than the larger community that defines the 'national' culture. This is especially how India's constitution-makers tried to model political community in Independent India. On the other hand, the court has also had to contend with a conceptualisation of a minority as being distinct along a *civilisational* continuum, and not simply or necessarily in numerical terms. The intersection of these different ways of thinking about community and the Supreme Court's efforts at resolving the challenge they raise, is well outlined in the cases of *Bramchari Sidheswar Bhai & Ors v State of West Bengal,*[20] *Sastri Yagnapurshdasji v Muldas Bhudardas Vaishya,*[21] and *Bal Patil & Anr v Union of India.*[22]

In *Bramchari Sidheswar Bhai v State of West Bengal,*[23] decided in 1995, the Ramakrishna Mission Residential College found itself in conflict with the revised policies of the Government of West Bengal regarding the College's management. The College was established by the Ramakrishna Mission in 1960 at the request of the West Bengal state Government and was partially funded by both the central and the state governments. The Ramakrishna Mission is a religious organisation devoted to the teachings of Sri Ramakrishna (Ramakrishna Paramahansa) (1836–1886). When the College was established, the state Government exempted it from rules pertaining to academic governance. However, the subsequent government action revoked this exemption, which the college challenged, claiming theirs was a minority institution under Article 30, and thus enjoyed special rights to administer the College autonomously and free of government interference.

The Ramakrishna Mission was founded by the Ramakrishna Order of supposedly 'Hindu' monks. But in advancing their claim to be a minority community, the Ramakrishna Mission argued that they constituted a world religion and were not simply a parochial sect within Hinduism. They noted that Ramakrishna Paramhansa, their spiritual founder, 'practiced various religions including Islam and realised the truth underlying these religions [...] That all religions are true [...] that all religions are only different paths leading to the same goal.'[24] Along these lines, the Mission was distinctive in that it allowed members and followers to retain their identity as a Christian, Muslim, Jew, Hindu, etc while also simultaneously being members of the mission. This particular distinction, they argued, differentiated them sufficiently from other religions, particularly Hinduism, and thus made them a religious minority in their own right and not simply a particular philosophical articulation of Hinduism.

Their argument was accepted by the High Court at Kolkata. On appeal, however, the Indian Supreme Court overturned the High Court decision, holding that the Ramakrishna Mission could not credibly claim to place itself apart from the broader Hindu community. And since the Hindu community constituted the majority religion of India, this meant that the Ramakrishna Mission did not enjoy minority status under Article 30.

[20] MANU/SC/0413/1995.
[21] AIR 1966 SC 1119.
[22] MANU/SC/0472/2005.
[23] *Bramchari Sidheswar Bhai* (n 20).
[24] *Bramchari Sidheswar Bhai* (n 20) para 24.

At the heart of the Supreme Court's reasoning was what it held to be the High Court's incorrect departure, on the question of Hindu identity, from an earlier and widely studied[25] Supreme Court decision in *Sastri Yagnapurshdasji v Muldas Bhudardas Vaishya*.[26] This case dealt with the followers of Swaminarayan, a nineteenth century social reformer. The Swaminarayans had built several temples, which they claimed should enjoy immunity on grounds of religious freedom, from the Bombay Hindu Places of Public Worship (Entry-Authorisation) Act 1956, which prohibited *Hindu* temples that were accessible to the general public from refusing entry to persons because they belonged to an untouchable Hindu caste or community.

The Swaminarayans limited rights of entry to their temples solely to members of their sect. They claimed that they were not covered by the Hindu Places of Public Worship Act because they constituted a religious sect that was distinct from that of Hinduism. They argued that even though they might be considered socially and culturally Hindu, they were not part of the Hindu 'religion' because:

> Swaminarayan, the founder of the sect, considered himself as the Supreme God, and as such, the sect that believes in the divinity of Swaminarayan cannot be assimilated with the followers of Hindu religion […] that the temples in suit had been established for the worship of Swaminarayan himself and not for the worship of the traditional Hindu idols […] [T] he sect propagated the ideal that worship of any God other than Swaminarayan would be a betrayal of his faith, and lastly, that the Acharyas who had been appointed by Swaminarayan adopted a procedure of 'Initiation' (*diksha*) which showed that on initiation, the devotee became a Swaminarayan and assumed a distinct and separate character as a follower of the sect.[27]

Quite like the Ramakrishna Mission, the Swaminarayans also claimed that their sect was open to all as long they were appropriately initiated. However, also as in the case of the Ramakrishna Mission, it was not clear whether and how this particular description of their religious practices set them apart from the Hindu 'religion' per se. This required inquiry into the essential nature of the Hindu religion, which formed a central part of Chief Justice Gajendragadkar's majority opinion disallowing the Swaminarayan claims and pronouncing them 'Hindus' subject to the demands of the Bombay Act.

However, Justice Gajendragadkar's opinion is ultimately built upon an unresolvable contradiction. On the one hand, he argued that the Hindu religion:

> does not claim any one prophet; it does not worship any one God; it does not subscribe to any one dogma; it does not believe in any one philosophic concept; it does not follow any one set of religious rites or performances; in fact, it does not appear to satisfy the narrow traditional features of any religion or creed. It may broadly be described as a way of life and nothing more.[28]

Despite its fuzziness, this is not an uncommon way to describe 'Hindu' religiosity or even a broader traditional sub-continental religiosity.[29] In other words, through this intuitive

[25] See also M Galanter, 'Hinduism, Secularism, and the Indian Judiciary' in R Bhargava (ed), *Secularism and its Critics* (Oxford, Oxford University Press, 1999) 233–67.

[26] *Sastri Yagnapurshdasji* (n 21).

[27] *Sastri Yagnapurshdasji* (n 21) 1123.

[28] *Sastri Yagnapurshdasji* (n 21) 1128.

[29] See, eg A Nandy, 'The Politics of Secularism and the Recovery of Toleration' in R Bhargava (ed), *Secularism and its Critics* (Oxford, Oxford University Press, 1999) 321–44; TN Madan, *Modern Myths, Locked Minds: Secularism and Fundamentalism in India*, 2nd edn (Oxford, Oxford University Press, 2009).

sociology, Justice Gajendragadkar characterises the term 'Hindu' as referring to the *civilisational* bond holding together and binding the traditions of the peoples of the Indian subcontinent.

On the other hand, however, Justice Gajendragadkar's opinion also advanced a much more formalist, reductive definition of Hinduism. Drawing significantly from the writing of Dr S Radhakrishnan and other modern commentators on the Hindu tradition, Justice Gajendragadkar went on to note that the wide variety of practices and philosophical reflections found in the Hindu tradition were nevertheless held together by a common philosophy of monistic idealism. That is:

> [b]eneath the diversity of philosophic thoughts, concepts and ideas expressed by Hindu philosophers [...] lie certain broad concepts which can be treated as basic. The first amongst these basic concepts is the acceptance of the Veda as the highest authority in religious and philosophic matters.[30]

In this way, Justice Gajendragadkar defined Hinduism, not in civilisational terms, but in terms of particular religious doctrines such as rebirth and predestination. It is this doctrinal account of Hinduism that he ultimately used to refute the Swaminarayans' claim that they were sufficiently distinct from Hinduism as to constitute a separate religion, which he dismissed as simply a product of 'superstition, ignorance and complete misunderstanding of the *true teachings* of Hindu religion and of the real significance of the tenets and philosophy taught by Swaminarayan himself'.[31]

In other words, Justice Gajendragadkar justified his rejection of the Swaminarayans claims by appealing to, and affirming, an *authoritative* version of Hindu belief and practice. His opinion was thus founded on a dogmatic and doctrinal conception of Hinduism as a unified communal entity that contradicted his earlier characterisation of Hinduism as describing ongoing forms of civilisational experimentation as found in the Indian sub-continent.[32]

It is here that the Swaminarayan case becomes salient to the case of the Ramakrishna Mission, as both these cases deal with similar tensions between a formal doctrinal account of the Hindu religion and sociological or civilisational accounts of the Hindu traditions that run at parallels to it. And in both cases there has been a judicial attempt to incorporate civilisational accounts into the doctrinal as far as might be possible. In doing so, the Supreme Court recognised the sociological reality of the enormous diversity of doctrines, practices, and traditions within what is considered to be the Hindu religion, but nevertheless proceeded to affirm an authoritative doctrinal conception of Hinduism that had little to do with any civilisational way of life.

Moreover, as between these civilisational and doctrinal definitions of Hinduism, the courts affirm the latter simply through the assertion of their judicial authority. That is, the courts in these two cases marshalled no argument to actively disarm the intuitive

[30] *Sastri Yagnapurshdasji* (n 21) at 1130.
[31] *Sastri Yagnapurshdasji* (n 21) 1135 (emphasis added).
[32] It could be argued that in moving to this more doctrinal definition, he was not denying a broader 'way of life' or civilisational conception of the Hindu traditions, but only emphasising that communities like the Swaminarayans are denominations within that broader tradition, and in this way are not analogous to more archetypically distinct religions—like, for instance, Islam or Christianity.

sociological appeal of the alternative civilisational account of Hindu religiosity. By contrast, it is useful to examine a later decision of the Court in *Bal Patil & Anr v Union of India*,[33] which actively engages with the civilisational conception of Hindu religiosity and the anxieties it produces for national conceptions of political community on which constitutionalism in India has been founded.

In *Bal Patil*, decided in 2005, the Supreme Court dismissed a petition of the Jain community arguing that the central Government ought to have declared them a 'minority' under the Minorities Commission Act 1992, a statute providing for the welfare of communities that have been formally classified as 'minorities' by the central Government for the purposes of that Act. The Government had denoted Muslim, Sikhs, Christians, Parsis, and Buddhists as constituting such 'minorities', but had left the Jains out of this list. The Jains then petitioned the Supreme Court to direct the Government to include them in this list.

It must be emphasised that, like *Sastri Yagnapurshdasji*, this case did not directly involve questions about definition of minority identity under Article 30. Even so, as with *Sastri Yagnapurshdasji*, *Bal Patil* offers important heuristic pointers on the judiciary's thinking about the issue of minority identity. In dealing with the Jain petition, the Court ultimately held that the power to declare a 'minority' was vested in the central Government and that it was inappropriate for the Court to second-guess this exercise of executive discretion. Nevertheless, a significant portion of the Court's opinion looked to justify the Government's exclusion of the Jains, and these dicta provide an important lens into examining the tense relationship between civilisational distinctiveness and the liberal nationalism of the Indian Constitution.[34]

In writing the opinion of the Court, Justice Dharmadhikari argued that Jains ought not to be declared minorities, not because of the absence of any civilisational or even doctrinal distinction, but simply due to the effect such a declaration would have on India's quest for constitutional unity. According to him, 'Hindu society [...] is itself divided into various minority groups [...] In a caste-ridden Indian society, no section or distinct group of people can claim to be in a majority. *All are minorities among the Hindus*' (emphasis added). Consequently, he argued, the Government should not act in ways that encouraged groups like the Jains to adopt what he called a 'minority sentiment'. Doing so would fragment the conceptualisation of political community on which constitutionalism in India was built.

Of course, Muslim assertion of a distinct 'minority' identity would presumably not trouble Justice Dharmadhikari as much as similar claims made by groups like Ramakrishna Mission, the Swaminarayans, and the Jains. In the history of Indian nationalism, Muslims and certain other groups have always been recognised as distinct from the dominant strands of national culture, without contention. But from Justice Dharmadhikari's vantage point, the Jains form part of that particular social spectrum that constitutes the Hindu-majority and the foundation on which constitutional nationalism is to be built. Consequently, any

[33] MANU/SC/0472/2005.

[34] In so far as their status as 'minorities' is concerned, the Jains have always been a hard case. They have sometimes been identified as being part of the broader Hindu community (see, eg the Hindu Marriage Act of 1955), at other times, however, they have been identified to be distinct (see S Radhakrishnan, *Indian Philosophy*, (London, George Allen and Unwin Ltd, 1948) Vol 1, 361). In fact, despite losing this case, the Jains would eventually succeed in persuading the Government to have themselves declared a minority community under the under the Minorities Commission Act in early 2014.

demand for minority status from these kinds of groups would fracture this foundation and its unifying force.

All in all, in their quest for national unity Indian courts have consistently and decisively crowded out civilisational conceptualisations of identification in favour of a rationalised political identity that comports with constitutional nationalism. However, the very fact that civilisational arguments continue to assert themselves in Indian courts suggests that aspirations to build a uniform nationalism have not been able to establish the desired conceptual hegemony. In fact, the continuing and wide-spread social appeal of these civilisational conceptualisations of community or a 'minority' community would suggest that constitutional practice cannot continue to ignore the force of these social intuitions and its implications for thinking about political community founded on a unified political community or nation.

To return to Loughlin's framework at this point, the present account of Indian constitutionalism would narrate the development of a state imagined as a *universitas* or at least an attempt to forge a *universitas*. Against this story of the development of constitutional community, it might perhaps be argued that the inability of the state to accommodate civilisational aspirations could be addressed by remodelling the state as a *societas*. However, this chapter argues that Indian society pushes the imagination of even the *societas* to its very limits. It is this aspect of Indian society and its conception of the ethical or political life that we must now elaborate through the thought of Mohandas K Gandhi. In doing so we illustrate the pitfalls of fashioning politics around a sovereign political community, the building block of Loughlin's public law and, to suggest alternative ground on which Indian society might locate the problem of constitutional politics, freedom and, national reconstruction.

V. Locating Loughlin against Gandhi's Rejection of the Nation

Among the most formidable opponents of colonialism in the twentieth century, Gandhi was unimpressed by the British colonial claim that freedom would be tied to learning to organise as a nation. On the contrary, his overwhelming concern was the alienating effects of colonial rule.[35] All pivotal institutions of colonial rule—ranging from parliamentary government, modern science and medicine, railways, lawyers and the political forms of organising community—were seen by Gandhi as producing alienating effects.[36] In total contrast to the preoccupations of modern and colonial politics, the location or the site of Gandhian politics was individual self-transformation through local practice and quotidian social forms interrupted by colonialism. And, the methodological route Gandhi offers for Indian freedom and home rule—*'Hind Swaraj'*—is not found simply in the transfer of state power from the British to Indians, but exhorting individual Indians to reconnect to the

[35] See A Bilgrami, 'Gandhi (and Marx)' in *Secularism, Identity, and Enchantment* (Cambridge MA, Harvard University Press, 2014) 122–74.

[36] MK Gandhi, *Hind Swaraj and Other Writings* (edited by A Parel) (Cambridge, Cambridge University, Press 1997) [hereafter Gandhi, *Hind Swaraj*].

autochthonous structures of experience and understandings that had been interrupted by colonial sensibilities, institutions, and forms of knowledge. Regarding the dislocations caused by colonial rule, it is important to note, as does Vivek Dhareshwar, that the target of Gandhi's attack was not the institutions and sensibilities of modernity that colonialism brought with it *per se*, but their occlusion of the autochthonous experiences and understanding in Indian society.[37]

A detailed theoretical discussion of the structures of experience that colonialism occludes, and how Gandhi thought India could best overcome this occlusion, will have to be reserved for another occasion.[38] Nevertheless, having isolated a key strand of Gandhi's thoughts on colonial constitutional politics, we have a vantage point from which to view the problem of political community as it was framed by the colonial state and adopted by the independence constitution though with small changes. That is, reframed in a Gandhian light, minority rights framed as a nationalist problem can also be seen as a particular example of a now post-colonial 'occlusion' inherited from colonial conceptions of constitutional community.

Gandhi's thoughts are rarely organised in neat logical argument and his reflections on the claims that colonial constitutionalism makes on Hindu practices are not as clearly enunciated as the manner in which we have just restated them. However, it is apparent that in Gandhi's thinking the category 'Hindu' had very little to do with what he termed 'exclusive nationalism'.[39] To Gandhi, Hinduism was merely an ethic that constituted individual and collective life in India. That is, he invoked the term primarily to identify a 'search after the truth through non-violent means [...] Hinduism is a relentless pursuit after truth'.[40]

In so far as he addressed the problem of factional or 'communal' conflict within the nation, Gandhi seemed to grant some credence to the nationalist view that the conflict between Hindus and Muslims was the defining problem for national unity. However, because he saw *swaraj*—freedom—as a process of 'self-transformation', 'to be experienced by each one for himself,'[41] his concern about Hindu-Muslim conflict can be described merely as a location where the occlusions of exclusive-nationalist understanding of identity had to be engaged with and resisted. This engagement he hoped would clear false understanding regarding these identities and reconnect Indians to the promise of self-transformation contained in terms like Hinduism, or for that matter in any religious tradition.

Thus, recognising the devastating effects of the Hindu-Muslim conflict, he notes that this much-touted socio-political enmity was a British invention and was by no means a defining problem of the Indian nation per se. He goes on to say that 'there are as many religions as there are individuals [...] [I]n no part of the world are one nationality and one religion synonymous terms: nor has it ever been in India.'[42] Most significantly, he also questions

[37] V Dhareshwar, 'Politics, Experience and Cognitive Enslavement: Gandhi's *Hind Swaraj*' (2010) 45 *Economic and Political Weekly* 51–58.

[38] See, eg US Mehta, 'Gandhi on Democracy, Politics and the Ethics of Everyday Life' (2010) 7 *Modern Intellectual History* 355–71.

[39] See S Bhattacharya, *Mahatma and the Poet; Letters and Debates Between Gandhi and Tagore 1915–1941*, 1st edn (New Dehli, National Book Trust, 1997) 30.

[40] M Gandhi, *Hindu Dharma* (New Delhi, Orient Paperbacks, 1978) 18–19.

[41] Gandhi, *Hind Swaraj* (n 36) 73.

[42] Gandhi, *Hind Swaraj* (n 36) 53.

why the conflict between Hindus and Muslims should be any more significant for national life in India than those conflicts between other communities, such as the Vaishnavites and Shaivites, or the Vedantins and Jains.

In other words, in thinking about social identity and social conflict, Gandhi made fervent efforts to dislodge socio-cultural traditions from exclusive nationalist identities and relocate them in traditions that allowed individuals the promise of ethical self-discovery. It was in this manner that he put his faith in India's civilisational or religious traditions and simultaneously sought to loosen the claims that constitutional nationalism made and continues to make on these traditions.

Constitutional practice for over the last half a century has, however, belied the Gandhian hope that Indians would come to think with and reflect on their problems through autochthonous categories and traditions of Indian thought and experience. On the contrary, the very logic of contemporary constitutionalism in India is founded on the need to transform Indian social categories so that they may become serviceable for the particular kind of national political community.[43] Even so, the judicial cases described earlier in this chapter demonstrate that India's autochthonous social imagination continues to interrupt or limit (albeit episodically and unsystematically) the reformist pedagogic ambitions of Indian constitutionalism. But as we have also observed, constitutional discourse is unable to draw on these social understandings in any meaningful way. It is against this background that Gandhi's diagnosis of the damaging pedagogic transformation that constitutionalism demands from Indian society that we must return to Loughlin to explore the problem that the cultural difference of India might pose for his account of public law.

VI. Searching for the 'Foundations' of Indian Constitutionalism

Gandhi's opposition to the pedagogy of Anglo-European state formation in India, and by extension, of the conceptual frames of public law in modern India, might invite two broad kinds of responses from Loughlin as a defence of his conception of the European public law tradition. In considering Loughlin's possible response to these challenges from Indian constitutional law and Indian society, we will conclude this discussion by examining the extent to which his model of public law can meet the socio-cultural challenge that India poses.

First, assuming—as Gandhi argues—that the modern Indian constitutional state alienates experience, Loughlin could well respond that this problem could entirely be resolved via a *societas* where the state merely facilitates various forms of autonomous striving. It must, of course, be noticed that as a matter of historical reality this has never really been the case. Even so, assuming that this might be a future aspiration, it must also be noted that Loughlin traces the modern state as a sovereign entity that brooks no rival even when it is fashioned as a *societas*.[44] Perhaps flowing from this conception of an undivided sovereign power, it

[43] See G Austin, *The Indian Constitution: Cornerstone of a Nation* (Oxford, Oxford University Press, 1966); Mehta (n 7).

[44] *Foundations* (n 1) Ch 7.

has to be remembered that the *societas* and the *universitas* draw on different dispositions that are simultaneously present in human consciousness, both of which play a role in securing the consent of a 'people' for the state that governs them. Thus, it is extremely difficult to untangle even the *societas* from the idea of a consenting people producing a sovereign unified public will which is the foundation of Loughlin's conception of public law.

It could of course be argued that there are few alternatives to the modern state in the organisation of contemporary politics. But even so it is important to note Gandhi's pointed disinterest for affective attachments that bind citizens to states. Akeel Bilgrami describes this in terms of a radical conception of democratic individualism, where Gandhi could not countenance that human freedom and self-reflection be sacrificed to disenchanted and abstracted forms of affection for a national community.[45] As Bilgrami argues, Gandhi aimed to recover a world where all human agents could individually discover the bonds of value and normativity that tied them to the world that they inhabited. Consequently, these individual ethical journeys could not take place in the folds of the modern state, which abstracts individuals from the world they inhabited; they can only take place in localised social settings like the village (which played a crucial role in Gandhi's thought).

The scholar and poet Rabindranath Tagore, one of Gandhi's most insightful interlocutors,[46] makes explicit this account of the state by arguing that the sovereign imagination of the modern state and the representational forms that it engenders are fundamentally antithetical to the civilisational forms in which human striving was organised in Indian society. In his lecture on *Swadeshi Samaj*, delivered at the height of the swadeshi movement at the turn of the twentieth century, he argued that:

> The (Indian) nation has protected itself through the concerted power of society [...] Thus the country belonged to the people, the king was only one part of it, just as a crown is on the head. In a centrally administered system where the ruler is all powerful, the heart of the country resides in the administration; in a socialist country the life of the nation is vested in the entire society [...] China and India have survived for a long time through national changes because its soul is disseminated all over society.[47]

This is further elaborated when he says that:

> [...] in the West the state is inseparably founded upon the consent of society, it is an expression of their natural custom. We cannot achieve it only by argument. However desirable, it is still unattainable for us.[48]

Of course, these are only small slivers drawn off the work of thinkers who said a great deal about Indian freedom and Indian renewal at the turn of the twentieth century. Furthermore, the political imagination they were fighting against has now actualised itself in the institutional scheme of the contemporary Constitution and its practice. Even so, assuming that contemporary politics may allow diverse social groups nothing more than the freedom of the *societas*, it is useful to understand the problems of politics as Tagore and Gandhi identified it. In particular, their indifference to the state and the abstracted idea of political

[45] A Bilgrami, 'Gandhi's Radicalism: An Interpretation' in Akeel Bilgrami (ed), *Beyond the Secular West* (New York, Columbia University Press, 2016) 222–30.

[46] For an excellent collection of their intellectual exchange, see Bhattacharya (n 39)

[47] R Tagore, *Swadeshi Samaj* (translated by A Guha) (Kolkata, Dey's Publishing 2013) 7–8.

[48] ibid, 8.

community with which the Indian state has encouraged identification illuminates the limits or the black spots of constitutional conversation conducted against a backdrop of either *societas* or *universitas*.

Loughlin's second response could perhaps even accept Gandhi's insights on the harmful effects of reorganising India as a unified nation or a political community that would found the constitutional state. However, he might argue that the pedagogic aspect of Indian constitutionalism does not quite set it apart from the public law framework that he has outlined. Quite the contrary, Loughlin could underscore the significance of pedagogy as the mode by which a multitude is transformed into a consenting people authorising the institutions and practices of public law in all contexts.[49] He could even recognise that this foundational moment is made intelligible by an arbitrary and even imagined act of constituting and delimiting a 'people'. Further, he could note that the administrative reach or infrastructural power of modern government founded on these arbitrary invocations of community covers vast swathes of human experience, with India being no exception. In other words, he could argue that pedagogy is in the nature of the modern state, and that the course of contemporary history has rendered its institutional manifestations entirely inevitable.

It is in this respect that we can perhaps once again notice a distinction between Loughlin's account and what we have sketched from Indian constitutional law. That is, whatever one might say of the pedagogic role of the state in Western Europe, it is also true to note that its infrastructural power (*potentia*) has deep social and cultural roots. As Loughlin shows, the religious and cultural force of Protestant ideas in local communities across Europe has played a very significant role in securing discipline and allegiance to governmental power.[50] It is this deeper allegiance to governmental power that we found missing in the account on minority rights in Indian constitutional law. That is, social groups like the Swaminarayans and the followers of Ramakrishna often prefer to choose above all else their own local forms of identification rather than governmentalised forms of political community idealised by the Indian state. In Loughlin's terminology, nothing like the 'disciplinary revolution' he narrates through the work of Gorski, Foucault, Weber, Mann and others has taken place or is likely to take place in India in the foreseeable future. In other words there is an absence of similar socio-cultural forces in India that have produced attachments and allegiance for the state in modern Europe.

As we have already discussed, it is moot whether the lack of socio-cultural roots for the institutional forms of modern public law will permit India to fashion institutions entirely beyond the conceptual imagination of modern state power. However, by juxtaposing the Indian constitutional experience in putting together a political community, we are also able to gather a glimpse at the limits of the public law tradition Loughlin outlines. Of course, this alternative outline garnered from the Indian experience requires more detailing than has been possible here. Nevertheless, our engagement with Loughlin allows us clarity on the challenge that the public law tradition faces when confronted with contexts where its building blocks have very limited social and cultural resonance. It is in this manner that this article has attempted to outline the challenge of comparative study that Loughlin's work raises when its building blocks are put to work in a non-European context like India.

[49] For instance, *Foundations* (n 1) 116, 176.

[50] *Foundations* (n 1) 409.

15

Uncovering the Foundations of Administrative Law?

DENIS BARANGER

I. Introduction

In such a world as ours, foundations are necessarily problematic. The world of yesterday was foundational. But foundations have been sapped. 'Modernity' would be a good word for this process of foundation sapping and the hope to build a world without foundations. This world would be a 'self-evident' one, one that does not need external justifications but stands as its own justification. Yet when the existing foundations are sufficiently eroded, there comes a generation of 'retrievers of ancient prudence'.[1] They attempt to uncover or rediscover foundations. Martin Loughlin is emphatically one of those 'retrievers of ancient prudence': 'This study,' he says, 'can […] be viewed as an exercise in retrieval',[2] and public law 'remains an essentially prudential discourse'.[3]

One can engage in historical pursuits for reasons other than foundational ones. In fact, the science of history has been an education of scepticism for many. Yet Loughlin's approach to the history of ideas is foundational. Let us take for granted that *Foundations* does what its title says it does, ie, it lays out the foundations of public law. My question is then the following: of what kind of public law is this the foundation? Does his 'architecture' of *droit politique* come up as a plausible foundation for our contemporary systems of public law? In order to answer this question, I will focus on the case of France and Britain as these two legal cultures are supposedly sufficiently different to test one of Loughlin's 'foundational' claims, namely, that the kind of public law he is talking about has become 'universal'.[4]

My starting point can be summed up as follows. Certainly, Loughlin excels at providing an account of a foundational structure for public law. And this foundation is obviously related to the phenomenon known as public law. It may be called the 'constitutional'

[1] The expression famously used by James Harrington in his *Oceana* about Machiavelli [*The Commonwealth of Oceana* and *A System of Politics* (edited by JGA Pocock, *Cambridge Texts in the History of Political Thought* (Cambridge, Cambridge University Press, 1992) 30].

[2] M Loughlin, *Foundations of Public Law* (Oxford, Oxford University Press, 2010) [hereafter *Foundations*] 10.

[3] ibid 406.

[4] ibid 2.

element in public law, the 'constitutional' foundations of public law. I find it more difficult, however, to use Loughlin's scheme when it comes to explaining what we generally mean by 'public law' in a modern context—namely administrative law: be it the framework of administrative action by the state, the blooming field of 'regulation' (the body of public law that regulates many fields of private action), or the judicial review of administrative action. Both in France and the UK, it is suggested, this dimension of public law has not evolved out of the kind of foundations that Loughlin envisages. In fact, it has not evolved from any foundation at all, in the sense that its development is not foundational in nature. In other words, *Foundations* is more a framework for studying the 'idealism of constitutional law' than the 'materialism operationalised through administrative law'.[5]

I am far from suggesting that Loughlin has overlooked the kind of development that I am referring to. In fact, his earlier works give it great attention. Moreover, even if *Foundations* is focused on another dimension of public law, its account of the destiny of public law as *droit politique* in the modern world clearly envisages the phenomenon of modern administrative law. This appears notably through Loughlin's careful readings of some continental scholars. For instance, he uses the French lawyer Léon Duguit as a witness of the post-metaphysical condition of man and society in which 'the modern inheritance of public law is in "a condition of dislocation" and in need of a new system to replace it'.[6] This dislocation is due to a massive, unanticipated, expansion of the governmental sphere. This expansion, in turn, is connected to the moral victory of ordinary life and terrestrial well-being over any sort of metaphysical background. Modern government increasingly 'intervenes in the provision of services, such as education, social security, transport and utility supply'.[7] This modern world of *services publics* (in French legal parlance) cannot be based on the foundational couple of sovereignty and human rights as first elaborated during the French Revolution. Prerogative, says Loughlin, is 'sublated', assimilated in the larger perimeter of the modern administrative state. And indeed 'prerogative' in the technical, British sense of residual, non-statutory, powers is a good example of this transformation. What was achieved by the case of *AG v De Keyser*[8] was exactly that. Prerogative was 'sublated' by statute law, at least in the sense that statute law was supposed to supersede prerogative whenever Parliament saw fit to set foot in the Crown's territory. But it took nearly 60 years and the *GCHQ*[9] ruling for prerogative to be fully sublated.

My argument is made in three parts. First, in section II, I will explain why administrative law resists a foundational approach. In section III, I will show how attempts to provide such a foundation have only been partly successful. Finally, in section IV, I will explore possible ways of extending Loughlin's understanding of public law as a 'distinctive juristic discourse'[10] to contemporary administrative law in France and Britain.

[5] ibid 370.
[6] ibid 404.
[7] ibid 405.
[8] *AG v De Keyser* [1920] AC 508.
[9] *Council of Civil Service Unions & Others v Minister for the Civil Service* (*GCHQ* case) [1983] UKHL 6, [1985] AC 374.
[10] *Foundations* (n 2) 2.

II. Public Law as (Essentially) 'Sporadic and Peripheral'

A. The Problem in Historical Terms

There is reason to think that modern administrative law has not evolved out of a foundational process. Both in France and the UK, administrative law as we know it is a fairly late development. The substantive law of administrative action only developed in the nineteenth century. And despite some heroic origins in the old regimes—eg, judicial supervision exercised over inferior courts by the King's Council in monarchical France and the prerogative writs in England—judicial review of administrative action is an even later development. *De prima facie*, it is not easy to relate the intellectual background of this development of administrative law to the kind of foundational process of *droit politique* as expounded in *Foundations.* Not only is this a fairly belated transformation, but it is also one that has been for the most part unanticipated. The great authors of *droit politique* that Loughlin so skilfully analyses envisaged a modern state which was mostly based on legislation. In this corpus, the role of the modern judge as a 'third giant' in the state was not really anticipated and even when it was, it was given only a subordinate, mechanical capacity. Nor, in fact, was the shift towards the primacy of case law, for the most part, anticipated. Bodin, Hobbes, or indeed Rousseau, would be surprised, and most probably astonished, at modern public law: namely, judges positioned in the driving seat. So a foundational-doctrinal approach to public law runs the risk of looking only at what the intellectual founders foresaw in their blueprints, while underestimating unanticipated developments—the twists and turns which have brought us to where we now stand. A quick exploration of the historical development of administrative law in France and the UK demonstrates this.

Let me begin with the French case. It is generally accepted that the birth of modern administrative law dates to an 1872 case named *Blanco.*[11] *Blanco* was not decided by the *Conseil d'Etat* case but by the *Tribunal des Conflits*. The *Tribunal des Conflits* is a court of exclusive jurisdiction appointed to rule on whether a case should be decided by a public law court or by a private law court. It does not decide on the merits of the case but only on the issue of jurisdiction. The *Blanco* judgment stands as authority for what is called the 'autonomy' of French public law (*droit administratif*). The autonomy of French public law is two-fold. First, the substantive rules of public law are separate and distinct from the private law rules contained in the *Code civil.* Second, this special body of rules is adjudicated by a special body of courts: the *juridictions administratives.* Thus, if you read the *Blanco* ruling literally, what you read is that:

> State liability for torts caused to private persons by [state] employees working in public services *cannot be governed by the principles of the Code civil*, [which regulates] the relations between two private persons. This liability is neither general nor absolute. It is governed by special rules, depending on the needs of public service.[12]

[11] Tribunal des conflits—8 février 1873—Blanco—1er supplt—Rec. Lebon 61.

[12] '[La] responsabilité, qui peut incomber à l'Etat pour les dommages causés aux particuliers par le fait des personnes qu'il emploie dans le service public, ne peut être régie par les principes qui sont établis dans le Code civil, pour les rapports de particulier à particulier. Que cette responsabilité n'est ni générale ni absolue; qu'elle a ses règles spéciales, qui varient suivant les besoins du service.' [Tribunal des conflits, Blanco, ibid.]

This ruling presents public law, not as something based on the kind of foundations that Loughlin envisages, but as a side development—a 'sideline' (for lack of a better word) body of rules. French public law thus arose as an adjunct development to the body of private law codified in the 1804 Civil Code. Historically and conceptually speaking, French administrative law does not stand as the *foundation* for the rest of the legal system. Rather, it aims at protecting the special 'rights of the state', to use the often overlooked standard set out in the *Blanco* ruling.

The history of administrative law in Britain, on the other hand, is markedly different from that of the French *droit administratif*. In fact, for a long time, the English system developed under the assumption that it had nothing resembling *droit administratif*. To describe the birth of a body of administrative law in Britain would be a massive task. But let me point out two features that should be as little controversial as possible. I do this in order to lend some legitimacy to the claim that the strategy at play in British efforts to understand public law does not always consist in 'reducing [public law] to a species of ordinary law,' a method which, according to Loughlin, 'ensure[s] that the nature, method and functions of public law will be misconstrued'.[13] The first of these features is the rise of quasi-judicial bodies, ie the acquisition of legislative and judicial functions by the executive. In *Justice and Administrative Law*, WA Robson noted in 1928 that

> [o]ne of the most striking developments in the British Constitution during the past half-century has been the acquisition of judicial powers by the great departments of State and by various other bodies and persons outside the Courts of law.[14]

He described the purpose of his study as one of 'examin[ing] in detail the nature and scope of the judicial functions exercised by government departments and other public and private bodies'.[15] In other words, administrative powers in Great Britain were initially seen as quasi-judicial powers. And the history of administration in the United Kingdom is a history of the rise of delegated legislation.

The second of these features involves the evolution of judicial review from what we might call 'weak' review to 'strong' review. It is common knowledge that there has long been an existing judicial framework for the review of administrative action, one based on the time-worn prerogative writs. But for a very long time—say from the heroic cases of the seventeenth century[16] to *Wednesbury*—this was a weak form of judicial review, one that consisted in a limited test for legality. Administrative entities were expected to come up with evidence that the power that they claimed to have was grounded either in statute or in common law precedent. I would call this the 'can you please show some ID?' approach to public law. If the public authority could show its jurisdictional ID, it could walk free and unfettered. Take the case of prerogative powers. For a long time courts were only willing to review the existence and extent of the prerogative but not its 'manner and exercise'. It took the *GCHQ* case (1983),[17] anticipated in 1976 by the Court of Appeal in *Laker*, to allow a move forward

[13] *Foundations* (n 2) 6.

[14] WA Robson, *Justice and Administrative Law: A Study of the British Constitution*, 2nd edn (London, Stevens and Sons Ltd, 1947) xxviii.

[15] ibid.

[16] Esp the *Case of Proclamations* (1611) 12 co Rep 74.

[17] *GCHQ* (n 9).

in this regard. As in the case of statutory powers,[18] this move was deeply connected to the greater concern for individual rights and especially for procedural rights.

The history of administrative law in the common law courts is thus deeply connected with the history of procedural rights. Although Dicey was very much concerned with 'private rights', he saw constitutional law guarantees as best suited to protect them. The failure of 'foundational' guarantees to sufficiently protect individual rights opened the path to 'non-foundational' forms of protection such as those offered by judicial review. This is a major shift. The topical case in this regard is *Dyson*.[19] *Dyson* explicitly acknowledges the failure of ministerial responsibility as a proper tool for the defence of individual rights: 'If ministerial responsibility were more than the mere shadow of a name, the matter would be less important, but as it is, the Courts are the only defence of the liberty of the subject against departmental aggression.'[20] *Dyson* then showed the way for courts to take over the business of defending individual rights. One could say that, in this move from weak to strong (or at least stronger) control, judicial review has to a significant extent ceased to be 'inevitably sporadic and peripheral', as Stanley de Smith famously put it.[21] Indeed, in the words of Maurice Sunkin, who in turn quotes other scholars:

> [I]t is now commonly assumed that: 'the effect of judicial review on the practical exercise of power has[...] become constant and central.' It is said that judicial review is a 'new and important stage in the public policy process'.[22]

Yet, however intense the review of administrative action in the UK might have become, it has not lost some of the core features that made it 'sporadic and peripheral'. It remains sporadic, despite the rising quantity of applications for judicial review (AJRs) and judicial review rulings, because it is court-based and thus inherently casuistic. It also remains essentially peripheral because it is very much based on 'remedies, not principles', to quote from the words of Lord Wilberforce in *Davy*.[23] It is only as remedies have evolved, that judicial review has evolved. In *O'Reilly v Mackman*, Lord Diplock famously stated that:

> [T]he distinction in substantive law between what is private law and what is public law has itself been a latecomer to the English legal system. It is a consequence of the development that has taken place in the last 30 years of the procedures available for judicial control of administrative action.[24]

This statement served as a preface to a narration of the change of administrative law, a change that took the form of a Dworkinian chain novel. First came *Shaw* (1952),[25] then the Tribunals and Inquiries Act (1958), culminating in the RSC Ord 53. In between, Diplock could mention such landmark cases as *Ridge* (1964),[26] *Anisminic* (1969),[27] and *Padfield* (1968).[28]

[18] *Cf Ridge v Baldwin* [1964] AC 40.
[19] *Dyson v Attorney-General* [1911] 1 KB 410.
[20] ibid.
[21] SA de Smith, *Judicial Review of Administrative Action*, 1st edn (London, Stevens and Sons Ltd, 1959) 1.
[22] S James, 'The Political and Administrative Consequences of Judicial Review' (1996) 74 *Public Administration* 613, quoting from SA de Smith, H Woolf & JA Jowell, *Judicial Review of Administrative Action*, 5th edn (London, Sweet & Maxwell, 1995) vii.
[23] 'English law fastens, not upon principles but upon remedies.' *Davy v Spelthorne* BC [1984] AC 262, 276.
[24] *O'Reilly v Mackman* [1983] 2 AC 237.
[25] *Shaw v DPP* [1962] AC 220.
[26] *Ridge* (n 18).
[27] *Anisminic Ltd v Foreign Compensation Commission* [1969] 2 AC 147.
[28] *Padfield v Minister of Agriculture, Fisheries and Food* [1968] AC 997.

That chain novel, as developed by other judges or scholars, could include *O'Reilly* itself, and be continued in later cases. In fact, many other chain novels (with new episodes continuously appearing in the form of sequels and prequels) could be written about other developments in this field such as the story of the 'taming of the prerogative', the rise of 'procedural fairness' from the ashes of 'natural justice' or the pre-Human Rights Act mythology of 'bringing rights home'. Is there a foundation to be found within such narratives? Directly? Or by reading between the lines? Or does the narrative (or, more generally, the narrative style in British public law) itself work as a foundation, a kind of mythical story of origins?

This raises a (deceivingly) simple question: why does this have to be a narrative at all? A narrative is a stylistic device adapted to the depiction of a series of events. Why does public law take such a shape? And why is there a story to tell? Why did it take so long for common law courts to move from weak to strong judicial review? And in the era of strong review, why did the strengthening begin only in the 1960s? And, finally, why is it itself an ongoing process and not one that has occurred once and for all, in a wholesale fashion? For instance, in the period spanning from *Keyser* (1920)[29] to *GCHQ* (1994),[30] why did the Appellate Committee of the House of Lords refrain from entering the field of the 'manner and exercise' of prerogative? Or, to take yet another example, why is it, in the terms of Lord Mustill, that as far as judicial review is concerned 'standards of fairness are not immutable'?[31] Is this true in the first place? Why was it (in the eye of the law) alright for administrative bodies to disregard procedural fairness in the (recent) past? Social sciences—especially history and sociology—can suggest answers, or at least patterns, to legal science and legal scholarship might be tempted to turn to the social sciences in order to solve such a quandary. For instance, the solution can be expressed in historical terms, but then the rationality of the entire process of change is hard to envisage, if only because we find it hard to understand why justice, which should be immutable, was not done from the beginning. And also because nothing (and especially not the reading of law journals and law reports) tells us that we stand at the end of history. Another case might come up, another statute. To say, with Oliver Wendell Holmes Jr, that 'the life of the law [...] has been experience' is to say that the law's logic is only apparent retrospectively, while conceding at the same time that new chapters (and thus new endings) can always be added. Thus, if narratives work as foundations, they are shifting ones that move across time. Common lawyers are used to the metaphor that the common law is constantly changing while at the same time immutable. But metaphors can work like drugs: they are likely to generate both delusion and addiction.

B. The Conceptual Problem: The State and its Avatars

The problem does not only appear in a historical form. It also appears in conceptual terms. This is emphatically the case with the notion of 'the state' in public law. I will first show that there are some very serious hindrances within administrative law to making the state a foundational concept and then argue that, although the state does indeed play a role

[29] See *Keyser* (n 8).
[30] See *GCHQ* (n 9).
[31] *R v Secretary of State for the Home Department, ex parte Doody* [1994] 1 AC 531, 560.

in administrative law, both in France and the UK, it is through more local conceptual instances—what I call 'avatars'—which, along the lines suggested above, operate in a way that is 'lateral' or 'peripheral' rather than foundational.

i. *The State as the* sine qua non *of Public Law?*

Loughlin defends the view, quite convincingly, that 'the concept of the state is [...] the *sine qua non* of public law'.[32] He makes further a plea for the 'indispensability of the concept of the state for public law'.[33] At least in the French and British cases, though, administrative law has done extremely well without a concept of the state. Of course, the state is not entirely absent: it lies hidden somewhere in the background, 'shrouded in darkness, veiling his approach with dark rain clouds', as the God of the Old Testament.[34] But the *Rechtsdogmatik* of administrative law has managed to keep it just there. At least in France and Britain, the state has not become a foundational concept of administrative law.

In France, to be sure, some authors in the Third Republic based the unity of 'public law' on the notion of the state. When Maurice Hauriou wrote his *Principles of Public Law* (1910), he found that the state was the unifying concept sitting between constitutional and administrative law: 'into legal reality (*dans la réalité juridique*), one has to distinguish a certain number of cases in which public lawyers (*publicistes*) have effectively dealt with the problem of the state as a whole.'[35] Carré de Malberg also noted that 'by public law, what is meant is the law of the state (*Staatsrecht*)'.[36] And this was not only a statement made by constitutional lawyers. Hauriou had built his *Principles of Public Law* on the general idea that there was a *régime d'Etat*—ie, a set of legal rules, principles and mechanisms specific to the state. Roger Bonnard, another important administrative lawyer of the Third Republic, had begun his *Précis de droit administratif* with the claim that 'one cannot reach a scientific understanding of administrative law without taking as a basis a theory of law and of the State'.[37] On the other hand, Olivier Beaud has more recently argued that the state is relatively absent from the vocabulary of public law. And while some authors of the Third Republic claimed that the state was the key concept of public law, others successfully defended the view that the state was unnecessary to the *Rechtsdogmatik* of French administrative law.[38] A careful sifting of cases and legislation established that rather than the state itself, what mattered for administrative law as suggested above, was simply its autonomy from private law

[32] *Foundations* (n 2) 183.

[33] *Foundations* (n 2) 183.

[34] Psalm 18–11. See also 97–2: 'Clouds and thick darkness surround him; righteousness and justice are the foundation of his throne.'

[35] 'il fallait découper dans la réalité juridique' un certain nombre de problèmes qui ont été traités par les 'publicistes qui [...] en France, ont véritablement traité le problème de l'Etat dans son entier', M Hauriou, *Principes de Droit Public* [1910, rééd] (Paris, Dalloz, 2010) 55.

[36] 'il faut entendre par droit public, le droit de l'Etat (Staatsrecht)', RC de Malberg, *Contribution à la Théorie Générale de l'Etat, 1919–1922* [rééd] (Paris, Dalloz, 2003) Vol I, 1.

[37] 'On ne peut pas arriver à une connaissance scientifique convenable du droit administratif sans prendre appui sur une théorie du droit et de l'Etat', R Bonnard, *Précis de droit administratif*, 3rd edn (Paris, LGDJ, 1940) 21.

[38] Olivier Beaud sees the Paris public law professor Gaston Jèze (1869–1953) as the main engineer of this 'disappearance of the state'. With Jèze, 'the state disappears, because it is replaced by service public and its ancillary concepts', in 'L'œuvre de Gaston Jèze signifie-t-elle un repli de la doctrine publiciste française sur la technique juridique?' (2013) *Jus Politicum* 11, 25.

(ie, the substantive autonomy of rules and procedural autonomy of a distinct body of administrative courts) and its distinctive 'process of public service' (*procédé du service public*).

In the United Kingdom, the relative absence of the state is even more apparent. British law knows of a Crown, or in the modern parlance of such lawyers as Diplock, Roskill, or Denning, an 'executive government'—which in fact has retained a great deal of the inherent features of the Crown. But it notoriously lacks an operational, legally meaningful, concept of a state, as Loughlin himself notes: 'In the British constitution [[…]] the crown or monarch (and there is still some confusion over these terms) continues to this day formally to represent the *Staatsgewalt*'.[39] One could even contemplate the possibility that there is nothing that corresponds to the German concept of *Staatsgewalt* in British law. Loughlin's approach in *Foundations* (which is more wide-ranging as it defends the notion of a 'universality' of public law), but also in previous works such as *Public Law and Political Theory*,[40] appears as a systematic, but highly counterintuitive, defence of the existence of *Staatsgewalt* in British law. And its level of systematic elaboration matches its degree of counterintuitiveness. Loughlin is not alone in taking this stance. His attitude is typical of what took place in British public law in this regard: if the state is to play a role at all in that branch of the law, it is always through a process of intellectual activism. Activist lawyers, judges or academics, come to believe that the state matters and, as a result, they defend a change of vocabulary—and beyond vocabulary, a transformation in the underlying political philosophy of public law. This has been the work of what Martin Loughlin has called 'the functionalist school' in the LSE and elsewhere. This is also the legacy of certain conspicuous (as well as relatively heirless) judges such as Diplock or Denning. But, be that as it may, the state has *never* been a self-evident feature of British law.

It is undoubtedly of interest to investigate the reasons for the disappearance of the state (for which we could re-use Hegel's magnificent phrase, 'the sleeping soul of the state'). One is certainly the triumph of case law. If case law has been so prevalent amongst the sources of administrative law, it is because legislation has failed. The massive development of enabling legislation, creating new powers as well as new public-law bodies, has not been met by the establishment of general, transversal, principles ruling the whole field. Legislators are notoriously bad at codifying. The codification of administrative law has thus been the business of judges. This is obvious in the French case as well—for instance through the line of cases establishing 'general principles of law' defining the core, unwritten, requirements of legality.[41]

Additionally, in both France and the UK, judges had symmetrical and equally powerful reasons to ignore the state as much as possible. In France, administrative judges stand at the very core of *Staatsgewalt*. There is no precise distinction between the executive government, the higher administrative bodies, and the administrative court system. The *Conseil d'Etat*

[39] *Foundations* (n 2) 223.

[40] M Loughlin, *Public Law and Political Theory* (Oxford, Oxford University Press, 1992).

[41] The new 'Code des relations entre le public et l'administration' (enacted in 2015 and in force since January 2016) does not really detract from this argument: it compiles existing legislation and codified case law. Despite some inevitable changes, it is far from amounting to a revolution or a 'clean slate'. The Code is part of an ongoing process of codification 'à droit constant' (with no changes in the law) in France since 1996. Yet case law has never stopped to shape French public law, maybe today more than ever.

is simultaneously legal counsel to the executive, the top administrative court and the place where many higher administrative officers come from. It has no need of the state because, in many regards, it is the state.

ii. A Process of Differentiation

The absence of a state that would be a visible, conspicuous foundation for administrative law is thus a feature of both the British and French public law systems. Yet, in both cases, the state can be viewed differently, representing different phenomenological 'strategies'. If one agrees with my suggestion that administrative law has developed as a non-foundational, lateral or indeed peripheral process, this leads to an investigation into smaller, less visible, manifestations or emanations of the state in the conceptual framework of administrative law. I would suggest that the keyword here is 'differentiation'. This process is central to an understanding of the *Rechtdogmatik* of both French and British public law. The legal identity of the state is found in this process of differentiation: the state is manifested in the process by which it struggles to distinguish its own rights, prerogatives, immunities, and so on, from the private rights that govern relations between private persons. The state's power (*Staatsgewalt*) thus appears in the negative, as simply a power to derogate from private law and private arrangements. It is not foundational. Intellectually, it is derivative in the sense that one needs to know what private law is before one can see the derogations from it that constitute public law.

The legal word for this in France is *dérogatoire*. It does not translate easily into English. Rules of public law *derogate* from rules of private law. They appear as deviations from the normal, common, rule applicable to private arrangements. Dicey may have overlooked this. He saw French public law as foundational: the state came first, it stood above the individuals and the law of the state was a kind of superior law administered by separate courts. French public law was a kind of institutionalised, judicialised, reason of state. Another term that would deserve a closer look here is that of *prérogatives*. As a French term of art, *prérogatives de puissance publique* are powers special to public authorities. In contract law, for instance, one such *prérogative de puissance publique* consists in the power to modify unilaterally the content of a contract. Another one, in the course of administrative action, is the power to execute one's own decisions without recourse to a court injunction. In other words: the sacrosanct autonomy of public law is an autonomy which has been gained from a pre-existing something else—namely private law. The autonomy of public law has been acquired at the expense of a previous inhabitant of the legal field. What has been acquired has been taken away from private law. As evidenced by *dérogations* and *prérogatives* (two words with the same Latin root: *rogatio*, *rogare*), the 'primacy' of public law is not absolute or foundational. In fact, as a close reading of the landmark *Blanco* case would suggest, French public law is lateral to a whole body of private law, which it actually presupposes. The state presupposes an existing civil society and public law presupposes the *Code Civil.*

This is not only a French phenomenon. 'Differential judicial protection' of public bodies and civil servants (*protection judiciaire différenciée*, in the words of Sabino Cassese[42]) is a common feature of British administrative law as well. But, despite this commonality, the

[42] S Cassese, *La construction du droit administratif. France et Royaume-Uni* (Montchrestien, clés, 2000) 144.

mental worlds and intellectual tools could not be more different. To say, as in Britain, that an administrative power is 'quasi-judicial' is to take a somewhat different course from pretending that it is 'exorbitant'[43] or *dérogatoire*, as in French legal parlance. In the British case, the power of administrative supervision is relegated, more or less artificially, to the function of common law courts through their capacity to administer the ordinary law of the land. In the French case, the administrative power is shown to be special and incommensurable with the ordinary law of the land, and thus assigned to a special court system. A similar asymmetry can be seen in the approach to state liability for torts. France has not moved away from the *Blanco* principle, which, as we might recall, holds that 'state liability for torts caused to private persons by [state] employees working in public services cannot be governed by the principles of the Code civil'. Conversely, the Crown Proceedings Act 1947 aims at treating the Crown as an ordinary litigant, and thus at bringing the Crown into the orbit of ordinary law. Despite this difference, however, in many tort cases the outcome of the case will be the same. In fact, both systems have created a 'differential judicial protection' of administrative action and even used similar language. While French administrative law granted 'privileges' to administrative bodies (*privilège du préalable*, *privilège de l'action d'office*), in Britain the Crown has been granted a 'Crown privilege' (albeit later to be termed a 'public interest immunity').

III. In Search of a Foundation

Both in France and the UK, there have been attempts to provide 'foundations' (and indeed constitutional foundations) for administrative law. These undertakings, both in their measure of (relative) success and of (relative) failure, are highly instructive. I will address them in turn.

A. France: The Search for the 'Constitutional Bases' of Administrative Law

Earlier on, I referred to the fact that, historically and conceptually, French administrative law does not stand at the foundation of the rest of the legal system. It was not born at the core, but in the penumbra of both private law and, to some extent, constitutional law. Yet this was an unsatisfactory state of affairs for French lawyers. They tried hard to find a foundation, preferably in line with the French culture of legal sources. Administrative law was based on case law: the case law of the *Conseil d'Etat*. This did not stand as a satisfactory foundation, if one were required. French law does not have a theory of precedent. Even worse, in its development, public law contravened the express rejection of the power of the judiciary to review administrative action as articulated in the Act of 16/24 July 1790. The search for foundations was initially a conceptual exercise. During the late nineteenth century, a school of thought supported the view that the basis of French administrative law was *service public*—ie, the particular ends that were pursued by administrative entities.

[43] An 'exorbitant' power is (etymologically) one that is 'outside the orbit' of ordinary law.

At the same time, another school of thought defended the different view that administrative law was based on *puissance publique* (public power)—the particular powers that administrative entities could use to pursue these ends.

It took Georges Vedel, an eminent public lawyer of the twentieth century, to formulate the issue in terms of foundations. In 1954, he expressed the view that it was 'the constitution [that was] the necessary basis of the [...] rules of administrative law'.[44] This, he took as self-evident: 'this results' he said 'from the very nature of the constitution, the foundation of the legal order and the charter of the state organisation'.[45] He then set out to uncover these foundations. He noted that *service public* was by no means a proper candidate: 'Not only is it in crisis, but also because it introduces a rupture between constitutional principles and administrative law.'[46] Vedel took the view that it was impossible to base administrative law on 'material'—ie, activity-based—concepts such as *service public*. Instead, he profferred the view that public law was built on more 'formal' foundations, namely Acts of Parliament, understood as a pure legal form, and the constitution, understood not substantively but merely as a certain legislative procedure endowed with the character of 'rigidity' (ie, entrenchment). Administrative law was thus based on *puissance publique* rather than *service public*. And *puissance publique* was in the main exercised by the executive power. 'Administration *stricto sensu*' said Vedel 'is nothing but the exercise of *puissance publique* by executive authorities'.[47] It remained for Vedel to identify a convenient constitutional peg upon which to hang this notion of *puissance publique*. He found it in Article 3 of the Constitutional Statute of 25 February 1875—even though this clause in fact said precious little about the actual power of the executive (except that the French President 'executed laws').

That this constitutional clause could appear as the constitutional foundation of the whole body of administrative law would come as a surprise to anyone not versed (and trained) in the French way of approaching the problem of legal empowerment. The authors of the Constitutional Statute of 1875 had not intended by any stretch of the imagination for Article 3 to found a system of administrative law. Vedel was certainly well aware of that, but in accordance with his theory of sources—drawn from Carré de Malberg—the intentions of the drafters was irrelevant and what really mattered was what courts made of the provision. This second observation provided Vedel with a second ground to warrant his claim—that of case law: 'We will not turn' said Vedel 'to theoretical speculations in order to point us towards the constitutional basis of administrative law. Rather, we will ask case law (jurisprudence) to do so.' According to Vedel, 'theory' was an easy target that could thus be quickly set aside. But, in fact, his anti-theoretical stance was intended to hide the very obvious fact that the Emperor was naked. The constitution said nothing about administrative law. Yet, given Vedel's theory of sources, the constitution *had* to say something about administrative law. So, even if the written law of the constitution seemed to remain silent, Vedel was theory-bound to make it talk through the 'oracle' of that law: the *Conseil d'Etat*.

[44] G Vedel, 'Les bases constitutionnelles du droit administratif' (1954) 8 *Etudes et Documents du Conseil d'Etat* 26–27, 36–43.

[45] ibid.

[46] ibid 26. Vedel says literally *solution de continuité*, using an originally medical term of art that refers to 'the displacement, rupture or dissolution of previously connected physical structures', see R Allen, *David Hartley on Human Nature* (Albany, SUNY press, 1999) 122. This medical meaning is now almost forgotten in France and the expression is widely used in non-medical contexts.

[47] Vedel (n 44) 37.

The proper reading of Article 3, for the sake of Vedel's argument, came from the *Conseil d'Etat* ruling in *Heyriès* (1918). The First World War and the extension of executive powers during the time of hostilities generated a certain amount of litigation before the administrative courts. In most cases, special Acts of Parliament with retroactive effect had validated wartime administrative measures that would have otherwise been bound to be annulled, as they were obviously *ultra vires* at the time at which they were adopted. A legislative draftsman's slip of the pen caused a *décret* (a regulation enacted by the *Président de la République*) to be omitted from the scope of a 1915 act of indemnity. The decree's purpose was to suspend some procedural rights granted by statute to civil servants, notably the right of access to their administrative file before a disciplinary sanction be issued against them. Suspension of Acts of Parliament is normally not a power which belongs to the *Président de la République*, not because of an explicit prohibition of the type contained in the British Bill of Rights of 1689, but, implicitly, because of the hierarchy of norms in the French legal system. There is in French administrative law a 'fundamental rule', namely the principle of legality, according to which 'regulations and decrees are subordinate to Acts of Parliament and cannot undertake anything against them'. At the same time, this hierarchy of norms reflected a hierarchy of state agencies and functions: how can a holder of a subordinate, 'administrative' function be able to set aside statutes passed by the 'representative of the national will', namely Parliament?

The *Conseil d'Etat* nevertheless managed to rescue the decree from illegality by first observing that Article 3 of the Constitutional Statute of 25 February 1875 placed the President at the head of the French administration and mandated him to execute laws. As a result, it argued, 'it was incumbent upon him to make sure that, at all times, public services [...] would be in working order'.[48] Wartime necessities certainly played a part in the reasoning which led to affirming the legality of the decree. But the *Conseil d'Etat* was careful to ground this decision, in want of an appropriate statute, on a constitutional basis. The decision was welcomed by Maurice Hauriou as a 'break with the unhealthy habit of defining the executive power [*sic*] only by the duty to carry statutes into execution'. 'This mission' continued the Toulouse professor

> is twofold: [first], to ensure the proper functioning of the administration (and also of government); [second], to carry statutes into execution. This truth [...] is now unveiled. It took the war. But, under such a light, some truths are glaring.[49]

Hauriou stood first among the holders of the minority view on the executive: he believed that executive power could not be reduced to an administrative function. Especially, he did not see it as subordinate: he saw it as the primary activity of the state. One could have taken another view of the matter. Indeed, if justified by necessity, executive suspension of procedural rights need not have been deemed illegal—or more precisely, its illegality could have been excused by relevant provisions in the constitution. But one could also analyse the decision of the *Conseil d'Etat* as a rather unconvincing attempt to find at any cost a legal basis for an administrative decision that was otherwise doomed to be annulled. Viewed in this light, it stretched the notion of how executive actions could be authorised by written

[48] Conseil d'Etat, 28 June 1918, n° 63412, Heyriès, Lebon, p 651.
[49] M Hauriou, 'Note sous Conseil d'Etat', 28 juin 1918, Heyriès, S 1922.3.49.

law (either statutory or constitutional) to the point where such a requirement had become entirely fictional. Under appropriate construction, Article 3 of the Constitutional Act of 25 February 1875 (which made no reference to war powers or 'necessity') could be made to justify almost anything.

Another case to which Vedel referred was *Labonne* (1919).[50] In *Labonne*, the *Conseil d'Etat* decided that the President enjoyed inherent (ie, non-statutory) national police powers over the whole territory. The facts (and the point of law) of this French case are remarkably close to those of the British *Northumbria Police* case.[51] Absent a statutory enactment empowering the executive to enact a police regulation, courts took recourse to a supposedly inherent police power that, in the UK, derived from the 'prerogative' (revived and probably extended despite its supposedly residual nature) and in France derived, despite the lack of a textual authorisation, from *pouvoirs propres*. Vedel himself acknowledged that *Labonne* did not mention the Constitution, that it is outside the 'visas' through which French courts formulate the premises of their judicial syllogism (*vu la constitution, et notamment son article 3, etc*). But, said Vedel, 'it is self-evident [*il va de soi que*] that this foundation cannot be other than the [written] constitution. Where else would the president draw such powers?'[52] He later said that this same theory also applied to the Constitution of 1946 and then to the Constitution of 1958.[53]

Vedel's theory of *bases constitutionnelle* is of interest for a number of reasons. First, it is based on the idea that administrative law should have a constitutional anchor. At the same time there is also the fact that precious little by way of such an anchor could be found in the actual texts of the written constitutional enactments of 1875, 1946, and 1958. What then should be done? What Vedel does is to amalgamate the constitutional text with *Conseil d'Etat* case law. He therefore does not need to cite the Constitution. Rather he can simply quote from *Conseil* decisions offering particular constructions of the constitutional text. If *Heyriès* is a shaky foundation for public law, *Labonne* is even worse. Indeed, proponents of the 'public service school' could have come up with equally convenient constitutional pegs for their particular theory of *services publics* as the constitutional foundation of administrative law. In fact, the 1946 Constitution expressly mentioned *services publics* in its Preamble, while it said *absolutely nothing* of *puissance publique.*

What is perhaps even more interesting about Vedel's reasoning is precisely how persuasive it turned out to be, despite the weakness of his 'philological' argument and the scant evidence he was able to muster in support. When he says about *Labonne* that 'it is self-evident [*il va de soi que*] that the foundation for this decision has to be the constitution' he is making as unconvincing an assertion as can be. Nevertheless, Vedel ended up setting out what would be accepted as the orthodox account of French public law for decades to come. His account of the 'constitutional bases' would become a kind of 'noble lie' or at least a remarkably efficient one. This may have been because Vedel himself was not an isolated intellectual without ties to the making of positive law. He was an 'embedded lawyer' very close to the higher circle of civil servants and judges and would become a member of the *Conseil constitutionnel* in the 1980s. What he has to say has almost always been approved

[50] Conseil d'Etat- 8 août 1919—Labonne—Rec. Lebon 737.

[51] *R v Home Secretary, ex p Northumbria Police Authority* [1988] 1 All ER 556.

[52] Vedel (n 44) 38.

[53] G Vedel, *Droit Administratif*, 7th edn (Paris, Presses Universitaires de France, 1980) Preface.

by judges in extra-judicial statements. And it has also frequently been confirmed by developments in the case law of French higher courts. For instance, while the Constitution was silent on the existence and limits of the jurisdiction of administrative courts, such jurisdictional delineations have been (belatedly) constitutionalised by the *Conseil constitutionnel* by way of unwritten, judge-made principles.[54] The normative category used for that purpose was that of *principes généraux reconnus par les lois de la République.* Was this a confirmation of the existence of *bases constitutionnelles* or an admission that there was nothing of the sort?

B. Britain: 'A Foundation with too much Sand and not enough Rock'[55]

Outsiders may have intellectual privileges that insiders don't enjoy. This may be the case when they come to observe at a certain distance a controversy in which insiders are fully immersed. Take for instance the debate over the foundations of judicial review in the UK. At the end of the day, it seems, what matters is not who is right and who is wrong. That is a question for insiders. What seems more relevant to the outside observer is the structure of the whole debate and what the adversaries have in common. Vedel's discussion of *bases constitutionnelles* in France and the conflicting theories developed in the course of the British *ultra vires* controversy have a major point in common. They are all source-based (or maybe should I say 'source-oriented'). They try to uncover a foundation of administrative law and/or of judicial review of administrative action in terms of sources. In so doing, they each reflect a deeply national and idiosyncratic approach to legal authority.

In France, the approach to legal authority is textual. For an administrative body to enjoy a certain power, there has (as far as possible) to be a written enactment. Other options—such as the '*pouvoirs propres*' in *Labonne*—are unsavoury and as a result marginalised. Wherever supporting text cannot be found, the courts will attempt to disguise what are best understood as inherent administrative powers under some cloak of a written authorisation, however implausible it might seem. In the UK, things have changed little since the *Entick v Carrington* formula: adequate legal authority of public bodies must come either from the common law or from statute. As a matter of fact, it is striking to note that the *Entick* formula is perfectly mirrored in the structure of the '*ultra vires* vs common law' controversy about the foundations of judicial review. Whereas the *ultra vires* school reads a whole set of substantive rules into enabling statutes, hence taking seriously the principle of parliamentary supremacy, the common law school identifies the common law, *Entick*'s second source of empowerment, as the principal basis of the supervisory power of courts over administrative decisions.

In both countries, legal scholars have sought to build the foundations of public law on a broader national theory of legal sources. And they have been trapped in that very theory, which is by necessity a formal theory of law. In both countries, the theoretical language is somewhat autocratic. The French understanding of sources (there *has* to be a constitutional

[54] Décision n° 86-224 DC du 23 janvier 1987, 'Loi transférant à la juridiction judiciaire le contentieux des décisions du Conseil de la concurrence'.

[55] J Laws, 'The Ghost in the Machine: Principle in Public Law' (1989) *Public Law* 27.

basis for administrative power and this constitutional basis *has* to be written) pointed exclusively towards one solution. Yet it was an extremely disappointing one, as the Constitution was silent on administrative power. In the UK, the 'Vedel approach' is more or less mirrored by the *ultra vires* school. What the theory of the written Constitution achieves in France, the supremacy of Parliament achieves in Britain. The solution *has* to come from the intention of Parliament. In Christopher Forsyth's approach, for instance, Parliament *must* have meant to say something about the framework for judicial review of the powers that it devolves to administrative bodies. As a result, in both countries, the religion of written law turns into the defence of an unwritten framework set up by the courts. Each formal theory of sources ends up justifying exactly the reverse of its very premises: courts, not legislators, make the law.

IV. Conclusion: Towards a Loughlinian Framework for Contemporary Public Law?

So far, in both France and the UK, attempts to reveal the foundations of public law—understood as the law controlling the exercise of discretionary administrative power and the management of public services—have not been entirely successful. In France, the discussion has foundered, mostly for lack of theoretical interest on the part of administrative lawyers. In the UK, it has taken a much more elaborate and analytical bent. Several important books and a wealth of articles have been devoted to the issue. But the external observer is bound to find that the controversy somewhat fades, maybe because of its inherent formalism. As I have said earlier in this essay, it is framed in formal terms—in terms of a national theory of which sources (statute law vs common law) govern it from above. This may be why some interesting attempts have been made (notably by Mark Elliott) to reframe the debate in terms of a 'constitutional foundation' of judicial review. It is also remarkable that the controversy should focus on judicial review rather than substantive administrative law. Stanley de Smith has prevailed and John Griffith—to whom *Foundations* is dedicated—has lost. And France never had a John Griffith in the first place.

At this stage, scepticism seems to be the most tempting option: should we not just accept that retrieving the foundations of public law *qua* administrative law is a lost cause? Should we not accept that while there is a foundational component to public law, which is generally called 'constitutional law', there is also a non-foundational dimension to that field? Moreover, administrative law may not be the only 'non-foundational' zone in the territory of public law. For instance 'government' and 'governmental powers', or the 'state of emergency' (*état d'exception*, *notrecht*) as objects dealt with by constitutional lawyers may also fall within that perimeter. But administrative law, especially when seen from the perspective of judicial review, is the legal framework that regulates most of the discretionary powers enjoyed by public bodies. Such 'discretion', however, is a notoriously elusive concept, for which foundational reasoning does not provide very satisfactory explanations. You simply know it when you see it—when its 'manner and exercise' has exceeded its limits, or has been unreasonable; when you are faced with particular, casuistic, occurrences of ultra vires or 'unreasonableness'. Such pessimism is not necessarily justified, however. Despite all that has been said above, there may still be reasons why certain foundations of (contemporary) public law should be framed in terms akin to those identified in *Foundations*. Let me just spell out here some avenues for future research.

A. Administrative Discretion: *Potestas* or *Potentia*?

Foundations' fascinating discussion of the modern theory of power in juristic discourse could shed some useful light on the field of administrative law. It would seem to me, at least *prima facie*, that the concept of 'power' at play in administrative law is a concept of power as *potestas*—that is, to follow Loughlin, power as 'rule-generated authority'.[56] Judicial review is based on that notion: administrative power is a *jurisidictio*; jurisdiction has, in the famous words of Lord Greene in *Wednesbury*, 'four corners'. This is very obvious in the case of statutory power, maybe less so in the case of prerogative. But even prerogative has limits, however indeterminate those limits may be. Conversely, constitutional law tends to approach power as *potentia*: as a kind of natural, self-generating, power; but also a kind of power over which law has a limiting, confining, capacity of some kind. Also, constitutional law is public law in the (Loughlinian) sense of a 'power-generating law'.[57] Most of the time, administrative powers are (or have to be) generated, not generating.

At the same time, as detailed above, the whole story of modern administrative law in both France and Britain shows us that discretionality is often a kind of Hobbesian *potentia* that is constantly eluding attempts to cabin it into a mere implementation of superior law. Administrative law is, in the words of Olivier Beaud, 'the state in action'. Here, the 'state' is employed not as a foundational concept, but as a body in constant motion, and correspondingly, the core concepts of legal thinking in the field of administrative law are not foundational but pragmatic. The state is approached through what it does (eg public services, public order, etc) and what it does is not predictable *a priori*. Legislation is continually buffeted by new changes in the needs of society. And its inevitable resulting pathologies are dealt with by case law. Yet, in this non-foundational process of state development, the original concern of constitutionalism—facing the state's *potentia* realistically in order to set some restraints on its tyrannical tendencies—has reappeared in administrative law. The governing concept of judicial review, in both our sample jurisdictions, is legality. In France, legality absorbs all the grounds of judicial review. In the UK, legality *stricto sensu* is only one of the main grounds of the superior court's supervisory jurisdiction of administrative action. But viewed *lato sensu*, legality—sometimes called lawfulness—actually covers all these grounds (ie legality *stricto sensu*, reasonableness, procedural impropriety and maybe today proportionality).

This process of a progressive building of a set of anti-arbitrary principles in administrative law is a possible explanation for that quest for a foundational narrative that I discussed earlier in this article. In this sense, the struggle for legality in administrative law is an almost exact counterpart to the earlier struggle for the 'rule of law' in the constitution of the state. The 'revolution of judicial review' almost explicitly mirrors the seventeenth century 'paper

[56] *Foundations* (n 2) 165.
[57] *Foundations* (n 2) 12.

wars' against the political absolutism of the Stuart State. This has been a common feature of judicial opinions for a long time. The Court's reasoning in *Dyson v Attorney General*[58] offers a perfect modern example: 'It has not, since the Commonwealth at any rate, been the practice of the Crown to attempt to defeat the rights of its subjects by virtue of the prerogative'. Since *Dyson*, such language has remained a commonplace of legal writing in Britain. The Human Rights Act is the modern Bill of Rights. And should the Act be abolished, common law rights—and more generally the common law itself—are ready to take over. The defence of a common law foundation for judicial review provided by Paul Craig and others could be read as a continuation of Coke's defence of the common law as the utmost guarantee against arbitrary power. The repeated attempts of the same eminent lawyer to establish a continuity between seventeenth century cases dealing with prerogative writs with modern judicial review is evidence of exactly the same phenomenon.[59] All-in-all, the phraseology of judges and scholars in modern Britain constantly refers back to the heroic era of the seventeenth century. This is probably not accidental, nor is it merely rhetorical. The birth of administrative law in Britain may have been 'sporadic and peripheral'. Yet it reflects a foundational quest for justice, or, in Loughlin's language, for 'right ordering' or *droit politique*.

B. The 'Right Ordering' of Administrative Law?

This is where Loughlin's position as a 'retriever of ancient prudence' is perhaps most remarkable. His claim that public law is about the 'right ordering' of society is very timely, precisely because it would appear as very untimely to most contemporary public lawyers. Contemporary public law has been dominated by a fear of embedding a certain theory of justice into positive law. Legal ordering should be a neutral ordering, one that does not choose between competing moral and political values. This rise of the neutral state has corresponded with the rise of the principle of equality as the core value of modern public law. Why not, however, approach the work of judges, administrators, and scholars in terms of a pursuit of 'right ordering' in the context of a blooming sphere of discretionary administrative powers? I take right ordering to mean the inherent, sometimes not completely elicited and self-conscious, notion of justice at play in a legal and political system. Modern lawyers in the field of public law have not given up the hope of identifying such a concept of political right or right ordering (the *recta ratio* of the modern age). But administrative law has not been built upon an existing theory of justice. It has been created along the way, by means of what Loughlin would call 'institutionalised practices':

> [H]istorical investigation often reveals that such institutionalised practices are partial, limited, and contingent expressions of more general ideas of right ordering [...] these practices incorporate the ways in which subjects themselves perceive the nature of the activity of governing.[60]

Why not apply this formula to the 'institutionalised practices' of British administrative tribunals, ministers and departments—in fact, the whole sphere of what Diplock called

[58] *Dyson* (n 19) 421.

[59] eg P Craig, 'Prerogative, Precedent and Power' in C Forsyth and I Hare (eds), *The Golden Metwand and the Crooked Cord: Essays in public law in Honour of Sir William Wade QC* (Oxford, Clarendon Press, 1998) 66–90.

[60] *Foundations* (n 2) 93.

'executive government' in his *GCHQ* ruling—and to judges of the superior courts of common law? And in France, of civil servants and *Conseil d'Etat* judges? In fact, it is quite evident that courts and scholars have pursued a certain idea of (political) justice in creating the modern framework of public law. This is the 'political right' element of administrative law. It is in part explicit, in part underdeveloped, and in all cases largely unexamined.[61] But the changes in the scope or intensity of review reflect parallel changes in the moral philosophy of the polis. Every judge is a Dworkinian Hercules. And while he or she often gets his or her timing wrong, at the end of the day some sort of 'updating' takes place. Take for instance the rise of proportionality. Or the way in which reasonableness has developed from a simple criterion of 'non-absurdity' in *Wednesbury* ('outrageous defiance of logic') into a keyword for a set of elaborate tests of legality[62] in response—sometime successful, sometimes less so (such as the apparently defunct 'super-Wednesbury'[63])—to the evolving demands of justice in the contemporary world. At the same time, the 'new architecture of public law'[64] is distinctive in the sense that it is at odds with some of the most foundational aspects of constitutional law—democracy being one of them. I will not develop this further in this article, but certainly what has been said about the 'non-foundational' nature of administrative law is very much in line with the discussions about the 'democratic deficit' not only of the EU but more generally of many fields of administration as well.

[61] Although there are some remarkable counterexamples, such as TRS Allan's *Law, Liberty and Justice* (Oxford, Oxford University Press, 1992), or indeed many of Loughlin's own works. It is remarkable that such works of legal literature have no obvious counterparts in French administrative law.

[62] Paul Craig's 'umbrella sense' of *Wednesbury* (*Associated Provincial Picture Houses v Wednesbury Corp* [1948] 1 KB 223); see PP Craig, *Administrative Law* (London, 1999) 537.

[63] Apparently because of the way in which some scholars seem to interpret *R (Rotherham MBC) v Secretary of State for Business, Innovation & Skills* [2014] EWHC 232 (Admin).

[64] *Foundations* (n 2) Ch 15.

Part VI

The Response

16

Excavating *Foundations*

MARTIN LOUGHLIN

I. Introduction

In the Preface to *Foundations of Public Law*[1] I explained that only after having embarked on the project did I realise its magnitude. I tried to make it more manageable by first presenting the conceptual framework, which was outlined in *The Idea of Public Law* (IPL).[2] But the task of explaining the fundamentals of the subject in *Foundations*, its companion volume, 'pushed me to the limits of my competence—cognitively, intellectually, linguistically'. I mention this because my gratitude that so many colleagues have been prepared to engage with the book's arguments is tempered by the scale of the task I face in trying to respond constructively to their insightful criticisms. Some commentaries require a response as long as they are and that would not do. Similarly, I have tried to resist the temptation to respond when authors have ascribed to me views I do not hold and which might result in the type of pedantic exchange that would not be constructive.

I begin by explaining what I was seeking to do. Although I see the editors' sense in organising the chapters according to methodological, normative, material, and comparative critiques, my response cannot so neatly be divided.

II. Approaches to Public Law

My basic aim has been a better understanding of public law than is common in the traditional professionally-prescribed account. This inquiry began with a simple observation that English common law denies the very existence of the subject I am employed to profess. The common law assumes the existence of a body of 'ordinary law' that determines all disputes, whether between private parties or between citizens and Ministers of the Crown. The distinction between public law and private law, a commonplace in continental European regimes, was not recognised in English law. And yet over the last three or four decades we have seen a distinct concept of public law emerging from common law practice; there is now a separate division of the High Court that deals with public law matters

[1] M Loughlin, *Foundations of Public Law* (Oxford, Oxford University Press, 2010) (hereinafter '*Foundations*').
[2] M Loughlin, *The Idea of Public Law* (Oxford, Oxford University Press, 2003) (hereinafter 'IPL').

and administrative dispute resolution has now been formalised into something like a system of administrative adjudication. A concept of public law is being formed in the British system through differentiation and formalisation.

I need not labour that point since it is concisely explained in Denis Baranger's article (chapter 15). Consequently, Mark Tushnet is not wrong to suggest that what he calls the authorial 'itch' is felt because of developments concerning 'the status of law in Great Britain today' (Tushnet, chapter 13). Marco Goldoni amplifies this point by placing me in a trajectory in British legal thought that runs from 'functional to reflexive jurisprudence' (Goldoni, chapter 11) and while I might quibble with the neatness of his evolutionary scheme, he captures my orientation in an insightful way. Assuming that the more general implications of these British developments are worth reflecting on, the question is: how should such an inquiry be pursued?

One obvious method is to carry out an anatomical examination of this new body of law. This is a necessary but rather basic task and a more challenging next step might be comparison with regimes in which the division between public and private law is well established. This too has been attempted by others.[3] But as Baranger suggests, the ambitious analyst might then be motivated to dig beneath local particularities to discover the 'elementary forms of public law', that is, the essential structures which enable all these bodies of municipal law to do their work. Such a structural analysis—think of Durkheim's *The Elementary Forms of Religious Life* or Lévi-Strauss' *The Elementary Structures of Kinship*—would indeed be an achievement, the equivalent perhaps of splitting the atom in public law. The analyst would have revealed public law as an autonomous system of institutions, procedures, rules and methods. This would be a science of public law in all its purity.

But Baranger is very clear on the difficulties. He doubts the possibility of a source-based foundation for administrative law, provides a fascinating critical appraisal of Vedel's attempt to do so in French administrative law,[4] and notes the difficulties of comparable attempts by English lawyers (notably, the *ultra vires* versus common law debate). Having always rejected the value of this type of anatomical account, I would endorse his view about the difficulties in finding a justificatory basis in source-based materials.[5] It is for this reason that I reject Vedel's proposition that: 'We will not turn to theoretical speculations'.[6] In 1992, I introduced the thesis of *Public Law and Political Theory* by examining the problems of this method, suggesting that the anatomical account begins with the questionable assumption that law is an autonomous discipline. A more fruitful way of proceeding, I proposed, is 'to start from the assumption that public law is simply a sophisticated form of political discourse; that controversies within the subject are simply extended political disputes'.[7] A theoretical account of the sort Vedel rejects is surely required.

[3] See, eg JWF Allison, *A Continental Distinction in the Common Law: A Historical and Comparative Perspective on English Public Law* (Oxford, Clarendon Press, 1996).

[4] Baranger, ch 15, 245–49.

[5] On my criticisms of *ultra vires* v common law, see: M Loughlin, 'Whither the Constitution?' in C Forsyth (ed), *Judicial Review and the Constitution* (Oxford, Hart Publishing, 2000) 425–26. In this short note, I argued that 'the main theme of the seminar concerns the foundations of judicial review' but once this question is raised then, 'it seems obvious that … a multitude of more basic questions lurk in its shadow'. And if, as seemed to be the case, 'the issue of the constitutionalisation of public law [is] a particularly important question for lawyers to address' then the questions include: 'What … are these foundational constitutional principles? Whence are they derived?'

[6] Baranger, ch 15, 245.

[7] M Loughlin, *Public Law and Political Theory* (Oxford, Clarendon Press, 1992) Ch 1.

This is relatively well understood. Goldoni, for example, experiences no difficulty in identifying my method of presenting public law as a scheme of intelligibility in which positive public law 'can only be conceived as local knowledge'.[8] But no matter how many times I make this point, some legal theorists persist in turning my argument into a structural claim about positive public law.[9] The problem lies with an unwillingness of analytical legal theorists to consider an argument drawn from a different philosophical tradition.[10] Andrew Halpin spares no energy in demolishing what he calls the 'uniform concept of public law'. This uniform concept, he tells us, 'detracts from the importance of local differences' which, when recognised, 'are considered subservient to the master concept of public law'. The concept produces 'a skewed analytical (descriptive) portrayal of public law', which 'distracts attention from the peculiar social and political conditions' and it 'elevates the legal to a position that may become unstable, or possibly even dangerous' (Halpin, chapter 3).

These are devastating criticisms, but they are pitched against a thesis entirely of Halpin's invention. He might have been diverted by what he calls his 'preliminary digression on Goldsmith and Levinson', for digression from *Foundations* it certainly is. It is so far from my purpose and method that all his subsequent criticisms are misconceived. Although this mantra of 'uniform concept' runs throughout his article, I can find no place at which he shows that this is a thesis I advocate.[11] Halpin evidently regards this 'uniform concept' as a type of positive law,[12] and I have repeatedly stated that the idea of public law I examine is not a subset of positive law.[13] My inquiry asks: what happens to the medieval idea of

[8] Goldoni, ch 11, 171.

[9] NW Barber, 'Professor Loughlin's *Idea of Public Law*' (2005) 25 *Oxford Journal of Legal Studies* 157–67. See also, P Craig, 'Theory, "Pure Theory" and Values in Public Law' (2005) *Public Law* 440–47. In reply: M Loughlin, 'Reflections on *The Idea of Public Law*' in E Christodoulidis & S Tierney (eds), *Public Law and Politics* (Aldershot, Ashgate, 2008) 47–68 (hereinafter '*Reflections*').

[10] For an indication of this tradition see section III below. See further, C Taylor, 'Interpretation and the Sciences of Man' in his *Philosophy and the Human Sciences: Philosophical Papers* (Cambridge, Cambridge University Press, 1985) Vol 2, Ch 1.

[11] In the almost 250,000 words of *Foundations* the notion of a 'uniform concept of public law' there is only one mention. It appears in the last chapter on 'The New Architecture of Public Law' in a section concerning the emergence of administrative law regimes in continental Europe. This led to the first wave of the great textbooks of Mayer, Orlando, and Hauriou 'so that by the latter-half of the nineteenth century a relatively uniform system of administrative law existed' (*Foundations* (n 1) 439). But this is an explanation of the development of positive administrative law which, as Baranger recognises, is the positive phenomenon that my argument is seeking to account for. It states a problem, not the solution.

[12] He states that 'even if public law is regarded as qualitatively different from *the rest of* municipal law …' (Halpin, ch 3, 35); that 'a variety of *forms of public law* [can be] distinguished by the constitutional arrangements responding to each set of individual circumstances …' (Halpin, ch 3, 37–38). It might be felt that Halpin's uniform concept of public law is pitched at the level of the state rather than positive law, but if so this can only be because he treats the state as a legal person rather than as a scheme of intelligibility, a limitation I examine further in section IV below.

[13] *Reflections* (n 9) 1: 'The most basic objective of the book [IPL], then, was to retrieve a subject that seems to have fallen off contemporary maps of knowledge. For want of a better term, I call this subject public law. But by public law I do not mean a categorical division within positive law …'. IPL (n 2) 155: 'A positive theory of public law cannot therefore be a theory of positive law.' *Foundations* (n 1) 2: 'Jurists today often draw a distinction between public law and private law, between the law that regulates relations between the individual and government and the law that regulates relations between individuals. In that sense, public law is being treated as a subset of ordinary positive law. The concept of public law adopted in this book is much broader. The entire body of ordinary positive law presupposes the existence of a prior source of authority—fundamental law, now public law. This inquiry into the foundations of public law deals with this more basic concept: it is an investigation into questions of "right" relating to the conferral of authority and legitimacy on modern governmental ordering.'

'fundamental law' in the modern world? This may have been inadequately answered, but if that basic point is not grasped any criticism of it is likely to fall wide of the mark.

III. Method and Objective of *Foundations*

My general method derives from a distinction between the natural and human sciences, between *Naturwissenschaften* and *Geisteswissenschaften*. In the natural sciences, the subject matter is inanimate or organic and the task is to determine causal laws. In the human sciences, the search for causal laws is not possible; in place of necessary laws the aim is to explain relations of meaning and value among social agents. The objective of the human sciences is not to demonstrate the truth of a law-like proposition. It is to gain an understanding of what is going on in a particular domain, to make more intelligible something about which we already have a certain level of understanding.

The subject of our limited understanding here is a body of law relating to the activity of governing. If the aim is to advance understanding, then an account that already posits the authority of 'the state' or presupposes the existence of legal order is unlikely to be of much value. Those are the assumptions underpinning the orthodox approach, which limits the province of jurisprudence to the study of positive law. This approach is evidently motivated by the desire to conceive law in the image of the natural sciences. But since there is so much that this approach cannot explain about the relations between law and governing, it cannot help us acquire a deeper understanding of the subject. From the perspective of public law, an account of law that equates state to legal order, presupposes a basic norm, or takes as a matter of fact a rule of recognition leaves too many puzzles unexplained. It not only tells us next to nothing about the function of law, which might seem a quite different, that is, sociological, inquiry; it also tells us very little about the nature of law, including the nature of the positive rules and prescribed methods of public law.

From the perspective of public law, source-based analysis halts the inquiry at an arbitrary point. Any satisfactory account of relations between law and governing must pose questions like: What type of association is the state? From where does the state draw its authority? What role does law perform in establishing the authority of the state? How do rules of law acquire authority? Obviously, something more needs to be said about state and law that the terms themselves do not clarify. I would suggest then that the key to advancing understanding of the nature of public law is to examine the fundamental question of how political authority is constituted.

This brings me to the general objective of *Foundations*. In IPL the aim was to elucidate the postulates of the discourse of public law, these being the concepts that are not often made explicit but which form the basis of the practice. This is why the book concludes by suggesting that the general conceptual framework revealed by these postulates outlines a pure theory of public law. In response to concerns expressed by Panu Minkkinen (chapter 4) and Mike Wilkinson (chapter 12), I should emphasise that this is not pure theory on the model of the natural sciences. Following the method of the human sciences, it presents the basic conceptual elements that any systematic account of public law must incorporate into its particular scheme. In *Foundations*, the challenge was to show how these elements are drawn into particular configurations by influential political jurists who account for the constitution of political authority using the language of rights, duties, powers and liabilities.

These jurists belong to a common school of political jurisprudence not because they present similar accounts of the nature of law, or the basis of political authority, or the relationship between the legal and the political. They are political jurists because they recognise that in the transition from the medieval to the modern world an autonomous domain of the political emerged. The common challenge is to devise a conceptual scheme through which the constitution of political authority can be explained.

IV. State Theory

One of the most basic concepts in this modern idea of public law is the state, my treatment of which is analysed by Bob Jessop (chapter 10). Jessop's contribution synthesises the conceptual aspects of his recent book on the state in a way that makes it accessible to legal scholars.[14] Jessop's criticisms of the analysis in *Foundations* are summarised in four questions: the basis for selecting texts for analysis, the factors influencing reception of concepts, whether discursive factors alone determine reception, and whether the answer to that last question can be tested by reference to the experience of different regimes.[15] For reasons I will explain, I can only address the first issue.

I should begin by noting that Jessop overestimates my ambition. The objective of *Foundations* is not to offer an account of the historical development of state and law. My aim is to examine the way that concepts shape a segment of political experience into a set of relations so that eventually that experience can be adequately expressed only through those concepts.[16] My objective is to advance understanding of the *concept* of public law. As suggested by IPL, a specific account of public law involves assembling a set of basic concepts into a relatively coherent framework with the aim of presenting a compelling justification of the authority of a regime. Specific accounts are politically contested, though at certain moments some of them become highly influential.[17] Jessop asks how the selection I have made can be justified.

The simple, though no doubt inadequate, answer is that it is an exercise of judgement. History mediates between empirical realities and ideas that are symbolic representations of those realities. To the extent that it requires the methodical assembling of knowledge, history is a science, but it cannot avoid using imagination to shape those materials into a narrative account. No author can avoid making a judgement about the historical experience

[14] B Jessop, *The State: Past, Present, Future* (Cambridge, Polity, 2016).

[15] Jessop, ch 10, 161–64.

[16] This is the gist of the point made by Reinhard Koselleck, '*Begriffsgeschichte* and Social History' in his *Futures Past: On the Semantics of Historical Time* (translated by K Tribe) (New York, Columbia University Press, 2004) 75–92, at 85: 'a concept bundles up the variety of historical experience together with a collection of theoretical and practical references into a relation that is given and can be experienced only through the concept'.

[17] See M Loughlin, 'The Constitutional Imagination' (2015) 78 *Modern Law Review* 1–25, 5–11 speculating on the influence of Hobbes, Locke and Rousseau on modern constitutional structures in Britain, USA and France respectively.

of reflecting on the constitution of political authority in juristic terms. More precisely, the purpose of my investigation was to offer an account of what historical experience tells us about the relative influence of certain constructions of public law.

It remains a challenging exercise, not least because the basic concepts are not just reassembled in each account; as they are modified they are invariably altered in meaning. Bodin, Althusius, Hobbes, Rousseau, Dicey, de Jouvenel, Schmitt and others, for example, place sovereignty at the core of their schemes, but that term neither carries a common meaning nor serves a similar purpose. The same observation can be made for such other concepts as rights, constituent power, representation—and the state. Consequently, there can be no escape from the exercise of judgement I make in presenting a narrative account of the idea of public law in European thought.

I will amplify this in later sections, but I should first explain that Jessop's other questions—what influences reception, whether discursive factors are compelling, what variation is exhibited across regimes—are questions of a sociological nature that lie beyond my objective. After chapters on the concept of the state and its constitution, I included in *Foundations* a chapter on state formation. I recognised there that since the 'juristic concept of the state provides a scheme of intelligibility' to count as a system of public law any such scheme must 'acquire a material existence'. I noted that this 'complicates any attempt to specify the general character of the state, not least because the processes of European state formation exhibit a high degree of variation' with each arrangement being 'shaped by particular local circumstances'.[18] Although that was all I needed to explain for my purpose, I then presented an overview of some of the most important analyses of political scientists and historical sociologists 'who have sought to identify the critical factors that determine levels of stability and power in the European system of states' which 'not only advances understanding of the processes of European state-building but also identifies the critical factors that explain variation in governing regimes'.[19] And, finally, I provided an account of the development of the British state from that perspective.

To ask for more is to ask for a historical sociology of European state formation. These are questions for sociologists like Jessop, from which public lawyers can learn a great deal. But the two ought not to be conflated. The great value of the hermeneutical method is to recognise different accounts of the same subject matter and that, provided one is attentive to the type of question being asked, each can be equally acceptable. That Jessop does not fully accept this is evident from his aim to 'put public law in its place' by situating the 'state idea' after territory, people and governing apparatus as a fourth element of the state. This is an advance in sociological theory, which has often been reluctant to include the symbolic within its discipline.[20] But if the juristic character of my exercise is acknowledged, the three

[18] *Foundations* (n 1) 238.

[19] *Foundations* (n 1) 239.

[20] It might be noted that Jessop includes the 'idea' of the state as a fourth element in his most recent book: above n 14, 49. He states there that the four-element definition is adapted from his leading work of 1990, but if we consult the definition then laid down, it is evident that ideational factors play almost no role. See B Jessop, *State Theory: Putting the Capitalist State in its Place* (Cambridge, Polity, 1990) 341: 'Any general definition of the state would need to refer to state discourse as well as state institutions. My own suggestion runs as follows. The core of the state apparatus comprises a distinct ensemble of institutions and organizations whose socially accepted function is to define and enforce collectively binding decisions on the members of a society in the name of their common interest or general will.' The reference to 'general will' might open the definition to the state idea but in common with

elements must be treated as aspects of an overarching idea, an idea that cannot be reduced to that of a fourth aspect. Jessop's method suggests that his model-driven account of the state seeks an explanation based on the standard of the natural sciences.

I have explained these points in some detail because the issues Jessop raises also touch on other comments, notably concerning the materiality of political jurisprudence. But before coming to those, I will comment briefly on James Penner's examination of how the state is justified in analytical jurisprudence and then on another facet of the modern concept of public law, the issue of secularisation.

V. State and Power in Analytical Jurisprudence

James Penner's contribution in chapter 7 poses an interesting question. He takes his cue from the claim in *Foundations* that the institution of the state expresses an unresolved tension between two irreconcilable dispositions represented by *societas* and *universitas*. He then aligns these two modes of association with the two modes of power expressed as *potestas* and *potentia* to ask whether my claim of irreconcilability can be refuted by analytical jurists. Examining the work of Kant, Raz, Rawls and Nozick he concludes that their work does not adequately account for and cannot be used to overcome this tension. They cannot provide a coherent moral justification for the modern state as it actually operates.

His contribution is of particular value because it explains the difficulties of presenting a moral justification of political authority from within the analytical tradition. Penner reinforces the arguments I made in IPL that analytical jurists who engage with these questions are involved in a political engagement that must be addressed in terms of political ethics and political authority.[21] In IPL I argued that when analytical jurists seek to transform these political issues into moral questions, they

> fail to heed Hegel's warning that the assumption that the claims of morality must succeed whenever there is a clash between politics and morality rests 'on superficial ideas about morality, the nature of the state, and the state's relation to the moral point of view'.[22]

many sociologists of the state it is hardly a central factor. *Cf* Pierre Bourdieu, *On the State: Lectures at the Collège de France, 1989–1992* (translated by D Fernbach) (Cambridge, Polity, 2014), in which Bourdieu presented an account of the state in standard idealist terms, that the state 'is the name we give to the hidden, invisible principles of the social order' (p7). Bourdieu never published these lectures, presumably because this idealist presentation of state theory was out of line with the rest of his sociological investigations.

[21] Penner, ch 7, 107–07, draws a distinction between the moral and the ethical that maps on to that we find in Hegel and on which I have previously invoked: see *Reflections* (n 9): 'we should … distinguish between … public and private morality … Morality is a modern creation expressing subjective freedom, and it is precisely because of its invention that the search for a science of political right commences. In this respect, the distinction that Hegel draws between an abstract, subjective morality (*Moralität*) and ethical life (*Sittlichkeit*), the concrete universal, is helpful. But … although in English the terms ethical and moral are generally used interchangeably, significant differences exist in German between *moralisch*, *ethisch*, and *sittlich*. While the first connotes a Kantian, universalistic approach to the question of what is right, the other two refer to notions of right or good that remain rooted in the customs of a particular society and express specific ways of being.'

[22] IPL (n 2) 147, citing GWF Hegel, *Philosophy of Right* [1821] (translated by TM Knox) (Oxford, Clarendon Press, 1952) §337.

Yet, this moral orientation permeates normativist accounts of public law that call for 'a fusion of constitutional law and moral theory'[23] and claim a 'necessary connection between law and justice, and between legal and moral obligation'.[24] These claims are at the core of recent attempts to promote what Jacco Bomhoff, in chapter 5, calls a 'legal theology'.

Penner's contribution is valuable for that purpose, but it has other merits. In *Foundations*, I did not present any definitive account of the relationship between *potestas* and *potentia* and his analysis clarifies that relationship.[25] His article shows how it may be possible to build a bridge between the interests of analytical and political jurists.

VI. The Secularisation Thesis

Bomhoff asks some penetrating questions about my claim that political jurisprudence is a 'kind of secularised natural law'. He holds that in advocating a prudential discourse of political right I do not take 'either religion or law sufficiently seriously' and that in seeking to deal with the question of political theology I do not pay sufficient attention to 'legal theology'.[26]

His evidence is recent work challenging the idea that 'public life today is "basically secular"'.[27] He maintains that I focus on theology and that 'theology is dogma', that I assert that 'true political freedom comes only with religion's demise',[28] and that basically I align myself with Mark Lilla's argument about 'the great separation' between politics and law on the one hand and religion on the other.[29] He suggests that I claim that secularisation 'provides the narrative in which the reign of absolute values, externally imposed, is replaced by a public discourse in which everything is always and continually up for prudential revision'.[30]

I certainly claim that public law is a modern concept formed as an autonomous discourse by a modern rupture and that this is an expression of modern secularising thought. But Bomhoff weakens his case by asserting it too strongly, and it is not assisted by Hauke Brunkhorst's allegation in chapter 6 that I 'casually dismiss [the constitutional advances of the Papal Revolution of the eleventh, twelfth and thirteenth centuries] as the "dark ages", a cliché that seems to be constitutive of the meta-narrative of state-sovereignty'.[31]

[23] R Dworkin, *Taking Rights Seriously* (Cambridge, MA, Harvard University Press, 1977) 149 (cited in IPL (n 2) 145).

[24] TRS Allan, *Constitutional Justice: A Liberal Theory of the Rule of Law* (Oxford, Oxford University Press, 2001) 283 (cited in IPL (n 2) 146).

[25] The only quibble I have with his analysis is his suggestion that 'the relationship between *societas* and *potestas*, and *universitas* and *potentia*, cannot be antagonistic all the way down as Loughlin has claimed, because the existence of the latter *depends* upon the existence of the former' (Penner ch 7, 106). He is right that *potentia* depends to a certain degree on *potestas*, but I think that since *societas* and *universitas* express two ideal-types, the latter does not rest on the former in the way Penner implies. His position comes from combining *societas-potestas* and *universitas-potentia* to a degree that, notwithstanding the obvious affinities, I have reservations about.

[26] Bomhoff, ch 5, 66.

[27] Bomhoff, ch 5, 68.

[28] Bomhoff, ch 5, 70.

[29] Bomhoff, ch 5, 70.

[30] Bomhoff, ch 5, 72.

[31] Brunkhorst, ch 6, 93.

Brunkhorst can make this claim only by overlooking the first chapter of *Foundations* where I show in detail how public law 'is formed as a distinct field of knowledge alongside the emergence of the modern state' but that 'no clear break in thought between the medieval and the modern exists'. I argue there that the 'modern idea of the state evolved through a process of continuous innovation in western European thought and practice between the twelfth and seventeenth centuries' and that, if we are to trace 'the juristic aspects of this process of state formation … we must travel back further still' and 'examine the ways in which the exercise of lawful authority to rule became bound up with theological questions'.[32] There is no mention of so-called 'dark ages' and, far from casual dismissal, the standing of the 'papal monarchy' is one of the chapter's main themes.

My argument in *Foundations* is that modern public law evolves from a series of tensions and struggles within Christian political theology and that it emerges in a recognisably modern form only because of this break, rupture, or separation. The main problem I have with Bomhoff's argument is that it does not respect the conceptual nature of the claim I make. Had I been writing a book about law in modern society his arguments might have force, but this was not my aim.

My argument with respect to the rupture that establishes the autonomy of the political is that the idea of public law to which it gave birth meant that it was no longer possible to make a legal claim to political authority based on divine right or revelation. This seems to me so obvious as to be non-controversial. The fundamental shift in thought was brought about by the work of political jurists during the seventeenth century: Grotius makes it in a subtle way with his *etiamsi daremus* statement, Hobbes explicitly in his construction of sovereign authority from a natural right of self-preservation, Pufendorf by removing God—and any point of external or transcendental point of reference—from natural law, and so on. Even John Locke, who held on to classical natural law longer than many, rejected the authority of revelation in his *First Treatise of Government*.

This point remains notwithstanding Bomhoff's criticism of what he refers to as the 'easy assumption that public life today is basically secular'.[33] Of course, there are established churches in certain states, Catholic holy days are sometimes given the status of public holidays, the UK Parliament opens with prayers, American presidents sometimes include 'so help me God' in their presidential oath, and so on. But none of this affects the basic fact that within the frame of modern public law the constitution of political authority does not rest on a theological foundation. The citizen's basic rights cannot be dependent on adherence to a particular faith.

Bomhoff would perhaps reply that that is a challenge to a theology and the religious, which he leaves undefined, concerns an altogether broader sensibility. I recognise this in Rousseau's assertion that political authority must be sustained by promoting a 'civil religion'. Yet, isn't this just the deployment of a religious impulse for secular purposes? Is, for instance, the promotion of nationalism as a means of bolstering authority an expression of the religious? Is Habermas' advocacy of the almost oxymoronic 'constitutional patriotism' an appeal to the religious? All systems of authority are sustained by the inculcation of belief systems, the propagation of a faith. The scheme of modern public law is no different.

[32] *Foundations* (n 1) 17.
[33] Bomhoff, ch 5, 68.

But surely this is no more than saying that religious beliefs, moral codes, works of art, and legal orders are, within the perspective of political authority, all matters of culture.

The problem with Bomhoff's argument is that he seeks to apply arguments about the role of religion in contemporary social life to the claims I make about public law. Like Jessop, he is raising empirical questions with respect to a conceptual argument.

VII. How is Public Law Law?

Bomhoff's main argument is about secular foundations but he also raises a question about 'the character of public law as political jurisprudence'. What makes a discourse juristic? What makes public law law? How do these studies on authority form a category of juristic thought?.[34] Such terms, he complains, 'are nowhere defined'.[35]

The short answer is that the concept of public law I am seeking to explain concerns the way in which the constitution of political authority is conceived as an assemblage of rights, duties, powers and liabilities. That is, I adopt the standard account of fundamental legal conceptions presented by an analytical legal scholar like Hohfeld and apply it to show how political jurists explain the constitution of political authority.[36] Adopting this approach, it seems clear that scholars who are often categorised as political philosophers, such as Hobbes, Spinoza, Rousseau and Hegel, are really operating as political jurists providing legal accounts of political authority. As I indicated above, their exercises in political jurisprudence yield quite particular accounts of the character of public law in which concepts acquire different meanings and perform different roles. This was the case with sovereignty and it is also the case with the concept of law.

What, after all, is law? By law do we mean the will of the sovereign, the set of customary rules and practices that have evolved among a professional cadre, or an expression of the principles of right instituted in the constitutional order? Political jurists give very different answers to this question: for Hobbes it is sovereign will, for Burke it is custom, for Rousseau it is an expression of principles of equal liberty.[37] Political jurists rummage around in the conceptual toolshed of political jurisprudence to construct their accounts of public law as particular structural formations.

In *Foundations* I used the metaphor of competing grammars with their own forms of life. Halpin thinks this is problematic since different grammars 'will produce different concepts of public law'.[38] The point I was making is that the way that political jurists draw general concepts into their own variants of a coherent scheme yields different accounts of *positive* public law and that in these different accounts concepts take on different meanings and occupy different roles. Michael Oakeshott has shown how the vocabulary we use to

[34] Bomhoff, ch 5, 73–74.

[35] Bomhoff, ch 5, 74.

[36] WN Hohfeld, 'Some Fundamental Legal Conceptions as Applied in Judicial Reasoning' (1913) 23 *Yale Law Journal* 16–59.

[37] I explained these in the three basic parts of an earlier work: M Loughlin, *Sword and Scales: An Examination of the Relationship between Law and Politics* (Oxford, Hart Publishing, 2000).

[38] Halpin, ch 3, 45–47; Goldoni, eg, also (p 174, n.56) notes a potential confusion between *langue* and *parole*.

identify the characteristics of the modern European state exhibits a considerable confusion of meaning.[39] I was using the term 'grammar' to indicate that these words only acquire a precise meaning as concepts when drawn into a coherent scheme. The various schemes produce different accounts of positive public law and deploy different usages of common terms. Only then, I suggest, is the vocabulary of political jurisprudence given a consistent grammatical form.

VIII. Is *Foundations* Conservative?

Having situated me in a tradition of British thought, Goldoni broadens his analysis to suggest that *Foundations* neglects 'the role of subjects and their subjectivation in the formation and development of modern constitutions'.[40] By focusing on right-ordering, he argues, I do not give sufficient consideration to the way that 'political action forges the material constitution'.[41] Since this has certain similarities to the criticisms of Minkkinen, Brunkhorst and Wilkinson, this is evidently a broader concern.

Minkkinen believes that I assume a 'consensual understanding of politics'[42] and that if I were to take seriously the claim that my argument is founded in the human sciences—this is what I assume he means by the term 'metapolitical'—I would place more weight on the way that French theorists insist on using 'law' as a synonym for 'justice' and therefore not 'as an instrument for social conservation but as a revolutionary source of authority'.[43] To put it more directly, 'Loughlin's theory runs the risk of promoting what Lefort would regard as the totalitarian tendencies of modern capitalism rather than putting them in question'.[44]

This assumes that I am making a normative argument rather than seeking to explain the characteristics of a modern phenomenon, that is, the way the institution of the state is conceived as a jural entity. Minkkinen's argument is that I cannot avoid being normative. I accept that *Foundations* could be classified as an exercise in rhetoric, that is, an art of persuading that this is the best way of understanding the subject. But the French thinkers Minkkinen invokes—Rancière and Abensour—seem to me to conflate rhetoric and polemic, and they do so for revolutionary political purposes. And why not? But, as I have explained elsewhere, their works are exercises in utopian abstraction that provide no practical guidance on how a political world is to be instituted.[45] Without that constructive element, I cannot see what—other than as external critique—they contribute to understanding public law.

My position receives some support from Goldoni, who accepts that the fact that 'political jurisprudence does not take into account disruptive politics … is a misplaced criticism'.[46] But before returning to his argument, I should address Brunkhorst's claim that my 'defence

[39] M Oakeshott, 'The Vocabulary of the Modern European State' (1975) 23 *Political Studies* 319–41.
[40] Goldoni, ch 11, 172.
[41] Goldoni, ch 11, 176.
[42] Minkkinen, ch 4, 53.
[43] Minkkinen, ch 4, 55.
[44] Minkkinen, ch 4, 57.
[45] M Loughlin, 'Droit Politique' (2017) 17 *Jus Politicum: Revue de Droit Politique* 299–335, at 327–30.
[46] Goldoni, ch 11, 176.

of *Staatsrecht* against the normativism of *Rechtsstaat* … demonstrates a clearly state-supportive attitude that prioritises the top-down perspective'.[47] He claims 'that Loughlin's polemical position in the discursive wars over the state is determined by a specific meta-narrative … of "state-sovereignty"'.[48] My impression here is that Brunkhorst wrongly assumes that by state I mean, as sociologists generally conceive it, *Staatsgewalt*. As I have already explained (section IV), that is not what I mean by the term. When the state is understood as a juristic idea—a scheme of intelligibility—my prioritising of the 'top-down' perspective is far from obvious.

That said, I accept that more consideration might have been given to the way that 'the emergence of public law can be reconstructed as a bottom-up political learning process that is mediated through legal revolutions motivated by egalitarian and emancipatory goals which established a law to cope with the paradox that modern law is freedom'.[49] These issues are not overlooked. I argue that 'the striving for equal liberty in solidarity' shapes 'the character of a political regime';[50] I address these matters in chapters 10 and 12 of *Foundations* and there is more in IPL.[51] But the orientation of my investigation is institutional in that it focuses mainly on the establishment of authoritative orders and some might wish that the struggles to make an actuality of the principles of liberty and equality had received greater prominence. Minkkinen, however, pushes this argument too far: when he suggests that law should be seen as a 'revolutionary source of authority' I confess that I am mystified.[52]

IX. The Material Critique

I come now to Goldoni's argument that all orders are supported by political and social forces.[53] I doubt anyone would deny that. But his specific claim is that I fail to examine 'the political economy that undergirds the material constitution',[54] that this means that 'political jurisprudence is in danger of leaving the domain of concrete order and landing in the field of political theology',[55] and that there is a risk that 'the autonomy of the political will not be able to maintain the productive tension between polarities but will sever its internal relation with the social in favour of a transcendental relation'.[56] He is joined in this critique by Wilkinson who asks 'how does the political ordering of public law stand in relation to the material reproduction of society?'.[57]

[47] Brunkhorst, ch 6, 92.
[48] Brunkhorst, ch 6, 92.
[49] Brunkhorst, ch 6, 94.
[50] Loughlin, ch 2, 18.
[51] See especially, *Foundations* (n 1) Ch 10, III ('Revolution and Constitution'); Ch 12, III ('Bills of Rights'), V ('Subjective Rights and Objective Law'); IPL (n 2) Ch 6 ('Constituent Power'), Ch 7 ('Rights').
[52] For an analogous point see M Loughlin, 'Santi Romano and the Institutional Theory of Law' in S Romano, *The Legal Order* (translated by M Croce) (London, Routledge, 2017) x–xxviii, at xxvi.
[53] Goldoni, ch 11, 176.
[54] Goldoni, ch 11, 176.
[55] Goldoni, ch 11, 178.
[56] Goldoni, ch 11, 179.
[57] Wilkinson, ch 12, 181.

When Wilkinson expands on this by suggesting that *Foundations* avoids all the issues concerning 'relations between capital and labour, debtors and creditors, core and peripheral nations …',[58] he allows me an easy answer. The book does not aspire to study the social forces that determine the public law—the form of political order—of any particular regime; it is a conceptual exercise in trying to understand how we use legal language to explain modern governmental authority. *Foundations* examines public law as an autonomous domain. It is accepted that causal laws 'whether those of Montesquieu (factors of climate, commerce, spatial location, etc) or Marx (generated between the forces and relations of production) undoubtedly exert considerable influence in structuring the domain of the political'.[59] But provided one accepts that 'political relations are not reducible either to moral or to socio-economic relations'[60] one recognises a domain whose mode of working deserves consideration on its own terms.[61] I emphasise that although from an internal perspective the political 'regulates all other domains of life', from the perspective of other discourses it 'is reduced to a specific and limited domain'. I also recognise that from within, the state is 'the entire scheme of intelligibility' but from outside 'it is merely the institutional apparatus of rule' which may be 'regulated by those other domains'.[62]

Much of Wilkinson's essay is a sketch of the sort of book he thinks should be written, one in which 'the material constitution of order and disorder can be explored and with it the fragility of public law'.[63] This would add to the pile of books that tell us a great deal about the contemporary crises of state and economy, a little about positive public law as a concrete order, and almost nothing about the modern *idea* of public law. But my argument should not be distorted. I don't say that the autonomy of the political is a 'one-off rupture' rather than a continuous struggle;[64] why otherwise would I argue that it is a historical achievement and the concepts by which it operates bear the scars of political struggles?[65] I don't present that rupture only as an immaterial process of secularisation;[66] I say the rupture has various dimensions.[67]

58 Wilkinson, ch 12, 182.

59 Loughlin, ch 2, 18.

60 Loughlin, ch 2, 21.

61 This point is most clearly made by French theorists, including those that the materialist critics invoke: see, eg, C Lefort, *Complications: Communism and the Dilemmas of Democracy* (translated by J Bourg) (New York, Columbia University Press, 2007) 113: 'In the first meaning, the political designates a particular domain of the social ensemble; it delimits the source of authority, the conditions and means of its exercise, and the range of its competences. In a second meaning, the political refers to the social ensemble itself, for the entire collectivity is affected by the nature of power and the mode of exercise of government. Decisions have effects in all domains of social life and the representation of authority in the sector of politics circulates in some manner throughout the entire social ensemble. In this second sense it becomes relevant to affirm a "primacy of the political", no matter the society under consideration. In other words, regime and political society are equivalent notions.'

62 Loughlin, ch 2, 27.

63 Wilkinson, ch 12, 193. This is most evident in his analysis of my later essay on *Nomos* where he seems to think that I have eventually woken up to the fact that the state is founded on a land-grab and the material organisation of distributive and productive forces: Wilkinson ch 12, 187–88, 205. All these factors are in fact introduced in *Foundations* (n 1) which begins by explaining that 'basic changes in the character of the medieval idea of fundamental law' were brought about by 'economic, social, political and technological development' (*Foundations* (n 1) 2). These factors are not examined in detail because the object of the exercise was not to analyse those factors; it was to explain 'the character' of the modern idea of public law.

64 Wilkinson, ch 12, 184.

65 Loughlin, ch 2, 22; *cf* Wilkinson, ch 12, 184: 'From a material perspective, the autonomy of the political is a fragile, ambiguous … achievement, rather than a one-off creation of the modern world'.

66 Loughlin, ch 2, 19.

67 Loughlin, ch 2, 21.

Neither do I suggest that material inequalities are 'hermetically sealed off or fully separated from the political' (p 191), only that those claims must be converted from noise into speech within the domain of the political. Wilkinson claims I 'insist[] on neutralizing Heller',[68] when in fact I offer a sympathetic account of his state theory and conclude that he identifies 'more precisely than any other legal scholar a juristic logic that makes sense of the constitution of the state'.[69]

Goldoni is nearer the mark when he suggests that 'by including a material dimension, political jurisprudence would shed an additional and different light on the governing art'.[70] Goldoni and Wilkinson have combined to sketch a prospectus for the study of 'the material constitution'.[71] That study is based on four factors: political unity, a set of institutions, a network of social relations, and a set of fundamental political objectives. But since 'social relations' must be converted into 'political relations' in order to count as constitutional discourse, then, contrary to what they assert, there is no obvious break with public law as political jurisprudence.

X. The Civic Republican Critique

I come now to the question of the social and its implications for contemporary public law. I first address Anna Yeatman's ambitious restatement in chapter 8 of the historical trajectory of public law in which she challenges my 'melancholic and pessimistic conclusion as to the current fate of public law'[72] by presenting a normative re-interpretation of that historical development. This is a rather different type of exercise.

My account of public law aimed to show how particular politically-driven interpretations of representation, sovereignty, rights, power, etc (that is, specific theories of public law drawn from conservative, liberal, republican, radical perspectives) were fought out within a distinctive worldview of the political. This involved historical interpretation but with the objective of explaining the phenomenon of the political in scientific terms, that is, as the systematic acquisition of knowledge of the subject. It is unclear whether I have adequately conveyed that or whether Yeatman regards it as an impossible task. But she certainly thinks that from a potentially sound account of the early-modern ambition I lost my way and adopted 'a liberal frame of reference',[73] leading me to a narrative that equates the rise of the social with the decline of public law.

Yeatman uses 'an evaluative criterion' as the basis of an alternative interpretation.[74] This is a historical reconstruction on civic republican foundations. It is an attractive story but rather one-sided. Rejecting the two-sided aspect of the state as a liberal construction, she

[68] Wilkinson, ch 12, 197.
[69] *Foundations* (n 1) 234–37.
[70] Goldoni, ch 11, 179.
[71] M Goldoni and MA Wilkinson, 'The Material Constitution' LSE Working Papers 20/2016.
[72] Yeatman, ch 8, 131.
[73] Yeatman, ch 8, 124.
[74] Yeatman, ch 8, 131.

presents the state in Hegelian terms as 'ethical life'.[75] But the tensions I identify are not purely liberal notions; many non-liberal scholars have expressed a similar dilemma. As Pierre Bourdieu presents it, one 'cannot have a Hegelian state without having a Marxist state', by which he means that the state is an ambiguous institution about which 'it is impossible to state a positive property without simultaneously stating a negative property'.[76] These two sides are the subjectivity of the idea and the objectivity of its products, the philosophical and the sociological respectively.

I have tried to convey these tensions not only with respect to the state as a mode of association but also more generally between ideals and actualities, between unity of common association and hierarchy of institutional form, between the ideal expression of sovereignty and the concrete existence of a sovereign. Bodin identified a similar problem when he drew a distinction between sovereignty and government. He noted that there is a 'great difference between the state and the government of the state'[77] and went on to explain that the distinction 'seems to me more than necessary for the good understanding of the state of every commonwealth, if a man will not cast himself headlong into an infinite labyrinth of errors'.[78] For good reasons, Yeatman places great store in Bodin's work, but she does not acknowledge the significance of Bodin's critical distinction.

One illustration. Yeatman presents an account of public law derived from Bodin as 'a system of public office'[79] and argues that the concept is of major importance in understanding the modern administrative state.[80] She is right on both counts, but the lineage is much more ambiguous than her argument about maintaining the purity of the idea suggests. Consider, for example, Alain Guéry's compelling argument that 'the history of offices' through to 1789 is 'the best place to start to understand how and why the notion of the public good took so long to become linked to the idea of public administration'.[81] The French did indeed establish a system of public offices but its history right until the Revolution is one in which public offices were sold by the king as a source of revenue. Early-modern juristic-political thought might have given an account of 'an anti-feudal ethics' based on the idea of public office.[82] However, the early-modern French Government's use of the system of public offices ensured that individuals became bound to one another in a manner not unlike a feudal arrangement.

The general point of this illustration is to highlight the problems inherent in a normativist treatment of conflating ideal and actuality. Such an account might form the basis of a normative political theory but it leads to a skewed treatment of the practical discourse of public law.

[75] Yeatman, ch 8, 119.

[76] Bourdieu (n 20) 85, 98.

[77] J Bodin, *The Six Bookes of a Commonweale* (translated by R Knolles, 1606 and edited by KD McRae) (Cambridge, Mass, Harvard University Press, 1962) 199.

[78] ibid, 249–50.

[79] Yeatman, ch 8, 116–17.

[80] Yeatman, ch 8, 117–19.

[81] A Guéry, 'The State' in Pierre Nora (ed), *Rethinking France: Les Lieux de Mémoire, Vol. 1* (translated by M Trouille) (Chicago, University of Chicago Press, 2001) Ch 1, at 22.

[82] Yeatman, ch 8, 127.

XI. The Rise of the Social

The issues Yeatman highlights about the modern welfare-regulatory state also raise a series of more general conceptual questions about public law. They return us to Baranger's observations in chapter 15 about the legal-technical difficulties in finding a foundation for the great body of administrative law that now exists. Baranger clearly explains the problems, whether founding it on a concept of state (that is, *Staatsgewalt*, institutional rule) or 'public service', interpreted by French jurists as executive power.[83] He recognises the need for a constitutional foundation, but notes that this leads jurists to a distorted interpretation of the French Constitution.

The answer to Baranger's question, I suggest, requires a constitutional solution, one not found in the constitution of government but in that of the state, that is, in Chapter 8 rather than in Chapter 10 of *Foundations*. This is where we find Yeatman's concept of public ethics, in what Heller calls 'the relativization of positive law by supra-positive, logical and ethical (*sittliche*) basic principles of law',[84] and where the discourse of 'political right' prevails. Yeatman believes I am too pessimistic in suggesting that political right is being subsumed in the technical efficacy of regulation. She thinks that 'policy and regulation do not substitute for law but complement it'.[85] I think it is more complicated than that, but I hope we might agree that it is in the discourse of political right that these issues are determined.

The rise of the social also raises questions for other commentators. Wilkinson asks about the crisis signified by the rise of the social, suggesting it cannot mean only the return of the religious. This is presumably because I wrote: 'The rise of the social marks the return of the religious, albeit in a different form'.[86] But I am not suggesting that 'the social' is 'just a stand-in for "the religious"'.[87] It refers to the idea of civil society explained by Hegel. As I wrote in *Foundations*, this expresses the rise of 'what Hegel calls "universal egoism" or "universality of abstract rights"' and the dominance of a sphere 'which finds its most typical form in economic interaction' where 'everyone acts in accordance with their perceived self-interest'.[88] The economic aspects are noted in the book's last chapter with reference, for example, to 'the extension of the disciplinary mechanisms of police to the central questions of government: fiscal rules devised in the regulatory network discipline ministers, monetary policies laid down by central banks constrain governments, audit regulations structure the programmes of public bodies …'.[89] The argument there is that these mechanisms are eroding the foundations of modern public law; these are material forces which are central to Wilkinson's conception of public law and according to which I should have spent more of the book analysing.

[83] Baranger, ch 15, 249.

[84] H Heller, 'Bermerkungen zur Staats- und Rechtstheoretischen Problematik der Gegenwart' [1929] in his *Gesammelte Schriften* (Leiden, AW Sijthoff, 1971) Vol 2, 249–78, at 275: '… der Begriff des Rechtes kann nicht gebildet werden ohne die keineswegs mit ihm identische Idee des Rechtes, die letztere aber nicht ohne die Relativierung des positiven Rechtes auf überpositive, logische und sittliche Rechtsgrundsätze'.

[85] Yeatman, ch 8, 128.

[86] *Foundations* (n 1) 465.

[87] Wilkinson, ch 12, 184.

[88] *Foundations* (n 1) 146.

[89] *Foundations* (n 1) 452.

The reference to the religious was intended to signify the return of 'overarching claims of the right and the true' to the political domain.[90] It is the problem which Bomhoff rightly identifies, while suggesting I do not address it in sufficient detail, as the rise of 'legal theology'.[91] It's not right to say I don't examine it, though part of the problem may lie in the book's structure, in that Parts III, IV and V are intended to address the three layers of state, constitution and government rather than be read as a historical sequence. In Chapter 12 on 'Constitutional Rights', the last chapter of Part IV, I highlight the implications that constitutional legality as a species of (positive) right has for legal practice and jurisprudential thought. On this, there is no doubt more to be said.

XII. The Post-National Critique

The other pressing feature of contemporary life that challenges the idea of public law is the growth of governmental power in international arenas. This is taken up by Neil Walker, in chapter 9. His aim is to convince us that in a debate 'between statists and postnationalists' there are 'no certainties … on either side' and 'more acknowledgement of that all-round might fuel a more constructive exchange'.[92] This is a smart rhetorical manoeuvre.

Walker undoubtedly identifies what some would consider to be the weak point of my account when he claims that *Foundations* 'retains and sustains from religious and non-religious imaginings of a natural order of things the very idea of a level and genus of law that is framing rather than framed, and that supplies an irreducible basis and encompassing framework for the organisation of social life'. His point is that the idea of the state at the core of the modern idea of public law 'may be understood as having filled a "God-shaped hole" in modern life'.[93] That is, my conception of public law rests ultimately on some faith-based claim.

I have addressed that issue above (section VI). The problem I want to take up is that rather than explaining and justifying their claim that recent developments in governing require a 'paradigm-shift' in the idea of public law, postnationalists see themselves not as advocates of a particular conception but as reasonable observers searching for a third way between two (often crudely presented) opposing positions. Walker does so here, invoking Mattias Kumm as another. The essay of Kumm to which he refers divides constitutional theory into 'nostalgic statists' and 'triumphalist cosmopolitans'. Walker suggests that Kumm's essay 'counsels against both attitudes'.[94] Actually, it is an analysis that comes down firmly on the side of the cosmopolitans.

There is, I would suggest, no third way here: one either operates inside the framework of modern political jurisprudence with all its contemporary stresses or makes that 'paradigm shift'. The issue is not about the fact that collective action seems to require extensive regulatory arrangements at the international level. The existence of these trends is

[90] *Foundations* (n 1) 465.
[91] Bomhoff, ch 5, 66 and above at 262.
[92] Walker, ch 9, 134.
[93] Walker, ch 9. 137.
[94] Walker, ch 9, 138.

not in dispute. The issue is: what are their implications for ways of conceptualising public law? Using terms suggested by Bodin's framework: when do governmental developments strike at the heart of the modern idea of a public law founded on sovereignty? In so far as cosmopolitans claim that this point has already been reached, my contention is that they are founding their claims on an impoverished, legal-positivist account of the so-called 'statist' position. The objective of *Foundations* is to show that this modern idea is much more nuanced and flexible than a legal positivist account would suggest.

I readily accept that once the modern idea of public law loses its authority by losing its imaginative power, the game is up. The point of reassessing its foundations is to show that the discourse involves a more sophisticated engagement. It encourages critics to pitch their claims against this richer account of the modern concept and to explain more clearly the consequences—both positive and negative—of making that paradigmatic shift in understanding what the idea of public law might mean today.

XIII. The Post-Colonial Critique

Jessop notes that the 'historical semantics of the state ... pose questions about the Eurocentric nature of state theory and, on this basis, the relevance of (Eurocentric) state theory to territorially organised forms of political authority beyond the centres of European state formation'.[95] I originally intended to include in *Foundations* a chapter on the imperial dimension of the form of the European state, but I quickly realised that the subject was too large and complicated to fit this study. *Foundations* therefore examined ideas about authority 'that emerged through a common European discourse'.[96] Consequently, I am particularly pleased that Mathew John in chapter 14 has taken on the task of commenting on the relevance of *Foundations* to the post-colonial setting of India.

In *Leviathan*, Hobbes deals mostly with sovereignty by institution but he acknowledges that a state can be established not only by consent but also by force. In the former case, the people who choose their sovereign 'do it for fear of one another' but in the latter 'they subject themselves to him they are afraid of'. Nevertheless, Hobbes then claims that 'the rights and consequences of sovereignty are the same in both'.[97] In a formal juristic sense that may be correct, but it cannot be denied that the conditions of authority are so different that it will have a major impact on conceptions of public law.

The impact of imperial conditions creates considerable complexities at the moment when a state removes an imperial ruler and seeks to refashion itself on a new constitutional foundation. Problems arise not only because of the challenge of using this constitutional moment as the occasion for restoration, for the promotion of inclusivity, or for bringing about social transformation. There are also problems with more basic matters of state. It is often the case, for example, that the inherited state (ie, *Staatsgebeit*: state territory) exists only as an imperial construction. In such circumstances, there might be no prior unity of a

[95] Jessop, ch 10, 163.
[96] *Foundations* (n 1) 2.
[97] T Hobbes, *Leviathan* (Cambridge, Cambridge University Press, 1991) Ch 20.

people in this territory (*Staatsvolk*) on which restoration or renewal can easily be founded. These basic questions of the constitution of the state present the building of a new order of the state through an independence constitution (*Staatsgewalt*) with a range of difficult political challenges.

John offers us a window into some of these complexities through an examination of the problems of adjudicating issues of 'minority rights' in post-colonial Indian constitutional law. He highlights the way that the promotion of social transformation through a modern legal discourse can be experienced as inauthentic, even alienating. For example, an exercise of constituent power by the newly-established sovereign nation might be perceived as a further barrier to realising *Swaraj*, that is, to reconnecting to 'the autochthonous structures of experience and understandings that had been interrupted by' colonialism.[98] John then suggests two ways in which the modern conceptual account of public law I outlined might be used to address these tensions.

I am ill-equipped to offer answers to his pertinent questions because each involves political challenges that can only be for local actors to address. I might offer only one, more conceptual, observation. It seems to me that in such a post-colonial context, the challenges for state-building are severe. The modern European state that provides the colonial edifice is constructed on a tension between ideal modes of *societas* and *universitas*. As a result of the combined experience of colonialism, modernisation and the emergence of a local elite educated in colonial manners, such tensions are likely to remain after independence. They will then be fought out in competing conceptions of how the constitution drafted on independence is to be interpreted and the role it is to play in the regulation of social life.

That is challenging enough. But below that modern discourse is a quite different tension, between the political struggle to establish an authentic expression of the meaning of a common life according to local traditions and its implications for the role of the modern state. This is a dimension of state construction that regimes which have not been subjected to alien rule have not experienced. This dimension requires a reconceptualisation of the colonial tradition of indirect rule in circumstances where the constitutional framing is Hobbes' sovereignty by institution rather than by conquest. But however formulated, the challenges faced by post-colonial states incorporate a new variant of a dual state: the modern post-colonial state and the native conception of 'being-in-common'.

XIV. American Exceptionalism

From the US perspective, Tushnet argues that scholars express little curiosity about foundations of public law since the answer is evident: the foundation of all public authority lies in the Constitution. I would not doubt that answer, but I would want to say that the fact that that answer is so readily accepted demonstrates the exceptional position of the USA. American constitutional scholars have difficulty in recognising the exceptional nature of their regime; even Tushnet, one of the scholars most open to comparative analysis, believes

[98] John, ch 14, 229–30.

that the question I raise 'is localised to the conditions of British constitutional theory'.[99] That I doubt. My argument is that the three basic layers of state, constitution and government are essential elements in the formation of any modern concept of public law. The fact that in the USA the constitutional dimension occludes systematic consideration of the relationship between the three indicates its unique circumstances, but it may also generate unique problems. So if the type of analysis in *Foundations* causes American scholars of comparative constitutional law to recognise the exceptional character of their regime rather than just holding it up as a model that others might strive towards, that would be achievement enough.

It is nevertheless surprising how reluctant a radical scholar like Tushnet is to move from a dominant American approach to constitutional theory. By dominant approach, I mean the assumption that the Constitution commands unquestioned authority and that therefore the subject of constitutional theory should focus on the logic of justification given in US Supreme Court constitutional decisions. This might seem unfair; after all, Tushnet has been a leading critical scholar of traditions of US constitutional law and questioned the court-centred focus many American scholars adopt with respect to constitutional issues.[100] But in his contribution here he writes that in the US the constituent states came together in 1789–91 'to create a new nation' and the 'Constitution was the act that did so'.[101] Did it? Or is this only so in retrospect?

From the perspective of political jurisprudence, I would suggest that during its first 70 or so years the USA existed in a state of irresolution over an essential foundational question, namely, where sovereign authority was actually located. It then required a civil war—the bloodiest in history to that point—to resolve the question of whether the USA was a federation or a sovereign state. These are issues about the state itself rather than about the constitution, however much the story has been told that the civil war was a dispute over constitutional interpretation. So while we can accept that today the Constitution, 'the written thing as assimilated into the political imagination',[102] is regarded as the foundation of public law, from the perspective of political jurisprudence the state-building processes by which identity is forged must be part of any account of the way authority was configured in the American state.

The contemporary dominance of constitutional thinking has affected not only the relationship between state and constitution; it also shapes thinking about the relationship between constitution and government. American constitutional scholars readily accept that constitutional analysis belongs to 'law's empire'. But their treatment of matters of government seems based on the assumption of what Adrian Vermeule calls 'law's abnegation'.[103] This is an almost schizophrenic state of affairs.[104] From the perspective of

[99] Tushnet, ch 13, 214.

[100] See, eg M Tushnet, *Red, White, and Blue: A Critical Analysis of Constitutional Law* (Cambridge, MA, Harvard University Press, 1988); M Tushnet, *Taking the Constitution Away From the Courts* (Princeton, Princeton University Press, 1999).

[101] Tushnet, ch 13, 212.

[102] Tushnet, ch 13, 213.

[103] R Dworkin, *Law's Empire* (Cambridge, MA, Harvard University Press, 1987); A Vermeule, *Law's Abnegation: From Law's Empire to the Administrative State* (Cambridge, MA, Harvard University Press, 2016).

[104] *Cf*, eg, P Hamburger, *Is Administrative Law Unlawful?* (Chicago, University of Chicago Press, 2014).

political jurisprudence, the dominance of the Constitution in the USA leads to a skewed understanding of the necessary relations between state, constitution, and government.

XV. Conclusions

The idea of public law advocated in *Foundations* should not be understood as a subset of positive law (section II), or based on a model of the natural sciences (section III), or derived from moral philosophy (section V), or conceived as normative theory (sections VIII and X), or presented as a 'nostalgic statist' account (section XII). The exercise undertaken in *Foundations* does not aspire to provide a historical sociology of European state-formation (section IV), nor to analyse the material forces that determine the governmental forms taken by particular regimes (section IX), nor to explain the role of religion in contemporary society (section VI). *Foundations* is a study of an idea that emerged in modern European thought (section XIII) that conceives the constitution of political authority in jural terms (section VII), is constructed on necessary relations between state, constitution and government (section XIV), and which today is threatened by the 'rise of the social' in the guise of dominant economic interests (section XI). The articles in this volume show that I need to be more precise if I am to get across the ambitions and limitations of that exercise. Consequently, I remain most grateful to my colleagues whose incisive comments in this volume have forced me to try and express my position more clearly.

BIBLIOGRAPHY

Abensour, M, *Democracy against the State. Marx and the Machiavellian Moment* (Cambridge, Polity, 2011).

Abrams, P, 'Notes on the Difficulty of Studying the State' (1988) 1 *Journal of Historical Sociology* 58.

Agamben, G, *State of Exception* (Chicago, Chicago University Press, 2005).

Allan, TRS, *Constitutional Justice: A Liberal Theory of the Rule of Law* (Oxford, Oxford University Press, 2001).

Allison, JWF, *A Continental Distinction in the Common Law: A Historical and Comparative Perspective on English Public Law* (Oxford, Clarendon Press, 1996).

Andersen, NÅ, *Discourse Analytical Strategies: Foucault, Koselleck, Laclau, Luhmann* (Bristol, Policy Press, 2003).

Anderson, B, *Imagined Communities: Reflections on the Origin and Spread of Nationalism* (London, Verso, 2006).

Anderson, G, 'Constitutionalism as Critical Project: The Epistemological Challenge to Politics' in S Gill and A Cutler (eds), *New Constitutionalism and World Order* (Cambridge, Cambridge University Press, 2014) 281.

Anderson, J, 'The Shifting Stage of Politics: New Medieval and Postmodern Territorialities?' (1996) 14 *Environment and Planning D: Society and Space* 133.

Anderson, P, 'The Intransigent Right at the End of the Century' (1992) 18 *London Review of Books* 7.

Ansari, I, 'Minorities and the Politics of Constitution Making in India' in D Sheth and G Mahajan (eds), *Minority Identities and the Nation-State* (Oxford, Oxford University Press, 1999).

Arendt, H, *The Human Condition* (Chicago, Chicago University Press, 1958).

——, *On Revolution* (New York, Viking 1963).

——, *On Revolution* (London, Penguin, 1973).

——, *Die verborgene Tradition* (Frankfurt, Fischer, 1976).

——, *Origins of Totalitarianism* (San Diego, Harvest, 1979).

Aron, R, *Democracy and Totalitarianism* (London, Weidenfeld and Nicolson, 1968).

Asad, T, 'The Construction of Religion as an Anthropological Category' in *Genealogies of Religion: Discipline and Reasons of Power in Christianity and Islam* (Baltimore, John Hopkins University Press, 1993).

Aulagnier, P, *L'apprenti-historien et le maître-sorcier. Du discours identifiant au discours délirant* (Paris, Presses Universitaires de France, 1993).

——, *The Violence of Interpretation. From Pictogram to Statement* (Hove, Brunner-Routledge, 2001).

Austin, G, *The Indian Constitution: Cornerstone of a Nation* (Oxford, Oxford University Press, 1966).

Avbelj, M, 'Theory of European Union' (2011) *European Law Review* 818–36.

Badiou, A, *Metapolitics* (London, Verso, 2011).

Bajpai, R, *Debating Difference: Group Rights and Liberal Democracy in India* (Oxford, Oxford University Press, 2011).

Bakhtin, M, *Speech Genres* (Austin, University of Texas, 1986).

Balakrishnan, G, *The Enemy: An Intellectual Portrait of Carl Schmitt* (London, Verso, 2002).

Barak, G, *Crimes by the Capitalist State: An Introduction to State Criminality* (New York, SUNY Press, 1991).

Baranger, D, 'The Apparition of Sovereignty' in H Kalmo and Q Skinner (eds), *Sovereignty in Fragments: The Past, Present and Future of a Contested Concept* (Cambridge, Cambridge University Press, 2010).

Barber, N, 'Professor Loughlin's *Idea of Public Law*' (2005) 25 *Oxford Journal of Legal Studies* 157.
Barkan, J, 'Law and the Geographic Analysis of Economic Globalisation' (2011) 35 *Progress in Human Geography* 589.
Bartelson, J, *A Genealogy of Sovereignty* (Cambridge, Cambridge University Press, 1995).
Beard, C, *An Economic Interpretation of the Constitution* (New York, Free Press, 1986).
Beaud, O, *Théorie de la* Fédération (Paris, PUF, 2007).
——, 'L'État' in P Gonod, F Melleray and P Yolka (eds), *Traité de droit administratif* (Paris, Dalloz, 2011).
Bell, C, *Ritual: Perspectives and Dimensions* (Oxford, Oxford University Press, 2009).
Bellamy, R, 'Political Constitutionalism and the Human Rights Act' (2011) 9 *International Journal of Constitutional Law* 86.
Berman, H, *Law and Revolution* (Cambridge MA, Harvard University Press, 1982).
Bernhardt, R (ed), *Encyclopedia of Public International Law, vol. 11. Law of the Sea, Air and, Space* (Amsterdam, Elsevier, 1989).
Bhattacharya, S, *Mahatma and the Poet; Letters and Debates between Gandhi and Tagore 1915–1941*, 1st edn (New Dehli, National Book Trust, 1997).
Bhuta, N, 'The Mystery of the State: State Concept, State Theory and State Making in Schmitt and Oakeshott' in D Dyzenhaus and T Poole (eds), *Law, Liberty and State: Oakeshott, Hayek and Schmitt on the Rule of Law* (Cambridge, Cambridge University Press, 2015).
Bickel, A, *The Least Dangerous Branch. The Supreme Court at the Bar of Politics* (New Haven, Yale University Press, 1986).
Bickerton, C, *European Integration: From Nation-State to Member State* (Oxford, Oxford University Press, 2012).
Biggs, M, 'Putting the State on the Map: Cartography, Territory and European State Formation' (1999) 41 *Comparative Studies in Society and History* 374.
Bilgrami, A, 'Gandhi (and Marx)' in *Secularism, Identity, and Enchantment* (Cambridge MA, Harvard University Press, 2014).
——, 'Gandhi's Radicalism: An Interpretation' in Akeel Bilgrami (ed), *Beyond the Secular West* (New York, Columbia University Press, 2016).
Biller, P, *The Measure of the Multitude: Population in Medieval Thought* (Oxford, Oxford University Press, 2000).
Blickle, P, *der Bauernkrieg* (München, Beck, 2006).
Böckenförde, EW, *Die verfassungsgebende Gewalt des Volkes—Ein Grenzbegriff desVerfassungsrechts.* (Frankfurt, Metner, 1986).
Bodin, J, *The Six Bookes of a Commonweale* (translated by R Knolles, 1606 and edited by KD McRae) (Cambridge MA, Harvard University Press, 1962).
Bonefeld, W, 'Freedom and the Strong State: On Ordo-Liberalism (2012) *New Political Economy* 633–56.
Bonn, EV, *Standard Texts on Social Market Economy: Two Centuries of Discussion* (translated by D Rutter and edited by HF Wunsche) (Stuttgart, Gustav Fisher Verlag, 1982).
Bonnard, R, *Précis de droit administratif*, 3rd edn (Paris, LGDJ, 1940).
Boukalas, C, 'No Exceptions: Authoritarian Statism, Agamben, Poulantzas and Homeland Security' (2014) 7 *Critical Studies on Terrorism* 112.
Bourdieu, P, *Sociology in Question* (London, Sage, 1993).
——, 'Rethinking the State: Genesis and Structure of the Bureaucratic Field' (1994) 12 *Sociological Theory* 1.
——, *On the State: Lectures at the Collège de France, 1989–1992* (translated by D Fernbach) (Cambridge, Polity, 2014).
Bowman, T and Stamp, R (eds), *Reading Rancière* (London, Continuum, 2011).
Bratsis, P, *Everyday Life and the State* (London, Anthem, 2006).

Breaugh, M et al (eds), *Thinking Radical Democracy. The Return to Politics in Post-War France* (Toronto, University of Toronto Press, 2015).
Breckman, W, *Adventures of the Symbolic. Post-Marxism and Radical Democracy* (New York, Columbia University Press, 2013).
Brenner, N et al (eds) *STATE/SPACE: A Reader* (Oxford, Blackwell, 2003).
Breuer, S, *Der Charismatische Staat: Ursprunge and Fruhfomen staatlicher Herrschaft* (Darmstadt, WBG, 2014).
Brunkhorst, H, *Critical Theory of Legal Revolutions. Evolutionary Perspectives* (New York, Bloomsbury 2014).
Buci-Glucksmann, C, *Gramsci and the State* (London, Lawrence and Wishart, 1980).
Burke, E, *Reflections on the Revolution in France* (edited by JGA Pocock) (Indianapolis, Hackett Publishing, 1987).
Cacciari, M, *The Unpolitical: On the Radical Critique of Political Reason* (New York, Fordham University Press, 2009).
——, 'Introduzione' in M Weber, *La scienza come professione. La politica come professione* (Milano, Oscar Mondadori, 2006).
Calhoun, C, Juergensmeyer, M and Vanantwerpen, J, 'Introduction' in C Calhoun, M Juergensmeyer and J Vanantwerpen (eds), *Rethinking Secularism* (Oxford, Oxford University Press 2011).
Campbell, T, *The Legal Theory of Ethical Positivism* (Aldershot, Ashgate, 1996).
Campesi, D, *A Genealogy of Public Security: The Theory and History of Police Powers* (London, Routledge, 2016).
Canovan, M, *Nationhood and Political Theory* (Cheltenham, Edward Elgar, 1996).
Carré de Malberg, R, *Contribution à la théorie générale de l'Etat* (Paris, Sirey, 1920).
Cartier, G, 'A Simple Common Lawyer: Essays in Honour of Michael Taggart' (edited by Dyzenhaus, D, Hunt, M, and G Huscroft) (2014) 64 *University of Toronto Law Journal.*
Cassese, S, *La construction du droit administratif. France et Royaume-Uni* (Montchrestien, clés, 2000).
Castoriadis, C, *Philosophy, Politics, Autonomy: Essays in Political Philosophy* (translated by D Ames) (Oxford, Oxford University Press, 1991).
Chignola, S, 'History of Political Thought and the History of Political Concepts': Koselleck's Proposal and Italian Research' (2002) 33 *History of Political Thought* 517.
Christodoulidis, E and Tierney, S (eds), *Public Law and Politics. The Scope and Limits of Constitutionalism* (Aldershot, Ashgate, 2008).
——, 'The European Court of Justice and "Total Market Thinking"' (2013) *German Law Journal* 2005.
——, 'Against Substitution: The Constitutional Thinking of Dissensus' in M Loughlin and N Walker (eds), *The Paradox of Constitutionalism. Constituent Power and Constitutional Form* (Oxford, Oxford University Press, 2007).
Cohen, G, *Rescuing Justice and Equality* (Cambridge MA, Harvard University Press, 2008).
Comaroff, J, 'Reflections on the Rise of Legal Theology: Law and Religion in the Twenty-First Century' (2009) 53(1) *Social Analysis* 193.
Connolly, WE, *Why I Am Not A Secularist* (Minneapolis Minn, University of Minnesota Press, 1999).
Constituent Assembly Debates: *Official Report, vol 4* (New Delhi, Lok Sabha Secretariat, 1999) 601.
Coupland, R, *Report on the Constitutional Problem in India: The Indian Problem, 1833–1935* (Oxford, Oxford University Press, 1943).
Cover, R, 'Nomos and Narrative' (1983) 67 *Harvard Law Review* 4.
Craig, P, 'Prerogative, Precedent and Power' in C Forsyth and I Hare (eds), *The Golden Metwand and the Crooked Cord: Essays in Public Law in Honour of Sir William Wade QC* (Oxford, Clarendon Press, 1998).
Crisafulli, V, 'Per una teoria giuridica dell'indirizzo politico' (1939) in *Prima e dopo la costituzione* (Naples, ESI, 2015).

Cristi, R, *Carl Schmitt and Authoritarian Liberalism: Strong State, Free Economy* (Cardiff, University of Wales Press, 1998).

Croce, M and Salvatore, M, *The Legal Theory of Carl Schmitt* (Abingdon, Routledge, 2012) 187.

Crouch, C, *The Strange Non-Death of Neoliberalism* (Oxford, Polity, 2011).

Curtis, B, 'Foucault on Governmentality and Population: The Impossible Discovery' (2002) 27 *Canadian Journal of Sociology* 505.

Dagan, H, *Reconstructing American Legal Realism & Rethinking Private Law Theory* (Oxford, Oxford University Press, 2013).

de Malberg, R, *Contribution à la Théorie Générale de l'Etat, 1919–1922* [rééd] (Paris, Dalloz, 2003).

de Smith, SA, *Judicial review of Administrative Action*, 1st edn (London, Stevens and Sons Ltd, 1959).

de Smith, SA, Woolf, H and Jowell, JA, *Judicial Review of Administrative Action*, 5th edn (London, Sweet & Maxwell, 1995).

de Spinoza, B, *Tractatus Theologico-Politicus, Tractatus Politicus* (translated by RHM Elwes) (London, Routledge, 1951).

de Vries, H, 'On General and Divine Economy: Talal Asad's 'Genealogy of the Secular and Emmanuel Levinas's Critique of Capitalism, Colonialism, and Money' in D Scott and C Hirshkind (eds), *Powers of the Secular: Talal Asad and His Interlocutors* (Stanford, Stanford University Press, 2005).

Dean, M, *The Constitution of Poverty: Towards a Genealogy of Liberal Governance* (London, Routledge, 1990).

Delaney, D, *Territory: A Short Introduction* (Oxford, Blackwell, 2005).

della Volpe, G, *Rousseau and Marx* (London, Lawrence & Wishart, 1978).

Deranty, J-P (ed), *Jacques Rancière. Key Concepts* (Durham, Acumen, 2010).

Desika Char SV (ed), *Readings in the Constitutional History of India 1757–1947* (Oxford, Oxford University Press, 1983).

Dhareshwar, V, 'Politics, Experience and Cognitive Enslavement: Gandhi's *Hind Swaraj*' (2010) 45 *Economic and Political Weekly* 51.

Dicey, AV, *Introduction to the Study of the Law of the Constitution* (London, Macmillan, 1885).

Dobel, JP, 'The Corruption of a State' (1978) 72 *American Political Science Review* 958.

Dowdle, M and Wilkinson, M (eds), *Constitutionalism Beyond Liberalism* (Cambridge, Cambridge University Press, 2017).

Du Gay, P, 'Is Office a Vocation in 'Post-Bureaucratic' Public Management?' in Yeatman, A (ed), *Neoliberalism and the Crisis of Public Institutions, Working Papers in the Human Rights and Public Life Program* (Sydney, Whitlam Institute 2015).

Dukes, R, *The Labour Constitution* (Oxford, Oxford University Press, 2012).

Dullien, S and Guérot, U, 'The Long Shadow of Ordoliberalism: Germany's Approach to the Euro-crisis' (2012) *European Council of Foreign Relations* 49.

Dupuy, J-P, *The Mark of the Sacred* (Stanford, Stanford University Press, 2003).

Duso, G, *La logica del potere. Storia dei concetti come filosofia politica* (Monza, Polimetrica International Scientific Publisher, 2007).

Dworkin, R, *Taking Rights Seriously* (Cambridge MA, Harvard University Press, 1977).

——, *Law's Empire* (Cambridge MA, Harvard University Press, 1987).

——, 'A New Philosophy for International Law' (2013) 41 *Philosophy and Public Affairs* 2.

Dyzenhaus, D, *Legality and Legitimacy: Carl Schmitt, Hans Kelsen and Hermman Heller in Weimar* (Oxford, Oxford University Press, 1997).

——, 'The End of the Road to Serfdom' (2013) 63 *University of Toronto Law Journal* 326.

Dyzenhaus, D and Poole, T, 'Introduction' in D Dyzenhaus and T Poole (eds), *Law, Liberty and State: Oakeshott, Hayek and Schmitt on the Rule of Law* (Cambridge, Cambridge University Press, 2015).

East India (Advisory and Legislative Councils, &c.), *Vol I: Proposals of the Government of India and Despatch of the Secretary of State* (London, His Majesty's Stationery Office, 1908).

Elden, SJ, 'Land, Terrain, Territory' (2010) 36 *Progress in Human Geography* 799.

——, 'How to Do the History of Territory' (2013) 1 *Territory, Politics, Governance* 5.

Eleftheriadis, P, *Legal Rights* (Oxford, Oxford University Press, 2008).

Elias, N, *The Civilizing Process: State Formation and Civilization* (Oxford, Blackwell, 1982).

Engdahl, FW, *Full Spectrum Dominance: Totalitarian Democracy in the New World Order* (Wiesbaden, Edition Engdahl, 2009).

Escolar, M, 'Exploration, Cartography and the Modernisation of State Power' (1997) 151 *International Social Science Journal* 55.

Esposito, R, *Living Thought: The Origins and Actuality of Italian Thought* (Stanford, Stanford University Press, 2012).

Ewing, K, 'The Resilience of the Political Constitution' (2013) 13 *German Law Journal* 2111.

Febbrajo, A and Corsi, G (eds), *Sociology of Constitutions: A Paradoxical Perspective* (London, Routledge, 2016).

Ferejohn, J and Pasquino, P, 'The Law of Exception: A Typology of Emergency Powers' (2004) 210 *International Journal of Constitutional Law* 333.

Festenstein, M and Kenny, M (eds), *Political Ideologies: A Reader and Guide* (Oxford, Oxford University Press, 2005).

Finer, S, *The History of Government 3 Volumes* (Oxford, Oxford University Press, 1997).

Flora, P (ed), *State-Formation, Nation-Building and Mass Politics in Europe: The Theory of Stein Rokkan* (Oxford, Oxford University Press, 1999).

Flynn, B, *The Philosophy of Claude Lefort. Interpreting the Political* (Evanston, Northwestern University Press, 2005).

Foucault, M, *Archaeology of Knowledge* (London, Tavistock, 1972).

——, *Power/Knowledge: Selected Interviews and Other Writings 1972–1977* (Pantheon, New York, 1980).

——, *Security, Territory, Population: Lectures at the Collège de France, 1977–1978* (Basingstoke, Palgrave Macmillan, 2007).

——, *Security, Territory, Population. Lectures at the College de France* (Basingstoke, Palgrave, 2008).

——, *The Birth of Biopolitics—Lectures at the College de France 1978–1979* (Basingstoke, Palgrave MacMillan, 2008).

——, 'The Subject and Power' in H Dreyfus and P Rabinow, (eds), *Michel Foucault. Beyond Hermeneutics and Structuralism* (Chicago, University of Chicago Press, 1983).

Freeden, M, *Ideology: A Very Short Introduction* (Oxford, Oxford University Press, 2003).

Fried, J (ed), *Die abendländische Freiheit vom 10 zum 14 Jahrhundert* (Siegmaringen, Thorbecke, 1991).

Friedrich, CJ, 'The Political Thought of Neo-liberalism' (1955) *American Political Science Review* 49.

Friedrichs, J, 'The Meaning of New Medievalism' (2001) 7 *European Journal of International Relations* 475.

Frost, S, *Lessons from a Materialist Thinker: Hobbesian Reflections on Ethics and Politics* (Stanford, Stanford University Press, 2008).

Galanter, M, 'Hinduism, Secularism, and the Indian Judiciary' in R Bhargava (ed), *Secularism and its Critics* (Oxford, Oxford University Press, 1999).

Gandhi, M, *Hindu Dharma* (New Delhi, Orient Paperbacks, 1978) 18.

Gandhi, MK, *Hind Swaraj and Other Writings* (edited by A Parel) (Cambridge, Cambridge University, Press 1997).

Gauchet, M, *Le Désenchantement du Monde* (Paris, Édition Gallimard, 1985).

——, *The Disenchantment of the World: A Political History of Religion* (Princeton, Princeton University Press, 1997).

——, 'Tocqueville' in M Lilla (ed), *New French Thought: Political Philosophy* (Princeton, Princeton University Press, 1994).

Gee, G, 'The Political Constitutionalism of John Griffith' (2008) 28 *Legal Studies* 20.

——, 'Rationalism in Public Law' (2013) 76 *Modern Law Review* 708.

Gee, G and Webber, G, 'A Grammar of Public Law' (2013) 14 *German Law Journal* 2137.

Gill, S, *Power and Resistance in the New World Order* (Basingstoke, Palgrave MacMillan, 2008).

Golder, B (ed), *Re-Reading Foucault: On Law, Power and Rights* (London, Routledge, 2013).

Goldoni, M, 'Rousseau's Radical Constitutionalism and its Legacy' in M Dowdle and M Wilkinson (eds), *Constitutionalism Beyond Liberalism* (Cambridge, Cambridge University Press, 2017).

Goldoni, M and Wilkinson, M, 'The Material Constitution' (2016) *LSE Working Paper Series*.

Goldsmith J and Levinson, D, 'Law for States: International Law, Constitutional Law, Public Law' (2009) 122 *Harvard Law Review* 1791.

Gordon, M, 'A Basis for Positivist and Political Public Law: Reconciling Loughlin's Public Law with (Normative) Legal Positivism' (2015) 6 *Jurisprudence* 1.

Gorski, P, 'Historicising the Secularisation Debate: Church, State, and Society in Late Medieval and Early Modern Europe, ca. 1300 to 1700' (2000) 65(1) *American Sociological Review* 138.

Gramsci, A, *Selections from the Prison Notebooks* (London, Lawrence and Wishart, 1971).

——, *Prison Notebooks* (New York, Columbia University Press, 2011).

Grant, J, *Times Literary Supplement*, 7 Oct 2010.

Green, P and Ward, T, *State Crime. Governments, Violence and Corruption* (London, Pluto, 2004).

Green, TH, in *Lectures on the Principles of Political Obligation and Other Writings* (Cambridge, Cambridge University Press, 1986).

Griffith, J, 'Why We Need a Revolution' (1969) 40 *Political Quarterly* 383.

——, 'The Political Constitution', (1979) 42 *Modern Law Review* 1.

Guéry, A, 'The State' in Pierre Nora (ed), *Rethinking France: Les Lieux de Mémoire, Vol. 1* (translated by M Trouille) (Chicago, University of Chicago Press, 2001).

Gursansky, D and Yeatman, A, 'Are Prisoners Clients? The Individualisation of Public Correctional Services' in A Yeatman, G Dowsett, M Fine, and D Gursansky (eds), *Individualisation and the Delivery of Welfare Services: Contestation and Complexity* (Basingstoke, Palgrave Macmillan, 2009).

Habermas, J, *Faktizität und Geltung* (Frankfurt, Suhrkamp 1992).

——, *Between Facts and Norms* (Cambridge, Polity Press, 1996).

——, *The Postnational Constellation* (Cambridge, Polity Press, 2001).

——, *Versuch über Glauben und Wissen* [unpublished manuscript] (Starnberg, 2016) [on file with author].

Halpin, A, 'Ideology and Law' (2006) 11 *Journal of Political Ideologies* 153.

Hamburger, P, *Is Administrative Law Unlawful?* (Chicago, University of Chicago Press, 2014).

Hammill, G, 'Blumenberg and Schmitt on the Rhetoric of Political Theology' in G Hammill and JR Lupton (eds), *Political Theology and Early Modernity* (London and Chicago, University of Chicago Press, 2012).

Hamrick, WS, *An Existential Phenomenology of Law: Maurice Merleau-Ponty* (Dordrecht, Springer, 1987).

Harding, M, *Charity Law and the Liberal State* (Cambridge, Cambridge University Press, 2014).

Hardt, M and Negri, A, *Empire* (Cambridge MA, Harvard University Press, 2000).

Harrington, J, 'The Commonwealth of Oceana and A System of Politics' in JGA Pocock (ed), *Cambridge Texts in the History of Political Thought* (Cambridge, Cambridge University Press, 1992).

Harvey, D, *The New Imperialism* (Oxford, Oxford University Press, 2003).

Hauriou, M, *Précis de droit administratif* (Paris, Sirey, 1892).

Hawker, G, *Who's Master, Who's Servant? Reforming Bureaucracy* (Sydney, George Allen & Unwin, 1981).

Hegel, GWF, *Philosophy of Right* [1821] (translated by TM Knox) (Oxford, Clarendon Press, 1952).

——, *Elements of the Philosophy of Right* (Cambridge, Cambridge University Press, 1991).

Heidenheimer, A, 'Politics, Policy and Policy as Concepts in English and Continental Languages' (1986) 48 *Review of Politics* 1.

Heller, H, 'Souveränität' in *Gesammelte Schriften* 2 (Leiden, Sijthoff, 1971).
——, 'Political Democracy and Social Homogeneity' from A Jacobson and B Schlink (eds), *Weimar: A Jurisprudence of Crisis* (California, University of California Press, 2002).
Hennis, W, *Max Weber: Essays in Reconstruction* (translated by K Tribe) (London, Allen & Unwin, 1988).
——, *Politics as a Practical Science* (translated by K Tribe) (Basingstoke, Palgrave Macmillan, 2009).
Hobbes, T, *Leviathan* (Cambridge, Cambridge University Press, 1991).
Hohfeld, WN, 'Some Fundamental Legal Conceptions as Applied in Judicial Reasoning' (1913) 23 *Yale Law Journal* 16.
Honnefelder, L, *Duns Scotus* (München, Beck, 2005).
Honneth, A, *The Pathologies of Individual Freedom: Hegel's Social Theory* (Princeton, Princeton University Press, 2010).
Hunter, I, *Rival Enlightenments: Civil and Metaphysical Philosophy in Early Modern Germany* (Cambridge, Cambridge University Press, 2001).
Isenstadt, S, *The Political Systems of Empires: The Rise and Fall of Bureaucratic Societies* (New York, Free Press, 1963).
Jacobsen, A and Schlink, B, *Weimar: A Jurisprudence of Crisis* (Berkeley, University of California Press, 2002).
James, S, 'The Political and Administrative Consequences of Judicial Review' (1996) 74 *Public Administration* 613.
Jamieson, F, 'Aesthetics of Singularity' (2015) 92 *New Left Review* 101–32.
Jayasuriya, K, 'Globalisation, Sovereignty and the Rule of Law: From Political to Economic Constitutionalism' (2001) 8 *Constellations* 442.
Jennings, WI, *Cabinet Government* (Cambridge, Cambridge University Press, 1936).
——, *Parliament*, (Cambridge, Cambridge University Press, 1938).
——, *The Law and the Constitution* (London, University of London Press, 1963).
Jessop, B, ——, *State Theory: Putting the Capitalist State in its Place* (Cambridge, Polity Press, 1990).
——, *State Power: A Strategic-Relational Approach* (Cambridge, Polity Press, 2007).
——, *The State: Past, Present, Future* (Cambridge, Polity Press, 2015).
——, 'Territory, Politics, Governance and Multispatial Metagovernance' (2016) 4 *Territory, Politics, Governance* 8.
Jèze, G, *Principes généraux du droit administratif* (Paris, Berger-Levrault, 1904).
John, M, 'Identity and the Social Revolution: On the Political Sociology of Constitutionalism in Contemporary India', *Jawaharlal Nehru University Centre for the Study of Law and Governance Working Paper* No. CSLG/WP/18 (New Delhi, Jawaharlal Nehru University, 2012).
Jones, GS, 'The Determinist Fix: Some Obstacles to the Further Development of the Linguistic Approach to History in the 1990s' (1996) 42 *History Workshop Journal* 19.
Judt, T, *Ill Fares the Land* (New York, Penguin, 2010).
Kaasch, O and Martens, K (eds), *Actors and Agency in Global Social Governance* (Oxford, Oxford University Press, 2015).
Kahn, P, *The Cultural Study of Law* (Chicago, Chicago University Press, 1999).
——, *Putting Liberalism in its Place* (Princeton, Princeton University Press, 2005).
Kant, I, *On the Old Saw that Might be Right in Theory but it Won't Work in Practice* (Philadephia, University of Pennsylvania Press, 1974).
——, *The Metaphysics of Morals* (Cambridge, Cambridge University Press 1996).
Keane, J, *Democracy and Civil Society* (London, Verso, 1988).
Kennedy, E, '"Ideology" from Destutt De Tracy to Marx' (1979) 40 *Journal of the History of Ideas* 353.
Kirk, GS, Raven, JE and Schofield, M, *The Presocratic Philosophers: A Critical History with a Selection of Texts*, 2nd edn (Cambridge, Cambridge University Press, 1983).

Kofele-Kala, N, *The International Law of Responsibility for Economic Crimes. Golding State Officials Individually Liable for Fraudulent Enrichment* (Aldershot, Ashgate, 2006).

Kommers, D and Miller, R, *The Constitutional Jurisprudence of the Federal Republic of Germany* (Durham, NC, Duke University Press, 2012).

Koselleck, R, '*Begriffsgeschichte* and Social History' (1982) 11 *Economy and Society* 409.

——, *Futures Past. On the Semantics of Historical Time* (Cambridge MA, MIT, 1985).

——, 'A Response' in Lehmann, H and Richter, M (eds), *The Meaning of Historical Terms and Concepts: New Studies on Begriffsgeschichte* (Washington DC, German Historical Institute, 1996).

——, '*Begriffsgeschichte* and Social History' in his *Futures Past: On the Semantics of Historical Time* (translated by K Tribe) (New York, Columbia University Press, 2004).

Koskenniemi, M, 'Constitutionalism as Mindset: Reflections on Kantian Themes about International Law and Globalization' in (2006) *Theoretical Inquiries in Law* 8/1 9.

Kratochwil, F, 'Of Systems, Boundaries and Territoriality: An Inquiry into the Formation of the State System' (1986) 34 *World Politics* 27.

Kriegel, B, *The State and the Rule of Law* (Princeton, Princeton University Press, 1995).

Kumm, M, 'The Best of Times and the Worst of Times: Between Constitutional Triumphalism and Nostalgia' in P Dobner and M Loughlin (eds), *The Twilight of Constitutionalism* (Oxford, Oxford University Press, 2010).

Laband, P, *Das Staatsrecht des deutschen Reiches* (Tübingen, Laupp, 3 vols. 1876–82).

Laclau, E and Mouffe, C, *Hegemony and Socialist Strategy. Towards a Radical Democratic Politics* (London, Verso, 2001).

Lacoue-Labarthe, P and Nancy, JL, *Retreating the Political* (London, Routledge, 1997).

Lassalle, F, *Qu'est-ce qu'une constitution?* (Paris, Dulliver, 1999).

Latour, B, *The Cult of the Factish Gods* (Durham NC, Duke University Press, 2011).

Laws, J, 'The Ghost in the Machine: Principle in Public Law' (1989) *Public Law* 27.

Lee, D, '"Office is a Thing Borrowed": Jean Bodin on Offices and Seigneurial Government' (2013) 41 *Political Theory* 409.

Lefort, C, ——, *The Political Forms of Modern Society: Bureaucracy, Democracy, Totalitarianism* (Cambridge MA, MIT Press, 1986).

——, '*Democracy and Political Theory* (Cambridge, Polity, 1988).

——, *Complications: Communism and the Dilemmas of Democracy* (translated by J. Bourg) (New York, Columbia University Press, 2007).

——, 'International Law, Human Rights, and Politics' (2013) 22 *Qui Parle* (2013) 117.

——, 'Politics and Human Rights' in JB Thompson (ed), *The Political Forms of Modern Society* 239 (Cambridge MA, MIT Press, 1986) 239.

——, 'The Question of Democracy' in *Democracy and Political Theory* (translated by D Macey) (Cambridge, Polity Press, 1988).

Levene, M, *Genocide in the Age of the Nation-State. Volumes 1 and 2* (London, IB Tuarus, 2005).

Levinson, S, *Framed: America's 51 Constitutions and the Crisis of Governance* (Oxford, Oxford University Press, 2012).

Lindahl, H, *Fault-Lines of Globalisation* (Oxford, Oxford University Press, 2014).

Locke, J, *Two Treatises of Government* [1680] (edited by Peter Laslett) (Cambridge, Cambridge University Press, 1988).

Loughlin, M, *Public Law and Political Theory* (Oxford, Clarendon Press, 1992).

——, *Sword and Scales: An Examination of the Relationship between Law and Politics* (Oxford, Hart Publishing, 2000).

——, *The Idea of Public Law* (Oxford, Oxford University Press, 2003).

——, 'Theory and Values in Public Law: An Interpretation' (2005) *Public Law* 61.

——, 'In Defence of Staatslehre' (2009) 48 *Der Staat* 1.

——, *Foundations of Public Law* (Oxford, Oxford University Press, 2010).

——, 'The Concept of Constituent Power' (2014) 13 *European Journal of Political Theory* 218.
——, 'A-legality or Jus Politicum: A Critical Appraisal of Hans Lindhal's Fault Line of Globalisation' (2014) 2 *Ethics and Politics* 965.
——, 'Modernism in British Public Law, 1919–79' (2014) *Public Law* 56.
——, 'The Constitutional Imagination' (2015) 78 *Modern Law Review* 1.
——, 'Droit Politique' (2017) 17 *Jus Politicum: Revue de Droit Politique* 299.
——, 'Erosion of Sovereignty' (2017) *Netherlands Journal of Legal Philosophy*.
——, 'Whither the Constitution?' in C Forsyth (ed), *Judicial Review and the Constitution* (Oxford, Hart Publishing, 2000).
——, 'Politonomy' in J Meierhenrich and O Simons (eds), *The Oxford Handbook of Carl Schmitt* (New York, Oxford University Press, 2007) 570.
——, 'What is Constitutionalisation?' in P Dobner and M Loughlin (eds), *The Twilight of Constitutionalism?* (Oxford, Oxford University Press, 2010).
——, 'Why Sovereignty' in R Rawlings, P Leyland, and A Young (eds), *Sovereignty and the Law* (Oxford, Hart Publishing, 2013).
——, 'Santi Romano and the Institutional Theory of Law' in S Romano, *The Legal Order* (translated by M Croce) (London, Routledge, 2017).
——, 'Politonomy' in J Meierhenrich and O Simons (eds), *The Oxford Handbook of Carl Schmitt* (Oxford, Oxford University Press, 2017).
Loughlin, M, and Walker, N (eds), *The Paradox of Constitutionalism: Constituent Power and Constitutional Form* (Oxford, Oxford University Press, 2007).
Luhmann, N, *Gesellschaftsstruktur und Semantik. Band 1* (Frankfurt, Suhrkamp, 1980).
——, 'Staat und Politik: Zur Semantik der Selbstbeschreibung politischer Systeme', *Politische Vierteljahresschrift* 15 (1994) *Sonderheft* 99.
——, *Law as a Social System* (Oxford, Oxford University Press, 2004).
——, *Ideenevolution: Beiträge zur Wissenssoziologie* (Frankfurt, Suhrkamp, 2008).
MacCormick, N, *Institutions of Law: An Essay in Legal Theory* (Oxford, Oxford University Press, 2007).
——, *Practical Reason in Law and Morality* (Oxford, Oxford University Press, 2008).
Machiavelli, N, *The Discourses* (translated by LJ Walker) (London, Penguin, 1970).
MacPherson, CB, *The Political Theory of Possessive Individualism—Hobbes to Locke* (Oxford, Oxford University Press, 2011).
Madan, TN, *Modern Myths, Locked Minds: Secularism and Fundamentalism in India*, 2nd edn (Oxford, Oxford University Press, 2009).
Madison, J, Hamilton, A and Jay, J, *The Federalist Papers* (edited by I Kramnick) (London, Penguin, 1987).
Majone, G, *Rethinking the Union of Europe Post-Crisis* (Oxford, Oxford University Press, 2014).
Malpas, J, 'Ground, Unity, Limit' in J Malpas (ed), *Heidegger and the Thinking of Place: Explorations in the Topology of Being* (Cambridge, MA, MIT Press, 2012).
Mann, M, 'The Autonomous Power of the State: Its Origins, Mechanisms and Results' (1984) 25 *Archives Européenes de Sociologie* 185.
——, *The Social Sources of Power* (Cambridge, Cambridge University Press, 1986).
——, *Incoherent Empire* (London, Verso, 2005).
Marchart, O, *Post-Foundational Political Thought. Political Difference in Nancy, Lefort, Badiou and Laclau* (Edinburgh, Edinburgh University Press, 2007).
——, 'The Second Return of the Political: Democracy and the Syllogism of Equality' in Bowman, P and Stamp, R (eds), *Reading Rancière* (London, Continuum, 2011).
Marks, S, *The Riddle of all Constitutions* (Oxford, Oxford University Press, 2000).
Marx, K, *A Contribution to the Critique of Political Economy* (Chicago, Charles H Kerr & Company 1904).

——, *MEW* 1 (Berlin, Dietz, 1988).
——, 'On the Jewish Question' in *Marx. Early Political Writings* (Cambridge, Cambridge University Press, 1994).
——, 'Critique of Hegel's Doctrine of the State' in *Early Writings* (London, Penguin, 2005).
Mauthe, B and Webb, T, 'Realism and Analysis within Public Law' (2013) 34 *Liverpool Law Review* 27.
May, T, *The Political Thought of Jacques Rancière. Creating Equality* (Edinburgh, Edinburgh University Press, 2008).
McAmhlaigh, C, Walker, N and Michelon, N (eds), *After Public Law* (Oxford, Oxford University Press, 2013).
McNicoll, G, 'Population' in P Demeny and G McNichol (eds), *Encyclopedia of Population* (New York, MacMillan, 2003).
Mehta, US, 'Gandhi on Democracy, Politics and the Ethics of Everyday Life' (2010) 7 *Modern Intellectual History* 355.
Meinecke, F, *Machiavellism: The Doctrine of Raison d'État and its Place in Modern History*, (translated by D Scott) (New Haven, Yale University Press, 1957).
Memos, C, *Castoriadis and Critical Theory. Crisis, Critique and Radical Alternatives* (Basingstoke, Palgrave Macmillan, 2014).
Merleau-Ponty, M, *Humanism and Terror* (translated by J O'Neill) (Boston, Beacon Press, 1969).
Miller, P and Rose, N, *Governing the Present: Administering Economic, Social and Personal Life* (Cambridge, Polity Press, 2008).
Mills, CW, *The Marxists* (New York, Dell, 1962).
Mills, CW and Gerth, HH (eds), *From Max Weber: Essays in Sociology* (New York, Oxford University Press, 1958).
Minkkinen, P, *Sovereignty, Knowledge, Law* (Abingdon, Routledge, 2009).
Mirowski, P, *The Road from Mont Pelerin: The Making of the Neo-Liberal Thought Collective* (Cambridge MA, Harvard University Press, 2009).
Mitchell, TJ, 'The Limits of the State: Beyond Statist Approaches and Their Critics (1991) 85 *American Political Science Review* 77.
Möllers, C, 'Les Gardiennes d'une Separation. Les Constitutions Comme Instruments de Protection des Differences Entre le Droit et la Politique' (2012) 7 *Jus Politicum* 1.
Montesquieu, *The Spirit of the Laws* (translated and edited by A Cohler, B Miller and H Stone) (Cambridge, Cambridge University Press, 1989).
Mortati, M, *L'ordinamento del governo nel nuovo diritto pubblico italiano* (Milan, Giuffré, 2000).
Müller, JW, *Contesting Democracy* (Princeton University Press, 2012).
Murkens, J 'Bundesverfassungsgericht (2 BvE 2/08): 'We want our identity back'—the revival of national sovereignty in the German Federal Constitutional Court's decision on the Lisbon Treaty' (2010) *Public Law* 530.
Nandy, A, 'The Politics of Secularism and the Recovery of Toleration' in R Bhargava (ed), *Secularism and its Critics* (Oxford, Oxford University Press, 1999).
Negri, A, 'Towards a Critique of the Material Constitution' in *Books for Burning* (London, Verso, 2005).
——, 'On the Constitution and Financial Capital' (2015) 32 *Theory, Culture & Society* 25.
Neocleous, M, *Administering Civil Society: Towards a Theory of State Power* (Basingstoke, Macmillan, 1996).
——, *Imagining the State* (Maidenhead, Open University Press, 2003).
Nickel, PM, 'Network Governance and the New Constitutionalism' (2007) 29 *Administrative Theory and Praxis* 198.
Nietzsche, F, *The Genealogy of Morals: A Polemic* (Cambridge, Cambridge University Press, 1994).
Oakeshott, M, *On Human Conduct* (Oxford, Clarendon Press, 1975).
——, 'The Vocabulary of the Modern European State' (1975) 23 *Political Studies* 319.

——, *The Politics of Faith and the Politics of Scepticism* [c.1952] (edited by T Fuller) (New Haven, Yale University Press, 1996).

——, 'The Rule of Law' in *On History and Other Essays* (Indianapolis, Liberty Fund, 1999).

Offe, C, 'The Theory of the Capitalist State and the Problem of Policy Formation' in LN Lindberg, R Alford, C Crouch and C Offe (eds), *Stress and Contradiction in Modern Capitalism* (Lexington K, DC Heath, 1975).

Orlando, VE, *Principii di diritto costituzionale* (Florence, Barbera, 1889).

——, *Principii di diritto amministrativo* (Florence, Barbera, 1891).

Palonen, K, 'Two Concepts of Politics, Two Histories of a Concept? Conceptual History and Present Controversies' (2006) 7 *Distinktion: Scandinavian Journal of Social Theory* 11.

Panitch, L and Gindin, S, *The Making of Global Capitalism: The Political Economy of American Empire* (London: Verso, 2012).

Pathan, S, 'A Historical and Theoretical Investigation into Communalism' (Manipal, India, Manipal University PhD thesis, 2009).

Penner, J, 'The Analysis of Rights' (1997) 10 *Ratio Juris* 300.

Penner, 'Autonomy, Religion and Politics: Reflections on Matthew Harding's *Charity Law and the State*' (2017) *Australian Journal of Legal Philosophy* 126–38.

——, 'The State Duty to Support the Poor in Kant's *Doctrine of Right*' (2010) 12 *British Journal of Politics and International Relations* 88.

Petit, V, *Counting Populations, Understanding Societies: Towards an Interpretive Approach* (Dordrecht, Springer, 2013).

Plot, M (ed), *Claude Lefort: Thinker of the Political* (Basingstoke, Palgrave Macmillan, 2013).

Pocock, JGA, *Politics, Language and Time: Essays on Political Thought and History* (New York, Atheneum, 1973).

——, 'Concepts and Discourses: A Difference in Culture' in Lehmann, H and Richter, M (eds), *The Meaning of Historical Terms and Concepts* (Washington DC, German Historical Institute, 1996).

Polanyi, K, *The Great Transformation: The Political and Economic Origins of Our Time* (Boston, Beacon Press, 2001 (1944)).

Poole, T, 'Tilting at Windmills?' (2007) 70 *Modern Law Review* 250.

Poulantzas, N, 'The Political Crisis and the Crisis of the State' in JW Freiburg (ed), *Critical Sociology* (New York, Halstead Press, 1979).

——, *State, Power, Socialism* (London, Verso, 1980).

Radhakrishnan, S, *Indian Philosophy* (London, George Allen and Unwin Ltd, 1948) Vol 1.

Ranciere, J, *Disagreement. Politics and Philosophy* (Minneapolis, University of Minnesota Press, 1999).

——, *Hatred of Democracy* (London, Verso, 2006).

——, *On the Shores of Politics* (London, Verso, 2007).

——, *Dissensus. On Politics and Aesthetics* (London, Continuum, 2009).

——, 'A Few Remarks on the Method of Jacques Rancière' (2009) 15 *Parallax* 114.

——, 'La méthode de l'égalité' in *La philosophie déplacée: autour de Jacques Rancière* (Paris, Horlieu Editions, 2006).

Rao et al, *The Framing of India's Constitution* (Dehli, Indian Institute of Public Administration, 1966) Vol 2.

Rappaport, R, *Ritual, Religion and the Making of Humanity* (Cambridge, Cambridge University Press, 1997).

Rawls, J, *A Theory of Justice* (revised edn) (Cambridge MA, Belknap Press, 1999).

——, *Political Liberalism* (expanded edition) (New York, Columbia University Press, 2005).

Raz, J, *The Morality of Freedom* (Oxford, Clarendon Press 1986).

——, *Ethics in the Public Domain* (Oxford, Clarendon Press, 1994).

Rehmann, J, *Theories of Ideology: The Powers of Alienation and Subjection* (Leiden, Brill, 2013).

Reno, Q, *Warlord Politics and African States* (Boulder, Lyme Regis, 1998).
Richter, M, 'Reconstructing the History of Political Languages: Pocock, Skinner and the *Geschichtliche Grundbegriffe*' (1990) 19 *History and Theory* 38.
Riesebrodt, M, 'Fundamentalism and the Resurgence of Religion' (2000) 47 *Numen* 266.
Ripstein, A, *Force and Freedom: Kant's Legal and Political Philosophy* (Cambridge MA, Harvard University Press, 2009).
Robson, WA *Justice and Administrative Law: A Study of the British Constitution*, 2nd edn (London, Stevens and Sons Ltd, 1947).
Rose, N, *Governing the Present. Administering Economic, Social and Personal Life* (Cambridge, Polity, 2008).
Rothe, DL, *State Criminality: The Crime of All Crimes* (Lanham MD, Lexington, 2009).
Rousseau, J-J, *Emile, or On Education* [1762] (translated by A Bloom) (New York, Basic Books, 1979).
——, *Du Contract Social* (1762) II, 7 (*Oeuvres Complètes, La Pléiade* III, 381).
Ruda, F, Hegel's Rabble: An Investigation into Hegel's Philosophy of Right (London, Bloomsbury, 2011).
Ruggie, J, 'Territoriality and Beyond' (1993) 47 *International Organisation* 139.
Saler, M, 'Modernity and Enchantment: A Historiographic Review' (2006) 111 *The American Historical Review* 692.
Satter, D, *Darkness at Dawn. The Rise of the Russian Criminal State* (New Haven, Yale University Press, 2003).
Scheuerman, W, *The Rule of Law Under Siege: Selected Essays of Franz Neumann and Otto Kircheimer* (Berkeley, University of California Press, 1994).
——, 'The Economic State of Emergency' (2000) 21 *Cardozo Law Review* 1869.
Schiavone, A, *The Invention of Law in the West* (Cambridge MA, Harvard University Press, 2012).
Schmitt, C, *Ex Captivitate Salus: Erfahrungen der Zeit 1945/46* (Cologne, Greven, 1950).
——, *The Crisis of Parliamentary Democracy* (Cambridge MA, MIT Press, 1988).
——, *The Concept of the Political* (translated by G Schwab) (Chicago, University of Chicago Press, 1996).
——, *The Nomos of the Earth in the Public Law of the Jus Publicum Europaaeum* (New York, Telos Press, 2003 [1950]).
——, *On the Three Types of Juristic Thought* (Westport CT, Praeger, 2004).
——, *Constitutional Theory* (translated by J Seitzer) (Durham NC, Duke University Press, 2008).
——, *Dictatorship. From the Origin of the Modern Concept of Sovereignty to Proletarian Class Struggle* (Cambridge, Polity Press, 2014 [1921]).
Schütze, R, *European Constitutional Law*, 2nd edn (Cambridge, Cambridge University Press, 2015).
Scubla, L, 'Est-il Possible de Mettre la Loi au dessus de l'Homme? Sur la philosophie politique de Jean-Jacques Rousseau' in J-P Dupuy (ed), *Introduction aux Sciences Sociales* (Paris, Ellipses, 1998).
Seidman, ML, *On Constitutional Disobedience* (Oxford, Oxford University Press, 2013).
Seligman et al, *Ritual and its Consequences: An Essay on the Limits of Sincerity* (Oxford, Oxford University Press, 2008).
Shortall, S, 'Lost in Translation: Religion and the Writing of History' (2016) 13(1) *Modern Intellectual History* 273.
Skinner, Q, *Liberty before Liberalism* (Cambridge, Cambridge University Press, 1998).
——, *Visions of History, Vol 1: Regarding Method* (Cambridge, Cambridge University Press, 2002).
——, 'State' in T Ball, J Farr and R Hanson (eds), *Political Innovation and Conceptual Change* (Cambridge, Cambridge University Press, 1989).
Skowronek, S, *The Politics Presidents Make* (Cambridge Mass, Harvard University Press, 1993).
Spruyt, H, *The Sovereign State and its Competitors: An Analysis of Systems Change* (Princeton, Princeton University Press, 1993).
Steinberger, P, *The Idea of the State* (Cambridge, Cambridge University Press, 2004).

Steinmetz-Jenkins, D, 'Claude Lefort and the Illegitimacy of Modernity' (2009) 10 *Journal for Cultural and Religious Theory* 102.

Stichweh, R, 'Professionen in einer funktional differenzierten Gesellschaft' in A Combe and W Helsper (eds), *Pädagogische Professionalität* (Frankfurt, Suhrkamp, 1996).

Streeck, W, 'Taking Capitalism Seriously: Towards an Institutionalist Approach to Contemporary Political Economy' (2011) 9 *Socio-Economic Review* 137.

——, *Buying Time: The Delayed Crisis of Democratic Capitalism* (London, Verso, 2014).

Sullivan, V, *Machiavelli, Hobbes and the Formation of a Liberal Republicanism in England* (Cambridge, Cambridge University Press, 2004).

Sullivan, WF, Yelle, RA and Taussig-Rubbo, M, 'Introduction' in WF Sullivan, RA Yelle and M Taussig-Rubbo (eds), *After Secular Law* (Stanford, Stanford University Press, 2011).

Sum, N-L and Jessop, B, *Towards a Cultural Political Economy: Putting Culture in its Place in Political Economy* (Cheltenham, Edward Elgar, 2013).

Supiot, A, *Homo Juridicus* (London, Verso, 2007).

Swedberg, R, *Max Weber and the Idea of Economic Sociology* (Princeton, Princeton University Press, 1998).

Tagore, R, Swadeshi Samaj, A Guha (trans) (Kolkata, Dey's Publishing, 2013).

Taylor, C, 'Interpretation and the Sciences of Man' in his *Philosophy and the Human Sciences: Philosophical Papers, vol.2* (Cambridge, Cambridge University Press, 1985).

Teschke, B, *The Myth of 1648: Class, Geopolitics, and the Making of Modern International Relations* (London, Verso, 2003).

——, 'Fatal Attraction: A Critique of Carl Schmitt's International Legal and Political Theory' (2011) 3 *International Theory* 179.

The Nehru Report: An Anti-Separatist Manifesto (New Delhi, Michiko & Panjathan, 1975) 27.

Thornhill, C, 'Carl Schmitt after the Deluge' (2000) *History of European Ideas* 225.

——, 'Martin Loughlin, Foundations of Public Law' (2011) *Public Law* 673.

Thucydides, 'The History of the Grecian War' in W Molesworth (ed), *The English Works of Thomas Hobbes* (London, Bohn, 1843).

Tomlins, C and Comaroff, J, '"Law As …": Theory and Practice in Legal History' (2011) 1 *UC Irvine Law Review* 1039.

Tribe, K, *Strategies of Economic Order: German Economic Discourse 1750–1950* (Cambridge, Cambridge University Press, 1995).

Tronti, M, *Operai e capitale* (Roma, Derive e Approdi, 2004).

Tuori, K and Tuori, K, *The Eurocrisis: A Constitutional Analysis* (Cambridge, Cambridge University Press, 2013).

Tushnet, M, *Red, White, and Blue: A Critical Analysis of Constitutional Law* (Cambridge, MA, Harvard University Press, 1988).

Vatter, M, *Between Form and Event. Machiavelli's Theory of Political Freedom* (Dordrecht, Kluwer, 2000).

Vedel, G, 'Les bases constitutionnelles du droit administratif' (1954) 8 *Etudes et Documents du Conseil d'Etat*.

——, *Droit Administratif*, 7th edn (Paris, Presses Universitaires de France, 1980).

von Gerber, CF, *Grundzüge eines Systems des deutschen Staatsrechts* (Leipzig, Tauchnitz, 1865).

Waldron, J, *Law and Disagreement* (Oxford, Oxford University Press, 1999).

Walker, H, 'Justice and the Dark Arts: Law and Shamanism in Amazonia' (2015) 117(1) *American Anthropologist* 47.

Walker, N (ed), *Sovereignty in Transition* (Oxford, Hart Publishing, 2003).

——, *Intimations of Global Law* (Cambridge, Cambridge University Press, 2015).

——, 'The Return of Constituent Power: A Reply to Matthias Kumm' (2016) 14 *International Journal of Constitutional Law* 906.

——, 'Surface and Depth: The EU's Resilient Sovereignty Question' in J Neyer and A Wiener (eds), *Political Theory and the European Union* (Oxford, Oxford University Press, 2010).

——, 'Sovereignty Frames and Sovereignty Claims in R Rawlings, P Leyland and A Young (eds), *Sovereignty and the Law: Domestic, European and International Perspectives* (Oxford, Oxford University Press, 2013).

Walsham, A, 'The Reformation and "The Disenchantment of the World" Reassessed' (2008) 51 *The Historical Journal* 497.

Walters, M, 'Is Public Law Ordinary?' (2012) 75 *Modern Law Review* 894.

Weber, M, *Economy and Society* (New York, Bedminster Press, 1968).

——, *Political Writings* (Cambridge, Cambridge University Press, 1994).

——, 'Politics as a Vocation' in HH Gerth and C Wright Mills eds, *From Max Weber: Essays in Sociology* (London, Routledge & Kegan Paul, 1948).

Wienrib, E, 'Poverty and Property in Kant's System of Rights' (2002–03) 78 *Notre Dame Law Review* 795.

Wilenski, P, 'Administrative Reform—General Principles and the Australian Experience' (1986) 64 *Public Administration* 3.

Wilkinson, M, 'Political Constitutionalism and the European Union' (2013) *Modern Law Review* 191.

——, 'Between Freedom and Law: Hannah Arendt on the Burden of the Tradition' in Goldoni and MacCorkindale (eds), *Hannah Arendt and the Law* (Oxford, Hart Publishing, 2012).

——, 'The Reconstitution of Postwar Europe: Liberal Excesses, Democratic Deficiencies' in M Dowdle and M Wilkinson (eds), *Constitutionalism Beyond Liberalism* (Cambridge, Cambridge University Press, 2017).

Wilson, E (ed), *Government of the Shadows. Parapolitcs and Criminal Sovereignty* (London, Pluto Press, 2009).

Wirth, W, 'Responding to Citizens' Needs: From Bureaucratic Accountability to Individual Coproduction in the Public Sector' in FX Kaufmann (ed), *The Public Sector: Challenge for Coordination and Learning* (Berlin, Walter de Gruyter, 1991).

Wittgenstein, L, *Philosophical Investigations* (Oxford, Wiley-Blackwell, 2009).

Wood, E, 'Logics of Power: A Conversation with David Harvey' (2006) *Historical Materialism* 19.

——, *From Lords to Citizens: A Social History of Western Political Thought* (London, Verso, 2011).

Yeatman, A, 'Democratisation and the Administrative State' in *Bureaucrats, Technocrats, Femocrats: Essays on the Contemporary Australian State* (Sydney, Allen & Unwin, 1990).

INDEX